Hollywood's Africa after 1994

# HOLLYWOOD'S AFRICA
# AFTER 1994

EDITED BY MARYELLEN HIGGINS

Ohio University Press • Athens

Ohio University Press, Athens, Ohio 45701
ohioswallow.com
© 2012 by Ohio University Press
All rights reserved

Cover art: Background photo, *courtesy istockphoto.com;* top: UH-60 Blackhawk,
*courtesy Suzanne M. Jenkins, USAF;* bottom left: Nelson Mandela in Johannesburg,
Gauteng, on 13 May 1998, *courtesy South Africa The Good News;* bottom right: A miner
in Kono District, Sierra Leone, searches his pan for diamonds, *courtesy USAID Guinea.*

Cover design by Beth Pratt

Printed in the United States of America
Ohio University Press books are printed on acid-free paper ⊗ ™

20 19 18 17 16 15 14 13 12    5 4 3 2 1

**Library of Congress Cataloging-in-Publication Data**
Hollywood's Africa after 1994 / edited by MaryEllen Higgins.
    p. cm.
Includes bibliographical references and index.
ISBN 978-0-8214-2015-7 (pb : alk. paper) — ISBN 978-0-8214-4433-7 (electronic)
1. Africa—In motion pictures. 2. Human rights in motion pictures. 3. Imperialism
in motion pictures. 4. Culture conflict in motion pictures. 5. Motion pictures—
United States—History—21st century. I. Higgins, MaryEllen, 1967–
PN1995.9.A43H65 2012
791.43'651—dc23

2012032543

# CONTENTS

# African Blood, Hollywood's Diamonds?

Hollywood's Africa after 1994

MARYELLEN HIGGINS

At the conclusion of Edward Zwick's *Blood Diamond,* Ambassador Walker lectures an audience about the complicity of Westerners in the human crises fueled by conflict diamonds in Sierra Leone. The target audience for Walker's speech is not the actors playing attendees at the staged meeting in Kimberley, South Africa, of course, but rather the spectators watching the film. Walker announces:

> The natural resources of a country are the sovereign property of its people. They are not ours to steal or exploit in the name of our comfort, our corporations, or our consumerism. The Third World is not a world apart, and the witness that you will hear today speaks on its behalf. Let us hear the voice of that world, let us learn from that voice, and let us ignore it no more.

Solomon Vandy, a humble Mende fisherman, approaches the podium. But before he utters his first word, the film ends, and the screen goes dark. In the film's postscript, viewers are urged to insist that their diamonds are conflict free. Ironically, Solomon's voice remains ignored as the film credits roll.

What are the messages conveyed in this moment? Does the severing of Solomon's speech suggest that there is not yet an African (or "Third World") perspective—that there are no grassroots African authorities, no African humanitarians who can take the microphone and offer a new perspective? Or does Zwick implicate Hollywood itself, so that the framing of Solomon's silence reads as a running commentary on Hollywood's perpetual denial of

African agency? Are we expected to fill in the blankness of Solomon's voice, rendering him an everlasting mute victim, unable to achieve liberation without our assistance?

We might also look at this scene in the context of another Hollywood blockbuster: *King Solomon's Mines*, based on H. Rider Haggard's best-selling 1885 novel, which has been adapted for movie and television screens on at least six occasions.[1] *King Solomon's Mines* epitomizes the imperial rationale: white adventurers arrive in Africa to locate hidden treasures that belonged to a biblical king, but also to save friendly, noble Africans from evil, monstrous tyrants. In 2006, *Blood Diamond* re-presents an African character named Solomon who reveals the location of a precious diamond in exchange for white protection against murderous African militants. In Zwick's reframing of the colonial narrative, Solomon is not an ancient king but a Mende fisherman, and diamonds are viewed not as glamorous jewels for the taking, but as catalysts for bloody conflicts linked to human rights abuses in Sierra Leone's civil war. Zwick transmits a new cast of characters onto the African scene: greedy European corporate magnates, shady international arms dealers, and human rights advocates in the Kimberley Process initiative.

In recent films set in Africa starring Hollywood celebrities, human rights issues have become a major thrust. A close inspection of some of the most interesting new "Africa films" reveals a mixing of human rights concerns with familiar figures from what V. Y. Mudimbe describes as the "colonial library" (1994, 17), figures that have been revived and cleverly revised in a new century. The legendary David Livingstone, a nineteenth-century Scottish missionary doctor, is resuscitated cinematically in 2006 through the figure of Nicholas Garrigan, a Scottish doctor who loses his way during a mission to Uganda in Kevin Macdonald's thriller, *The Last King of Scotland*. There is a twist here, too. Previous Hollywood films tended to glorify Livingstone's "civilizing mission" in Africa: the tagline of Henry King and Otto Brower's 1939 *Stanley and Livingstone* reads, "The most heroic exploit the world has known! Into the perilous wilderness of unknown Africa . . . Heat . . . fever . . . cannibals . . . jungle . . . nothing could stop him!" In contrast, the Scottish protagonist in *The Last King of Scotland* befriends the tyrannical Ugandan president Idi Amin Dada, provides information that leads to the execution of Amin's opponents, and fails to save anyone. Dr. Livingstone's "three C's"—commerce, Christianity, and civilization—are replaced by Dr. Garrigan's covetousness, corruption, and complicity.

This collection questions whether recent cinematic depictions of Africa adapt colonial fictions in order to subvert them, or whether they serve, ultimately, to reproduce colonialist ideologies. Crafted and reinforced by European and North American missionaries, travel writers, and filmmakers, colonial narratives consistently referenced Africa as a dangerous or exotic territory, as the pinnacle of horror and savagery, and as the recipient of the West's benevolent, heroic humanitarianism. The argument here is not that all of the films examined in the volume fall neatly under the rubric of Hollywood cinema; instead, our focus is on the fate of what Kenneth Cameron calls the "complex of received ideas" about Africa that Hollywood has perpetuated (12). The chapters that follow examine big-budget, celebrity-studded films produced and distributed by major Hollywood studios but also independent films and transnational films that engage with Hollywood's "Africa" archives. When recent films set in Africa revisit narratives of empire, are they recycled reinforcements of an imperial enterprise, nostalgic renderings of the past, revisionist engagements, creative attempts at atonement, anti-imperialist subversions, distractions, a blend?

The collection sets out not just to trace what remains of the colonial legacy in Hollywood, but to contemplate what has changed in Hollywood's updated projections of Africa. How do we read twenty-first-century projections of human rights issues—child soldiers, genocide, the exploitation of the poor by multinational corporations, dictatorial rule, truth and reconciliation—within the contexts of celebrity humanitarianism, "new" military humanitarianism, and Western support for regime change in Africa and beyond?[2] Do the emphases on human rights in the films offer a poignant expression of our shared humanity, do they echo the inequities of former colonial "civilizing missions," or do human rights violations operate as yet another mine of grisly images for Hollywood's dramatic storytelling? Does the continent serve as a stage for redemption and reconstituted intervention during a time when American and British military operations abroad have received intense global scrutiny?

The year 1994 was selected as a starting point for several reasons. The Rwandan genocide of 1994 pricked the consciousness of human rights advocates worldwide, and Hollywood celebrities responded. Human rights activists have looked to film as a medium to circulate images and interpretations of human rights violations in Africa, and to motivate viewers to participate in human rights campaigns. The DVD version of Annie Sundberg and Ricki Stern's *The Devil Came on Horseback* (2007), a documentary about US marine captain Brian Steidle's travels through Darfur, promises that for every copy sold, a dollar is donated to Save Darfur. Terry George's *Hotel Rwanda* (2004) would not be released until a decade after the Rwandan genocide, yet the prominent media presence of *Hotel Rwanda*'s leading actor, Don Cheadle, in the Save Darfur movement underscores the role of Western filmmaking and Western celebrities in the process of "raising awareness" about African conflicts—what Heike Härting describes as the development of a Western "humanitarianist consciousness" (2008, 63). On the DVD version of *Hotel Rwanda*, Don Cheadle speaks about the heroism of the nonfictional Paul Rusesabagina, whose character he plays in the feature film. Immediately after, Cheadle urges viewers to take action for victims in Darfur. The Save Darfur movement saw film as a vehicle to prompt agitation against oppression in Africa, yet what kind of activism is generated when the exposition of the Darfurian context is based not on historical or political knowledge, as Mahmood Mamdani observes, but on the Rwanda analogy?[3] Several contributors to this volume perceive that films about human rights violations in Rwanda, Darfur, and Sierra Leone base their pleas on analogies, disturbing images, and sentimental narrators; the assumed humanitarian gaze is dictated by the camera's frame in a move that privileges what Mamdani calls "evidence of the eyes" over substantive understanding of complex African political histories (2009, 7).

At the African Studies Association Conference in 2007 and at the African Literature Association Conference in 2008, Ken Harrow and Thomas Turner organized a series of panels titled "What's Wrong with Human Rights Films?" At first glance, one may wonder: What could be wrong with a film that advocates human rights? To address this question, contributors look critically at the types of awareness that human rights films set in Africa invite. The Hutu militia that killed Tutsis and moderate Hutus attempted to dehumanize their victims by portraying them as "cockroaches." What are the effects of the U.N.'s General Roméo Dallaire's assertion that Hutu militiamen have eyes that are "not human" in Peter Raymont's documentary, *Shake Hands with the Devil* (2004)—a film that won the Audience Award for Best World Documentary at the Sundance Film Festival? What are the effects of the references to "devils on horseback" in the Sudanese context? Do references to demons function to elicit a particular emotive impact, and if so, what are the implications? If human rights films are truly invested in bringing about positive change, is generating sympathy for one side and outrage against the other the best means of persuasion? Three scholars who have worked extensively on human rights issues in Africa—Margaret Higonnet, Joyce Ashuntantang, and Ken Harrow—investigate these questions much more elaborately in their contributions to the volume.

We also look at Hollywood's Africa in the aftermath of Nelson Mandela's historic inauguration as president of South Africa in 1994. The earliest "Africa films" in the Hollywood archive concentrated on South Africa: How has Hollywood interpreted South Africa's transformations after the end of apartheid, and how have South Africans challenged Hollywood? What is the imprint left by one of Hollywood cinema's most prominent icons, Clint Eastwood, in his direction of *Invictus* (2009), a film that narrates Mandela's struggle against the kinds of widespread expectations of African catastrophe that Hollywood has traditionally reinforced? Do the massive explosions in Darrell Roodt's *Dangerous Ground* (1997) signal the breaking of new ground in cinema's South Africa, or is the spectacle of violence in the film just another staple of Hollywood-style filmmaking? Gillian, Robyn, and Shawn Slovo— the daughters of the late South African activists Joe Slovo and Ruth First— also intervene in Hollywood's Africa through their writing and production in Tom Hooper's *Red Dust* (2004) and Phillip Noyce's *Catch a Fire* (2006). How do these activist-inspired films mediate the new South Africa for global audiences? Given the star power of American celebrities (Hillary Swank and Tim Robbins) in these films, how do we situate them vis-à-vis Hollywood's Africa? In terms of its cinematography and the absence of Hollywood stars, one of the most unusual films set in South Africa is Neill Blomkamp's *District 9* (2009); but in terms of its depictions of alien "Others" and decadent Nigerians, does it offer anything significantly new to Hollywood's Africa?

Just as Edward Said argued that Western articulations about the "Orient" reveal more about the articulator's "battery of desires, repressions, investments, and projections" than anything substantial about the East (1978, 8), the contributors argue that Western film images of Africa express more about the West than anything substantial that could be said about actual Africans. In terms of the number of films produced, box-office success, and visibility at the Academy Awards ceremonies, Mandela, who is arguably Africa's most celebrated political icon, has been upstaged on Hollywood screens by figures such as Idi Amin, the Rwandan *génocidaires,* and militant rebels in Sierra Leone. In the wake of debates over the American military withdrawal from its operations in Somalia, the failure to prevent genocide in Rwanda, and widely publicized massacres in Sudan, it is not surprising that so many Hollywood films set in Africa after 1994 present us with images of humanitarian crises and questions of Western intervention. Ridley Scott's *Black Hawk Down* (2001) would be invoked by Vice President Dick Cheney to argue for continued American force in Iraq. At a town hall meeting in Milwaukee in

2004, he referenced *Black Hawk Down* to illustrate two lessons he thought should be gleaned from the withdrawal of American forces in the world: "one, they could strike us with impunity; and two, if they did hit us hard enough, they could change U.S. policy" (qtd. in Lawrence and McGarrahan 2008, 448). Even the vice president recognized the potential of Hollywood images of Africa, not just in their reflections of our national preoccupations, but in the shaping of popular opinions.

The contributors see Hollywood's Africa not as a series of detached fantasies that offer pure entertainment, but as projections—entertaining as they may be—that reflect various national and international investments, both material and ideological. Hollywood's interest in Africa has surfaced at a time when the American Council of Foreign Relations asserts that "Africa is becoming steadily more central to the United States and the Rest of the World in ways that transcend humanitarian interests" (Lake and Whitman 2006, 5). Two publications of the Council on Foreign Relations—*More than Humanitarianism: A Strategic U.S. Approach toward Africa* (Lake and Whitman 2006), and *Beyond Humanitarianism: What You Need to Know about Africa and Why It Matters* (Lyman and Dorff 2007), argue for more aggressive intervention on the continent. Stephen Ellis, in his chapter "How to Rebuild Africa," calls American intervention in Africa "tough love" (Lyman and Dorff 2007, 160). In 2007, the Bush administration created the U.S. Africa Command, or AFRICOM. AFRICOM's 2011 Posture Statement includes the aim of reducing threats to American citizens "by helping African States to provide for their own security."[4] Concurrently, the website seems to be very engaged in the winning of hearts and minds through humanitarian appeals. AFRICOM's first commander, General William E. Ward, states, "Years from now we want Africans and Americans to be able to say AFRICOM made a difference—a positive difference."[5]

When we watch Hollywood films set in Africa, do they also participate—consciously or unconsciously—in the winning of hearts and minds, the fostering of resolve to intervene in humanitarian crises in Africa, the building of support for American-enforced security in Africa and elsewhere? U.S. Army Rangers and Delta Force operators in *Black Hawk Down* (2001), characters based on the soldiers who fought the Battle of Mogadishu, swoop into Somalia to assist the Red Cross and to capture the Somali warlord Mohamed Farrah Aidid and his allies. The Navy SEALs in Antoine Fuqua's *Tears of the Sun* (2003) rescue a humanitarian doctor from brutal rebels and help reinstall the friendly heir to the presidency. We could read these films as Hollywood projections of well-intentioned military humanitarianism and regime change—or, if one wishes to read them more skeptically, as "philanthropic imperialism" (de Waal 1997, 179) and "humanitarian bombing" (Weiss 2007, 10). We could contemplate the good-hearted, democratic American protagonists (played by the likable actors Josh Harnett in Scott's film and Bruce Willis in Fuqua's); contrast them with their one-dimensional, tyrannical African foils; and read the films as promotions of what Uzodinma Iweala calls "the West's fantasy of itself" (2007, B07). We might also look at the critical responses to the films: Why was *Black Hawk Down*, a film in which powerful, armed Americans can save only each other in the end, much more successful than *Tears of the Sun*, which glorifies American-enforced regime change and provides uplifting images of thankful Africans?

In 1994, Ella Shohat and Robert Stam argued that American celebrities who play British colonial heroes imply a "historical lap-dissolve by which the British-dominated imperialism of the nineteenth century faded into the US-dominated imperialism of the twentieth" (113). Beyond 1994, American action heroes—embodied by actors such as Bruce Willis in *Tears of the Sun*, Matthew McConaughey in Breck Eisner's *Sahara* (2005), or Michael Douglas in Stephen Hopkins's *The Ghost and the Darkness* (1996)—step in to rescue endangered European characters, suggesting that the transfer of imperial power from Europe to the United States has fully materialized. If, as Ruth Mayer argues, films are "indefatigably adjusting the symbolic repertory of yesterday to the conceptual and ideological frameworks of today" (2002, 1), what do recent cinematic reshapings of the colonial archive suggest about the world's most powerful nations? What is the impact of celebrity heroines in Africa after 1994—Jennifer Connelly in *Blood Diamond*, Gillian Anderson in *The Last King of Scotland*, Rachel Weisz in *The Constant Gardener*, Monica Bellucci in *Tears of the Sun*, Naomi Watts in *King Kong*, Penelope Cruz in *Sahara*—who, like their predecessors, engage in romantic relationships with the heroes, but who also guide the films' humanitarian consciousness? If new "Africa films" adapt Hollywood's proven formulas (for example, *King Solomon's Mines* meets *Heart of Darkness*) to make a profit, why is it that these formulas work (or fail) today? And what, if anything, had to be tweaked in the colonial formulas to render them appealing and acceptable to audiences after 1994?

Films about Africa that have been nominated for Academy Awards after 1994 project new affairs with Empire that replace the "ideal imperial figure" (Shohat and Stam 1994, 110) with flawed tragic heroes. The morally suspect treasure seeker (Danny Archer in *Blood Diamond*) and the parody of the colonial savior (Nick Garrigan in *The Last King of Scotland*) suggest a conscious reshaping of the colonial archive. *Hotel Rwanda*, which diverges from the status quo in its emphasis on a black African hero, casts shame on former colonizing nations (especially Belgium) and the most powerful countries in the United Nations for their abandonment of Rwandan victims of genocide. The practices of Western corporations in Africa are likewise held up for popular scrutiny: Fernando Meirelles's *The Constant Gardener* (2005) scorns human rights abuses by Western pharmaceutical companies; Andrew Niccol's *Lord of War* (2005) places American arms dealers at the center of African tragedies; and *District 9* ridicules the multinational corporations that would harvest the very bodies—the raw materials—of "Others" to extract fuel (for example, African uranium) in their pursuit of the deadliest weapons.

But perhaps Western cinematic condemnations of imperialist exploitation in Africa function also as trickster narratives, as Christopher Odhiambo Joseph argues in his chapter on *The Constant Gardener*. In this interpretation, Hollywood-style trickster films seem to point toward African independence from Western dominance, but then switch gears and advocate revised Western intervention. Through characters like Ambassador Walker in *Blood Diamond* or Tessa in *The Constant Gardener*, trickster films criticize the treatment of Africans by powerful Western nationals and multinational corporations. Yet within these same narratives, African characters who are initially resistant to European or American partnership, like Solomon Vandy in *Blood Diamond*, discover that they depend on Western humanitarian heroes and heroines for their survival. Thus, Solomon refuses Danny Archer's positioning as master, but ultimately learns that he can trust his fate to Archer when his actions are monitored by the well-intentioned American journalist, Maddy Bowen. Another example emerges in the *Last King of Scotland* when Nick Garrigan initially scorns British imperialist meddling in Uganda. Nick's anti-British alliance with Amin proves to be too dangerous, and this time it is the Scottish anti-imperialist who needs the British to help him escape from the terrifying Ugandan leader. The interventionist impulse is thus modified: colonial exploitation is scorned, but the complete withdrawal of dominant Western influence is projected as dangerous, unconscionable, and cowardly.

In order to further analyze the tensions between African independence and Western influence in the films, we might examine the portrayals of menacing African despots who resist Western intervention. In *The Last King of Scotland*, the tyrant is embodied by the anti-imperialist Idi Amin; at the commencement of *Hotel Rwanda*, he is the voice of a genocidal RTLM "Hutu power" radio announcer who explains that he hates Tutsis because they were collaborators for the Belgian colonists; in *Blood Diamond,* he is the menacing Captain Poison, who trains child soldiers; in *Tears of the Sun,* he is the genocidal commander Terwase, who insists that his people did not embrace "the religion of the colonists" and "will never be pawns for anyone." The toppling of these villains through Western intervention is depicted as a pathway toward peace, while the voices of anti-imperialism and African struggles for independence from the West are contained within the rhetoric of the ruthless despot bent on vengeance.

To set the stage for Western intervention, a number of films after 1994 echo what James Ferguson describes as "Africa talk," which characterizes the history of the continent as "a series of lacks and absences, failings and problems, plagues and catastrophes" (2006, 1–2). In *Blood Diamond,* the veteran Danny lectures the idealistic Maddy: "Peace Corps types only stay around long enough to realize they're not helping anyone; government only wants to stay in power until they've stolen enough to go into exile somewhere else; and the rebels, they're not sure that they want to take over, otherwise they'd have to govern this mess. But T.I.A. . . . This Is Africa." In *The Last King of Scotland,* the Scottish doctor initially defends Idi Amin's oppressive regime: "This is Africa: you meet violence with violence or you're dead." In *Black Hawk Down,* the pilot Michael Durant's Somali captor reinforces T.I.A. talk from within: "We know this: without victory, there can be no peace. There will always be killing, you see? This is how things are in our world." In Michael Katleman's horror film *Primeval* (2007), it is an African American cameraman who concludes, "I would never say this in front of a bunch of white people. . . . Slavery was a good thing. Anything you gotta do to get the fuck out of Africa is OK with me." Celebratory denouements for African characters are often imagined as Western-assisted escape, rather than a locally orchestrated peace, whether it be *Blood Diamond*'s Solomon Vandy, *Hotel Rwanda*'s Paul Rusesabagina, *Primeval*'s Jojo, *Shooting Dogs*' Marie (Michael Caton-Jones, 2005), or the televised film *24: Redemption*'s schoolboy refugees (Jon Cassar, 2008). As Binyavanga Wainaina writes in his satirical comments aimed at Western narrators in Africa: "Africa is to be pitied, worshipped or dominated. Whichever angle you take, be sure to leave the strong impression that without your intervention . . . Africa is doomed" (1995).

Colonial formulas, Africa talk, and Western rescue fantasies still permeate representations of Africa in films after 1994, but films set in Africa are not essentially and inevitably the product of social and political forces that control the scriptwriters' pens, the cinematographers' gazes, or the directors' decisions. It is interesting that a notable exception to the African catastrophe formula in Hollywood's Africa emerges from the direction of Clint Eastwood, who takes the pessimism of Africa talk head-on in *Invictus* (2009). *Invictus's* Nelson Mandela is quite familiar with predictions of African failure, and like the South African national rugby team depicted in the film, Mandela is determined to defy the widespread expectations of postapartheid devastation and collapse. And he does so without the intervention of Western saviors. Mandela's recitation of lines from William Ernest Henley's eponymous poem could apply not only to his character but also to a wider vision of African agency: "I am the master of my fate / I am the captain of my soul."

The science fiction film *District 9* offers a more playful cinematic commentary on "Africa talk" in the rendering of the authoritative white guide, Wikus Van De Merwe. Wikus's obviously flawed exposition on aliens, nicknamed the prawns, mimics self-proclaimed "experts" on African affairs in the apartheid era: Wikus positions himself as "Mr. Sweetie" while he lures prawn children out of their homes in order to force them into concentration camps. His claims to humanitarianism—and by extension the assumed humanitarianism of those who view themselves as experts on "Others"—are ridiculed by the camera as Wikus's blithe, amused, and self-serving disregard for the lives of prawns under his control becomes increasingly apparent. Even when Wikus transforms into a prawn and rescues one of them, his desire to save himself from becoming alien overrides any concern about the fate of the tortured prawns in Johannesburg. It is difficult to determine whether we are ever supposed to take Wikus—or the film—seriously. Do the ubiquitous cameras embedded in the film's mise-en-scène suggest a metacommentary on Western filmmaking about Africa? Is Blomkamp's stereotypical portrait of bloodthirsty, menacing Nigerians in the film so overblown as to call attention to its ridiculouness?[6] Or is the portrait yet another troubling example of the demonization of "Others," as Kimberly Nichele Brown suggests?

The question of whether new "Africa films" films are ultimately viewed as repetitions, reinforcements, or subversions of the colonial archive is not, in the end, determined by the films themselves, but by how we interpret them. If we follow the suggestion of Harry Garuba and Natasha Himmelman and look for "images that arrest us precisely because they do not fit into the structures of our expectations," we might detect curious moments that open up new creative avenues for our readings of Hollywood's Africa. For example, as I remark in a subsequent chapter, I was struck by the Somali character

Atto's reference to John Sturges's Hollywood western, *Gunfight at the O.K. Corral* (1957), in *Black Hawk Down*. Why did the scriptwriter, Ken Nolan, insert an amused Somali character who asks, "What is this, the K.O. Corral?" Atto's inversion of the "O.K." seems to foreshadow the reversal of the Americans' presumed easy victory in the gunfight. Looking at this moment prompts an investigation into further references to the American western film genre, from Scott's staging of Bakara Market as the "Wild West," to Nolan's invention of the character Hoot Gibson, who carries the same name as an American cowboy rodeo champion who turned to Hollywood film acting in the 1920s. Thus, an alternative reading of the film might see the soldiers' interpretations of their roles in Somalia as part of the fictions and fantasies of American cinema.

Western studios have the power to frame events in Africa for global audiences—and to revise, edit out, voice in, and distribute the final product to mass audiences. Africans in Western cinema are still, to use Edward Said's terms, "*contained* and *represented* by dominating frameworks" (1978, 40). However, Africa is not framed in the exact same way throughout the films, and some of the differences emerge as we recognize the competing narratives and metacommentaries within the films themselves. There are also several overt exceptions to Hollywood cinema's typical reliance on European and American heroes. *Invictus,* unlike typical Hollywood films that filter South African history through the figure of a white hero, presents Nelson Mandela as its central protagonist and a white rugby captain as his cooperative partner. Phillip Noyce's *Catch a Fire* concentrates on the political awakening of the black South African ANC activist, Patrick Chamusso, who takes over the film's voiceover in the concluding shots as he appears beside the actor Derek Luke, who portrays him. The "white consciousness" that used to drive Hollywood films about South Africa dissolves as events on screen are filtered through the points of view of significant black African characters. In her chapter on *Catch a Fire* and *Red Dust,* Jane Bryce argues that these films "perform the important gesture of making visible aspects of the past which were repressed under apartheid, and bringing these to the attention of audiences. Moreover, they do this by to an extent reversing the usual terms of engagement—focusing on what South Africa offers to the world as opposed to what the world offers Africa." Of course, for over half a century, African directors have presented local perspectives as they employ African writers, cinematographers, and actors. A full discussion of African cinema is well beyond the scope of this book, but the concluding chapters consider African cinema's critical engagements with Hollywood's Africa.

How can Hollywood's Africa be characterized after 1994, and how has it been challenged? There is not a single conclusion, as the various chapters in the volume demonstrate. In order to provide a broad range of perspectives on Hollywood's Africa, I asked scholars in Barbados, Kenya, South Africa, and the United States to contribute to the book project. To my delight, they agreed. The resultant volume includes analyses by interdisciplinary scholars situated within departments of African studies, English, film and media studies, international relations, and sociology across continents. Several contributors grew up, have resided, or currently live in countries represented in *Hollywood's Africa after 1994*. The international contributors to this volume offer a variety of suggestions for interpretation, but the goal of the volume is not to offer definitive conclusions. Rather, by reading the various strategies and multiple contexts in which Hollywood's Africa and its counterparts can be studied, we hope to inspire readers to develop their own creative interpretations.

NOTES

1. See Ruth Mayer (2002) on *King Solomon's Mines* and "trick translation," 30–40. Kenneth Cameron discusses Haggard's influence on American and British cinema in his chapter, "The White Queen and the Hunter" (1994, 17–32). See also Peter Davis on Haggard and "Zooluology" (1996, 124 and 147). For an exploration of representations of monstrosity in film adaptations of *King Solomon's Mines*, see Paul Ugor (2006). For a study of "the purification of imperialism" in *King Solomon's Mines*, see Jeff Bass (1981).

2. Several books contemplate the transition from neutral humanitarian endeavors that aim to provide relief from human suffering to a "new humanitarianism" that allows the taking of sides and seeks to remove the causes of suffering through intervention. For much more detailed discussions of the debates surrounding "new humanitarianism" and humanitarian intervention, see Alex de Waal (1997), David Chandler (2001), Thomas Weiss (2007), Margaret Denike (2008), Michael Barnett and Thomas Weiss (2008), and Nathan Hodge (2010).

3. For more on Save Darfur's use of analogy, see Mahmood Mamdani (2009). For a related discussion of the problematic generation of "understanding" of human rights issues in *Hotel Rwanda*, see Renate Kahlke (2007).

4. AFRICOM's 2011 Posture Statement was written by General Carter F. Ham. At the time of writing, AFRICOM is situated in Stuttgart, Germany. Its website is located at www. Africom.mil.

5. Ward, www.Africom.mil/africomDialogue.asp?entry=20.

6. Dayna Oscherwitz contemplated what she saw as the deliberate insertion of cameras and the overblown representation of Nigerians in *District 9* in her presentation at the African Literature Association's annual conference in Athens, Ohio in 2010: "Re-globalizing Africa: Reversal and Renegotiation in Recent African Films."

Barnett, Michael, and Thomas G. Weiss, eds. 2008. *Humanitarianism in Question: Politics, Power, Ethics*. Ithaca: Cornell University Press.

Bass, Jeff. 1981. "The Romance as Rhetorical Dissociation: The Purification of Imperialism in *King Solomon's Mines*." *Quarterly Journal of Speech* 67 (3): 259–69.

Bickford-Smith, Vivian. 2006. "Picturing Apartheid: With a Particular Focus on 'Hollywood' Histories of the 1970s." In *Black and White in Colour: African History on Screen*, edited by Vivian Bickford-Smith and Richard Mendelsohn, 256–78. Athens: Ohio University Press.

Cameron, Kenneth. 1994. *Africa on Film: Beyond Black and White*. New York: Continuum.

Chandler, David. 2001. "The Road to Military Humanitarianism: How the Human Rights NGOs Shaped a New Humanitarian Agenda." *Human Rights Quarterly* 23 (3): 678–700.

Davis, Peter. 1996. *In Darkest Hollywood: Exploring the Jungles of Cinema's South Africa*. Athens: Ohio University Press.

Denike, Margaret. 2008. "The Human Rights of Others: Sovereignty, Legitimacy, and 'Just Causes' for the 'War on Terror.'" *Hypatia* 23 (2): 95–121.

de Waal, Alex. 1997. *Famine Crimes: Politics and the Disaster Relief Industry in Africa*. Bloomington: Indiana University Press.

Douzinas, Costas. 2007. *Human Rights and Empire: The Political Philosophy of Cosmopolitanism*. New York: Routledge-Cavendish.

Ferguson, James. 2006. *Global Shadows: Africa in the Neoliberal World Order*. Durham: Duke University Press.

Haggard, H. Rider. 1885. *King Solomon's Mines*. London: Cassell.

Härting, Heike. 2008. "Global Humanitarianism, Race, and the Spectacle of the African Corpse in Current Western Representations of the Rwandan Genocide." *Comparative Studies of South Asia, Africa, and the Middle East* 28 (1): 61–77.

Hawk, Beverly G, ed. 1992. *Africa's Media Image*. New York: Praeger.

Hodge, Nathan. 2010. *Armed Humanitarians: The Rise of the Nation Builders*. New York: Bloomsbury.

Iweala, Uzodinma. 2007. "Stop Trying to 'Save' Africa." *Washington Post*, July 15, B07.

Kahlke, Renate. 2007. "Understanding Genocide? Western Cinematic Depictions of Rwanda and Bosnia." *Politics and Culture* 2. Retrieved from http://aspen.conncoll.edu/politicsandculture.

Lake, Anthony, and Christine Todd Whitman, chairs. 2006. *More than Humanitarianism: A Strategic U.S. Approach toward Africa* (Report of an Independent Task Force). New York: Council on Foreign Relations.

Lawrence, John Sheldon, and John G. McGarrahan. 2008. "Operation Restore Honor in *Black Hawk Down*." In *Why We Fought: America's Wars in Film and History*, edited by Peter C. Rollins and John E. O'Connor, 431–57. Lexington: University Press of Kentucky.

Lyman, Princeton N., and Patricia Dorff, eds. 2007. *Beyond Humanitarianism: What You Need to Know about Africa and Why It Matters*. New York: Council on Foreign Relations.

Mamdani, Mahmood. 2009. *Saviors and Survivors: Darfur, Politics, and the War on Terror*. New York: Pantheon.

Mayer, Ruth. 2002. *Artificial Africas: Colonial Images in the Times of Globalization*. Hanover: University Press of New England.

Mudimbe, V. Y. 1994. *The Idea of Africa*. Bloomington: Indiana University Press.

Said, Edward W. 1978. *Orientalism*. New York: Vintage.

Shohat, Ella, and Robert Stam. 1994. *Unthinking Eurocentrism: Multiculturalism and the Media*. New York: Routledge.

Ugor, Paul. 2006. "Demonizing the African Other, Humanizing the Self: Hollywood and the Politics of Post-imperial Adaptations." *Atenea* 26 (2): 131–50.

Wainaina, Binyavanga. 1995. "How to Write about Africa." *Granta* 92. Retrieved from http://www.granta.com/Magazine/92.

Weiss, Thomas G. 2007. *Humanitarian Intervention*. Cambridge: Polity Press.

# ONE

# The Cited and the Uncited

### Toward an Emancipatory Reading of Representations of Africa

HARRY GARUBA AND NATASHA HIMMELMAN

> Orientalism is . . . a system for citing texts and authors.
>
> —Edward Said

In *The Last King of Scotland* (Kevin Macdonald, 2007), a newly qualified Scottish medical doctor sits in front of a map of the world pondering where he should go to escape from the stifling world of his boring, conventional bourgeois family. The map, a little globe, sits on his table like a plaything. And playfully, with a child's glee, he spins it round like a toy. When it comes to a halt in front of him, the country he sees is Canada. No, not exotic enough, he thinks; and then he spins the globe again. When it stops once more, he places his finger on the point right in front of him. This time it is Uganda, in the eastern heart of Africa. And it is to Uganda that he and the film go.

This sequence, of course, echoes the famous scene in Joseph Conrad's *Heart of Darkness*[1] where the narrator, Marlow, speaks of his childhood fascination with maps and his longing to visit the blank, unexplored spaces on the maps of the world. By the time he grows up, Marlow tells us, those blank spaces will have become places of darkness. Here is how Marlow describes it in Conrad's classic tale:

> "Now when I was a little chap I had a passion for maps. . . . At that time there were many blank spaces on the earth, and when I saw one that looked particularly inviting on a map (but they all look that) I would put my finger on it and say, When I grow up I will go there. . . . I have been in some of them . . . well, we won't talk about that. But there was one yet—the biggest, the most blank, so to speak—that I had a hankering after.

"True, by this time it was not a blank space any more. It had got filled since my boyhood with rivers and lakes and names. It had ceased to be a blank space of delightful mystery—a white patch for a boy to dream gloriously over. It had become a place of darkness." (2006, 7–8)

By reiterating and foregrounding the Marlow-and-maps scene from *Heart of Darkness, The Last King of Scotland* suggests right from the beginning that by the time our young doctor "grows up," Uganda will also have become a place of darkness. And by the time our young—now "grown-up"—doctor leaves the country at the end of the film, Amin's rule has transformed Uganda into "a place of darkness."[2] We will return to these images later.

If, as Edward Said claims in his classic study of representations of the Orient in Western texts, "Orientalism is . . . a system for citing texts and authors" (1979, 23), Hollywood's Africa is also discursively anchored on a similar system of citations. In this sense, representations of Africa in Hollywood or Hollywood-influenced films are massively cited. Representations of Africa in these films work on a referencing system of citations in which the present image builds on a previous, always already known image of Africa (see Mayer 2002 and Ebron 2002), sometimes of maps and exploration and conquest, or of adventure or safaris, but more often of savagery and sexuality, cannibalism and concupiscence, drumming and dancing, and so on; in short, depictions that show an excess of physicality and primitive passion. Cited from text to film or from film to film, these tropes define an Africa inscribed as both discursively known but also inscrutable to reason (see, for instance, Hickey and Wylie 1993).

They constitute an archive that V. Y. Mudimbe famously referred to as the "colonial library" in his study of the invention of Africa in European discourse (see Mudimbe 1988). The colonial library is a library of citations, a readily available archive in which all the significant information worth knowing about Africa is stored.

One way to critically read films that depend on this archive of images is to focus on retrieving the "citations" that enable and give authority to each frame, image, or sequence of the film. Such a reading is certainly of great benefit in uncovering the circuits of citation—the process of iteration and reiteration—through which cultural meanings are created, disseminated, and consolidated or subverted. However, in some of these films, there are also images and sequences that stand outside this dominant system of citations, images that arrest us precisely because they do not fit into the structures of our expectations. Often highly marginal to the narrative and discursive thrust of these films, these images are puzzling precisely because there is no narrative explanation for them in these films, and they do not appear to be based on any discursive authority; they appear to stand outside the discursive economies that structure the narrative and give the film its coherence. These kinds of images or sequences are what we will be referring to as the "uncited," invoking that notion of citations that Said speaks of in connection with Orientalist discourse. Although citations may be said to invoke the already known, the image that can be tracked through previous representations in antecedent texts and narratives, the "uncited," based on this understanding, is the unknown, the image not dependent on or anchored on an archive, or a body of knowledge that is easily retrievable through recourse to available discourses.

Said's notion of citation is highly valuable as a methodological tool for identifying and studying representations of Africa, especially when the preoccupation is with the examination of the genealogies and circuits of dissemination through which particular images are enunciated, circulated, and consolidated. What we propose to do in this chapter is to elaborate on the many modalities of citation at this postcolonial, postmodern moment and to add to it the previously ignored idea of the uncited. As citation became a dominant mode of knowledge production about Africa, it was inevitable that several modalities of citation would emerge, often to consolidate this knowledge or in true postcolonial, postmodern fashion to question its authority and undermine its foundations. However, although it is important to identify the ways in which citations function in textual and visual representations of Africa and in narratives of Africa in general, it is important that attention also be given to those rare moments when the uncited emerge within these narratives, marginal as they may be.[3] For, by falling outside the archive of representations, the uncited challenges us to read beyond the archive or to "discover" and highlight the new, alternative archives that may provide discursive authority for these uncited representations. The uncited, therefore, is not dependent on the subversive, counterdiscursive move; it is the blank, uninscribed space that is still outside of discursive representation, to borrow Conrad's metaphor.[4] The uncited is that which is disarticulated from discourse. The ultimate aim is to suggest that reading films of this kind for instances of the "uncited" may be a more emancipatory approach to the criticism of films that rely on and derive their authority from a hegemonic system of citations.

In his well-known essay on Conrad's *Heart of Darkness,* Chinua Achebe begins with an anecdote about his encounter with "an older man" who happened to have been walking alongside him on the campus of the University of Massachusetts in the fall of 1974 when he was teaching at the university. After some casual remark about how young undergraduates are these days, the man asks Achebe if he is also a student. Achebe answers that he is a teacher—of African literature. The man finds this funny; he says he knows a fellow in a certain community college who also taught something like African history. "It always surprised him, he went on to say, because he never thought of Africa as having that kind of stuff, you know" (1989, 2). Achebe ponders about the reasons for this man's opinion of Africa and concludes that:

> Ignorance may be a more likely reason; but here again I believe that something more willful than a mere lack of information was at work. For did not the erudite British historian and Regius Professor at Oxford, Hugh Trevor-Roper, also pronounce that African history did not exist? (1989, 2)

The question of knowledge and ignorance has always been central to the evaluation of Western discourses about Africa. This question is premised on the understanding that "knowledge" translates into more accurate, "truer" representations while ignorance is the source of "false" representations. False representations are based on misconceptions and assumptions that knowledge will dispel as it steers us to the truth. Truth, by this understanding, is out there in the world waiting to be known.

On the premise that ignorance is a lack of information, young, enthusiastic students of Africa often think of the images of Africa they encounter in the West as representations based on ignorance. This, we suggest, turns the logic of discursive representation on its head. By believing that these representations are based on ignorance, we miss the fact that there is a kind of knowledge present in these images which makes them so readily understandable; we miss the fact that there is a knowledge regime within which representations of Africa function and acquire meaning, one built on centuries of knowledge production on Africa that is immediately available to comprehension. This is the dilemma that Achebe identifies when he says in the quote above that "something more than a lack of information is at work."

What we wish to propose is—first—that we uncouple the equation of ignorance/knowledge in representation with falsity/truth, ignorance translating to falsity and knowledge to truth. A more productive approach is to view these representations as based on certain kinds of knowledges about Africa, produced, circulated, and consolidated throughout the history of Western knowledge production about Africa in the age of modernity. It may be useful at this point to illustrate this with reference once again to Conrad's text. If we use the Conrad analogy of "blank spaces" as opposed to "rivers and lakes and names" with which this essay begins, what we are proposing is that we equate the "blank spaces" with genuine ignorance while the latter should be seen as knowledge, no matter how flawed. The point of ignorance is that a discursive regime of representation has not been imposed on a territory or a people; they are blank spaces, not only signifying lack of textual inscription but also standing in for the absence of "names" and thus reminding us that we are at the limit of representational coding, whether in language or in cartographic mimesis.

This is the reason that blank spaces are inviting to the protagonist and to us; they call attention to the unknown, to that which we are ignorant of, that which is outside of discourse. When we accept this ignorance, we leave the spaces on the map blank; when we refuse to accept it, we may still choose to draw it into the ambit of discourse and knowledge anyway. In *Journey without Maps,* his travelogue about his journey through Liberia in 1935, Graham Greene records one such instance of a refusal to leave any blank spaces.[5]

> I could only find two large-scale maps for sale. One issued by the British General Staff, quite openly confesses ignorance; there is a large white space covering the greater part of the Republic. . . . The other map is issued by the United States War Department. There is a dashing quality about it; it shows a vigorous imagination. Where the English map is content to leave a blank space, the American in large letters fills it with the word "Cannibals." (1936, 43–44)

This is a well-known strategy that simply imposes textual security to counter the real insecurities of our ignorance by imposing a discursive grid on the unknown.[6]

Our aim in drawing on this analogy is to suggest that we reverse our usual perceptions of representations of Africa in Western texts and see them as based on "knowledge" rather than ignorance. The analogy we have tried to invoke shows that the unrepresented is what is actually based on ignorance. This reversal is central to the argument we make in this chapter about reading filmic citation and adopting an emancipatory approach to the question of the uncited.

The kind of filmic citation that we have highlighted is of course a form of intertextual referencing that literary critics have been well aware of since the work of Julia Kristeva.[7] Said's *Orientalism* anchored the notion of intertextuality and citationality within a Foucauldian frame by aligning it to the production and consolidation of discourses. It is important to note, if only in passing, that Said was particularly concerned with the discourse of Orientalism; but in his emphasis on representation and the loss/recession of the referent (the Orient) his work unwittingly reinstitutes the ignorance/falsity (of representation) perception that we are trying to undo.[8] Since all of this work is fairly well known, we will focus here on the modalities through which contemporary, postcolonial filmic citation operates. The expression "well known" is important here because images of Africa have been in circulation for centuries, and they function within a regime of representation that has been an object of study from the period of the anticolonial struggle to the postcolonial present.[9] Not only were these representations built upon by the cultural pundits of empire, they were also deployed in a variety of ways and for multiple purposes by postmodern, postcolonial writers who were seeking either to affirm the "synchronic essentialism" of these representations or interrogate their epistemological foundations.[10] The modalities of citation have thus multiplied over time with their increasing deployment as signs and sites of ideological affirmation or contestation.[11]

For the purposes of this chapter, we wish to identity five ways in which citations may function in literary and filmic texts. These are: reinscription /reaffirmation; subversion/counterdiscourse (metanarrative thrust—to dislodge); parody/irony; fragmenting/reframing; and splitting/doubling—deploying the discourse or fragments of it in a Janus-faced manner, so to speak. These may, in fact, be deployed together in practice. We must also be reminded that the overarching framework within which representations of Africa function is a system of contrasts and antinomies that sets up the continent and its people as the space of radical difference, the site of alterity.[12] The schema of Self and Other that is the driving logic of this form of representation is founded on binarisms.[13]

The first manner of citation that we have identified is the simple instance of reinscription / reaffirmation. Reinscription / reaffirmation occurs when the particular trope deployed in a film feeds into a recognizable strategy of representation. For example, the trope of unrestrained sexuality[14] may clearly feed into the strategy of debasement and negation or the strategy of idealization and aestheticization,[15] in which case it merely reaffirms itself. It may even simply be an instance of an unfettered sexual appetite feeding into the strategy of sexualization in general, in which case people, landscapes, mores, and manners may be highly sexualized as a racial trait, in character with the environment and climate; in short, a part of the habitus, to use Bourdieu's term (Bourdieu 1977). However, reinscription / reaffirmation may invoke more than one strategy at a time. Indeed, we would argue that the level of sophistication of the film depends on its ability to simultaneously invoke several strategies of representation through the use of a single trope. We will at a later stage give examples of this in *The Last King of Scotland.*

The dynamics of subversion / counterdiscourse —our second identified modality—is best described in the famous phrase of postcolonial discourse as "the empire writes back" (see, e.g., Ashcroft, Griffiths, and Tiffin 2002). Again, subversion occurs when an image or trope is deployed only to subvert it or question its validity. By subverting the validity of the trope, the film "writes back" to its authorizing discourse and its institutional agencies, thus creating a counterdiscourse. The counterdiscourse seeks to dislodge the authority of the normative discourse; one of its conventional strategies is to take the mini-narratives of the previous discourse, then focalize and elevate them to become the main objects of attention. Famous instances of this in literature include Jean Rhys's *Wide Sargasso Sea,* which brings the first Mrs. Rochester (the madwoman in the attic) of *Jane Eyre* into focus, and George Lamming's *Water with Berries,* which rewrites the Caliban story. Less directly focused on specific texts and characters are the novels of Chinua Achebe, which are counterdiscursive at a more general level of creating alternative discourses to challenge Western representations of Africa.

As a modality of citation, reinscription / reaffirmation is more allied to colonialist discourse, and its objective is often to naturalize representations, whereas subversion / counterdiscourse represents the postcolonial, and the objective is to create an alternative discourse and an alternative archive, often by contextualizing and historicizing. The other three modalities of citation may be said to recall the strategies of postmodernist parody and pastiche; rather than naturalizing or contextualizing, the main thrust here appears to be performative. The trope or strategy becomes a site of creative performance that may involve parody or irony, satire or caricature, double entendres, and so on. Postmodernist citation often tends to work along these lines (see Hutcheons 1988). Like the subversive mode, irony and parody imply that these citations are used against the grain of the dominant discourse. Rather than reaffirm, parody highlights for playful scrutiny, and irony destabilizes authority. However, the purpose is usually not to create a counterdiscourse but to either bring the dominant discourse to disrepute or caricature its authority, or its authorizing agencies and institutions.

Beyond parodic playfulness and ironic reversal, a trope or image may be fragmented and reframed in a citation. This happens, for example, when a trope is split from its representational strategy and reframed within another. This kind of recoding is a modality that is similar to what we have called "splitting/doubling," but distinct because for the latter, the conventional framing is retained but extended to also call unflattering attention to the prejudices of the framer. We will give examples of these in the next section.

Standing in contrast to these many ways of employing citation is the uncited—the image or sequence that is disarticulated from discourse, one not explained by the discursive economies of citation and their archive. The uncited is that which leaves us blank. Rather like the map in *Heart of Darkness*, it invokes the blank spaces that make us wonder and challenge us to seek a discourse within which it will acquire meaning.

THE CITED AND UNCITED IN *THE LAST KING OF SCOTLAND*

*The Last King of Scotland* so massively cites other works that it is impossible to avoid the echoes of other images and texts that surface as the film unfolds. Perhaps the most significant thing about this film is its evocation of a host of images of Africa, its almost total dependence on other texts and representations of Africa.[16] To appropriate a phrase from theorists of literary intertextuality, this film is largely "a tissue of quotations" (Barthes 1978, 142–48). From the motif of the outward journey to Africa, which becomes an inward journey of psychic and psychological exploration for the European protagonist, this initial Conradian resonance announces the density of embedded texts and images that we will encounter in this film, which is saturated with citations of African excess, spanning the entire spectrum of representations of Africa from the benign and lovable to the malignant and loathsome.

The historical figure of General Idi Amin Dada (played by Forest Whitaker) provides, both in his body and his person, an archive from which to explore the range of these representations. And Giles Foden's novelistic rendition of those years in his novel of the same title furnishes director Kevin Macdonald with material enough to interweave the demands of recognizable historical fact with the freedom of the imagination on which representations of Africa typically depend.[17] This grounding in historical fact, which also leaves enough space for the creative imagination, is important because it allows for the consolidation of the discourse of Africa around an invocation of documentary truth that is empirically verifiable but creatively reconstructed. The flights of fantasy and imaginative manipulations then appear to be anchored to an incontestable core of truth. This articulation of history with fiction within the same domain of textuality is central to representations of Africa.

The film begins with shots of a sedate Scottish countryside life; the sense of a settled social order in which the trajectories of life are already well mapped is clearly evident—from growing up within a nuclear family, acquiring an education and getting into a profession, the horizons of individual and social life are fairly well established. And then we move to Africa and all that changes. If you turn your eyes away from the screen in the brief moment of transition from Scotland to Uganda, you can tell that the protagonist has arrived in Africa because the music changes to a loud roll of drums and percussion. Turn to the screen and a rush of colors—brilliant, primary colors—replace the mild and mellow sunlight of Scotland and its muted tones.[18] The auditory and visual contrasts place a world of natural and social quietude beside a thunderous, chaotic one defined by its noise and exuberance. These binary oppositions set the scene for what is to follow: the African adventure of a European protagonist. Form and content collaborate here to reinscribe and reaffirm the trope of Self and Other, which is the overarching system within which representations of Africa function in discourse.

Having made the point, the film immediately moves beyond simple reaffirmation to juggling between this and more sophisticated forms of citation. Now in Africa, Dr. Nicholas Garrigan (played by James McAvoy), our Scottish medical doctor, is in a bus traveling from the Kampala airport to a rural village where he is to resume duty. He looks out the window and notices some vaguely familiar animals, and he turns to the young woman sitting beside him to ask what they are. The noise threatens to drown conversation, but, above the din, she tells him that they are monkeys and then in her turn asks: "Do you have monkeys in Scotland?" He answers: "No, if we had monkeys in Scotland, we'd probably deep-fry them." The pervasive trope of Africa and animals is here cited along with the idea that Africans hunt and eat wild game. This simple citation, however, is also parodied and ironized in Garrigan's response. The trope becomes for him a site of performance; by spinning it around, so to speak, he simultaneously registers his awareness of the conventional reading that Africans eat monkeys and parodies it by ascribing the deep-frying to Scotland.[19]

Soon after this, the young woman suggestively tells Garrigan that the next bus stop is her stop, her destination. The suggestion of sexual availability is taken up and the next scene is one of wild lovemaking between this African woman and the white man she has just met in a bus. This scene of transitory sex sets in motion the trope of African female sexuality, which will be reinscribed / reaffirmed again and again in the film in contrast to the sexual restraint of Sarah Merrit (played by Gillian Anderson), the white woman in the film who is also clearly attracted to the protagonist. The fun and adventure that our medical doctor came to Africa for begins even before he arrives at his destination, and, once back in the bus to continue his journey, he exclaims: "I am a medical officer overseas!" The country is in the midst of celebrating a military coup that they expect will liberate them from the tyranny of the previous Obote regime; Dr. Garrigan is celebrating his freedom from father, family, and the expectations that circumscribe his life in Scotland. Nicholas's exclamation proclaims his liberty in Africa, a space where he is free from the conventions and moral proprieties that govern his life back home.

This juxtaposing of two frames of reference, simultaneously invoking identity and difference, will be one of the significant strategies of representation that the film will rely on. Juxtaposition may sometimes highlight contrasts as in the placing of the hospital scene of immunization beside shots of the mchawi[20] healing routine, which consists of chanting and dancing and the magical. Here the biomedical is clearly contrasted with the traditional animist; but the shot of Garrigan observing the practice of the other through the wire fencing that separates them emphasizes both this difference and the social and spatial contiguity of modern medicine and ancient magic in Africa, and this suggests—as the film later shows—that this sense of difference and dichotomy may in fact be tenuous and fragile. In true Conradian fashion, the collapse of one into the other is a theme that runs through the film.

It is this representational strategy that creates openings for the deployment of the citational modality of fragmenting/reframing. While the medicine doctor/mchawi dual frame reinscribes / reaffirms, the exchange of clothes between the dictator and the doctor sets the fragmenting/reframing logic of representation in motion. It begins with small acts (the shooting of the cow)[21] and the exchange of material objects—the military uniform for the

Scottish shirt, the ride in the presidential limousine and the people "mistaking" him for the president and waving. Finally, Nicholas is in the presidential palace, and Idi Amin walks in and commands his aides: "Hold on to your guns everyone. Hold on to your guns!" The dictator jocularly suggests that the doctor is the unstable one likely to pick up your gun and shoot you. The significance of this registers when we recall that in an earlier episode Nicholas had instinctively picked up Amin's gun to shoot the dying cow. Though it is Amin's gun, it is the doctor who uses it; the shooting is supposed to be a mercy killing not a brutal murder, but in this instance mercy is murder.

With care and sophistication, the trope of the brutal, instinctive savage is fragmented and reframed; the trope of murderousness is fragmented and reframed within the ethic of mercy. This is a trick that Idi Amin and the film will continually play on the hapless doctor through a strategy of endless troping and reframing. Amin appoints him his personal physician and family doctor,[22] buys him a fancy sports car, makes him attend a meeting in his place when he travels to Libya,[23] and draws him into an African replication of the Oedipal cycle[24] that he was fleeing from when he left Scotland.

As we earlier affirmed, the physical figure of Idi Amin provides a site for the reinscription/reaffirmation of many of the stereotypical images of African grossness, and the film takes advantage of this in many instances. A few examples of these are his buffoonery, his gluttony, the loud constipated fart,[25] his mood swings between the loud laughter of unrestrained physical mirth and the loopy-eyed depression that follows the next second.[26] But just as often as these instances of reaffirmation/reinscription occur, there also are layered on them the modalities of fragmenting and reframing and sometimes spitting/doubling, a metaphor physically realized in the image of Muyenga, Amin's body double, and the metonymic doubling games (exchanging clothes, exchanging cars) that he plays with Garrigan, which almost results in the assassination of both of them. Thus while Muyenga is his physical body double, Nicholas, the film suggests, is his real metonymic double, the physically unprepossessing European who slips into the shoes of the African giant without fully realizing it. Literally speaking, he wears Amin's military uniform, briefly becomes Amin in the chauffeured limousine, and even represents Amin at an important meeting. While it is Amin's men who do the torturing and killing as the case of the minister attests, Garrigan is the informer who leads them to their prey.

The instance of masculine bonding between Amin and Garrigan when they discuss his unwillingness to take up the job of personal physician is characteristic of this reframing that occurs again and again in the film. When Amin suggests to Nicholas that he does not want to take up the job he has been offered because of "the woman," the latter replies:

> "It's not that simple. It's complicated."
> "Why, is she married?"
> "Yes, she is."

The shared laughter that follows affirms a shared male identity, beyond the lines of color, nationality, age, and so forth. Note here though that it is not the black man's sexuality that is under discussion, it is the young white man's, and it is the white man who will later have an affair with Amin's wife, Kay (played by Kerry Washington).[27] The trope of sexuality is fragmented and reframed, but by a skillfully manipulated doubling, we realize later that the joke is on Amin, who is the one who gets cuckolded. But then throughout the tables always turn in unexpected ways.

As Amin's acts of brutality increase, and the horror of it all dawns on Garrigan, he attempts to distance himself from the atrocities, to claim his true identity, and return home to the Scotland he left for this African adventure. "This isn't me," he says, "I have to go home now." Like a lost schoolboy, he tries to recapture this receding identity by mentioning his name and place of birth:

> "Am Nicholas Garrigan.
> "And I'm from Scotland.
> "It's my home. I want to . . ."
> "Your home is here."

It is important to note that it is Amin, the African, who is telling him that "Africa" has claimed him for its own, not some voice of European reason. Amin explains to him, with a psychoanalytic understanding that is almost professional, the process of his descent, the workings of his own subconscious desires. He uses Garrigan's question about the killing of Jonah Wasswa (played by Stephen Rwangyezi), the Health Minister, as his cue. The minister's meeting with some representatives of a South African pharmaceutical company had earlier been reported to Amin by Garrigan, who was suspicious of what was being planned at the secret meeting. Amin replies that at the subconscious level, Nicholas knew what he doing when he reported the meeting to him. The following dialogue ensues between them:

"Do not pretend to yourself that you did not know. You are a stronger man than that."

"I didn't want him to die though."

"But you . . . you did it."

Amin explains to him: "You did it because you love me. You have stepped deep into the heart of my country. . . . Uganda embraces you." The echoes of J. M. Coetzee's *In the Heart of the Country* and the canonical Conrad text *Heart of Darkness* are unmistakable here. In the conventional manner of the trope of the European swallowed by the "African darkness," Garrigan descends into the country's darkness, but it is not the voice of another white man that tells him this or finds him, it is the African voice of the "African darkness" that has claimed him. The voice of psychoanalytical reason issues from the heart of darkness itself. The Faustian transaction is sealed when Garrigan has a Ugandan passport delivered to him, in his home. We may recall that when Amin tells Garrigan the story of his youth and his days in the British army, he ends the narration by saying "The British Army, it became my home." While Amin claims a British home, mimics the folk culture of Scotland, and gives his children Scottish names,[28] he tells his unwitting conscript from the real Scotland, his "white monkey," that he is Ugandan.[29] The reversals, the splitting and doubling go on and on.

Perhaps there is no better example of this splitting and doubling than during the State dinner to which Amin invites Garrigan. In front of an audience of white diplomats and black government officials, Amin begins his speech by evoking all the glories of ancient African civilization, speaking of the African origins of civilization, and the subsequent European plunder and exploitation of the continent. This is the regular rhetoric of pan-African, Afrocentric, nationalist discourse with its simple schema of Self and Other. After this opening, he proceeds to talk about the special dishes that have been prepared for the dinner guests. He assures them in the same nationalist tone that it is all local food. Though it is local and special, he says, he can also assure his guests that none of it is human flesh. The mention of human flesh changes the modality of citation in subtle ways. This descent from the Afrocentric podium, so to speak, to invoking the stereotype of cannibalism, as it is usually attributed to Africans in colonialist discourse, becomes even more interesting against the background of stories of Amin's own cannibalism.[30]

By foregrounding the putative cannibalism of Africans, the deployment of the trope calls attention to the prejudices that guide European representations of Africa when placed beside the glories of ancient African civilizations. At the same time and from another perspective, it is difficult to ignore the attention it calls to apocryphal tales of Amin's cannibalistic practices. It would appear that the ironizing goes in two directions simultaneously, split and doubled, as it were, between the Self and the Other. This parodying of the cannibalism trope inserted within the context of the representational strategies of Afrocentric discourse also inscribes and parodies the strategies of colonialist discourse in its representations of African cannibalism. This endless layering of citational modalities, one upon the other, is perhaps the major characteristic feature of this film.

To return to what we highlighted earlier in this chapter, unlike the citation, whether simply reinscribed or nuanced with levels of citational complexity, the uncited is the speech, dialogue, scene, sequence, for example, that cannot be abstracted into our conventional categories of analysis. During Amin's first appearance in the film when he joins local villagers in celebrating the coup and does his populist warrior's dance on the stage, everything is as it should be: the burly general erupting on the stage like a force of nature; the crowd cheering as he mimes the movements of the warrior's dance, complete with spear and shield; and then the deliverance of his rousing speech about the new Uganda that his rule will usher in for the people. The earthiness of his speech and performance is neither lost on the crowd nor on us. All of this goes according to the script of African citation. But then amid this noise and dance and celebration, the camera momentarily focuses on the face of an unnamed soldier. There is a close-up, but the expression on his face is inscrutable; he is looking at the crowd because his eyes are moving, and here there is a hint of an interiority that is unavailable to us. It is clear that he is not part of the excitement of this crowd of people, nor does he seem to particularly care about the Amin phenomenon. This is clearly a frame that falls outside of our conventional categories of analysis and understanding. Why does the camera take a close-up of this lowly soldier with the suggestion that something is going on in his mind—a something we will never have access to and will never know because the camera and the narrative move on? But we are left with only a blank space where we may ask the question: Why does the narrative pause to look closely at this "philosophical" soldier in all his insignificance to the larger narrative scheme of the film? The silent commentary of his face is one significant moment of the uncited in this film, so disarticulated from the dominant citational thrust of the film that it is in fact easy to miss the moment.

But another such moment that we are unlikely to miss is the moment when Amin tells Garrigan that he knew all the while about the latter's affair with his wife. He speaks of this only when Garrigan is being tortured.

> Listen to me Nicholas, I know, I know about you . . . and Kay. How could you do that to me? I am the Father of the nation, Nicholas, and you have most grossly offended your father.

The Freudian reference here is clear and we also know that the Oedipus complex[31] is one of the categories of analysis that the film asks us to draw upon. But then, the questions remain and multiply because we know the character of Idi Amin, we know the discourses in which representations of Africa function, and we know the knowledge regimes that give them authority and through which they acquire meaning. Given knowledge of these discourses and their regimes of knowledge production and, knowing who Amin is, we are still prompted to ask: If he knew, why did he not act? Why did he continue to accept medication from him when he was fully aware of this? And Amin, the vengeful vicious killer, is no fool.

To understand the full import of his knowledge and the implications of an adulterous relationship, we should recall what he did to his wife when he found out: he killed her. The cold-blooded way he tells Garrigan about the killing is characteristic: "I made an example of Kay because she betrayed me." But there is no evidence in the film that his attitude toward his doctor changed after this knowledge. When Nicholas is being tortured toward the end of the film, he emphasizes the gravity of his adultery within the context of the traditional beliefs and practices of his people.

> In my village, when you steal the wife of an elder, they take you to a tree and they hang you by your skin. Each time you scream, the evil comes out of you. *Sometimes it can take three days for your evil to be spent.* (Emphasis added)

Yet he did nothing all the while until the doctor tried to poison him. Again the oblique reference in the quote to the Christian crucifixion and resurrection is not lost on us in the hanging by the skin and the three days it take takes for the evil to be spent. It is another example of the complex modalities of citation on which the film depends. But then what is not explained is why it took so long for him to act. Our usual categories for explaining this character and representations of Africa in general are inadequate in this instance. Something has dropped out of this orbit of discursive representation and knowledge. Here the uncited confronts us in all its blankness. To deal with these instances of the uncited we need to seek another archive, a new discourse that will provide us with the "rivers, and lakes and names"—as Conrad's Marlow would say—that would fill this blankness.

## THE SIGNIFICANCE OF THE UNCITED

There is a long history of representations of Africa and Africans in films and an even longer history in the other forms of textuality and performance that preceded filmic representation. In fact, Roland Barthes argues that in France, the government and the mainstream media have developed an AfricanSpeak which he refers to as "African Grammar" in his essay of the same title (Barthes 1979). There is now also a fairly extensive bibliography of scholarship on these representations and works that affirm and consolidate these representations, as well as works that examine, interrogate, and critique them. These images and counterimages and the categories of comprehension and analysis that have developed alongside them have thus become fairly established. Just as there is an archive of these representations, there is also an archive of the analytic tools that we need to understand them. It is therefore tempting to simply read representations of Africa through the frames that these categories have bequeathed to us. This is a temptation that this chapter urges us not to give in to. Rather it is more profitable and beneficial to read, first, for the complex articulations between various modalities of citation currently in use in several domains of textuality and performance and in society and culture as a whole. And second, we must also read for the uncited; for the uncited is the site from which we extend the archive or develop new archives of knowledge beyond that currently provide by our theories and discursive practices.

### NOTES

1. Further reinforcing the "cited" archive, Conrad's title appears more than once in reviews of the film, but is used as a "descriptive phrase." See, for instance, Stein 2006. For more on the influence of Conrad, see Brantlinger 1988, 173–97; Mayer 2002; and Ebron 2002.

2. These images are best expressed in film reviewer William Arnold's (2006, 1) description of the genre: "Africa-is-hell movie." For a more in-depth study and analysis of how Africa is represented, see, for instance, Hawk 1992.

3. While we agree that "imperialism has monopolized the whole system of representation," as Edward Said (1994, 27) asserts, we argue that some moments remain outside of this system of representation.

4. As Amy Novak argues (2008, 40), Africa continues to signify as one of the few remaining "blank spaces on the earth" (Conrad 2006, 7): an indistinguishable, violent, disease-ridden, uncivilized, and unknowable presence in the Western imagination. In this Western narrative, Africa is trauma—a stereotype repeated again in 2006 in the popular and critically acclaimed US films *The Last King of Scotland* and *Blood Diamond*.

5. Several reviewers of the film note connections with the work of Graham Greene: "The story's sexual thread feels very '70s . . . with a dash of Graham Greene intrigue" (Phillips 2006, 1). "The film replays the old Graham Greene trope of Europeans acting out their fascination and guilt amid Third World chaos" (*"The Last King of Scotland,"* 2007, 91).

6. For a fuller discussion of this point, see Garuba 2002.

7. See Kristeva 1986, especially "Word, Dialogue and Novel."

8. Robert Young makes this point in his chapter on Edward Said (Young 2003).

9. For this sort of study, see Pieterse 1998.

10. For instance, works emerging out of the Négritude movement.

11. A recent text that looks at the ways in which white, male writers deploy the tropes of colonialist discourse is Brenda Cooper's *Weary Sons of Conrad* (2002).

12. For an in-depth analysis and theorization of "alterity," see Mbembe 2001.

13. For a complete exploration of this logic, see JanMohamed 1983.

14. Unrestrained sexuality appears throughout the film, but is perhaps most blatantly portrayed in a scene toward the end of the film in which "Amin watches 'Deep Throat' and seeks Nicholas' expert advice on the physiological possibility of Linda Lovelace's purported clitoral condition" (McCarthy 2006, 3).

15. For an elaboration of these strategies of representation see, among others, Spurr 1993.

16. Whether or not the film is successful in problematizing this archive is beyond the scope of this essay. However, in his review of the film, J. R. Jones (2006, 2) praises the director for "unpack[ing] the ignorance and arrogance that still characterize the West's attitude toward Africa." However, he also acknowledges that "no Western director can make a movie about Africa without being accused of colonialism himself, and some critics have faulted *The Last King of Scotland* for focusing on its white hero as black corpses pile up around him" (Jones 2006, 3).

17. It is important to note here that Giles Foden, once an editor of the *Times Literary Supplement,* is not merely a novelist but brings to his craft a wealth of knowledge about literature and literary and cultural traditions of representation; and Kevin Macdonald has a background in documentary filmmaking. On a broader note, it needs to be emphasized that from the travel and exploration writing of the early modern period to more contemporary depictions of Africa, this layering of the fictional and the documentary has been standard practice.

18. As reviewer Michael Phillips (2006, 1) points out, "Shooting in Uganda with cinematographer Anthony Dod Mantle, Macdonald offers high-contrast, deeply saturated images of a poor country dominated by rich greens and browns." Of significance is also the fact that the film was shot in Kampala, making *The Last King of Scotland* "the first Western

production to shoot in Uganda since the second unit of "The African Queen' 56 years ago, and certainly the first time its main city has been shown" (McCarthy 2006, 2).

19. The monkey trope resurfaces on a different register later on when Nicholas Garrigan is told: "You know what they are calling you? His white monkey." Here again, the trope is turned around and the white man rather than the black is the monkey.

20. Traditional healer.

21. "After an accident involving Amin's motorcade and a cow, Garrigan is called upon to fix Amin's injured hand. When no one else will kill the injured cow, who is bellowing in pain, Garrigan snatches the president's gun and disposes of the beast himself" (Voynar 2006, 1).

22. Although "Nicholas Garrigan" is a fictional character, "Amin did have a Scottish doctor" (Schwarzbaum 2006, 1). The Ugandan president also had "a kind of real-life counterpart in a former British soldier named Bob Astles, who became one of Amin's closest advisors and was known in the British press as 'Amin's white rat'" (Chocano 2006, 1). According to David Denby (2006, 3) of the New Yorker, author Giles Foden "concocted the doctor out of several real world figures, including a Scot who treated Amin for a while."

23. During this meeting he is asked to select "an architect to design a building for the upcoming Pan-African Conference" (Veltman 2007).

24. As Stina Chyn (2006, 1) reinforces in her review of the film: "The Last King of Scotland . . . present[s] the unlikely friendship and father-son relationship that develops between two people of very different backgrounds."

25. "When Amin becomes convinced that he's been poisoned (an early indication of his paranoia) and demands medical attention in the middle of the night, Nicholas correctly diagnoses severe flatulence and has his patient relieve the symptoms by bending over a stick held tightly against his pot belly" (Stein 2006, 1).

26. As Teresa A. Booker (2008, 187) reinforces in her review, "At one moment [Amin] is as innocent and charming as a school boy and, in the next, brutal and callous."

27. The Washington Post reviewer Stephen Hunter (2006, 2) describes Nicholas's "constant agitating for sexual satisfaction" as "feckless and disreputable."

28. Moreover, "director Macdonald, a Scotsman himself, stages a hilarious scene in which Amin appears at a public ceremony wearing a kilt surrounded by Africans performing a Scottish song" (McCarthy 2006, 2).

29. In her FilmThreat review of The Last King of Scotland, Chyn (2006, 1) explains that the film "is as much about the Ugandan dictator as a historical figure as it is about Nick Garrigan, a signifier of the white 'Other.'"

30. "Smiling into cameras, [the Ugandan president] dropped provocations like bombs: 'I don't like human flesh. It's too salty for me'" (Dargis 2006, 1).

31. Earlier in the film, Amin tells Nicholas, "You are like my own son."

REFERENCES

Achebe, Chinua. 1989. "An Image of Africa: Racism in Conrad's Heart of Darkness." In Hopes and Impediments: Selected Essays, 1–20. New York: Doubleday.
Arnold. William. 2006. "'Last King of Scotland' Is a Fanciful Take on a Ruthless Tyrant." Seattle Post-Intelligencer, October 6. http://seattlepi.nwsource.com/movies/287697_scotland06q.html.

Ashcroft, Bill, Garth Griffiths, and Helen Tiffin. 2002. *The Empire Writes Back: Theory and Practice in Post-colonial Literatures.* 2nd ed. New York: Routledge.

Barthes, Roland. 1978. "The Death of the Author." In *Image-Music-Text.* Translated by Stephen Heath. New York: Hill and Wang.

———. 1979. "African Grammar." In *The Eiffel Tower and Other Mythologies.* New York: Hill and Wang.

Booker, Teresa A. 2008. "Film Reviews: The Last King of Scotland." *Teaching Sociology* 36 (2): 187.

Bourdieu, Pierre. 1977. *Outline of a Theory of Practice.* Translated by Richard Nice. Cambridge: Cambridge University Press.

Brantlinger, Patrick. 1988. "The Genealogy of the Myth of the Dark Continent." In *Rule of Darkness: British Literature and Imperialism, 1830–1914,* 173–97. Ithaca: Cornell University Press.

Chocano, Carina. 2006. "Movie Review: 'Last King of Scotland': Forest Whitaker Portrays Ugandan Dictator Idi Amin, Gillian Anderson and James McAvoy Costar." *Los Angeles Times,* September 27. http://www.calendarlive.com.

Chyn, Stina. 2006. "The Last King of Scotland." *FilmThreat,* October 13. http://www.filmthreat.com.

Conrad, Joseph. 2006 [1899]. *Heart of Darkness.* Edited by Paul B. Armstrong. A Norton Critical Edition. 4th ed. New York: W. W. Norton.

Cooper, Brenda. 2002. *Weary Sons of Conrad: White Fiction against the Grain of Africa's Dark Heart.* New York: Peter Lang.

Dargis, Manohla. 2006. "An Innocent Abroad, Seduced by a Madman." *New York Times,* September 27. http://movies.nytimes.com/2006/09/27/movies/27king.html.

Denby, David. 2006. "The Current Cinema: Power Players: 'All the King's Men' and 'The Last King of Scotland.'" *New Yorker,* October 2. http://www.newyorker.com/archive/2006/10/02/061002crci_cinema?.

Ebron, Paulla A. 2002. *Performing Africa.* Princeton: Princeton University Press.

Garuba, Harry. 2002. "Mapping the Land/Body/Subject: Colonial and Postcolonial Geographies in African Narrative." *Alternation* 9 (1): 87–116.

Greene, Graham. 1936. *Journey without Maps.* London: Heinemann.

Hawk, Beverly G. 1992. *Africa's Media Image.* New York: Praeger.

Hickey, Dennis, and Kenneth C. Wylie. 1993. *An Enchanting Darkness: The American Vision of Africa in the Twentieth Century.* East Lansing: Michigan State University Press.

Hunter, Stephen. 2006. "'Last King of Scotland' Usurps the Story of Idi Amin." *Washington Post,* October 4. http://www.washingtonpost.comm/wp-dyn/content/article/2006/10/03/AR2006100301617_pf.html.

Hutcheons, Linda. 1988. *The Poetics of Postmodernism: History, Theory, Fiction.* New York: Routledge.

JanMohamed, Abdul. 1983. *Manichean Aesthetics: The Politics of Literature in Colonial Africa.* Amherst: University of Massachusetts Press.

Jones, J. R. 2006. "Movies: A Place in the World." *Chicago Reader,* October 6. http://www.chicagoreader.com/features/stories/moviereviews/061006/.

Kristeva, Julia. 1986. *The Kristeva Reader.* Edited by Toril Moi. New York: Columbia University Press.

"*Last King of Scotland, The.*" 2007. *Time* 169 (17), April 23, p. 91.

Macdonald, Kevin, dir. 2007. *The Last King of Scotland*. Beverly Hills, CA: Twentieth Century Fox Home Entertainment.

Mayer, Ruth. 2002. *Artificial Africas: Colonial Images in the Times of Globalization*. Hanover, NH: University Press of New England.

Mbembe, Achille. 2001. *On the Postcolony*. Berkeley: University of California Press.

McCarthy, Todd. 2006. "The Last King of Scotland." *Variety*, September 6. http://www .variety.com/story.asp?i=story&r=VE1117931479&c=31.

Mudimbe, V. Y. 1988. *The Invention of Africa: Gnosis, Philosophy and the Order of Knowledge*. Bloomington: Indiana University Press.

Novak, Amy. 2008. "Who Speaks? Who Listens? The Problem of Address in Two Nigerian Trauma Novels." *Studies in the Novel* 40 (1–2): 31–51.

Phillips, Michael. 2006. "Movie Review: 'The Last King of Scotland.'" Chicago Metromix. http://chicago.metromix.com.

Pieterse, Jan Nederveen. 1998. *White on Black: Images of Africa and Blacks in Western Popular Culture*. New Haven: Yale University Press.

Said, Edward. 1979. *Orientalism*. New York: Vintage.

———. 1994. *Culture and Imperialism*. New York: Vintage.

Schwarzbaum, Lisa. 2006. "Movie Review: The Last King of Scotland (2006)." *Entertainment Weekly*, September 27. http://www.ew.com/ew/.

Spurr, David. 1993. *The Rhetoric of Empire: Colonial Discourse in Journalism, Travel Writing, and Imperial Administration*. Durham, NC: Duke University Press.

Stein, Ruthe. 2006. "Whitaker Mines Amin's Heart of Darkness in 'King.'" *San Francisco Chronicle*, October 6. http://www.sfgate.com/cgi-bin/article.cgi?f=/c/a/2006/10 /06/DDG97LHNJA1.DTL.

Veltman, Chloe. 2007. "Review of the Week: When Doctor Meets Dictator." *British Medical Journal* 334 (100). January 13. http://www.bmj.com/cgi/content/full/334/7584/100.

Voynar, Kim. 2006. "The Last King of Scotland." *Telluride Review*, September 3. http:// www.cinematical.com/2006/09/03telluride-review-the-last-king-of-scotland.

Young, Robert. 2003. *Postcolonialism: A Very Short Introduction*. Oxford: Oxford University Press.

## TWO
# The Troubled Terrain of Human Rights Films
*Blood Diamond, The Last King of Scotland,* and *The Devil Came on Horseback*
MARGARET R. HIGONNET, WITH ETHEL R. HIGONNET

> What filmmakers should do is get as much authenticity
> as possible.
>
> —Robert F. Worth, "Another Round of Explosions,
> but This Time It's Fake"

The last decade has witnessed a proliferation not only of low-budget documentary films but of mass-market cinema with an apparent human rights agenda. This phenomenon invites a number of questions about the uses of cinema as a vehicle to effect social change. How has film become the dominant vehicle for getting out the message about human rights? Kevin Rozario suggests this question in his study of the Red Cross's paradoxical use of "delicious horrors" to make humanitarian appeals (Rozario 2003). Whereas nineteenth-century realist fiction staked claims first to mirroring and later to photographing reality, mass-market adventure films stake claims to telling us the truth about humanitarian calamities by literally embedding cameras in the narrative. In turn, as documentary films have developed, they have appropriated older narrative structures borrowed from those of historical fiction. Fact and fiction, naked truth and narrative seem to be in tension with each other, but in fact they are blurred, as Hayden White has argued in his study of the relation between narrative and historical representation. We may expect to find the "true" and "real" in "the chaotic form of 'historical records,'" but we also are driven to organize these into the "formal coherency of a story" in order to shape meaning (White 1987, 4). To extend Hayden White's thesis that historians draw on four types of narrative to shape meaning—tragedy, romance, comedy, and irony—we may ask whether the documentarist who depicts the violations attendant on violence must draw on tragedy, romance, or irony (White 1973). If we look at films about the violence that has beset Africa in recent decades, it appears that loosely humanitarian films on the topic often fall prey to paternalistic and sentimental narrative forms, precisely the flaw that critics have identified in humanitarianism itself. While Richard Rorty links the cultivation of human rights to sentimental education (Rorty 1993, 122–23, 128–29), Beran (2008), Kennedy (2004), and Rieff (2002) all by contrast indict the sentimental failures of humanitarianism. The ethnographic cinematographer Jean Rouch has commented on "the paternalism characteristic of even the films made with the best intentions" (Rouch 2003, 66). Most fall into a class that Josef Gugler calls "humanploitation" (letter to the author, 2008).

These problems become visible from the outset in the figures selected as the central focalizers to mediate our imaginative reconstruction of events. Whose voices, in brief, are heard? As we shall see, cinematic effects may build on narrative strategies familiar in print, such as romance to provide closure, or instead they may seek to engage the viewer "beyond the ending" by cutting short conventions of resolution or by implying a cycle that returns. Can such films shape an empathetic response to humanitarian crises and propel viewers toward active intervention? To explore these questions, this chapter examines three films that span the strategies visible in high to low budget productions.

### HOW HAS FILM BECOME THE DOMINANT VEHICLE
### FOR GETTING OUT THE MESSAGE ABOUT HUMAN RIGHTS?

Ethnographic work on Africa using the vehicle of film dates back to the late forties (*Au pays des pygmées*, 1948), and starting in the 1950s, film in Africa became "an essential medium of mass communication" (Rouch 2003, 67). In *Africa Shoots Back*, Melissa Thackway explores the genre of sub-Saharan Francophone "memory-history films" that blur the boundary between documentary and fiction, a form that continues to dominate production, if not the market (Thackway 2003, 97–119). In the last thirty years, human rights advocacy concerning Africa has increasingly turned to the documentary film, exploiting the power of the visual to awaken the audience's emotions.

Humanitarians have drawn on the shock of the image for over two centuries to effect reforms. Enlightenment philosophers such as Rousseau and Adam Smith theorized links between images and moral emotions, as Richard Wilson and Richard Brown explain in their introduction to *Humanitarianism and Suffering: The Mobilization of Empathy:* "The emotional nature of compassion is closely linked to visual and literary images of suffering and innocence" (2009, 3). Around 1800, for example, visual representations of torture suffered by slaves, such as engravings by William Blake, mobilized readers on behalf of abolition. Victorian newspaper xylographs of half-clad women and children crawling through tunnels in coal mines mobilized readers to support legal restrictions on child labor. Early photography likewise from the nineteenth century onward depicted the harsh circumstances of rural labor and urban poverty, a century before the right to be free from hunger was declared by the UN. The contradictory use of the visual in defense of human rights emerges, however, when we consider that nineteenth-century photographers officially documented colonial acts such as the execution of chained Sepoys by cannon fire, following violence against English colonial women and children.[1] Such images may become double-edged swords.

With the advent of moving pictures, the great early cinematographer Sergei Eisenstein in *The Battleship Potemkin* (1925), his historical reenactment of a 1905 mutiny, made use of montage, close-ups, dramatic angles, and the movement of large masses to dramatize the psychological impact of summary executions and of a massacre by Cossack soldiers in order to suppress a popular demonstration. Yet film has served totalitarian as well as humanitarian interests: Walter Benjamin in the thirties had good reason to critique the powerful effects of film used for fascist political ends (Benjamin 1968). The critical use of cinematic documentation to analyze current human rights violations came to the fore at the middle of the twentieth century. Indeed, since the seventies, activists have begun to capitalize on cinematic media to mobilize political intervention in human rights crises. Thus, filmmaker Lisa Jackson's HBO report on rape in the Congo, *The Greatest Silence* (2008), uses interviews not only with victims but also with "warrior-rapists" to try to change their attitudes and to expose the shame attendant on their systematic brutalities.

Cinema as a modern medium brings with it certain baggage: early twentieth-century theorists relished its capacity to capture action and transformation scenes. Speed, change, and machinery all met in this new technology for projecting images and narrative. Many early silent films record travel—by locomotive, boat, tramcar, or automobile—and they depict touristic scenes of all kinds, from the piers of "Manhatta" to exotic locales in the Pacific and in Africa. Thus, the seductions of technology and the power of film to bring the world "home" fostered exotic voyeurism that seems to come into play when film is the vehicle chosen to depict human rights violations.

Still, the turn in the last three decades toward movies about human rights marks an innovation. Here the documentary impulse may be rooted in the very early use of still photographs to record the losses incurred in wars: in the Crimea (the birthplace of the Red Cross), during the American Civil War, in the Boer War, and during the Chinese civil war in the late twenties, photographs of the dead documented not only death but the grotesque suffering of many. It is not accidental that many of the human rights crises that challenge us today arise in the context of civil wars, and that in an era of realpolitik photography testifies to the fact that modern wars have become more, rather than less, violent in their impact on civilian bodies and minds, as Susan Sontag (1993) and others have observed.

## IS DOCUMENTARY FILM A GENRE? HOW DO HISTORICAL REENACTMENT AND FICTION INTERSECT IN DOCUMENTARY FILMS?

The boundary between documentary and fiction is readily blurred in "documentary" films, which rely on the narrative structures of history, as well as in films that deliberately reenact historical events around a fictional core and insert stock news footage (Thackway 2003). Not only does documentary by ethnographers such as Jean Rouch draw on techniques of fiction such as narrative focused on an individual, but it may subordinate the presentation of facts to a humanitarian appeal to sentiment, since it aims to mobilize the viewer. These are issues that this essay addresses by examining the uses of visual evidence, the insertion of a narrative with a protagonist (often supported by a romance motif), the representation of victims, and the specifically cinematic treatment of visual materials.

Christian Johnston, director of a film dramatizing the Lebanese civil war of 1975–1990, for example, in 2008 used as extras men who had fought on opposite sides in Lebanon twenty or thirty years earlier. Emil Zir, now thirty-eight, returned from exile, notes: "It brings back the memories" (Worth 2008, A4). And one of the foreign actors comments, "When you're standing next to someone who's actually been on the front line, that's a reality check." Although equipped with a permit, the actors were interrupted by soldiers who heard them fighting once again in a hospital that had been burned out decades ago. According to journalist Robert Worth, Lebanese Army platoons were drawn to the site of the filming, believing the gunfire was real. Johnston's previous film, *The September Tapes* (2002), was likewise "mistaken for a documentary, both during the filming and at the Sundance Film Festival"

(Worth 2008, A4). Historical action films thus deliberately seek to achieve the effects of documentary through the accurate details of setting and costume that were formerly the hallmarks of the realist novel.

As Johnston's films suggest, the context of war in which human rights and humanitarian issues have arisen has special seductive power for the narrative medium of film. The earliest film shorts demonstrate a remarkable concern for both everyday details of motion and melodrama—trains and thieves; Eisenstein's *Potemkin* moves dramatically from passivity to mutiny, and from massacre to a confrontation of battleships at sea. The traits of speed, violent destruction, and mass events (especially the romance of motion) continue to be important in leftist films after World War II (such as *Z* and *The Battle of Algiers*) that turned to themes of political oppression and colonial injustice. The energy necessary to bring about change, formerly incarnate in a Hollywood sheriff on horseback, finds symbolic representation in metal vehicles—cars, trains, and airplanes. The individualization of historical narrative may draw its force from "action" adventures that require the protagonist to run down streets amid the outbreak of fire and gunfire. The palpable violence of the setting and the speed of the tracking camera transfer metonymically to the central actor in films that unite entertainment with empathy, where the individual protagonist has displaced the broader cast of Eisenstein's experimental films.

## *BLOOD DIAMOND:* AN ACTION ADVENTURE WITH ITS HEART ON ITS SLEEVE

The films discussed here stand at several different points on a spectrum of choices about the representation of historical fact. The first example, Edward Zwick's *Blood Diamond* (2006), presents a contemporary historical fiction about the civil war in Sierra Leone. Skewered by Manohla Dargis as an "exceptionally foolish thriller . . . gilded in money and dripping with sanctimony," this action flick turns misery into a backdrop, underscored by "documentary-like images of children roaming a mound of garbage, by the blank-looking men and women sitting in trash-strewn streets and by the periodically brandished arm and leg stumps" (Dargis 2006).[2] As Dargis shows, historical elements within the fiction are easily overlooked. Although the title refers to a rare pink stone found by Solomon Vandy, a Mende fisherman enslaved by the rebel Revolutionary United Front (RUF) to pan in a river for diamonds, the term draws on the familiar language of activists who have condemned the trade in diamonds that has fed violent internal conflicts in Africa as well as the historic oppression of Africans by white colonizers. While the fictional Solomon (Djimon Hounsou) and Danny Archer (Leonardo DiCaprio), a Rhodesian mercenary who trades diamonds for arms with the RUF, stand in the foreground, in the background we find a plausible version of the chaos in 1999–2003 of mercenaries, smugglers, rebel abductions of women and children, and massacres on all sides. Particularly disturbing are realistic scenes that portray the rebels amputating people's hands to stop them from voting in upcoming elections.

By contrast, white violence portrayed in the film fits largely into conventional tropes of a military battle in an "action-adventure" film. Archer and his ruthless middleman Coetzee, a white South African mercenary employed by an international diamond company CEO, are both plausibly veterans of the historical "32 Battalion," a prominent unit in the South African Border War, made up of Angolan and Rhodesian soldiers and white South African officers. In conjunction with the political thesis that rebel violence is generated by the diamond trade (De Beers is indirectly indicted), the film also alludes pointedly to the 1995 hiring of the mercenary South African security firm Executive Outcomes by the provisional government of Sierra Leone.

In contrast with the groveling poverty and mutilation shown early in the film, the escape of the fisherman with his son to London is totally unrealistic, as are the subsequent events of their being reunited with family and helping an idealistic American journalist, Maddy Bowen, document her story about links between the diamond industry and the civil war. Zwick imposes optimistic closure: Solomon Vandy prepares to deliver a speech in South Africa, a reference to a 2000 meeting in Kimberley that led to the Kimberley Process Certification Scheme (2003) to curb the trade in conflict diamonds. By implication, individuals can change history. As MaryEllen Higgins has pointed out, however, Solomon does not in fact utter a word.

THE LAST KING OF SCOTLAND: DOCUMENTARY EMBEDDED IN FICTION

Halfway along the spectrum of historicity, *The Last King of Scotland* (2006), directed by Kevin Macdonald, lays out the narrative of fictional young Dr. Garrigan, a Scot who has accepted his first post at a clinic in Uganda, and then finds himself swept up in the entourage of President Idi Amin, seduced by the attractions of luxury, cars, and attention from this powerful political leader. By contrast to Barbet Schroeder's 1974 documentary, *General Idi Amin Dada: A Self Portrait*, the author of the 1998 book from which the film is drawn, Giles Foden, says that 80 percent of the narrative is fiction, but 100 percent is truth (Macdonald 2006, interview on DVD). Dr. Garrigan is an invention, but he draws us into the bizarre world of Amin, and his immature weakness gives an ironic twist to the usual white protagonist's role. The film frequently inserts documentary clips apparently taken from TV news footage about the rise of Amin and the growing international concern about his deployment of violence against rivals. The climax of the film is framed by the turning point in Amin's career: a scene at the airport Entebbe, where a plane seized by Palestinians in fact landed with its hostages. The centrality of the Amin character to the drama pushes this film closer to reenactment than to the tradition of historical fiction shaped by Sir Walter Scott, in which the historical leaders who appear are usually secondary to the action. Moreover, the actors and advisers to the film (who appear in the documentary supplements on the DVD) consider changes made to the historical record to be exceptions to the overall attempt to shape an accurate account.

Director Kevin Macdonald aimed at a nuanced version of the history that would be more complex than any simple narrative of Amin's evil. Stephen Rwangyezi, who played the role of Wasswa, comments that the film should not simply demonize Idi Amin, and a relatively young man who played a bodyguard suggests, "We should strive to make the country bigger than Amin" (DVD). These divergent goals driving those who participated in making the film leave traces of inconsistency as well as complexity in Amin's characterization, although they do not free the film from a Western-oriented depiction of a dictator, a black Kurtz at the "heart of Africa."

*THE DEVIL CAME ON HORSEBACK:* REENACTMENT-DOCUMENTARY

The third film considered here, *The Devil Came on Horseback* (2007), whose directors have won five awards, including the Silverdocs Festival "Witness Award," is anchored by documentary photographs, handheld video, and film, as well as news clips that offer a layered history from 2004 to 2006, reenacting and analyzing the experiences of Marine Captain Brian Steidle in the Sudan. The reenactment absorbs into its own frame the primary documentary narrative about Steidle's first job in the Nuba mountains monitoring the Sudanese ceasefire of 2003, and then his decision to volunteer with the African Union forces monitoring the conflict in Darfur. Photographs are filmed, as if they were moments in action that the cameraman is viewing, stop-shot rather than snap-shot. Boundaries blur. From a documentary point of view, a certain historical specificity in the images is lacking: in spite of occasional references to a map of the region, the emphasis in the insertion of grisly photographs is more on the shock of what Steidle saw in the months he was in the Sudan than on tallying the suffering and losses of the individual towns he visited. The relationship between film and photograph, then, is somewhat troubling. Nonetheless, it must be underscored that historical documentaries make artistic choices, some more powerful than others. Just as Ken Burns interweaves interviews with photographs or film footage, so too Sundberg and Stern interweave newsreels and interviews with Steidle, with prints and footage that he himself took. As we shall see, their highly self-conscious artistry exploits powerful narrative and cinematic devices that serve their human rights agenda.

### WHO MEDIATES OUR IMAGINATIVE RECONSTRUCTION OF EVENTS?

Across the spectrum, it is striking that these quite different films rely on white Western men as the protagonists who mediate the viewers' experiences of events. Not only are they central to the plot, but their ability to recognize the human rights disasters that they encounter is central to the positioning of the viewer. Thus they become the "focalizers" through whom the African situation is filtered. They may also become the heroes whose purpose in the plot is to offer solutions to these crises. Their masculine authority is reinforced by the insertion of romance elements into the plot.

*Blood Diamond* typifies the action-adventure propensity to focus on a white protagonist who must assume responsibility for solving the problems set up by the predictable plot. While the narrative begins with the destruction of Solomon Vandy's world, the introduction of Danny Archer, the diamond smuggler whom we might well consider one of the causes of Solomon's problems, is the first step toward reconstructing Solomon's family. Archer's own early loss of his parents humanizes him, as the attractive journalist Maddy Bowen discovers. But his most important actions are usually undertaken running and firing a gun. As Dargis comments, "The faces remain obscured, the voices muted, even as Danny comes sharply into focus." His last stand on a hill above the Kono diamond fields establishes his status as hero, as he holds off soldiers trying to seize Solomon, Dia, and the pink diamond. In perfect mimicry of Hemingway's *For Whom the Bell Tolls*, Archer sacrifices himself for others, laconically telling Maddy on his cell phone, "It's a real story now, and you can write the hell out of it." This stock

Western action plot is the mold that Hollywood films with a humanitarian focus must break.

Some recent Hollywood blockbusters have reworked the theme of the orientalizing white protagonist ironically, while still privileging Western civilization and using camerawork to perpetuate an orientalist gaze. Thus in *The Last King of Scotland* (2006), director Kevin Macdonald frames the naive young Dr. Nicholas Garrigan's story in a way that embraces tropes about exotic and erotic Africa and about Western solutions to African problems. Unlike the usual white knight in shining armor, however, Nicholas Garrigan is a callow postadolescent medical school graduate who chooses to join an older doctor at a clinic in Uganda, not because he shares a calling to help immiserated people who have no access to medical services, but because he wants to get as far away as possible from his domineering doctor father. His initial perception of Africa corresponds to an exotic dream: children laugh along dirt roads down which his bus rides, and a beautiful young woman invites him to spend the night with her before he continues to his destination. In a classic paternalistically colonialist scene, he is contrasted to a witch doctor performing in the street nearby. Yet this narrative overturns the stock plot about a heroic white observer of human rights violations in significant ways, most importantly through Dr. Garrigan's refusal to observe anything, and his careless sacrifice of other lives, as order breaks down around him. Actor James McAvoy's center-part hairstyle, slight build, and dazzled gaze at social functions and political theater contribute to the characterization of his personal and political immaturity. In an interview, McAvoy explained that he worked to capture Garrigan's contradictions: although Garrigan means well, he lacks self-awareness and is both arrogant and morally weak (*Last King* 2006). The aim of McAvoy's portrayal is to shape identification by the audience with the youth—"He is you"—while inviting our transformation. Only after Garrigan's passport has been stolen does he study photographs that document the individual and group murders through which Amin has maintained power. The massacres of roughly 300,000 rivals and other ethnic groups flash across the screen in a blurred sequence of photographs.

The documentary *Devil Came on Horseback* exposes the tragedy taking place in Darfur as seen through the eyes of an American witness whose initial naïveté functions to draw the reader into his story. Whereas the morally weak Dr. Garrigan of *Last King* probably repels many viewers, most American viewers are probably attracted to former US marine captain Brian Steidle, as we learn along with him. Steidle is the central hero and narrator of this autobiographical documentary about his experience in Darfur and about what he has done since returning to the US to take action against the genocide there. Using the exclusive photographs and firsthand testimony of Steidle, the film, directed by Annie Sundberg and Ricki Stern, takes the viewer on a jolting ride into the heart of Darfur, Sudan, where the government of Omar Al-Bashir is giving military support to "Janjaweed" militia whose raids systematically wipe out the black African Muslim residents of this western region. As an official (but unarmed) United Nations monitor and then African Union observer, Steidle had access to parts of the country that no journalist could penetrate. In his own words, "I was totally unprepared for what I would see" (*Devil* 2007). Unarmed except with a camera, he experiences being fired upon, taken hostage, and barred by his own commander from intervening to save the lives of young children. Ultimately frustrated by the inaction of the international community, Steidle resigned and returned to the US to expose the images and tell his story to journalists, politicians, students at universities, and even prosecutors at the Hague.

In a linear opening account, a flashback shows Steidle as a blond toddler playing by the ocean; a proud summary of his volunteering to become a Marine narrates how he broke his neck and both feet. These credentials establish him as a quintessentially admirable young American: an innocent, patriotic, courageous (white) man. Almost by accident he volunteers to go to Darfur. The film explores Steidle's transformation from soldier to observer to witness and activist, and ultimately to central character of the film. We see a man at first confounded by his naïveté and then confronted by the urgency of a humanitarian catastrophe that he sees unfolding firsthand. An everyman figure (and hence one that American viewers will find it easier to identify with), Steidle is initially unequipped to absorb the horror around him. His background as a soldier shapes part of his discomfort in his assignment: "If I were looking through a scope and not through a camera we could end this." At an attack he witnesses on Hamada, he is restrained by his commander: "We weren't even supposed to protect the people," he comments. Exhausted, Brian leaves for the United States, where his sister encourages him to show his photographs and tell his story. In a second odyssey performing relief work with her, he travels to Chad, Rwanda, and finally back to the United States. His effort to get the story out is the most complex moment in the narrative for the viewer, as first his father and then officials at the State Department urge him not to show his photographs, and he expresses his despair at his impotence to bring about change. Near the end, he is asked if he is a whistleblower. No, he answers, in a heroic understatement, "I wouldn't call it that. I'm just some guy who tried to wake up the conscience of the people."

Gayatri Chakravorty Spivak has famously asked, "Can the Subaltern Speak?" and the question is certainly pertinent to these films. Whatever their good intentions, Western films that raise issues of human rights often fall into a striking pattern that recapitulates the colonialist and paternalist representation of the white man who saves the people of color from themselves. The voice of the white witness frequently overrides the voices of eyewitnesses and actual victims of violation. But this issue of paternalism may be more complicated than appears at first glance.

The implausible story of Solomon Vandy, a Mende fisherman, stands in for the suffering of civilians in Sierra Leone caught in the grindstone between the government and rebel groups such as the RUF. Although the role is played with dignified reserve by Djimon Hounsou, and Solomon's situation as fisherman and father is carefully established, as a representative of African suffering he is little more than a cardboard cutout, largely a silent victim as rape, pillage, and mutilation surround him. In this case, an attempt to individualize mass suffering fails signally, and the final satisfaction of Solomon's desire for his family may foreclose the kind of humanitarian outreach that can flow from an effective presentation of injured innocence.

Ironically, in *The Last King of Scotland*, Dr. Garrigan's blindness to the brutality of Idi Amin's rule explains and cinematically justifies the blindness of the camera to the suffering of Ugandans. Even everyday life in Uganda remains almost invisible, compared with the ultramodern hospital in Kampala that Dr. Garrigan visits briefly. Significantly, the weight of visual representation plays down the human rights issues on which the actual history of Idi Amin rests. To be sure, Amin himself is humanized in his craving for admiration as well as in his demented rage, and the role is brilliantly played by Forest Whitaker, who won an Oscar for his performance. But the massacres of an estimated 300,000 political rivals, intellectuals, and ethnic groups under Amin are selectively flashed on the screen and blurred in a sequence of photographs through which the doctor flips. At the home of the British diplomat to whom Garrigan turns for help, the camera shows a rapid succession of photos that pile up the evidence of assassinations, without granting any single instance of suffering emotional weight. The hallucinatory sequence of scenes that leads to Kay's body in a morgue blurs her body and erases her individual experience of pain. By contrast to the hundreds of thousands dead in Uganda, the sadism of Amin's guards directed at the doctor draws the close and prolonged attention of the camera. The line between black and white is grotesquely simplified. One must turn to supplementary interviews with extras and advisers on the DVD to gain a sense of the lived history of this period.

Particularly important indices of the film's ultimately orientalizing gaze are the quick steps through which the script brings the narrative to closure. Despite his torture, once Dr. Garrigan has been released and washed up a bit, he can walk and merge into the crowd of hostages who have gathered at the Entebbe airport. It is not a Ugandan whom we see tortured, but Garrigan. And he is serendipitously freed at just the right moment to return to Europe. To be sure, our last glimpse of the doctor shows an exhausted victim, not a transformed healer of political trauma who will be believed because he is a white man—the reason given by the Ugandan doctor for freeing Garrigan. Instead, the political solution to the local crisis, intertitles explain, will come from an Israeli offer to negotiate with the Palestinians who had abducted the plane, then a successful raid on Entebbe—a white intervention to end the crisis. As the sun begins to rise, a flashback reminds us of the children who were loping beside the bus when Dr. Garrigan first arrived in Uganda, their youthful gaiety promising a better future ahead. But the plane takes off. Uganda is a problem that Garrigan can leave behind. How is the viewer to engage this unresolved ending?

Until the final moments of *The Devil Came on Horseback,* Brian Steidle's voice dominates his account of the genocide in the western Darfur region. Pictures rather than people speak. In his documentation of a conflict that has claimed 400,000 lives and displaced 2.5 million people, only a few Darfuris speak directly to the camera for more than a few seconds. Upon Steidle's arrival in Darfur, he rushes to gather information about a massacre that has just taken place in El Fashir, where a townsman explains the attack on a market day and shows the results. In this segment, the team collects forensic evidence such as bullet shells and is led to the bodies of the dead.[3] Two inhabitants describe the attack, guiding the monitors; we are told that people are being killed here because they are Africans, black—in a violation of the 1948 Hague Convention on Human Rights condemning as genocide the "intentional destruction" of a group because of its racial or religious identity.

In the next sequence Steidle visits a camp for internally displaced persons (IDPs). Here he records the testimony of traumatized victims, their sentences broken up as they obsessively list their losses. One woman who speaks English explains they have "no bowls, no seeds, no water . . . no nothing" (my ellipsis). In an incomplete lament, she says, "If today I say I am a teacher . . ." She has lost her mother, her son, her job, her dog, and her town. "We are scattered like seeds." Intercut in the background are boys playing with a soccer ball, their relish of life not yet lost. Another woman weeps, "We didn't understand why [they] did this." Houses collapsed on the old members of the community; she lost her fourteen-year-old son.

A defector from the Janjaweed is "not afraid to tell you the way it is." Filmed for his own protection from behind, the boy replies to questions about who trained the Janjaweed: "Government." Who gave them weapons? "Government. They are pay us" [sic]. He describes his experience: "The order is to go kill . . . whistle . . . they spread about . . . repeating slogans . . . all attack directly." Sobbing, the boy explains that the slogan is "Kill the slaves."

After leaving Darfur and presenting his photographs to reporter Nicholas Kristof, the State Department, and audiences at the Holocaust Museum as well as college campuses, Brian Steidle returned to Africa, visiting refugee camps in Eastern Chad and in Rwanda. In Chad, three refugees speak briefly: a young man who recounts the loss of his little brothers and father, a woman who lists her losses in broken speech, and an eloquent older man who tells the story of an attack by Antonov fire bomber, explaining that his people have received no help from Arab countries, even though they are Muslim. Dignified, he turns the corner of the house and wipes his eyes, as the camera follows him. His silence speaks as powerfully as his story. In Rwanda, a survivor of the massacre tells us about the "safe haven" Murambi, where the Interahamwe police came in and killed all who had sought refuge there, including his wife and five children. He himself had been stripped naked "because they thought I was dead." At the very end, the director of a refugee camp and Pastor Habimana speak about rape and HIV—topics "we do not talk openly about." Thus, they become the mediators who shield the victims from exposure and the persecution entailed when they bear witness to such violations—for even reporting rape may cause punishment for illegal sexual activities.

Ultimately, for all the pathos of each of these tales, the childhoods and families and personalities of the Africans who speak in this earnest film remain blanks in the "heart of darkness." They turn to Americans, who, they hope, will act to bring them help. That dependence structures the narrative, as their accounts are chopped up and spliced into the story of the American witness who wants to mobilize his audience. Their voices are mediated, and their own stories stay shrouded in mystery.

Steidle's survivors point toward a question that is not usually asked in this context of the usurpation of voice. When the camera follows the thin, elderly man in the Chad refugee camp as he walks around the corner of the house to wipe his eyes, the viewer is eavesdropping, intruding voyeuristically on his grief. When the Rwandan survivor tells about surviving by playing dead, he comments, "It was terribly hard to see." The trauma of the eye-witness marks the broken sentences of some and the silences of others. Although the prosecutor Luis Moreno Ocampo declares, "We're empowering them," to testify for the camera can itself be traumatic, not therapeutic, as Dembour and Haslam have argued about judicial proceedings at the International Criminal Tribunal for the former Yugoslavia at the Hague (2004, 160). In cases like this, what should be the norms of respectful documentation?

HOW DO CINEMATIC VISUAL DEVICES SHAPE AN EMPATHETIC RESPONSE TO HUMANITARIAN CRISES TO PROPEL VIEWERS TOWARD ACTIVE INTERVENTION?

*The Last King* deploys theatrical motifs to dramatize the theater of power. Cinematically, these appear first in celebrations of Amin's rise to power, in which women dance on raised platforms while villagers gather in a mass to watch, and Amin himself makes demagogic speeches. If masculinity is destabilized, visual violence is inscribed as the reality on which power rests. After the murder of Kay and Garrigan's involuntary betrayal that he had attempted to poison Amin (he grabs a bottle of pills from the servant who has been ordered to try one), the dictator excoriates the young imperialist for thinking to himself "I will play a white man with the natives." This line forcibly reminds us that orientalizing attitudes entail a theater of power, just as Amin's own mimicry of imperialist rituals through his display of guards in Scottish uniforms "si(g)nifies on" British displays of power. The theme of theater and empty role-playing here echoes a scene that juxtaposes proxies dressed up as Amin to ward off assassination attempts. Amin continues his denunciation of his treacherous "son," however, with a claim to power that will be anchored in violence against the flesh: "We are not a game, Nicholas . . . we are real." As a driving antagonist whose presence fills the screen, Amin recenters the narrative.[4]

Among the three films considered here, *The Devil Came on Horseback* makes the most complicated use of visual devices to engage the reader. At the outset, the camera is set on the passenger seat of a car, filming Brian Steidle as he drives down an African road, telling us why he is there. Visually the movie situates us beside him in the car, seeing with a camera what he is seeing, focusing on him as our intermediary. As the driver, he is the agent who drives the narrative we will hear, and (as we will learn quickly), he is also the cameraman whose photographs taken in 2004 flash onto the screen as if they were what we were looking at as we pass by. Steidle plays the role here not exactly of the author, although he is credited for his "exclusive photographs and firsthand testimony," but rather the role of "engaging narrator" (Warhol 1986) who invites the viewer to enter the world he is about to re-create.

The cinematographer in effect re-creates or reenacts the exploration of the Sudan that Steidle undertook in 2004. His vision becomes ours as the film projects onto widescreen many of the 1,000 plus photographs he took—images mediated from his eye to his camera to the film screen to our eyes. Our closeness to him in the car situates us as if we were his sister, listening firsthand to a recapitulation of the piecemeal e-mail narrative that she had received in 2004, when she accompanied him on his return to the region in 2006, to interview refugees in the camps in Chad. In the car, the camera turns from Steidle to the side, to view villages as they flash by, catching traces of the violence that are visible everywhere. With striking effect, the camera also swivels to the rear, looking back, to suggest the retrospective distance between the filmed account and the still photographs that are contemporaneous with the acts of violence that Steidle directly witnessed. "I was totally unprepared for what I would see." That phrase, "what I would see," introduces filmed images of Steidle's snapshots of wounds and dead bodies.

This layering underscores the multiple types of visual documentation that texture the narrative in an analogue of "thick" description. Most important are the thousand photos[5]—Steidle's documents—that serve to support his testimony to the journalist Nicholas Kristof, to US representatives in Congress, and to the prosecutor Luis Moreno Ocampo at the Hague. Black-and-white or color clips from TV newscasts anchor the narrative firmly in a recognizable history. UN testimony about the conflict in Sudan in 2004 and other intercut news reports, such as Colin Powell's declaration that Sudan was responsible for genocide in Darfur, set Steidle's witness to us within the broader context of a reality recognized by world politicians, including Kofi Annan. The color videos of Steidle's past point to the middle-class American world he came from, loving the sea, but now finding himself in the desert. Intercut maps, a standard feature in these films about Africa, provide analytic representations of the geopolitical relations of power. But they also serve to localize Sudan and Chad on the larger space of the globe for Americans who are not well versed in geography.

One of the most seductive cinematic gestures of the film is the alternation between color and black-and-white photography. Set against the playful scenes of Brian and Gretchen chasing each other, when Brian decides to join the Marines we see black-and-white recruiting clips inserted as documentary—and as a clue to the dark experience of adult life in Iraq that lies ahead. Pace, too, plays a role in bringing these images to life: the photography may be run fast or slow, sped up or frozen. Some photographs of dead bodies may be shown first in color—a scrap of green cloth—and then in black and white, as if the lived experience of real death had become objective documentary. When Brian recounts a July 2004 African Union report on schoolgirls who were chained and burned, we see photos of burned bodies and an entire village in ashes, turning to black. Conversely, when Brian gives Nicholas Kristof his hard drive, Kristof comments, "Photos made this a little more vivid"— and the black-and-white images turn to color.

When Brian recounts the motives of the rebel groups at war against the Janjaweed, explaining the attack on Al Fahir in 2003, the film zooms in for close-up photos of their faces, humanizing those men who seek the rights others have won. Most strikingly, the film opens and closes with a sequence capturing the faces of children who peer into the camera, which appears to have been set on the ground. As the children themselves zoom in from many angles they are above, looking back at the camera, interrogating the camera and interrogating us, the viewers.

These metanarrative devices entangle the viewer in Steidle's situation. As a cameraman, he is a representative viewer, standing in for our own position as viewers. But that position, he discovers, is problematic. The last section of the film turns to this problem, which threatens Steidle and menaces us as well. "It makes me feel hopeless," he says. "The fact that I had to stand around watching these things happen." In theories of social recovery and healing, such as *Testimony* by Shoshana Felman and Dori Traub, bearing witness, even standing witness to the witness, often carries high moral weight. Steidle challenges this assumption.

The complex visual effect that accompanies the opening credits metaphorically represents the difficulty presented to the viewer, who must decode layered images. We read the title and other information through what seems to be wet glass but is probably a montage of sand splattered with blood, overlaid on orange figures of Janjaweed fighters on horseback carrying machine guns. Our vision is symbolically obscured. The ground of all we will see is the desert: poverty, drought, and blood.

Reviews of *Blood Diamond* raised the question whether the film conformed to audience demands or defied them. It was nominated for five Academy Awards but won none. In his web review, James Berardinelli complained, "It's hard to imagine there's much of an audience for a movie fueled more by the politics of African atrocities than the adrenaline and testosterone cocktail that typically characterizes this sort of film" (Berardinelli 2006). By implication, a documentary without enough testosterone will inevitably fail.

In the conclusion of *The Devil Came on Horseback*, Steidle indicts the viewer. "Watching is nothing: it's just watching." Although he speaks of himself, his message is metanarrative: we, the film-spectators, are "just watching." One of the underlying humanitarian premises is that compassion can mobilize action. Yet this, too, is in doubt. "And all the other people here," he goes on. "I'm compassionate," but "I have no idea what it's like." Although he wants to support them in their pain, what most hurts him is his inability to change the situation: "And that's that." When Brian then weeps, he weeps for all of us.

The vocabulary we use to invoke this emotional relationship—*compassion, sympathy,* and *empathy* (Wilson and Brown 2009)—is rooted in the concept of sharing "with" the other, entering into the situation of the other. But compassion does not equal the assumption of responsibility. Indeed, the narrative vehicles through which we present these stories undercut their transformative goals. Saturated by action-adventure films and by adventure-romance films in which political harmony is symbolically achieved through sexual relationships, audiences may not actually seek change. Even the tragic mode, in which calamitous errors in judgment and criminal actions can be exposed, then wiped clean through aesthetic catharsis, becomes a double-edged sword. An aesthetic of closure in which the playful children who have been seen at the beginning of a film return at the end—the trope on which both *The Last King* and *Devil* rely—inhibits the call to action by the audience that leaves the theater.

Filmmakers who shape humanitarian narratives by assuming the authority of a third-person narrator and who focus their films on Western interventions may shut down questions that Western audiences should be asking themselves. The crises these directors purport to be highlighting disappear into the background, as they blur rather than clearly articulate what has happened, in order to achieve an aggregative effect. The desire to foster identification by a white audience with a central white actor evacuates the suffering, courageous endurance, and persistent activism of those on the ground who are represented simply as victims.

## NOTES

This essay arose from Ethel Higonnet's work documenting violence against women in the Ivory Coast and surrounding nations. Her film, *Invisible Crime* (Capa 2010), is based on her interviews. Ethel laid out large questions about documentary film that launched the essay; Margaret developed the historical argument and critical analyses.

1. The role of victim ostensibly justifies mass violence that in retrospect clearly violates human rights.

2. Amputees in fact figured among the child and teenage film extras. Scandalously, a promise by Warner Bros. Pictures to provide prosthetics for the twenty-seven children was delayed for publicity purposes.

3. Steidle's African Union team may have videotaped the evidence, or the scene may have been reenacted. The same ambiguity marks all the interviews.

4. It is perhaps not an accident that Cowboy Films was coproducer of the film, as the focus on Amin flirts with American audiences' infatuation with emblems of patriarchal power.

5. Apparently videotapes were used as well, as when the burning of villages by the Janjaweed is filmed from a helicopter monitoring the violence as it occurs.

## REFERENCES

Benjamin, Walter. 1968. "The Work of Art in the Age of Mechanical Reproduction." *Reflections*, 217–51. New York: Schocken.

Beran, Michael Knox. 2008. "Hearts of Darkness: Trendy Paternalism Is Keeping Africa in Chains." *City Journal* 18, no. 1. http://www.city-journal.org/2008/18_1_paternalism.html.

Berardinelli, James. 2006. Review of "Blood Diamond." *Reel Reviews* 2006. www.reelviews.net/movies/b/blood_diamond.html.

*Blood Diamond*. 2006. Directed by Edward Zwick. Warner Virtual Studio. Story by Charles Leavitt and C. Gaby Mitchell. Warner. DVD 2007.

Dargis, Manohla. 2006. "Diamonds and the Devil, amid the Anguish of Africa." Review of *Blood Diamond*. *New York Times*, December 8. movies.nytimes.com/2006/12/08/movies/08diam.html.

Dembour, Marie-Bénédicte, and Emily Haslam. 2004. "Silencing Hearings? Victim-Witnesses at War Crimes Trials." *EJIL [European Journal of International Law]* 15 (1): 151–77.

*Devil Came on Horseback, The.* 2007. Directed by Annie Sundberg and Ricki Stern. Performed by Kevin Steidle. Break Thru Films. DVD 2008.

Felman, Shoshana, and Dori Laub. 1992. *Testimony: Crises of Witnessing in Literature, Psychoanalysis, and History.* New York: Routledge.

Gugler, Josef. 2003. *African Film: Re-imagining a Continent.* Bloomington: Indiana University Press.

*Last King of Scotland, The.* 2006. Directed by Kevin Macdonald. Performed by Forest Whitaker, James McAvoy, Kerry Washington. DNA Films. DVD 2007.

Jackson, Lisa. 2008. *The Greatest Silence: Rape in the Congo.* HBO Jackson Films.

Kennedy, David. 2004. *The Dark Sides of Virtue: Reassessing International Humanitarianism.* Princeton: Princeton University Press.

Rieff, David. 2002. *A Bed for the Night: Humanitarianism in Crisis.* New York: Simon and Schuster.

Rorty, Richard. 1993. "Human Rights, Rationality, and Sentimentality." In *On Human Rights: The Oxford Amnesty Lectures,* edited by Stephen Shute and Susan L. Hurley, 112–34. New York: Basic.

Rouch, Jean. 2003. "The Situation and Tendencies of the Cinema in Africa." In *Ciné-Ethnography,* edited and translated by Steven Feld. Minneapolis: University of Minnesota Press.

Rozario, Kevin. 2003. "Delicious Horrors: Mass Culture, the Red Cross, and the Appeal of Modern American Humanitarianism." *American Quarterly* 55 (3): 417–55.

Sontag, Susan. 1993. *Regarding the Pain of Others.* New York: Picador.

Spivak, Gayatri Chakravorty. 1988. "Can the Subaltern Speak?" In *Marxism and the Interpretation of Culture,* edited by Cary Nelson and Lawrence Grossberg, 271–313. Urbana: University of Illinois Press.

Thackway, Melissa. 2003. *Africa Shoots Back: Alternative Perspectives in Sub-Saharan Francophone African Film.* Bloomington: Indiana University Press.

Warhol, Robyn. 1986. "Toward a Theory of the Engaging Narrator: Earnest Interventions in Gaskell, Stowe, and Eliot." *PMLA* 101 (5): 811–18.

White, Hayden. 1973. *Metahistory: The Historical Imagination in Nineteenth-Century Europe.* Baltimore: Johns Hopkins University Press.

———. 1987. *The Content of Form: Narrative Discourse and Historical Representation.* Baltimore: Johns Hopkins University Press.

Wilson, Richard Ashby, and Richard D. Brown. 2009. Introduction to *Humanitarianism and Suffering: The Mobilization of Empathy,* edited by Richard Ashby Wilson and Richard D. Brown. Cambridge: Cambridge University Press.

Worth, Robert F. 2008. "Another Round of Explosions, but This Time It's Fake." *New York Times,* February 22, A4.

# THREE

# Hollywood's Representations of Human Rights

The Case of Terry George's *Hotel Rwanda*

JOYCE B. ASHUNTANTANG

In recent years, Hollywood has produced "human rights" films—films that expose egregious abuses inflicted on ordinary people who do not receive support from local systems of justice and who do not have the means to articulate their stories to wide audiences. A number of recent films in the human rights genre are set in Africa, including *Hotel Rwanda* (2004), *Lord of War* (2005), and *Blood Diamond* (2006). The appellation "human rights film" itself is debatable, since Hollywood movies have to negotiate between advocacy for global human rights, presumed audience preferences, and box office figures, which in turn may trump the very rights the films are meant to uphold. In several cases, these films fall more adequately under the rubric of what Elizabeth Swanson Goldberg calls the "counter-historical dramatic film." According to Goldberg, "Crossing generic boundaries, the counter-historical dramatic film employs adventure, romance, suspense, courtroom drama and war narrative conventions to represent instances of historical atrocity. Over and above these generic classifications, however, it refers to a historic event or a true story, presenting a counter-narrative to an official version of history or to a perceived silence surrounding a historical event" (2007, 29). *Hotel Rwanda*, directed by Terry George, is a good case in point.

Despite its weaknesses, the role of cinema as a viable medium for the dissemination of human rights education cannot be underestimated. Human rights films can produce what Goldberg has called "long distance witness observers thousands of humans removed in time and space" (2007, 4). *Hotel Rwanda* revisits the 1994 Rwandan genocide—the mass killing of an estimated 800,000 people within a period of 100 days. The story is based on the experiences of Paul Rusesabagina, a hotel manager at the Hotel des Mille Collines in Kigali during the period of the genocide. The Hutu protagonist, Paul (played by Don Cheadle), sets out to save his Tutsi wife, Tatiana (played by Sophie Okonedo), and his children, but before long he finds himself with 1,200 Rwandans, both Tutsis and Hutus, who have sought refuge at the hotel. Using the resources at his disposal—money, drinks and sheer wit—Paul is able to keep the Hutu militia at bay. As it becomes apparent that the international community will not intervene in their rescue, Paul takes charge of the situation and refuses to seize an opportunity to save only himself and his family. With the help of the UN peacekeeping force led by Colonel Oliver (played by Nick Nolte), Paul and the 1,200 refuges are saved and taken to various refugee camps. It is in this vein that *Hotel Rwanda* has been called the African *Schindler's List,* in reference to Steven Spielberg's film, which is based on the story of Oskar Schindler, who managed to save 1,100 Jews from being gassed at the Auschwitz concentration camp (Graydon 2005, 34).

According to George, after learning about Rusesabagina's story and eventually visiting the genocide site at Murambi where over 40,000 people were massacred, he wrote in the guest book, "I promise to tell the story of the genocide to the world" (2005, 25). This particular telling of a story of the genocide has received extraordinary reviews. The film earned three Oscar nominations, and has won over twelve awards, including the Humanitas Prize in 2005. This is a screenwriter's award that honors "stories that affirm the human person, probe the meaning of human life, and enlighten the use of human freedom. The stories reveal common humanity, so that love may come to permeate the human family and help liberate, enrich and unify society."[1] To confirm its status as a human rights film, Amnesty International created a teachers' guide to encourage and aid educators to use *Hotel Rwanda* to teach human rights.

Human rights representation in this film brought to the fore some of the issues plaguing human rights pledges and activism. Despite developments in international law and human rights fueled by the United Nations Charter of 1945, the Declaration of Human Rights drawn in 1948, and the United Nations Convention on the Prevention and Punishment of the Crime of Genocide (also in 1948), tragic events after World War II have proven that the promise of "never again" has been broken many times over. Established crimes against humanity and massacres amounting to genocide in the former Yugoslavia, Cambodia, Rwanda, and elsewhere have shocked people around the world. One of the focal points of international human rights is to make people aware of the abuses of human rights so that those perpetrating these abuses can be shamed and passive observers can be turned into human rights activists. Thus, after people watch the film *Hotel Rwanda,* they are expected to react negatively to the genocidal activities depicted in the film and canvass for a better world. Considering that *Hotel Rwanda* was released ten years after the Rwandan genocide, and in the light of the massacres going on in Darfur, one can argue that one of the goals of *Hotel Rwanda* is to compel viewers not to ignore genocide yet again, especially when one notes the role of Don Cheadle, the principal actor in *Hotel Rwanda,* in television ads meant to sensitize Americans about the mass violence in Darfur.

*Hotel Rwanda* certainly brings to the big screen the difficulty of translating into action some of the human rights declarations drawn up by the United Nations, in addition to postdeclaration hypocrisies. George prompts viewers to examine to what extent the lack of intervention was due to race or to perceived classes of nations. In the film, Colonel Oliver, who is largely constructed on the nonfictional Canadian general Roméo Dallaire (head of the United Nations Assistance Mission for Rwanda [UNAMIR] during the genocide), believes that a United Nations intervention is necessary and could have been, if implemented, quite successful in lowering the number of Rwandan deaths. In the film, the lives of the refugees in the Hotel des Milles Collines are dependent on this kind of intervention. The following conversation between Paul and Jack, a Western journalist, elaborates on this argument.

> PAUL: I am glad that you have shot this footage—and that the world will
> see it. It is the only way we have a chance that people might intervene.
> JACK: Yea, and if no one intervenes, is it still a good thing to show?
> PAUL: How can they not intervene—when they witness such atrocities?[2]

One may apply Jack's question to human rights films. This scene suggests that George is indeed aware of the risk that images of human suffering may, ultimately, be exploited as a source of compelling yet problematically lucrative storytelling. Just as Paul implores his hotel guests to call the influential people they know abroad to shame them into action, George's film likewise engages in the politics of shame. The film criticizes the United Nations for failing to live up to the promises of its declarations, in addition to individual countries with a history of political intervention in the region, such as Belgium, France, and the United States. When Paul solicits help from his employers at the Belgian company, Sabena (the Société Autonyme Belge d'Exploitation de la

Navigation Aérienne), he gets temporary relief as the attacking Interahamwe is told to retreat because of a call from France. But the frustrated Sabena Airlines president, Tillens (played by Jean Reno), later tells Paul: "I pleaded with the French and the Belgians to go back and get you all. I'm afraid this is not going to happen. . . . They're cowards, Paul. Rwanda is not . . . worth a single vote to any of them. The French, the British, the Americans. I am sorry, Paul." George postulates some unflattering reasons for the more powerful UN member countries' unwillingness to intervene. Colonel Oliver tells Paul he has been abandoned because "the West, all the superpowers, everything you believe in, Paul. They think you are dirt. They think you're dumb. You're worthless . . . you're black, you're not even a nigger, you're African. They're not gonna stay, Paul. They're not gonna stop the slaughter."

The film also opens the question of whether "humanitarian" military intervention is merely a pretext for Western nations to ultimately gain influence in other nations for their own gain. If Rwanda offered the prospects of valuable raw materials such as oil, nuclear capabilities, or a strategic geographical location, would Western "interest," and the Western response, have been different? The answer is a possible "yes," based on the deputy assistant secretary for defense, James Woods, from 1986 to 1994. In a documentary aired on PBS titled *Frontline: The Triumph of Evil*, Woods explains:

> In the spring of '93 when the Clinton administration came in . . . we were asked to develop lists of what we thought would be serious crises this administration might face and forward that to the new Secretary of Defense, Mr. Aspin. I put Rwanda-Burundi on the list. I won't go into personalities, but I received guidance from higher authorities, "Look, if something happens in Rwanda-Burundi, we don't care. Take it off the list. U.S. national interest is not involved and we can't put all these silly humanitarian issues on lists, like important problems like the Middle East and North Korea and so on. Just make it go away." (2005, 64)

The kind of blatant disregard for African lives displayed in the quote above becomes visible in *Hotel Rwanda* when Prudence Bushnell (played by Debra Winger, and based on the US deputy assistant secretary of state for African affairs of the same name) tries in vain to convince American officials that preventing further murders in Rwanda is in the American national "interest."

Another human rights issue represented in *Hotel Rwanda* is the extent of the responsibility of the individual within a nation-state with regards to human rights. By constructing the whole film around Paul, George has employed what Robert Toplin has identified as one of the four principal methods of presenting cinematic history, which is "employing a documentary style to develop the 'Great Man' perspective on the past" (1996, 14). In presenting stories of the past, Hollywood filmmakers usually zoom in on the exploits of one or two characters. This is the case with counterhistorical dramatic films such as *Schindler's List*. As Toplin indicates, "This approach brings history to a personal level, portraying it through the experiences of fascinating and often heroic people for whom audiences are encouraged to show sympathy" (1996, 20). In the case of *Hotel Rwanda*, George considered Rusesabagina "a shining example of humanity."[3] Rusesabagina proved that individuals could intervene to stop human rights abuses. To make this point, George presents a growth in Paul's character where he moves from someone who cares about only his immediate family to one who finally accepts the whole of Rwanda as family. In the beginning, when Tatiana asks him to intervene in the torture and kidnapping of their neighbor Victor, Paul answers, "He's not family. Family is all that matters. Please . . . please leave things to my good judgment." But at the end of the film, Paul decides to stay behind with the rest of the refugees. As the truck leaves with his family, and his frantic wife cries out in anguish questioning his action, Paul answers, "I cannot leave these people to die. I cannot leave these people to die." It is a befitting chorus for human rights advocacy and one that affirms for the viewer that yes, one person can make a difference in the face of a human rights crisis. On another level, it reads as a critique of those individuals—or perhaps nations—that cannot see beyond their own immediate interests.

Despite its success in sparking debates about the politics of international human rights and the contradictions of national governments that claim to value those rights, George's representation of human rights in *Hotel Rwanda* also bears the marks of what goes wrong not only with the human rights movement itself, but the way human rights are constructed and disseminated with reference to Africa. These include the projection of the savage / victim / savior paradigm, ignoring the historical and cultural contexts of human rights abuses, and downplaying the severity of the genocide in order to obtain maximum entertainment value for the film. According to George, he decided to tell Paul's story because "it was a perfect story to be told on film—a riveting political thriller, a deeply moving romance, and, most of all, a universal story of the triumph of a good man over evil."

How do George and his team manipulate history and the elements of cinematography like setting, lighting, and characters to mediate, by extension, Africa to the world? The film opens with a black screen. The audience is thus psychologically prepared to enter what Conrad has classically called the "heart of darkness," a darkness which for centuries has been a symbol of Africa. In presenting this image George participates, even if unwittingly, in what Paul Ugor has described as the "continuous reproduction of the monstrous African racial other in contemporary American Hollywood films" (2006, 132). This darkness projects Africa as another world, the opposite of Europe and America, and as such, a locale devoid of "civilization." This is the same darkness that had earned the continent the title "dark continent" in the nineteenth century, which led to colonization being dubbed a "civilizing mission." But the darkness is not just of color, it is a representation of the presumed evil that lurks within that darkness, evil that the film is going to uncover. As if to confirm the metaphoric importance of this darkness, there is a voice that comes through the dark screen. It is a voice of rage, a voice that menaces. The voice declares:

> When people ask me, good listeners, "Why do I hate the Tutsi?" I say, "Read our history." The Tutsi were collaborators for the Belgian colonist. They stole our Hutu land, they whipped us. Now they have come back, these Tutsi rebels. They are cockroaches. They are murderers. Rwanda is our Hutu land. We are the majority. They are a minority of traitors and invaders. We will squash the infestation. We will wipe out the RPF rebels. This is RTLM, Hutu power radio. Stay alert—watch your neighbors.

The monstrous voice in the darkness—a staple of Hollywood horror films—creates the anticipation of savage "evil" hiding in the dark, especially when the voice is urging for all the Tutsi "cockroaches" to be killed. This frightening voice punctuates the film at different intervals, spewing hate and inflaming anti-Tutsi sentiment. This darkness in a way helps to strip the audience of any real surprise because it is a "known" darkness which is expected. Francesco Casetti argues that both film and literature can "be considered as sites of production and circulation of discourses; that is, symbolic constructions that refer to a cluster of meanings that a society considers possible (thinkable) and feasible (legitimate)" (2004, 82). Hence film and literature serve not only as forms of mass entertainment and education but also as avenues for hegemonic viewpoints. In a scene that scrutinizes Western apathy, the journalist Jack Daglish (played by Joaquin Phoenix) predicts that when people in the West watch the horrors they'll say, "'Oh, my God, that's horrible,' and then they go on eating their dinners." This is because where Africa is concerned, these horrors are no longer seen as outrageous but rather as allegedly commonplace. This is the same point Susan Sontag makes when she explains that

> postcolonial Africa exists in the consciousness of the general public in the rich world of unforgettable photographs of large-eyed victims, starting with figures in the famine lands of Biafra in the late 1960s. . . . These sights carry a double message. They show suffering that is outrageous, unjust and should be repaired. They confirm that this is the sort of thing that happens in that place. (2002, 71)

Ironically, the darkness at the beginning of *Hotel Rwanda* becomes all too familiar and blunts the shocking impact of the genocide.

While the film adequately demonstrates the significant role that hate radio has played in the perpetuation of genocide, the ahistorical representation of Hutu rage feeds into Western stereotypes about Africa. It is this oversimplified, decontextualized portrayal that plagues the framing of human rights abuses. George builds on the theory that the genocide started with the shooting of President Habyarimana's plane, which killed him and the president of Burundi. But even cursorily conducted research should have shown that the roots of the genocide were planted during the colonial era when the minority Tutsi ethnic group was privileged by the Belgians over the Hutus, who form approximately 85 percent of the Rwandan population. When the Belgians left and the Hutus won over the government, there was an atmosphere of revenge that led to the exile of over 400,000 Tutsis. The exiled Tutsis later formed a rebel army in exile, the Rwandan Patriotic Front (RPF). This army was responsible for several mass killings and the destabilization of several communities in Rwanda. In August 1993, the reigning Hutu government signed a peace accord with the RPF, but some Hutus were against power-sharing with the RPF, whom they feared would rule the country with further vengeance. When President Habyarimana was killed in April 1994, Hutu militants organized the systematic murders of Tutsis suspected to be involved in the shooting. In that same month, the killing took on a wider scope, and an estimated 800,000 Tutsis and moderate Hutus were massacred. Of course, colonialism is not a valid excuse for a genocide, and the perpetrators should be brought to justice. However, *Hotel Rwanda* barely considers colonial history, which implicates the West and the Tutsis. And when it does reference Belgian colonialism, it is through the hateful, anticolonial voice of a Hutu power radio announcer. Maybe George can be excused for omitting major historical events because he spotlights instead the unethical desertion of Rwandans by UN powers and the failure to uphold the vows of the Geneva Convention. But as one can conjecture, any deliberate ignorance of African history provides an excuse to lump Africa as "déjà vu." As Snow holds, "*Hotel Rwanda* is a work of fiction. As a cultural artifact produced by an affluent industry in the West, and for affluent Western consumers, the focus on a distant exoticized culture about which the affluent Western consumers know very little, it serves to consolidate ideological pillars of disinformation that came before it, and upon which it was built" (2005).

*Hotel Rwanda* exemplifies another pitfall of international human rights activism: the danger of assigning sweeping labels to victims and perpetrators. These are categories that need to be handled with care in order to give an opportunity for peaceful conflict resolution. In *Hotel Rwanda,* the Tutsis are represented as the innocent victims and the Hutus as criminal savages—with the exception of Hutus who "believe in" the West, who adapt their style, and behave like "one of them," such as Paul. The menacing voice that opens the film is identified as Hutu. Therefore, while the blackness that opens the film may be reminiscent of the tropes used to characterize the continent of Africa, within the locus of the film it is synonymous with the Hutus. To present an angry and hateful radio announcer without a substantial historical context of Hutu and Tutsi political relations is certainly misleading and facilitates the creation of oversimplified binaries. It is a verifiable fact that the RTLM was a hate radio station run by Hutus, but George intersperses this extremist voice throughout the film to underscore general Hutu genocidal savagery and sweeping Tutsi victimhood. Simplistically framing the conflict along the lines of "good guys/bad guys" does not help the cause of human rights because it refuels anger, reinforces polarizing dichotomies, and makes conflict resolution difficult. These binaristic labels (savage/victim and evil/good) are sustained throughout the film—labels that are satirized by Raoul Peck in *Sometimes in April* (2005) when an American reporter asks which side—"Tutus or Hutsis"—comprises "the good guys."

Constance Morrill argues that "many thoughtful analyses of the genocide have emerged over the last twelve years, in different languages, about the complex origins and international dimensions of this politico-ethnic conflict. And most useful studies suggest that what happened in Rwanda more than a decade ago was not as simple as 'Tutsi victim, Hutu perpetrator'" (2006, 16). Yet this alternative truth is not revealed in movies like *Hotel Rwanda*, nor in several other accounts of the genocide, such as Philip Gourevitch's book, *We Wish to Inform You That Tomorrow We Will Be Killed with Our Families* (1998). The Rwandan Patriotic Front, which was a rebel Tutsi force, is represented in the movie as very responsible, despite reports of violent Tutsi reprisals and abuses against Hutus. In the film, Tutsi rebels form an army that protects civilians and helps a UN convoy of refugees successfully drive through enemy lines. From this perspective, Snow holds, "The Hutus are the devil incarnate. The Tutsis are saintly. Indeed they are beyond reproach, because they are victims of genocide" (2005). This highlights another wrinkle in human rights activism; although many human rights groups advocate universalist human rights language, they have historically used it to promote special interests. As Michael Ignatieff explains, "There's nothing wrong with particularism in itself. . . . The problem is that particularism conflicts with universalism at the point at which one's commitment to a group leads one to countenance human rights violations toward another group. Persons who care about human rights violations committed against Palestinians may not care so much about human rights violations committed by Palestinians against Israelis, and vice versa" (2001, 19). What this proves is that while human rights are often espoused as apolitical and neutral, in practice, as Ignatieff argues again, "Human rights activism means taking sides, mobilizing constituencies powerful enough to force abusers to stop. As a consequence, effective human rights activism is bound to be partial and political" (2001, 9). And the film invites spectators to take sides. In a move that seems to be a deliberate attempt to enhance Christian sympathy for Tutsis, *Hotel Rwanda* depicts the Tutsis as Christians, despite the fact that the vast majority (over 90 percent) of Rwanda's population—Hutu and Tutsi—are Christians. The preponderance of nuns with their crosses and orphans in the Tutsi camp—and the absence of Christian symbols associated with Hutu characters—makes this quite obvious. Tatiana, Paul's wife, a Tutsi, wears a visible cross on her neck; a cross that her Hutu husband fondles at one point in the movie as if it will sanctify him. Hutus, in contrast, are viewed as part of Satan's army.

As soon as lights come up and the film proper begins, the symptomatic darkness now reveals itself in the chaos that becomes visible. There are people everywhere and traffic jams. Then, Paul and his driver run into the Interahamwe marching past. The militia is presented as barbaric. In the shooting script, George describes the Interahamwe parade as *a mass of men and women,*[4] most in the same color uniform. Line after line, waves, all performing the Interahamwe war dance, in *wild hypnotic sync.* Many wave sticks, spears, wooden imitation of guns. (2005, 121)

The description in the shooting script is aptly translated into action in the film because what the viewers see is a chaotic group of people wielding every imaginable weapon from sticks to guns. The camera pans through them in quick succession, leaving no individual profiles. As Goldberg argues, "The failure of the Western world to represent others as individuated humans rather than undifferentiated masses has a long history, infamously expressed in Marlow's explanation of his grief at the death of his helmsman during the journey to the interior in Conrad's *Heart of Darkness*" (2007, 189). Conrad's Marlow explains, "Perhaps you will think it passing strange this regret for a savage who was no more than a grain of sand in a black Sahara" (as cited in Charters 2007, 302). Indeed, this is the kind of representation that George conjures up in this scene. The weapons and disorganization of the Interahamwe also mark them as out of modern civilization. While George calls the dancing a "wild hypnotic sync," Conrad refers to the dance of the Africans in the Congo as a "frenzy" (as cited in Charters 2007, 290). The colorful uniform can be read as a stereotype, too, a presentation of the exotic in Africa. But even that uniform becomes a symbol of savagery, especially when we see Georges Rutaganda, the Interahamwe boss, wearing it, as he is the one who receives machetes from China, which will be used in the killing. While this essay does not propose that George, or Hollywood, is racist, it is evident that the legacy of racism in Hollywood cinema has not been fully shaken. As Chinua Achebe explains, "It may well be that what is happening at this stage is more akin to reflex action than calculated malice" (1989, 18). Yet this does not make the situation any more tolerable.

In the midst of this victim/savage dichotomy is the metaphor of the savior who needs to come to rescue the victims. *Hotel Rwanda* is a film that castigates the failures of the savior, but nonetheless the savior image is constructed through the Western journalists and the UN general played by Nick Nolte. The presence of the Western journalists in the hotel provides security for Paul and the other refugees. In fact, throughout the film Paul hopes for a rescue from the West. He solicits help from Sabena, the owner of the hotel, and the Sabena boss summons someone in France. This image of the white man as a "savior" is stretched in *Hotel Rwanda* to the point that when a convoy of refugees, including Paul's wife and children, are held up by the Interahamwe, according to the film, it is the UN general who saves the day by using his gun. However, according to an eyewitness account by Amadou Deme, a Senegalese army officer who served in the intelligence of the UN mission for Rwanda from August 1993 to July 1994, General Roméo Dallaire was nowhere near that incident. Instead, it was Georges Rutaganda, the second in command of the Interahamwe militia, who eventually calmed the Interahamwe. As Deme explains, "In the film, a UN officer resembling General Dallaire of Canada takes George's place as savior . . . using a gun. In fact, there were no white commanders there that day, and General Dallaire was not even in Kigali but in Rwamangana" (2006). Yet to reinforce this image of the West/ white man as savior, the climax of the film comes when the UN peacekeeping forces have to leave, taking with them all of the foreigners. The despair and frustration that sets in because the savior does not act is represented in the scene where Paul is standing in the rain, soaked, with all the refugees standing behind him looking on helplessly. This image heightens the way Western countries have framed the human rights corpus, which George exploits. This is the point Makau Mutua underscores when he reiterates that

> the grand narrative of human rights contains a subtext which depicts an epochal contest pitting savages, on the one hand, against victims and saviors, on the other. The savage-victim-savior construction is a three-dimensional compound metaphor in which each dimension is a metaphor in itself. The main authors of a human rights discourse, including the United Nations, Western States, international non-governmental organizations and senior Western academics, constructed this three-dimensional prism. This rendering of the human rights corpus and its discourse is unidirectional and predictable, a black and white construction that pits good against evil. (2002, 10)

The film reinforces the belief that American and Western European heroes—rather than international UN soldiers, including the Senegalese soldier, Amadou Deme—must always play the role of "big brother coming to the rescue." There is a brief scene that acknowledges the rescue of endangered Tutsis by the Rwandan Patriotic Front, but these soldiers are not presented as individual saviors with substantive roles.

Yet one can argue that in George's portrayal of Paul he might have undercut this stereotype, since Paul is Rwandan, and he ends up taking over as the savior who rescues 1,200 people. Nevertheless, this argument doesn't hold up to scrutiny because Paul's dependence on the West for his freedom is quite central to the film. The Belgians who help negotiate his fate own the Hotel des Mille Collines, which becomes a sanctuary for Paul and the rest of the refugees. In addition, the money Paul uses to buy his family and friends is ostensibly Western currency. So in spite of George's commendable choice to make a film about Africa which for once does not have a Western protagonist, the development of the plot still reveals the bias of a Western framework. To reconfirm this bias, not only is Paul rescued, but the viewer finds out that Paul and his family will resettle in Belgium. Thus, the West becomes a final haven for Paul and his family. To complicate matters, the cloying Hollywood ending in which the family reunites robs the film of the sting of the genocide. This sort of ending is repeated in *Blood Diamond* (2006), where Solomon Vandy can save his family from war-torn Sierra Leone only by going physically to London and relying on Maddy, the American journalist, who is writing a story about the exploitation of diamonds in Sierra Leone.

Furthermore, though fictionalized, *Hotel Rwanda* is fiction based on a true and disturbing story; as a Hollywood film it is going to reach millions of people who will arguably view the film as their source of information on the genocide. There is no denying that the question of accuracy will always plague any film that purports to be historical, although this has been protested by film critics such as Rosenstone, who holds that what one should do is to attempt to see if the film's "overall portrait or vision has something meaningful and important to say about our past" (2006, 49). But a film paraded as a human rights film has to be sensitive to facts, because by not representing the facts objectively the film perpetuates anger and resentment. Amadou Deme's resentment is a case in point.

> "Truth and Reconciliation" is said to be part of the mandate of international justice. Averting our eyes from the truth because it is personally or politically awkward is bad for our collective conscience. Georges Rutaganda is today serving a life term for crimes against humanity. I would like to hope that Paul Rusesabagina would join me in acknowledging that on May 3rd, 1994, Georges Rutaganda risked his life to save refugees, including Paul's wife, at a roadblock in Kigali. (2006)

The lack of complexity of certain aspects of the film grossly distorts the context, which is essential to understanding the genocide. What George provides are short vague snippets of the sociopolitical context of the genocide between "suspenseful" scenes of Paul's many attempts to stop the "wild" Hutu Interahamwe from gaining access to the Hotel des Mille Collines. Not centralizing the historical context of the genocide in the film does a disservice to the viewers. This representation contrasts sharply with Peck's *Sometimes in April*, which takes colonialism into account in his retelling of the story of the genocide. Peck also refrains from demonizing any groups and highlights heroic acts by Hutu and Tutsi women during the genocide.

The representation of one individual's story of perseverance unintentionally undermines the struggle of an entire nation. Thus, it is Paul's ability to bargain through bribery, flattery, personal interest, and his wit that comes into focus and not the several thousands of Hutus and Tutsis who struggled to survive during the genocide, thereby revising the story of the genocide and casting it within the framework of Hollywood aesthetics and values. This puts *Hotel Rwanda* in the subcategory of Hollywood films dubbed "biofilms," or films that bring to light a traumatic historical past by concentrating on an individual life as a way of presenting a collective historical event. Therefore, instead of representing the specific qualities of the Rwandan genocide, *Hotel Rwanda* manipulates the cinema medium to transform the image of the genocide to a Hollywood product that creates the illusion that this medium can successfully interpret the genocide to the world. At its best, however, *Hotel Rwanda* facilitates productive discussions about the Rwandan genocide, how human rights are promoted and articulated, and human agency.

NOTES

1. "About the Prize." http://www.humanitasprize.org/.
2. This quotation and all subsequent quotations are derived from the DVD version of *Hotel Rwanda*.
3. See George 2005.
4. The italics in this quote are mine.

REFERENCES

Achebe, Chinua. 1989. "An Image of Africa: Racism in Conrad's *Heart of Darkness*." In *Hopes and Impediments: Selected Essays*. New York: Doubleday.
Amnesty International. Human Rights Education. Film Curriculum Guides. *Hotel Rwanda*. http://www.amnestyusa.org/sites/default/files/rwanda_brochuredivided_0.pdf.
Burgoyne, Robert. 2008. *The Hollywood Historical Film*. Malden, MA: Blackwell.
Butcher, Teal Goler. 1992. "Human Rights: Promise and Reality." In *International Perspective on Human Rights: The Legacy of George Mason*, edited by Jack R. Censer,

Daniel Shumate, and Josephine Pacheco, 93–146. Fairfax, VA: George Mason University Press.

Casetti, Francesco. 2004. "Adaptation and Mis-adaptation: Film, Literature, and Social Discourses." In *A Companion to Literature and Film*, edited by Alessandra Raengo and Robert Stare, 81–91. Malden, MA: Blackwell.

Charters, Ann. 2007. *The Story and Its Writer: An Introduction to Short Fiction*. Boston: Bedford Saint Martin.

Deme, Amadou. 2006. "Setting the Record Straight: Hotel Rwanda." *CounterPunch*, April 24. http://www.counterpunch.org/deme04242006.html.

George, Terry, ed. 2005. *Hotel Rwanda: Bringing the True Story of an African Hero to Film*. New York: New Market Press.

———.2005."Director'sStatement."http://ascotelite.ch/modules/obomovie/detail.php?page_id=2&lang=2&navTitle=Filme&print=1&suisa=1005.323&zusatz=text1.

Goldberg, Elizabeth Swanson. 2007. *Beyond Terror: Gender, Narrative, Human Rights*. New Brunswick, NJ: Rutgers University Press.

Gourevitch, Phillip. 1998. *We Wish to Inform You That Tomorrow We Will Be Killed with Our Families*. New York: Farrar, Straus and Giroux.

Graydon, Nicola. 2005. "The Rwandan Schindler." In *Hotel Rwanda: Bringing the True Story of an African Hero to Film*, edited by Terry George. New York: New Market Press.

*Hotel Rwanda*. 2004. Directed by Terry George. California: United Artists Films.

"Hotel Rwanda 'West Wing' Writers Win Humanitas Award." 2005. June 25. http://www.cbc.ca/arts/story/2005/06/30/artsbriefs050630.html.

Ignatieff, Michael. 2001. "Human Rights as Politics." In *Human Rights as Politics and Idolatry*, edited by Amy Gutmann, 3–52. Princeton: Princeton University Press.

Morrill, Constance. 2006. "Show Business and 'Lawfare' in Rwanda: Twelve Years After the Genocide." *Dissent* (Summer): 14–20.

Mutua, Makau. 2002. *Human Rights: A Political and Cultural Critique*. Philadelphia: University of Pennsylvania Press.

Rosenstone, Robert A. 2006. *History on Film/Film on History*. Harlow: Pearson Longman.

Snow, Harmon Keith. 2005. "Hotel Rwanda: Hollywood and the Holocaust in Central Africa." December 8. http://www.allthingspass.com.

Sontag, Susan. 2002 [1993]. *Regarding the Pain of Others*. New York: Farrar, Straus and Giroux.

Toplin, Robert Brent. 1996. *History by Hollywood: The Use and Abuse of the American Past*. Urbana: University of Illinois Press.

Ugor, Paul. 2006. "Demonizing the African Other, Humanizing the Self: Hollywood and the Politics of Post-imperial Adaptations." *Atenea* 26 (2): 131–49.

United Nations Charter. http://www.un.org/aboutun/charter/.

Universal Declaration of Human Rights. Preamble. http://www.un.org/Overview/rights.html.

Woods, James. 2005. "Frontline/PBS: Triumph of Evil." In *Hotel Rwanda: Bringing the True Story of an African Hero to Film*, edited by Terry George, 61–89. New York: New Market Press.

# FOUR

# Hollywood's Cowboy Humanitarianism in *Black Hawk Down* and *Tears of the Sun*

MARYELLEN HIGGINS

In *Reading Humanitarian Intervention,* Anne Orford observes that "legal texts justifying interventions in the name of human rights protection offer a narrative in which the international community as heroic savior rescues those passive victims who suffer at the hands of bullies and tyrants" (2003, 34–35). At first blush, Ridley Scott's film *Black Hawk Down* (2001), which stages the 1993 battle of Mogadishu in Somalia, appears to craft a similar narrative, but with a significant modification. In Scott's film, it is not only the Somalis, but also the humanitarian internationals themselves—the Red Cross and the United Nations—who appear to be powerless. The opening sequences present a series of grim images of silent, starved, and dead Somalis, and the equally silent Red Cross workers who try to nourish the living. The visual displays of suffering on screen are accompanied by text crawls: "300,000 civilians die of starvation. . . . Mohamed Farrah Aidid, the most powerful of the warlords, rules the capital of Mogadishu. . . . He seizes international food shipments at the ports. . . . Hunger is his weapon."

The US military first enters the scene through the handsome figure of Sergeant Eversmann (Josh Harnett), who from his helicopter witnesses Aidid's militia confiscating bags of food marked "USA" at gunpoint from a Red Cross food distribution center. Because the area is under the UN's jurisdiction, the soldiers are prevented from engaging in conflict and saving the starving victims. The initial shots invite viewers to feel outrage at the antagonists' merciless disregard for starving people, to recognize the fragility of humanitarian internationals in need of muscular protection, and to share the heroes' frustrations with villains who appear to take advantage of international rules that prohibit violent engagement. In later scenes, US military elites will position themselves as the ultimate international frontier marshals of global law and order.

The combination of weak humanitarian internationals in Africa in need of muscular protection, helpless African victims, American military heroes, and the accompanying call for outlaw justice also appear in Antoine Fuqua's *Tears of the Sun* (2003). In Fuqua's film, the fictional muscular humanitarians are American Navy SEALs who protect an international missionary doctor and cooperative "Christian Ibo" victims from "Muslim Fulani" insurgents. In the DVD commentary, Fuqua states that *Tears of the Sun* is about "man's inhumanity to man" and "good men who are doing something about evil." The story line illustrates what Mahmood Mamdani describes as the international humanitarian order: African subjects are not "active agents in their own emancipation," but "passive beneficiaries of an external 'responsibility to protect'" (2009, 275).

What is intriguing about both films' representations of American military intervention overseas is their evocation of the classic Hollywood western, this time with its outlaw heroes discovering a new "Wild Wild West" on African frontiers. In the classic western genre, eastern laws are viewed as insufficient tools to enforce justice when lawless or rogue villains circumvent the prescribed rules; thus, the western cowboy hero or fast-firing lawman must step in to restore order through "rough justice" (Lusted 2003, 46). In *Black Hawk Down* and *Tears of the Sun,* it is the American military that represents what Orford describes as "the hard body of the international community," which swoops in to impose order on lawless states. Through its association with humanitarian internationals, American military intervention is coded in the films as the administration of global justice (172).

For Richard Slotkin, the resuscitation of the themes of the western in contemporary films responds to a nostalgia for "old assurance of American progressivism"; the dominant appeal "is not to the memory of historical experience but to the remembrance of old movies" (1992, 640). One might recall George W. Bush's call to capture Osama Bin Laden at any cost: "I want justice. And there's an old poster out West that says, 'Wanted: Dead or Alive'" (Harnden 2001). Yet it is also possible to regard the revival of western film icons as a conscious illumination of the very nostalgia for the Old West of Hollywood movies. The references to the western genre in *Black Hawk Down* are not necessarily indicative of a national yearning for comforting narratives of American progress in which American heroes tame and "civilize" the (global) "wilderness." Instead, Scott's film holds the conjuring of Hollywood fictions up for evaluation through the characters' glorification and imitation of mythic western outlaw heroes, and through their disillusionment as they are hit and encircled by the Somali resistance in Mogadishu. The possible embedded ideologies within the film, then, can be interpreted through a reading of how the western genre itself influences the characters' perceptions of their roles in the world.

## COWBOY HUMANITARIANS

Of the young soldiers in the Mogadishu battle, Mark Bowden, whose book inspired the film, writes, "It didn't matter that none of the men in these helicopters knew enough to write a high school paper about Somalia. They took the army's line without hesitation. Warlords had so ravaged the nation battling among themselves that their people were starving to death. When the world sent food, the evil warlords hoarded it and killed those who tried to stop them. So the civilized world has decided to lower the hammer, invite the baddest boys on the planet over to clean things up. 'Nuff said" (2000, 10). The army's line frames American engagement abroad in terms that echo André Bazin's analysis of the western film genre as "the great epic Manicheism which sets the forces of evil over against the knights of the true cause" (1971, 145). In Bowden's book, Sergeant Paul Howe perceives his Delta Operators as "modern knights and true" (34). The veteran soldiers in the film version of *Black Hawk Down* are associated with knights—those precursors to cowboy heroes—as the senior Delta, Wex (Kim Coates), sketches what is described in the script as "a medieval knight dragging an enormous sword through a dense forest" (15). Furthermore, Bowden's descriptions of "Aidid-controlled territory" summon the landscapes and themes of the western that the Rangers and Delta Force Operators have absorbed: "Hundreds of thousands of clan members lived in this labyrinth of irregular dirt streets and cactus-lined paths. There were no decent maps. Pure Indian country" (6). In the film, Lieutenant Colonel McKnight (Tom Sizemore) explicitly draws the analogy to the western as he warns his fellow soldiers that "Bakara Market is the Wild West." In the initial logic of Scott's *Black Hawk Down*, it will be up to the Rangers and the Delta Force Operators—Captain Steele (Jason Issacs) refers to the "D-boys" as "a bunch of undisciplined cowboys"—to band together and capture the warlord Aidid.

The US Army Ranger Eversmann, after seeing the Red Cross mission in peril, demonstrates his humanitarian credentials as he muses on the necessity for the American intervention: "Look, these people, they have no jobs, no food, no education, no future. I just figure that we have two things we can do. We can either help, or we can sit back and watch a country destroy itself on CNN." Yet as *Black Hawk Down* progresses, competing narratives emerge about the kind of "help" that is achieved. What begins as a typical Hollywood fantasy of humanitarian rescue in Africa transforms into a fantasy gone awry: the capture plot is turned around as the elite American forces fail to extract Aidid, and, as in the western genre's captivity narrative, are imperiled by fierce "Others" who surround and imprison them. In the spirit of Bowden's book, *Black Hawk Down* attempts to reconstruct events through the soldiers' perspectives—that is, through their imagining of their roles in the world through the prism of Hollywood movies and video games. Describing his conversations with the soldiers, Bowden writes that they "remarked again and again how much they felt like they were *in a movie*, and had to remind themselves that this horror, the blood, the deaths, was real" (qtd. in Wetta and Novelli, 442, emphasis in Bowden's original).

References to the classic Hollywood western in Ken Nolan's script for *Black Hawk Down* read, at close inspection, like a deliberate framing of events as a myth in the making. The character Hoot Gibson (Eric Bana) recalls the American rodeo champion Hoot Gibson (1892–1962), who became a stuntman and actor in several early westerns, such as John Ford's *The Fighting Brothers* (1919), *Action* (1921), and *The Horse Soldiers* (1959), as well as Otto Brower's *Spirit of the West* (1932). Lawrence and McGarrahan note that while there are similarities between the character "Hoot" and Delta Sergeant Norm Hooten (like "Hoot," Norm Hooten was reportedly scolded for holding his weapon without the safety on), he is a character largely invented for the film, one who "points toward a cowboy film star of several decades' duration" (2008, 444). Beyond the insertion of Hoot Gibson, the most intriguing reference to the American western in Scott's film is made by Osman Atto (George Harris), Aidid's Somali financier. In one of the few scenes in which Somali characters participate in the dialogue, Atto mocks US attempts to capture Aidid: "You put up your wanted posters. $25,000. . . . What is this, gunfight at the K.O. corral?" Major General Garrison (Sam Shepard), who in Bowden's book clearly enjoys the prospect of a "heart-pounding, balls-out gunfight" (24), is amused by Atto's K.O. analogy, and replies, "It's the O.K. Corral." While the American characters in the film view themselves uncritically as outlaw heroes, it is the Somali financier who recognizes the connection between what will become a variously interpreted Mogadishu gunfight and the legendary Tombstone, Arizona, showdown between the Earps and the Clantons in 1881, which became famous through its multiple, and likewise conflicting, versions in western films and television series, among them Allan Dwan's *Frontier Marshal* (1939), John Ford's *My Darling Clementine* (1946), John Sturges's *Gunfight at the O.K. Corral* (1957), the ABC series *Life and Legend of Wyatt Earp* (1955–61), Sturges's *Hour of the Gun* (1967), Frank Perry's *Doc* (1971), George Cosmatos's *Tombstone* (1993), and Lawrence Kasdan's *Wyatt Earp* (1994).

As Allen Barra observes, the story of Wyatt Earp in the Old West is summoned in popular culture "when the question of the influence of the frontier on our national character or the relation of force to law" (1998, 335). In Scott's *Black Hawk Down*, two main characters—the idealistic Ranger Eversmann and the rule-breaking, sharp-shooting Delta Operator Hoot (who, like Wyatt Earp's partner Doc Holliday, generally prefers to work alone)—team up to engage in a climactic battle with a Somali clan in Mogadishu. Hubert Cohen writes that "just as Westerns function as our Arthurian legend—the cowboy hero as the Knight who rides forth from the Roundtable to perform good acts and affirm justice—Wyatt and his lawmen are seen as Knights called away from the cardtable to preserve civil order against a gang of Mordreds" (2003, 205). The modern knights in the film engage in various friendly games (chess, Scrabble) before they are called into battle. The use of veteran knights and youthful cowboy heroes may function to couch violent intervention abroad in familiar, romanticized myths, yet the reference by a Somali character to the Wild West calls attention to how the battle itself is mediated through the western's iconic images and characters.

On one level, *Black Hawk Down* seems to conjure the memory of the fictionalized O.K. Corral gunfight to romanticize the American outlaw intervention in Somalia. The conclusion to *Black Hawk Down* is infused with dramatic irony as the badly injured Ruiz (Enrique Murciano) asks Captain Steele, "Are we going after them?" Steele responds, "You bet your ass we will. We gotta regroup." The spectator likely knows better: Aidid was not captured in the battle, and President Clinton, under pressure from a protesting Congress and a public discouraged by images of slain soldiers dragged through the streets of Mogadishu, would withdraw the troops. After learning that they would leave, Eversmann recounts talking to Blackburn, who asks, "What changed? Why are we going home?"—and despite his response—"nothing"—he confesses that "everything's changed." The implied shame extends to the civilian public that displays a lack of nerve in a nation that will not "cowboy up" and support a continuation of the fight when it meets fierce local resistance. In his foreword to the shooting script, Bowden remarks, "The Mogadishu battle had prompted not just a sudden end to the mission in Somalia, but a withdrawal of American military force from the world. The world had paid a terrible price for that—in Rwanda, Bosnia, and Kosovo" (Nolan 2002, xv).

Nonetheless, the multiple references to the western genre suggest that Scott and Nolan are quite aware that their story, like the O.K. Corral gunfight, participates in the creation of mythical tales of American gunfighters, this time on an African frontier. The articulation of the analogy by the Somali financier in the film also suggests that the Somalis are equally conscious of how the battle will be incorporated into American mythology. The film exposes the flaws in the idealist Eversmann's belief that violent intervention will achieve humanitarian aims—attempts to restore "order" by toppling Aidid's regime lead to violence, chaos, suffering, and death. The reception of Scott's film tends to run along the lines of Bowden's assertion that "what viewers see is without question the most authentic depiction of modern soldiering ever filmed" (Nolan 2002, xi), yet the soldiers' interpretations of the battle are obviously influenced by Hollywood fictions. How do we read, then, the "authenticity"? Is it grounded in the film's use of realistic props and stunts provided by the Pentagon, or in its authentic representation of a flawed fantasy?

## YIPPEE-KI-YAY INTERVENTION

In Antoine Fuqua's *Tears of the Sun,* the very presence of Bruce Willis, who stars as Navy SEAL Lieutenant A. K. Waters, evokes the image of the updated cowboy hero. Recalling Willis's famous role as John McClane in *Die Hard* (John McTiernan, 1988), Joseph Tirella (2007) writes, "Like John Wayne before him, Willis has come to define a certain archetype in American cinema. He's the modern-day equivalent of a cowboy." Willis's famous line (in response to the name "Mr. Cowboy")—"Yippee-ki-yay, motherfucker"—merges the resuscitated cowboy with the more recent figure of the masculine action hero (see Lichtenfeld 2007). Tarak Barkawi reads *Tears of the Sun* as a narrative crossover from Ray Kellogg and John Wayne's film, *Green Berets* (1968), in which Wayne stars as the leader of a small number of humanitarian-minded American Special Forces who protect a village threatened by villainous (Vietnamese) insurgents (Barkawi 2004, 135). At the conclusion of *Tears of the Sun,* after the villains are destroyed, Lieutenant Waters coaches a compliant African leader on how to rule correctly: "Become a fucking a man," he commands, and "cowboy the fuck up."

As in *Black Hawk Down*, the first sequences in *Tears of the Sun* feature merciless African villains who terrorize helpless African victims. In this case, the villains are Nigerian "Muslim Fulani" rebels who shoot the defenseless wife and daughters of an "Ibo Christian" Nigerian president. A British newscaster's voiceover explains that the Muslim rebels have assassinated the president, who ran a democratically elected government. Within this constructed context, American Navy SEALs are ordered to evacuate an American doctor, Lena Kendricks (Monica Bellucci), as well as European nuns and a priest from the chaos. As in *Black Hawk Down*, *Tears of the Sun* perceives conventional laws that restrain protective American gunpower as ineffective and ultimately immoral. Unlike *Black Hawk Down*'s Sergeant Eversmann, however, Lieutenant Waters does not arrive on the scene with humanitarian ideals. Waters and his crew initially view the abandonment of Africans at the missionary hospital as just another part of their duties—the scene in which the European doctor is extracted recalls moments in *Hotel Rwanda* in which foreign nationals are ushered to safety while tearful Rwandans are left behind. Lieutenant Waters becomes uncharacteristically moved after witnessing the rebels' pillaging of a village, and has, like the spectators watching the film, what one of the soldiers describes as "ringside seats to an ethnic cleansing." In the DVD commentary, Willis explains that spectators are not spared from grisly images so that they can see "what tribal warfare looks like." Clearly, viewers are expected to celebrate as the Navy SEALs disobey orders, gunfight their way through the Nigerian forest, and pave the way for a future democracy.

As in early cowboy westerns, *Tears of the Sun* defines its enemy as savage. One of the refugees characterizes the Muslim rebels: "This is what they do. They cut off the breasts of nursing mothers, so that they can never feed their own babies." *Tears of the Sun* presents a variation of the Hollywood western's captivity narrative, where the white woman—revised here as the white humanitarian international—"symbolizes the values of Christianity and civilization that are imperiled in the wilderness war" (Slotkin 1992, 14). When Dr. Kendricks refuses to leave "her [African] people" behind, Waters urges her: "Do you have any idea what's gonna happen to you and these young women once the rebel forces get here?" Africa is painted as a wilderness that has, according to Waters, been abandoned by God ("God left Africa")—a statement that is echoed cinematically by Danny Archer in *Blood Diamond* ("God left this place a long time ago"). And as Slotkin argues of the "savage war" in the classic western film, "To avoid defeat in such a war, the hero must be licensed to use whatever force of violence may be necessary. The taboos and moral prohibitions that limit the use of force do not apply" (95). The *mission civilisatrice*, or the *mission salvatrice* is accomplished when US air power swoops in to carpet bomb the rebels. The absolute evil of the Fulani Muslim enemy in *Tears of the Sun* functions to code the violent destruction of anti-Western Muslim rebels as an act of heroism.

As Tarak Barkawi observes, Hollywood's display of "muscular humanitarianism" in films such as *Tears of the Sun* functions much like the rhetoric of the Bush administration during the Iraq War: it depends on the construction of oppressed victims who yearn for freedom, and positions the US military as their liberators (2004, 137). For Barkawi, public disapproval of American military force abroad is not, as it is frequently assumed, based on a lack of public resolve, or on an unwillingness to shed blood. Rather, the objection is based on the suspicion that others do not want American intervention; resistance is "a direct assault on the self-perception of many American citizens and their view of the United States in the World" (131). To regain public support, then, the interventionist's narrative insists that suffering locals desperately desire military rescue (131–36). The denouement of *Tears of the Sun* thus reads like a neoconservative fantasy, one that is not realized in *Black Hawk Down:* When oppressive leaders are destroyed and replaced by the American military's sanctioned favorites, order is restored, the victims bless the heroes gratefully, victory is unambiguous, and nothing is expected in return.

Just as the classic Hollywood western typically portrays cowboy heroes as the tamers of rogue villains during the colonization of North America, the Navy SEALs in *Tears of the Sun* are depicted as the forces that restore law and order to a chaotic Nigeria. *Tears of the Sun* bears an interesting resemblance to another piece of colonial fiction: The character Arthur Azuka (Sammi Rotibi) walks in step, a century later, with Umbopa of Rider Haggard's *King Solomon's Mines*. Azuka is, in a confusing plot twist, the king of "the Ibo Nation" and the heir to the Nigerian presidency; the African Umbopa in *King Solomon's Mines* is also an exiled heir to the throne, who relies on British colonial adventurers for protection against the evil tyrant, Twala. Both heirs initially disguise their identities, and both are saved by Westerners who slay their African opponents. The resultant image is of powerful Westerners who heroically enforce regime change in a dangerous world of rogue states. Here I'd like to turn to Barbara Harlow's question, "What makes the difference in the end between a 'civilizing mission' and 'humanitarian interventionism?'" (1996, 45). The connection between the colonial adventure novel and the humanitarian intervention film here echoes Mamdani's comparison between the rhetoric of the international humanitarian order and the colonial order: Human rights violations in Africa are emphasized to "turn the victims into so many proxies whose dilemma would legitimate colonial intervention as a rescue mission" (2009, 277).

### THE DISTRACTION OF THE WESTERN: OMISSION AND SUBSTITUTION

Orford argues that in the humanitarian interventionist's rendering of the plot of rescue, "the international community is absent from the scene of suffering until it intervenes as heroic savior" (2003, 85). Just as Western states craft narratives of humanitarian intervention that omit their imperial histories and their previous connections to oppressive regimes in African states, the films present an international community that arrives on the scene in Africa only to intervene as humanitarian heroes. Orford writes, "The assumption that international actors played no role in causing the crisis is central to establishing the fault of the target state. . . . Raising such questions would threaten the progress of the narrative" (176). The overt references to the western in *Black Hawk Down* signals an awareness of the popular framing of American imperialism as a civilizing mission, yet the projection of the fantasy/myth eclipses other significant historical references and readings, particularly the previous roles of Western states in Somalia (and throughout Africa) and their economic support for dictatorial regimes.

The lens in Scott's film does not spare the viewer from disturbing images of the suffering caused by Aidid's callous disregard for starving Somalis, but blurs previous histories of colonialism, superpower proxy wars, and American military blunders that led to the suffering of Somali civilians. In his foreword to Nolan's screenplay, Bowden recalls producer Jerry Bruckheimer's advice as he drafted an early version of the script: "Every scene should advance the story, and should end in a way that propels you into the next scene," and "You can lose an audience very quickly if you confuse or bore them, and once that happens, you can't get them back" (2002, vii). Ken Nolan asks on writing the script: "How much politics do we put in without boring the audience?" (2002, xix). Whether cinematic omissions of colonial and postcolonial power are confusing, boring, or do not propel the narrative, the end result is a convenient reduction. The production notes in *Black Hawk*

*Down: The Shooting Script* reduce the civil war in Somalia to illogical African feuds: "The U.S. Troops come to Somalia with good intentions, hoping to save lives, not take them. Increasingly mired in Somalia's incomprehensible feudal politics—in which one clan has been pitted against another for a millennium—the soldiers are destined for a brutal education" (Nolan 2002, 151).

In a commercial Hollywood film like *Black Hawk Down*, the absence of potentially "boring" historical contexts is not so surprising. It is well understood that filmmakers have poetic license to tamper with the evidence. An analysis of what is omitted from the film's plot, dialogues, and mise-en-scène, however, demonstrates not just the well-known and accepted fact that films do not accurately represent history, but how the narrative of pure American heroism depends on the erasure of previous US involvement in the scene of suffering. Omitted from the contexts given in the on-screen inscriptions is Siad Barre, the dictator with an extended record of human rights violations who ruled Somalis for twenty-two years, and who was able to sustain and build his power through foreign donors during the Cold War until he was overthrown by Aidid and his supporters in 1991. Tripodi (1999) reports that the United States provided Barre's Somalia $20 million in military aid in 1980, a figure that was raised to $34.1 million by 1985, and later diminished as the Cold War fizzled. As Alex de Waal notes, the resources that were spent on the interventions in Somalia in the 1990s "transformed Somali politics by feeding inflated expectations of the return of the aid machine that had sustained Siad Barre" (1997, 185). While the film establishes the guilt of Aidid's financier Atto (Garrison scorns him: "you pay for [Aidid's] beds, much less his militia"), the payments by European and American governments that boosted Barre's military forces are never mentioned.

Also omitted is what de Waal calls "the drumbeat for intervention" in Somalia that might explain the general hostility toward humanitarian workers. Philip Johnson, CARE-US's president, recommended in 1992 that "the international community, backed by UN troops, should move in and run Somalia because it has no government at all" (de Waal 1997, 181). Further eclipsed in the film is the role of the Egyptian UN secretary-general, Boutros Boutros-Ghali, who argued in favor of nation building, which would necessitate the disarming of Somali clans (Tripodi 1999, 142). As Lawrence and McGarrahan observe, the film does not include Bowden's report on the misguided US missile attack on a Habr Gidr meeting of elders, spiritual leaders, professors, Somali judges, and the poet Moallim Soyan, which killed the eldest member of the clan and several others (Lawrence and McGarrahan

2008, 434; Bowden 2000, 72). It does not recount the outrage of Somalis after the attack, or the anger caused when black hawk helicopters, in their search for Aidid and his allies, damaged Somali homes.

As Thomas Doherty remarks, "Unlike the book, the film provides little explanation as to why a city should erupt in spontaneous rebellion against good-hearted Americans who want only to deliver food and medicine to a starving people" (2005, 217). As if to explain what possesses Somali children to serve as Aidid's lookouts when the helicopters arrive, Jimi Hendrix's "Voodoo Child" (played by Stevie Ray Vaughan) pipes in as the black hawk helicopters take off. The music continues as Atto calmly picks up a shaking glass of tea, and the "Voodoo Child" refrain kicks in just as (read "possessed") Somali boys spot the helicopter and phone the militia leader. This moment echoes a description by Bowden in his book: "Telephone poles leaned at ominous angles like voodoo totems topped by stiff sprays of dreadlocks—the stubs of their severed wires" (2000, 7). Like the villains of the western genre, Somali military figures are portrayed as criminals who bring perpetual violence and chaos. Inside the mosque where the pilot Mike Durant (Ron Eldard) is held captive, Firimbi (Treva Etienne) asserts, "In Somalia, killing is negotiation. Do you really think if you get General Aidid, we will simply put down our weapons and adopt American democracy? That the killing will stop? We know this: without victory, there can be no peace. There will always be killing, you see? This is how things are in our world." The film edits out details from Bowden's book that would humanize Firimbi: in the book, Firimbi helps to wash and bandage Durant's wounds, gives Durant a radio to listen to the BBC World service, allows a visit by a representative from the Red Cross, provides Durant with a doctor and home-cooked meals, and manages to communicate with him using Spanish and Italian (Bowden 2000, 319). Images of mosques and the calls of the muezzin punctuate the film, suturing the fear of captivity by Somali mobs with the Muslim call to prayer.

In its appeal for military intervention in Africa's devastating civil wars, it is substitution, rather than omission, that abounds in Tears of the Sun, as if one set of African antagonists can seamlessly stand in for another. In his writing on the Save Darfur movement, Mamdani asserts that the appeal for forceful humanitarian intervention in Darfur was grounded not on understanding but on the Rwandan analogy (2009, 64). What replaced an investigation of the causes for civil war in Darfur was "an assault of images without context" (56), a reliance on "the evidence of the eyes" where pictures replaced explanation (7). In the DVD commentary for Tears of the Sun, producer Arnold Rifkin describes the film as "a metaphor for what is happening today in the world." As A. O. Scott (2003) argues, *Tears of the Sun* projects a fictional "collage of recent real-world African atrocities, evoking wars in places like Rwanda, Liberia and Sudan." Scott writes,

> [Nigeria's] disintegration is staged to allow the West—specifically the United States military—to atone for its failure to halt those other slaughters. It is often said that politicians and generals are always fighting the last war; in this case, Alex Lasker and Patrick Cirillo, the screenwriters, and Antoine Fuqua, the director, appear to be applying Rambo-style revanchist methods to a Clinton-era debate about humanitarian intervention.

The film's distorted collage—which muddles histories of insurgency and counterinsurgency in Africa—stretches not only across African space, but also through time. As *Tears of the Sun* intertwines images reminiscent of Sierra Leone, Rwanda, and Darfur, it presents the figure of the Nigerian general Yakubu, a character who recalls Major General Yakubu Gowon, a prominent figure during the 1967–70 Nigerian Civil War. To summarize it all, the Nigerian character Musa explains to the African American soldier, Silk: "Cultural differences and the quest for economic power are turning Africa into a killing field."

In this case, the "cultural differences" are inscribed as religious differences, and Western colonial and neocolonial quests for economic power resonate only as a faint echo. With the exception of a few comments about the rebels' reliance on financing from American suitors through payments for access to Nigerian oil, postcolonial meddling in Africa by Western states is swept out of *Tears of the Sun*'s historical exposition. When the specter of colonialism does emerge, it appears fleetingly in oblique references performed through the vitriolic speeches of the film's evil antagonists. The rebel Terwase (Peter Mensah) addresses his militia: "As Hausa and Fulani, we have a responsibility to protect our people, our way of life, and our nation. The Ibo do not have the faith that we do. They do not believe in our religion. They have taken the religion of the colonialists. We will never be pawns for anyone. Never. We will cleanse this nation of this Ibo and the American vermin." Here, colonialism is depicted as the benign spread of Christianity, while anti-imperialist motivation to decolonize is coded as the ideology of a genocidal enemy.

Frank Joseph Wetta and Martin A. Novelli perceive a "New Patriotism" in war films that lauds soldiers' loyalty to each other in combat, one that "[does] not revive patriotism so much as turn it inside out so that the private motivations and goals of the individual soldier supersede any stated or understood national or public rationales for whatever war is being fought" (2003, 861). In *Tears of the Sun,* as the Navy SEAL Slo (Nick Chinlund) is dying, he pleads with Lieutenant Waters to defeat the antagonists, so that his sacrifices are "not for nothing." In *Black Hawk Down,* Hoot asserts that he will not respond to people at home who ask why he goes to war because he is sure that "they won't understand." Yet the fictional Hoot does, in fact, explain his reasons to the spectators watching the film at home: "It's about the men next to you," and "that's all it is." The idealist Eversmann's hopes for humanitarian rescue fall apart; the tagline, "leave no man behind," replaces the call for the rights of suffering humans internationally. The embedded argument in the films, like the ubiquitous "support our troops" bumper stickers during the Iraq War, is that the viewing public should, like Hoot, cast aside the larger political questions and rally behind the valiant efforts of self-sacrificing soldiers.

In Hollywood filmmaking, one expects omissions, analogies, and distortions. Serious human rights advocacy, however, requires an awareness of relevant political complexities and historical contexts. How then, can a film advocate human rights as it eschews political understanding, and as it reduces, demonizes, and dehumanizes entire groups of people? In these constructed African contexts, it would seem that the perpetually vilified, "reel bad Arabs" analyzed by Jack Shaheen (2009) have been cinematically transformed into reel bad Muslims. In the worlds of both *Black Hawk Down* and *Tears of the Sun,* the viewer is invited to share the elite soldier's desire: the disempowerment of rogue Muslim African generals through American firepower. The perceived resolutions to the humanitarian crises in both films, achieved or not, entail the destruction of those who would oppose American intervention, which is read as global humanitarianism. Perhaps the memory of American support for compliant African dictators during the Cold War and the imbalance of economic power might not just compromise the entertainment value of the films, but might also risk unsettling the perception of the United States as the world's frontier marshal and humanitarian savior.

That said, *Tears of the Sun* has generally been dismissed by critics as a fantasy.[1] If DVD commentaries are an accurate representation of the perceptions of the writers, actors, and producers, *Tears of the Sun* was not intended to appear under the genre of fantasy but as a metaphor for "what is happening in the world." *Black Hawk Down*, in contrast, calls attention to the fantasies of veteran soldiers who see themselves as knights, and young Rangers who perform their duties like cowboys in movies. *Black Hawk Down* would be applauded by critics for its verisimilitude. So as not to miss the complexities of filmmaking, one fruitful interpretation of Hollywood's cowboy military humanitarians would recognize the tension between fantasy and authenticity, between myth-making à la Hollywood westerns and the insistence that the myth is authentic history.

## NOTES

1. For example, Scott (2003) asserts that "the movie's real setting is a sentimental fantasy world."

## REFERENCES

Barkawi, Tarak. 2004. "Globalization, Culture, and War: On the Popular Mediation of 'Small Wars.'" *Cultural Critique* 58 (Fall 2004): 115–47.
Barra, Allen. 1998. *Inventing Wyatt Earp: His Life and Many Legends*. New York: Carroll Graf.
Bazin, André. 1971. "The Western, or the American Film Par Excellence." In *What Is Cinema? Essays Selected and Translated by Hugh Gray*. Vol. 2. Berkeley: University of California Press.
*Black Hawk Down*. 2001. Directed by Ridley Scott. Produced by Jerry Bruckheimer. Sony Pictures, Revolution Studios Distribution Company. DVD.
Bowden, Mark. 2000. *Black Hawk Down: A Story of Modern War*. New York: Penguin.
Cohen, Hubert. 2003. "Wyatt Earp at the O.K. Corral: Six Versions." *Journal of American Culture* 26 (2): 204–23.
de Waal, Alex. 1997. *Famine Crimes: Politics and the Disaster Relief Industry in Africa*. Bloomington: Indiana University Press.
Doherty, Thomas. 2005. "The New War Movies as Moral Rearmament: *Black Hawk Down* and *We Were Soldiers*." In *The War Film*, edited by Robert Eberwein, 214–21. New Brunswick, NJ: Rutgers University Press.
Harlow, Barbara. 1996. "From the 'Civilizing Mission' to 'Humanitarian Interventionism': Postmodernism, Writing, and Human Rights." In *Text and Nation: Cross-Disciplinary Essays on Cultural and National Identities*, edited by Laura García-Moreno and Peter C. Pfeiffer, 31–47. Columbia, SC: Camden House.
Harnden, Toby. 2001. "Bin Laden Is Wanted: Dead or Alive, Says Bush." *Telegraph*. Sept. 18. http://www.telegraph.co.uk/.
Lawrence, John Sheldon, and John G. McGarrahan. 2008. "Operation Restore Honor in *Black Hawk Down*." In *Why We Fought: America's Wars in Film and History*, edited by Peter C. Rollins and John E. O'Connor, 431–57. Lexington: University Press of Kentucky.
Lichtenfeld, Eric. 2007. "Yippee-Ki-Yay . . . The Greatest One-Liner in Movie History." *Slate* June 26. http://www.slate.com/id/2168927/.

Lusted, David. 2003. *The Western*. New York: Pearson Longman.

Mamdani, Mahmood. 2009. *Saviors and Survivors: Darfur, Politics, and the War on Terror*. New York: Pantheon.

Nolan, Ken. 2002. *Black Hawk Down: The Shooting Script*. Foreword by Mark Bowden. New York: Newmarket Press.

Orford, Anne. 2003. *Reading Humanitarian Intervention: Human Rights and the Use of Force in International Law*. Cambridge: Cambridge University Press.

Scott, A. O. 2003. "*Tears of the Sun* Film Review: Americans Atoning for African Slaughters." *New York Times*, March 7. http://movies.nytimes.com/movie/review?res=9804E4DC133FF934A35750C0A9659C8B63.

Shaheen, Jack. 2009. *Reel Bad Arabs: How Hollywood Vilifies a People*. Northampton, MA: Olive Branch.

Slotkin, Richard. 1992. *Gunfighter Nation: the Myth of the Frontier in Twentieth-Century America*. New York: Harper Perennial.

*Tears of the Sun*. 2003. Director's extended cut. Directed by Antoine Fuqua. Produced by Michael Lobell, Arnold Rifkin, and Ian Bryce. Sony Pictures, Revolution Studios Distribution Company. DVD.

Tirella, Joseph. 2007. "Yippee-ki-yay! Bruce Willis' Best and Worst." *Today Movies*. June 25. http://today.msnbc.msn.com/id/19378043/ns/today-entertainment/t/yippee-ki-yay-bruce-willis-best-worst/.

Tripodi, Paolo. 1999. *The Colonial Legacy in Somalia*. New York: St. Martin's Press.

Weiss, Thomas G. 2007. *Humanitarian Intervention*. Malden, MA: Polity Press.

Wetta, Frank Joseph, and Martin A. Novelli. 2003. "'Now a Major Motion Picture': War Films and Hollywood's New Patriotism." *Journal of Military History* 67 (3): 861–82.

# FIVE

# Again, the Darkness

## Shake Hands with the Devil

KENNETH W. HARROW

> As the genocide raged, Dallaire was condemned to peer
> into the heart of darkness, to witness the failure of
> humanity, to shake hands with the devil.
>
> —*Shake Hands with the Devil: The Journey of Roméo
> Dallaire*

To prepare for a recent talk on human rights films, I decided to view
two documentaries on Rwanda, *Shake Hands with the Devil: The Journey of
Roméo Dallaire* (Peter Raymont, 2004) and *Ghosts of Rwanda* (Greg Barker,
2004, Frontline-PBS), and one popular feature film, *Hotel Rwanda* (Terry
George, 2004). My decision to create a series of roundtables titled "What's
Wrong with Human Rights Films" for the 2007 African Studies Association
and 2008 African Literature Association was made in reaction to a screening
of Michael Caton-Jones's *Shooting Dogs* (2005), for which I had been asked to
be a respondent on my campus. That film centered on a self-sacrificing British priest who saves "his" Tutsis but is ultimately killed. As the film is deeply
flawed, especially in its celebration of the Catholic priesthood, whose actual
behavior in this massacre was generally the contrary to that presented in the
film, I thought it would be important to ask whether the flaws in *Shooting
Dogs* were merely random or something intrinsic to the whole enterprise of
making human rights films. For these purposes, I just as easily could have
chosen *Hotel Rwanda*, another film that reduces the historical event to a
Hollywood Manichean binary of good and evil. This was partly the subject
of my earlier essay, "Un Train Peut en Cacher un Autre" (2005), in which
I address the ideological effects of the genocide narrative in its occlusion
of historical evidence that muddies the purity of the binary. To be specific,

the focus on the genocide of the Tutsis occludes the range of human rights abuses directed against the Hutus, and especially directs us away from the role of the Rwandan government and its Tutsi militias in wreaking havoc in the Democratic Republic of Congo (DRC) after 1998, and in sharing a large part of the responsibility for the eventual deaths of more than five million people. (Disclosure: I also worked on the creation of *Forsaken Cries,* the first Amnesty International film on the Rwandan genocide made in 1997 by Kathy Austin [Institute of Policy Studies]. In that film our narrative never addressed claims of abuses suffered by Hutus at the hands of the Rwandan Patriotic Front [RPF].)

In films about the genocide we find the following typology:

—A teleological history in which the events are presented in the form of an African historical determinism. The framing inevitably explains African history as entailing endless "tribal warfare"; this is what we might call the Western newspaper headline version of Africa, dating back to colonial times.

—The centering of a Western protagonist through whose eyes the horror is duly registered (as in *The Constant Gardener* [Fernando Meirelles 2005])—typically, a white man or woman through whose eyes the dominant perspective of the film is purveyed. This is not entirely the case in *Hotel Rwanda,* although the figure of Paul Rusesabagina, through whom the focalization is directed, is seen as somehow succeeding in remaining above the fray, unlike the others trapped in the killings. He is like a European, because of his link to the European hotel, and is still presented as a victim because of his Tutsi wife. Secondarily, the figure of the Nick Nolte character, the UN colonel, reinforces this perspective. Paul's relationship to those threatening him is inevitably represented in black-and-white terms.[1]

—A code of characters and issues cast in familiar binary terms, an inevitable feature of human rights discourse. As an Amnesty International country specialist, I know all too well how it becomes necessary in mobilizing support for a cause not to muddy the appeal by suggesting that the ones on whose behalf an appeal is made are anything but pure victims of those who are to be seen as perpetrators. From such ratiocination is inevitably built the binary logic that Jan-Mohamed would define as a "Manichaean aesthetic," characteristic of colonial ideology, and, in lock step with its logic, that of a modernist ideology.[2]

Ironically, as American activists, we can currently embrace this self-righteous position of the human rights petitioner by repressing knowledge of our own country's complicity in the very abuses against which we have been protesting for decades. The standpoint of our enunciation as human rights spokespersons has been compromised.

So what's "wrong" with human rights films is that they have to be seen by an audience who can share the outrage of the director, that is, of the one who is presumed to have constructed the film's implied point of view—and that standpoint is not, and in fact has never been, a place that is free from its ghosts of shame. Nonetheless, even without our own personal support for the invading armies of the night that the United States is determined to deploy around so much of the world, we cannot avoid the interpellation generated by the current crop of films about genocide and attempt to formulate a responsible critique. After all, even a "liar" can speak the "truth"—as many an African trickster tale has taught us.

The film I wish to explore, *Shake Hands with the Devil,* I would feign call Dallaire's, though it was directed by Raymont. Raymont begins the film with an account of the Rwandan genocide that for one and a half hours details how hard it was on Dallaire, the Canadian general in charge of the UN peacekeeping forces—how hard it was for him to have witnessed and lived through the genocide, to have failed to stop it. In a sense, it is a handbook on genocide clichés, like "What right did I have to live when so many died?"; and, especially, "My failure was that I could not convince others to stop it." Or, addressing the African characters, "No one cared because you are black, unlike Yugoslavians." Or that the killings were so horrific, they were incomprehensible. There is a litany now that is driven by a set of expectations of responses that translate into a symbolic code for the human rights film, with its own discourses, filmic practices and shots, its own narrative trajectory, its own underlying logic, and finally, its own relations of production and exhibition that constitute what we could call the human rights industry. This is not a judgment on its motives, but a constatation.

This litany can now be recognized in the words of the UN colonel in *Hotel Rwanda*—indeed, echoing Terry George's bitter observations—that no one cares about the genocide of blacks. The words are shocking in their directness for an American audience for whom the entire discourse around blackness is fraught with tensions and prohibitions. So when *Shake Hands with the Devil* begins, its initial image on the screen presenting a heavily mottled though recognizably African face, accompanied by a semi-incomprehensible voice, the code is clear: Africa, menacing, impenetrable. This is then followed by Dallaire's flat Canadian tones baldly announcing on the plane that his return, now ten years after the genocide, was a return to hell.

As *Shake Hands* unfolds, we hear Dallaire recount his recollections of the earlier events; and as others comment on Dallaire's decency and on how painful he found the experience, it becomes increasingly difficult to maintain the emotion we are being asked to experience, that is, sympathy for Dallaire.

Mr. Kurtz he dead. A penny for the old guy.

In a sense, Dallaire's account of the events is no different from that of anyone else, despite his unique role in this history. He uses the same tropes of the genocide narrative, the same explanations of the sequence of events and the major players. He is a little more direct than some in vilifying the French and Belgians, the latter of whom turn and accuse him of failing to protect the ten Belgian peacekeepers who were killed at the outset of the genocide. But when we are brought back into the narrative's chain of events, it is essentially the same.

What is different, what is astonishing, is Dallaire's own personal discourse. Not his honesty—that being the most banal aspect of the film—but rather his eventual collapse into the very state of said Mr. Kurtz. Dallaire describes the key moment when he meets and shakes hands with the leadership of the Interahamwe. The encounter is made dramatic by the way in which he describes it.

As he begins, we see a man coming over a rise, the head off-frame, the feet not yet visible as he walks toward us, a machete in hand. A stark figure of menace. "From when I shook their hand, their hands were cold. But they weren't cold as a temperature." (Music comes up, a running vibrato of danger.) "They were cold as if an other body. Although they had a human form, theirs were not human." (Speaking directly to his Rwandan interlocutor, behind whose shoulder the camera is situated; we see Dallaire's clear blue eyes, his yellow-white mustache; his blue shirt, tie, and jacket. An ordinary dress code for the ex-soldier.) Dallaire, the general, addresses us, tells us of his encounter with evil. He has clearly not read *Heart of Darkness,* will not join in with Conrad's ironic dismemberment of Kurtz's rationalizations, because he is *not* Marlow. Nor is the film's intended audience or the Rwandan interlocutor a Marlow who, after all, finds he has to lie to the Intended, in the end, so as to protect her and to maintain the fiction of Kurtz's "mission." Dallaire is Kurtz. So, when he pronounces the words "not human," we are led by all that is given us to trust in the film, to that moment of The Encounter with Evil—the fundamental raison d'être for human rights films. This is the moment of truth, and its image will speak this truth along the lines of hundreds of years of racialized, Europeanized codes.

What follows is focalized through Dallaire's eyes and words: We see Him. And He is black, He is frowning, staring directly at us; He has his black, angry followers behind Him. And in His hand, menacing us directly, He holds a machete. "Their eyes were reflecting the most evil that I could ever imagine. It was being personified, and that personification, coming from my . . . religious background" (now it is the same African man's body we see again, walking toward us, machete clearly visible, as the music trills in danger) "was the devil." (Cut to sight of skull and bones, shocking in state of semidecomposition. In background, another skull and corpse. Next to skull, bright white plastic container, its open mouth, like that of the skull, gaping, pointing to us, calling to us—see what the Devil hath wrought. Music, solemn, as we pan over the remains of the decomposing bodies.)[3]

As the apocalyptic vision reaches its apotheosis, we pass to the humanist's response, embodied by Stephen Lewis, UN envoy for Africa: "There comes a moment in time when human behavior is capable of the most ferocious and irrational activity" (pan of bodies in hideous states of decomposition, bloated in death). "This capacity to go berserk [stressed], to have no semblance of feeling for the human condition at all, apparently it lies in us; apparently it lies in human behavior. I don't know what is so crazed as to trigger it, but it is there." Thus Dallaire's melodramatic fanaticism, which peers out at us in his words, is tempered by the international envoy whose humane, semibewildered, pseudoscientific explanation works in tandem with Dallaire's account to evoke and explain that black, menacing image whose satanic work is displayed in the detritus of the genocide. The Evil, the Devil for Dallaire becomes the familiar, normalized figure of the crazed human, one whose cinematic image, in its silent work of revelation, its truth-function, becomes plainly visible for us to witness: it is Him, again: "the horror, the horror." The darkness is within, to be sure, but figured as the menace repeatedly evoked by Marlow in the long voyage up the winding river that snakes into the heart of the continent, and that is now given the name "Interahamwe."

According to Dallaire, it was his religion that enabled him to understand that that fearful African man, his enemy whom he was touching and seeing, was really the devil. Later, Dallaire deplores the evacuation of the foreign nationals, leaving the desperate Tutsis behind, and it becomes clear that the wrong committed by all those French, Italian, and Belgian armed troops that led the evacuation was that they did not remain with him, under his command, so as to assist him. His mission was to serve as the bulwark against the evildoers. He, even he, the film tells us, the best of the white men gone to Africa to save the natives from themselves, could not help but couch his assignment in the language of the crusades. And he reinforces that by evoking the Christian appeal to paradise as the counterbalance to the evil that he fought and failed to defeat.

As his defeat stretched into months, he gradually goes crazy. His helplessness to stop the genocide unfolding before his eyes maddens him. He describes the stench of the dead bodies in the street, evokes his feeling of accountability, repeating twice, "for the rest of my life." And so, he tells us, "It's catching up with me. I'm being pushed too much." He stares stoically ahead, in his car, as the voice of his military assistant Major Philip Lancaster describes the breakdown: "You could see it happen in little things. I guess the first signs to me, in his writing that came apart at the seams. There were days when he would sit down to write an order of some kind, which would make no sense" (Lancaster's expression of concern, eyebrows raised); "incoherent, bits and pieces slammed together." Dallaire, intercalating, musing, "Try to take command of forces . . ." Then cut to Lancaster: "It became clear to me around the middle of July, he had just become too tired. His eyes were just glazed over. He didn't recognize me. He'd hit the wall. Finally he had given everything he had, and had nothing left." Dallaire: "I'd become aggressive, unreasonable. I'd take off for two to three hours" (image of driving into the night in Kigali). "I would be daring the Hutus to try to kill me. I felt I was starting to put the mission at risk, so I felt I had to be released."

Mr. Kurtz, he dead.

It would not be too difficult to imagine this new version of Kurtz, this Marlon Brando in another steamy jungle, slowly turning into the very evil he came to obliterate, his mission to save the natives turned into a personal nightmare. As his orders became incoherent, as he became a creature of the night, ready to attack and destroy the beasts or be killed, as he witnessed the bodies piled high before the morgue and felt both rage and remorse, we can picture the final signs of Kurtz's madness, the gruesome sight of the skulls of Africans posted on top of the poles around his compound. And as the opening intertitle tells us, he experienced his own heart of darkness: "As the genocide raged, Dallaire was condemned to peer into the heart of darkness, to witness the failure of humanity, to shake hands with the devil." Kurtz died. Dallaire was evacuated, eventually hospitalized and treated, given pills so that he would not fall prey definitively to his dark demons of evil.

When the Rwandan genocide is the failure of one man, of the one white man sent to save the Africans from evil, then we are in the quintessential imperial narrative. However, in this case, unlike Kurtz whom Marlow judged to be an extraordinary man, Dallaire strikes the spectator as the most ordinary and even banal of figures. Ironically, it was the exceptional political leader, Bill Clinton, who was shown in the film as "apologizing" for not having "appreciated the extent of the massacre" at the time, an untruth of proportions that can only leave the decent Dallaire aghast. Marlow would have understood the lie, the necessity to cover what would have undermined civilization were it to have been exposed.

If the narrative would have it that it is the white man's fault not to have stopped the genocide, then the black man, even in his worst of crimes, cannot be held responsible, fails to bear his responsibility. What has emerged as the Rwandan Genocide Narrative always places the blame for the genocide on "history," finding the fault to lie first with the Germans and Belgians with their colonial distinctions of ethnic groups and ID cards, then with the Belgian priests who favored the Hutus on independence, and finally with the international community that failed to intervene at the crucial moment. In all this sea of blame, no Rwandans seem to have any agency in the affair. The exception to this apportioning of blame elsewhere can be found in Mamdani's account *When Victims Become Killers* (2002), where he actually asks *the* hard question, what did the Rwandans feel they had at stake that led them to decide to assume the roles of génocidaires?[4]

If the burden of the human rights film is to leave us with the impression that Rwandans were not responsible for their actions—not in 1994, ten years before this film was made, or even earlier, in the past, back to colonial times—then they must not be responsible for coming to terms with it in the present. That is, they are not responsible for constructing this narrative, this fundamental human rights narrative, that functions to explain the past and the import of what happened. We could say, they remain not responsible for constructing their own history, and therefore their own roles, their own subjectivity, their own standpoints. Not even their own crimes. Be they devils or be they angels, that is not their work, but rather is the white man's burden. Thus, the obscene lament that for Dallaire it had all become too much for him to bear.

What's wrong with human rights films is the simple expression of their undercurrent of self-pity, the affect inherent in the phrase "pauvre de nous."[5] The genius of Oyono and Kourouma lay in their ability to exploit the deep irony in that expression, or its equivalents.[6] The trouble with human rights films is that they have no access to that irony. That is, to be clear, they are sure of their ownership of the truth. That was the problem with Phillip Gourevitch's earlier account, *We Wish to Inform You That Tomorrow We Will be Killed with Our Families* (1998). And it is the problem in this film of Dallaire's sad story, where the truth appears so clarion clear. It is also the clarion call of *Hotel Rwanda* and its peers, its *Constant Gardeners, Blood Diamonds,* and so on, films that leave no room to hear even a whisper of the words of doubt, to perceive the edges of the shadows cast so close by what was to occur in East Congo and five million dead; no edge to the frame of responsibility.[7]

Frontline advertises the film *Ghosts of Rwanda,* another documentary film that marks the tenth anniversary of the Rwandan genocide, as an account of one of the worst atrocities of the twentieth century. In it, the narrative voiceover of Will Lyman tells us that the story we will see is to be the Rwandans' account, including those on both sides of the issue. But Lyman's voice is American, and the filmmaker Greg Barker's point of view is the same as that in *Shake Hands* or *Hotel Rwanda*. The film's focalization is created almost immediately through the figure of Dallaire, making points that are identical to those in *Shake Hands with the Devil*. In short, there is the Definitive Version that emerges, albeit with different packaging.[8]

With *Hotel Rwanda,* one might have wondered how we could say that the point of view and focalization are developed through a European or American figure when the principal character is a Rwandan. Don Cheadle plays Paul Rusesabagina. He is the "ghost," in French the "nègre," in the film—that is, the absent ghostwriter whose presence Cheadle simulates in performing the cultivated, Westernized version of the "civilized" Rwandan, the ultimate figure of the resistant victim of the genocide. The Cheadle character is the multicultural exemplum, that is, the Hutu married to the Tutsi, and not the stereotype of either. His tie to the white UN colonel (played by Nick Nolte) permits us to return to the underlying Western human rights truths: that there is no real difference between Hutu and Tutsi (as demonstrated in the scene at the bar where Nolte can't tell the difference between two beautiful women), and the demonization of Bagasora, leaving us with the certainty that there is no valid reason for the Hutus' vicious hatred of the Tutsis. Thus, the violence remains incomprehensible, which implies its perpetrators must have been possessed, if not by the devil, then by drugs and hatred induced by evil leaders. With this tendentious description, we are left with the impression that the perpetrators had no thoughts, gave no consideration to their actions, had no rational motives to which we could ascribe a comprehensible political agenda. In a sense this requires us to downplay their apprehension over being reconquered by the Tutsis. Even if that apprehension were turned into propaganda used to demonize the Tutsis, it still represented a historical conjunction that cannot be conjured away. In 1990 the RPF did invade Rwanda, and during the four years before the genocide, it did represent a threat to the regime. The international community's mediation did take the form of a compulsory agreement in which the RPF was to assume an important role in the government and military. In short, there is nothing to say that after four years of war, and fear of an imposed agreement, the Hutu political class or population had nothing to fear from the RPF or their Tutsi supporters. To be sure, the Hutu extremists played on this fear as did the Nazis when demonizing the Jews. But *Hotel Rwanda* is not about whether there was something to fear in the RPF, not about the complexities generated in history, but about the shock of a genocide, about the goodness of Rusesabagina set against the evil of the killers. It is fair to say that this same combination of shock and legitimate resistance marked the best-known, most powerful written account of the genocide, Gourevitch's *We Wish to Inform You That Tomorrow We Will Be Killed with Our Families* (1998).

Like that account, the film must turn us to the question of ethics and human nature posed to the Western consciousness by the Holocaust, whose shadow inheres in the very words we use to describe and frame these genocides. Its issues, like the very concept of human rights as an intellectual domain produced in the Western academy and legal system, mark out the stakes of these films from the outset. It is all the more striking, then, to see a black American actor play the role of a Rwandan, indeed embodying the drama of his life, in a depiction that purports to give us that account as seen through African eyes, when those very eyes are conceived and created by an Irish director, Terry George. There is a real dialogic relationship at play in this heteroglossia, or these heteroglossias, that marks the interplay between George and his character Rusesabagina, the character Rusesabagina and the real life Rusesabagina on whom he is based, and finally Don Cheadle and

Rusesabagina whom Cheadle both plays at and returns, gives back, to Rusesabagina. The play of simulation never ends as Rusesabagina's Cheadle made Rusesabagina famous, whereupon the latter then publicly voiced his critique of the film for its indiscriminate embrace of the RPF. This was followed by Kagame's angry responses. In the end, Rusesabagina criticized Kagame's government for throwing the election, and Rusesabagina became persona non grata in the country for which he had become a virtual hero.[9]

What's wrong with human rights films is that the film's frame cannot begin to accommodate this declension of the heroic savior to the political man. Perhaps Nelson Mandela could avoid this reduction to the human, but his wife Winnie showed how difficult it could be to maintain that status. Ironically, as Terry George got caught up in the controversy between the real Rusesabagina and Kagame, he concluded, "Hotel Rwanda 2 is a sequel I never want to make" (George 2006, A25).

The voiceover in *Ghosts of Rwanda,* the intertitles of the human rights films that state the facts—these are the ghosts through whose eyes we are made to see the truth. We need to accommodate the ways we are led into films via conventionalized techniques, establishing shots, opening sequences, that create the space for the characters' voices, or intertitles, to whom we are sutured—that is, through whose point of view we are made to see the events unfold. The manner of establishing the suture has to be familiar to the audience to work—resistance is only possible by an audience that has determined to read against the grain, in this case one that begins with a doggedly afrocentrist standpoint. Without that resistance, the laying out of a sequence of events that follows will be accepted as truth, and the idea that this, or any other, truth is being constructed will be hidden. We should call this normalization of the one truth, the one Rwanda genocide film, the one human rights film whatever its variants, the work of ideology. It interpellates us as sympathizers, so that we will accept the hegemony not only in its account, but especially in its *manner of accounting* for the truth. If, like the real Rusesabagina, we refuse to play our roles, resist the interpellation, fail to assume the predetermined subject position, we will have marked ourselves as rebels to the established truths being purveyed. That is, we will be marked as insensitive to the worst of crimes committed against humanity. Perhaps this is why Kagame would regard Rusesabagina as a traitor.

It has taken no more than these ten years, after the productions of Dallaire's film, *Hotel Rwanda, Ghosts of Rwanda, Shooting Dogs,* and many other films that have joined this parade, for it to have become clear that human rights films are now an integral part of the industry of genocide. It is beyond all irony that those of us who turned early to film as another weapon in our feeble arsenal against oppressive regimes should have participated in the construction of an apparatus of truth-making that has proven all too resistant to the complexity inherent in human conflict. Just as a film's conditions of production and technology of filming are invisible, just as the voiceover is heard from a speaker we cannot see, so too are the processes set in motion that "manufacture consent" to "hegemony," Gramsci's term for the way in which a dominant intelligentsia establishes its ideology. What's wrong with human rights films is that their intentions and causes might be good, thus making it all the easier for us not to question their assumptions and standpoints unless they are pointing a finger at us. After all, all those dead bodies are there for us to see—how can we question someone like Dallaire for whom this is indubitable evidence of the devil's evil work? But then, we've had eight long years of Bush's rhetoric, and maybe we have no excuse for not being inoculated against its interpellations, the call of the crusades all over again. Or else, once again we will see the darkness.

NOTES

1. Other films that fit this typology in which the film's principal point of view is focalized through a Western protagonist include *The Last King of Scotland, Tears of the Sun, The Devil Came on Horseback,* and, as mentioned, *The Constant Gardener.* I am grateful to MaryEllen Higgins for pointing this out to me.

2. Central to all modernist thought is the binary split on which the notion of modernism itself is grounded: to be modern is not to be . . . traditional, old-fashioned, or, most significantly for us (or JanMohamed, in this instance), uncivilized. The ideological weight of modernity being normally associated with the West, and lack of civilization with the Other, is fundamental to the project of colonialism, as it is to that of modernism. For this reason, postcolonial theorists have referred to colonialism and the contemporary postcolonial moment as the incomplete project of the Enlightenment.

3. The textual citations are of Dallaire's words in the film. That this figuration of evil lends itself so easily to the Western public discourse can be seen in this citation on the *Shake Hands* website reflecting the current journalese wording: Satan shows his real face in Peter Raymont's chilling documentary *Shake Hands with the Devil: The Journey of Roméo Dallaire,* in which the courageous Canadian general returns to Rwanda a decade after he was abandoned by the world to command a wholly inadequate UN force during the 1994 massacre. Only Dallaire (who ended up guilt-ridden and traumatized), his men, a handful of Rwandans, journalists, and doctors emerge creditably from this film. See French 2005.

4. In her comments on this essay to me, MaryEllen Higgins writes: "It reminds me of the film *Stanley and Livingstone,* with Spencer Tracy. In it, Africans are depicted as irresponsible, wayward children who are too susceptible to devilish temptations (and,

following the colonialist line, Livingstone is celebrated as the missionary who is there to guide and save them)" (personal communication, 2008). Similarly, one can evoke a host of Hollywood films that depict this pattern, like *Sanders of the River* (1935), a film that is almost unbearable to watch in its reduction of Africans to childish savages—all the more unbearable in that the central figure of the Africans in the film is played by Paul Robeson. In an attempt to reverse this pattern, Bassek ba Kobhio created an ironized portrayal of the paternalistic figure of Albert Schweitzer in his *Le Grand blanc de Lamberene* (1995). As Ba Kobhio works within the logic of paternalism, albeit attempting to oppose it, he winds up less with a subversion than what strikes me as an awkward parody.

   5. Examples of this turn of pity and self-pity can be seen in Nolte's character who expresses disgust not only with the treatment of the Tutsis, but with his own inability to do anything about this (*Hotel Rwanda*). Similarly, Dallaire's expressions of affect verge on the maudlin, and ultimately turn us toward his own suffering in seeing the violence of genocide enacted before his eyes, and in his helplessness to do anything about it. Others in the film vocalize our need to pity the poor Dallaire, but he opens the way for this continually by presenting his own feelings of reentering the hell that is Rwanda. The ultimate expression of this might be understood in our historical relationship to the Holocaust as an event whose horrors can be rehearsed in film and text, but never changed. The pity we feel for its victims becomes self-pity when we experience similar helplessness before the unfolding events of genocide that are closer to our lives. This is the source of Philip Gourevitch's claims (1998) about ethical obligations laid on us by the experiencing of the evidence of the genocide in Rwanda.

   6. The phrase is used explicitly and frequently in Oyono 1956. It also conveys the dominant affect in most of Kourouma's work, starting especially with *Les Soleils des indépendances*.

   7. Within three years of the end of the genocide, the RPF government of Paul Kagame decided to put an end to the harassing incursions of the remnants of the former Rwandan government and its militias from across the borders in the DRC. The refugee camps there had been used as bases for the now opposing Rwandan Hutu forces to regroup, rearm, and constitute an attacking force, albeit not a major menace. As Mobutu chose not to prevent those attacks, and as the UN chose not to monitor and police the camps, Kagame took it upon himself to overthrow Mobutu's government in 1997. He used Laurent Kabila's movement, rallied Ugandans to the cause, and marched his troops across the continent to oust Mobutu. As Kabila came to power, he eventually repudiated his Rwandan sponsors who were now advisers and generals in his government. He sent the Rwandans packing, but Kagame refused to accept the situation. Thus, in 1998 he fomented a rebellion in East Congo, using RPA troops as well as militias he created and supported, most notably the RCD-Goma. It was this unleashing of warfare in East Congo that eventually cost the Congolese some five million lives, and its conflict is still not totally resolved. See Amnesty International Report 2000. See also Human Rights Watch Report 2002.

   8. Tellingly, the episodes of *Ghosts of Rwanda* posted on their website include the following: Excerpt 1: "The Warning"; excerpt 2: "In the Face of Evil"; excerpt 3: "Heroes and Bystanders"; excerpt 4: "Epilogue." The pattern is the same; the markings of the major episodes follow the predicted binary.

   9. Some of this fascinating postproduction brouhaha is revisited by Terry George in a piece he wrote for the *Washington Post* on May 10, 2006. George recounts the smear

campaign mounted by Kagame against Rusesabagina following the election in which Kagame won 90.5 percent of the vote. (Amnesty International detailed the ways in which Kagame made it impossible for the opposition parties to mount a campaign.) Paul Rusesabagina became a critic of the regime that had stopped the genocide in which he had become a cinematic hero; and he could not return home after this.

REFERENCES

Amnesty International Report 2000. "Democratic Republic of Congo: Killing Human Decency." May 31. Ref. number Afr/62/007/2000. http://www.amnesty.org/en/library/info/AFR62/007/2000/en.
Barker, Greg. 2004. *Ghosts of Rwanda.* Frontline-PBS, BBC, Silverbridge Productions. United States/Canada. DVD.
Caton-Jones, Michael. 2005. *Shooting Dogs* (US: *Beyond the* Gates). UK, Germany. Cross-Day Productions. DVD.
French, Philip. 2005. "Shake Hands with the Devil: The Journey of Roméo Dallaire." *Observer,* August 7. http://www.whitepinepictures.com/dallairesite/dallaire-observer.pdf and http://film.guardian.co.uk/News_Story/Critic_Review/Observer_review/0,,1543957,00.html.
George, Terry. 2005. *Hotel Rwanda.* United Artists. UK, USA, Italy, S. Africa. 35 mm.
———. 2006. "Smearing a Hero." *Washington Post.* 10 May. www.washingtonpost.com/wpdyn/content/article/2006/05/09/AR2006050901242_pf.html.
*Ghosts of Rwanda.* http://www.pbs.org/wgbh/pages/frontline/shows/ghosts/video/.
Gourevitch, Philip. 1998. *We Wish to Inform You That Tomorrow We Will Be Killed with Our Families.* New York: Farrar, Straus and Giroux.
Harrow, Kenneth W. 2005. "Un train peut en cacher un autre: Narrating the Rwandan Genocide." *Research in African Literatures* 36 (4): 223–32.
Human Rights Watch Report 2002. *Democratic Republic of Congo: War Crimes in Kisangani: The Response of the Rwandan Backed Rebels to the May 2002 Mutiny.* August, vol. 14, no. 6 (A). http://hrw.org/reports/2002/drc2/.
JanMohamed, Abdul. 1983. *Manichean Aesthetics: The Politics of Literature in Colonial Africa.* Amherst: University of Massachusetts Press.
Kourouma, Ahmadou. 1970. *Les Soleils des indépendances.* Paris: Seuil.
Mamdani, Mahmood. 2002. *When Victims Become Killers: Colonialism, Nativism, and the Genocide in Rwanda.* Princeton: Princeton University Press.
Oyono, Ferdinand. 1956. *Le Vieux nègre et la Médaille.* Paris: Julliard.
Raymont, Peter. 2004. *Shake Hands with the Devil: The Journey of Roméo Dallaire.* White Pines Pictures; Canadian Broadcasting Corporation; Société Radio-Canada. Canada. DVD.

# SIX

# Ambiguities and Paradoxes

Framing Northern Intervention in *The Constant Gardener*

CHRISTOPHER ODHIAMBO JOSEPH

This chapter explores how ambiguity and paradox as framing strategies have been wittingly, deceitfully, and ingeniously deployed in the film *The
Constant Gardener* (2005) to simultaneously legitimate external intervention
in Africa and implicitly reiterate and "normalize" imaginations, attitudes,
myths, stereotypes, and perceptions of the North about Africa, as part of
that continuum in the tradition of Hollywood films that persistently portray
Africa as a place literally on its knees, begging for intervention. In "reading" the claims of intervention that this film both represents and makes, two
theoretical constructs are privileged: William Empson's (1949) interpretation
of the deployment of the literary mode of ambiguity, on the one hand; and
Paulo Freire's (1972) and Augusto Boal's (1979) ideas of sociocultural, economic, and political intervention, on the other.

Empson's conceptualization that "an ambiguity, in ordinary speech, means
something very pronounced, and as a rule witty or deceitful . . . which gives
room for alternative reaction to the same piece of language" (1) is important in reading the claims of intervention as framed in this film as it draws
attention to doublespeak, the main domain of the "trickster," inviting alternative reactions and interpretations in the manner of the trickster tales
found in Africa.[1] Freire's and Boal's ideas, in contrast, are invaluable in reading this film because they provide perspectives of interpreting how intervention is meaningfully structured to bring about conscientization. For instance,
Freire strongly argues for collaboration between the intervening agents and
the targets of such intervention. For him, it is through such collaborations
that the culture of silence can be challenged and contested, resulting in real

conscientization in the communities targeted by such interventions. And Boal, following closely on Freire's ideas, emphasizes the centrality of the victims of oppression and exploitation in the structures of intervention as espoused in his *Theatre of the Oppressed*.

Arguably, *The Constant Gardener* explicitly frames intervention in Africa against the greed and exploitation of a Western multinational drug company as its raison d'être. However, a more critical reading reveals that it still falls within that template of films in the Hollywood tradition which imagine Africa as the other: abject, desolate, and derelict, in direct opposition to the universalized, normalized, and orderly Euro-American civilization and modernity. As such, consciously or otherwise, it frames and imagines Africa as a site literally waiting for external intervention. This portrayal is both problematic and disturbing as it borders on racism, revealing to some extent the attitude and deeply held perceptions of the West about Africa. "Today the colonial image of the black man continues to characterize white mental projections, revealing a profound racist unconscious," writes Olivier Barlet (2000, 5). Thus, implicit within the assumedly well-intended intervention vision are the perpetuation and circulation of the normalized Western stereotypes and myths of the African continent, its people, and its various scapes. But what is interesting about this film is the subtle way that it normalizes Western racist imaginations of Africa through its ambiguous framing, to "trick" the viewer into accepting it as serious, sensitive, and genuine in its representation and exposition of Africa's myriad socioeconomic and political problems. As Grace Musila (2008, 157), for example, has aptly observed, "This film at first sight appears to present a sensitive view of the continent." Implicit in Musila's observation is the assumption that like other cultural productions it has some other meanings tacitly inscribed within its framing(s) that continue to circulate and perpetuate the ideologies originating from its source, of Africa as a premodern and purposeless place, whose inhabitants lack agency. In this regard, it repeats, for example, the sentiments and views such as those of the British historian Anthony Froude (1888, 306), who in relation to the West Indies declared, "There are no people there in the true sense of the word with a character and purpose of their own." As such, it is by deliberately emphasizing the derelict image of Africa that this film ends up undermining its own apparently well-meaning intervention enterprise against Western global capitalism and its attendant acts of greed and exploitation of third world nations.

In fact, a more attentive and critical viewing/ "reading" of the visual images that this film projects reveals its interventionist endeavor as both ambiguous and paradoxical: perhaps to conceal the Western normalized imaginations of Africa as the "Dark Continent." It is for this reason that it becomes instructive to read it as a strategy of signification that, like the trickster, employs ambiguity both as an encoding and decoding strategy. Like the trickster in traditional African folklore, this film plays tricks on the viewer/"reader" through a conscious deployment of ambiguity and paradox to seduce the viewer/"reader" to accept it as a genuine medium of intervention. Overtly, this film appears to criticize the Western world for perpetuating abjection and suffering that pervades Africa. Thus, at one level the film seems to be a sensitive and empathetic representation of Africa as a continent more sinned against than sinning, but the film employs the same visual images that imagine Africa as a dysfunctional, diseased, corrupt, and insecure place.

Perhaps before delving into strategies that this film deploys to frame intervention, a brief outline of its plot is called for. *The Constant Gardener* presents the story of Tessa and her revolutionary ideas: her strong aversion to social injustice, human rights abuses and exploitation of the poor of the third world by the more advanced and prosperous Western nations. The film begins in Africa where we find Justin Quayle seeing off his wife Tessa Quayle at Wilson Airport in Nairobi. We learn that in spite of her husband's reservation she is determined to travel to Lokichoggio to listen to the local social justice and human rights activist Grace Makanga. Later on it is revealed that together with the driver and Dr. Arnold Bruhm, she has been killed. Thereafter the film becomes a web of intertwined series of activities: the investigation of her death; an exposition of her love life with her husband, Justin; the conspiracy of the Western pharmaceutical companies colluding with the British, Canadian, and Kenyan governments. Through flashbacks, Tessa's activism, as well as her romantic life, is laid bare. Through these flashbacks we discover that she is an avowed social and economic activist who does not let pass any opportunity to engage, confront, and challenge those involved in social injustice. This is aptly demonstrated in the scene in which she confronts Justin after he has just finished reading the lecture on diplomacy and civilization that seems to shape the West's international diplomacy policies toward third world people. Tessa's questioning and critique of these policies at the end of the lecture signals the film's ideological intervention enterprise.

The film's visual plotline seems to magnify her concerns. The plotline is enhanced by the romantic relationship that develops between Tessa and Justin—a relationship that eventually, within the logic of the film, acts as a credible catalyst, prompting her to travel to Kenya, an apt site for her to engage in activism and intervention. It is therefore unsurprising when we see her in Kibera slums worried about the test trials of the TB drug on unsuspecting Africans by the Western pharmaceutical firm as well as her active involvement in the investigation of this conspiracy, which consequently leads to her death, that of Dr. Bluhm, and that of her husband, Justin. The romance story that adds suspense, tension, and anxieties also diverts the attention of viewer from the narrative of vulgar Western capitalist exploitation: that is, the effects of the pharmaceutical drug company trials on the unsuspecting victims and the colluding governments' conspiracy against the poor living in the slums. It is this romance subplot that ensures that Tessa remains within the center of the film's frame long after her death, which occurs at the beginning of the film. Arguably, the entire film takes place in Justin's mind, reconstructed through the use of flashbacks and his stream of consciousness in an attempt to understand the death of his wife.

Having outlined the plotline of the film, I now turn to the ways that ambiguity and paradox have been deployed, as framing strategies, to generate the alternative and contrastive perspectives in the frame of this film. This begins with Tessa questioning the logic of the Western international relations policies, then transportation of the viewer through the first flashback to a significant moment in the film's narrative plot: the first meeting between Justin and Tessa. Then immediately after, the viewer is led to the point where Justin receives the news of Tessa's death. Justin's immediate connection of Tessa's death with their first meeting is important as it links the various subplots of the film's narrative: Tessa's intervention in the drug trial scandal and the romance drama. It is also a critical point in the film's plot because it reveals Tessa's character as an outspoken and determined activist-interventionist. It is at this point that it is also revealed that she is the only one who stood up to a very hostile audience to challenge the accepted notions of Western diplomacy and civilization. She openly criticized the lecture read by Justin, questioning its moral probity especially when it claimed that Western diplomacy was the mapping and marker of civilization. It was only Tessa who seemed to correctly understand the hypocrisy of the policies of Western diplomacy that perpetuate the exploitation and abjection of the third world countries to sustain the very high standards of living in Western economies. Indeed, the hostility that Tessa's questioning elicits from the other participants clearly showed how people in the West refuse to acknowledge that the comfort and modernity they enjoy are a result of their nations' unjust and unfair policies, portrayed later in the depressing visual images of Kibera and Lokichoggio in the film's frame.

A critical interpretation of these visual images is important in exposing both the overt and tacit meanings in this film. Admittedly, these visual images magnify Tessa's strong feelings about the exploitation of poor third world countries to cushion the ostentatious lifestyles that define the West, focusing especially on how these visual images are projected and played out in this drama of intervention against the injustices wrought by vulgar Western capitalism. It is interesting to note, for instance, how the visual images are manipulated to magnify Tessa's argument on how these Western international relations policies lead to dereliction and abjection in the third world; the camera wittingly zooms beyond the confines of the room where the lecture is taking place, focusing on a panoramic view of the expansive city, zeroing in on the magnificently complex state of the city's architectural aesthetics that valorize the West's civilization and modernity, built, perhaps, through the exploitation of the third world's resources.

This play of visual images as a backdrop to Tessa's criticism of the lecture read by Justin is one of the strategies of intervention ingeniously designed to prick the conscience of the citizens of the Western world. Thus the juxtaposition of Tessa's sharp criticism pitted against these imposing concrete architectural structures acts as a reminder of the unequal socioeconomic relation that exists between the North and South. Framing intervention in this way is meant to elicit feelings of guilt in the West through the employment of these contrastive visual images that keep shifting from specific locations in Africa and Europe. The camera seems to be deliberately and ingeniously deployed to focus selectively on extremely elaborate images of abjection in Africa, exposing it as a place that is disorderly, cacophonous, desolate, derelict, apathetic, and lethargic; in contrast, the camera's lens when zoomed on the Western metropolis reveals an image of a world that is orderly, serene, civilized, modern, and prosperous. More significantly, these contrastive images suggestively give credibility to Tessa's argument that Western prosperity is a result of the exploitation of third world countries. For instance, the archaic railway, a relic of the colonial legacy, which passes through Kibera slums and which children play along, is similarly juxtaposed with the more sophisticated and ultramodern rail system found in the Western world. The overcrowded schools in Kibera slums are contrasted with the tidy, less crowded, and meticulously organized ones in Europe. The noisy and overcrowded hotel where Justin meets with Ghita makes a sharp contrast with the calm high-class hotel where Justin meets Pellegrin. Other contrastive images that reflect the effects of the Western world's exploitation of the African continent and its people are revealed through the images of the general transport system found in Nairobi, reflecting its very chaotic and disordered traffic system full of *matatus* (the popular public means of transport) competing for space in an unplanned, overcrowded street, while the traffic system in Europe is presented as a perfectly functioning system with clearly defined parking spaces, well marked, and orderly. The images of derelict and dilapidated hovels and traditional huts in Kibera and Lokichoggio, respectively, sharply contrast with the imposing, concrete modern buildings of the Western cities. The cacophonous open-air markets in Kibera are contrasted with the ultramodern supermarkets in Europe. In general, the civilization and modernity of the well-developed and maintained infrastructure(s) of the Western world are juxtaposed with the desolate, derelict, poorly managed, and dysfunctional ones in Kenya. That this film is a criticism of the debilitating effects of global capitalism on the poor victims of the third world cannot therefore be overstated. The deployment of these contrastive visual images appears to be a conscious attempt at exposing the wide disparities that exist between countries of the North and those of the South. This strategy, that emphasizes the binary opposition of worlds through visual images, seems to remind the West that the prevailing socioeonomic inequalities are a direct result of the exploitation by unscrupulous, greedy multinational companies from the West such as KND and 3BEE. These contrastive visual images act as a mirror for the Western populations, to look into and reflect on how their civilization and modernity adversely affect the people and places in the third world. This situation is expressed eloquently by a number of individuals in the film such as Grace Makanga (the only local activist), Tessa, Sandy, and Hammond.

Yet what initially appears as a well-intentioned desire of the film is acutely undermined eventually by its ambiguous and paradoxical framing. Indeed, *The Constant Gardener* is in the tradition of the Hollywood films such as *Cry Freedom* (based on the relationship between Black consciousness leader Steve Biko and liberal newspaper editor Donald Woods). While expressing appreciation for the antiapartheid sentiments of the film, black critics like Professor Mbulelo Mzamane point out that the "conventions of Hollywood, but also a long tradition of racism, demand that [Hollywood movies] look through the eyes of a white star, a white hero. . . . [*Cry Freedom* . . . does] not avoid the trap that Biko was teaching about: the tendency of white liberals to appropriate the struggle of black people and enunciate it in terms that are palatable to them" (qtd. in Dixon 1995, 2). This observation is in sync with the framing of intervention in *The Constant Gardener.* Two instances from the film confirm this: At the beginning of the film we are told that Tessa Quayle is flying to Lokichoggio to listen to the local socioeconomic rights and justice activist/interventionist Grace Makanga speak about the exploitation by Western pharmaceutical drug companies of the poor people in the third world. Later in the film there is the image of Makanga on a TV screen speaking about these issues. Unlike Tessa, she does not participate actively in the frame of the film as her activities are recorded and only reported to the film's viewers. Through this strategy she is doubly marginalized from the center of the film's frame though a very vocal activist, ironically only introduced because of Tessa's interest in her speech. Second, it is implied that Dr. Arnold Bluhm is also involved in investigation on the test trial of the TB drug on the poor masses of Kibera, but his intervention, like that of Makanga, is obliterated by the more prominent role assigned to Tessa's activism and intervention in the film's frame. Though the film acknowledges local intervention efforts, these are given less prominence in the frame of the film with the entry of Tessa. Her stepping into the center of the frame indicates that intervention can be initiated yet again only by the leadership of the white community, as has been the tradition of Hollywood intervention films on Africa. Even though this film tells a story of the exploitation of Kenyans by Western global capitalism, it does very little to show the efforts of the Africans in the fight against their exploitation apart from the token presence of Grace Makanga and Dr. Arnold Bluhm. (It is instructive to note that Dr. Bluhm, though black, is actually not a local.) Whereas *The Constant Gardener* alerts the world to human rights violations committed by the Western pharmaceutical companies in a third world country, it nevertheless remains fixated on the traditional notions of Africa as a world suffering from paralysis, and in the process circulates, reiterates, and affirms the Western imaginaries of Africa that presuppose its inferiority.

If we take into consideration the current thinking on arts and cultural productions on intervention, the framing adopted in this film is obviously problematic. Such thinking in fact reveals that apt and meaningful intervention must not only involve the target audience but also use local aesthetics and episteme. For instance, Freire's seminal writing on intervention, *Pedagogy of the Oppressed,* argues that the beneficiaries of intervention should not be construed as empty vessels waiting to be filled with knowledge, as is so evident in this film. Musila (2007, 68) accentuates this anomaly in the film as follows:

The passive victimhood is best captured in a scene when Quayle engages in a tense chase with a colleague at the High Commission, Tim Donahue, whom he assumes to be a hit-man hired by the pharmaceutical company. The two engage each other in a dramatic race across the dry landscape of Northern Kenya, as the Turkana pastoralists and their livestock watch in ignorant fascination by the roadside. This scene poignantly captures the core ideological problem with the film: that local people are passive victims throughout the film, who, like the herdsmen, stand by and watch, while the various Western powers fight over their destiny; whether in benevolent humanitarianism or corporate greed.

Making Africans passive spectators in a drama that concerns them in many ways entrenches the culture of silence that the intervention should be expected to eliminate. This passivity is manifested several times in the film when Tessa visits Kibera. On all these occasions she is hardly seen connecting with those people on whose behalf she claims to be intervening. The closest that she seems to relate directly is when she asks Jomo to go for an HIV test. However, her alienation is graphically captured, when together with Dr. Bluhm, she is standing on top a pedestal, watching the victims from that privileged position. This image contradicts Boal's overarching principle that victims of oppression and their interveners should occupy similar levels in the process of intervention. As observed by Musila (2007, 68–69):

> Tessa Quayle, for instance, despite her passionate commitment to the cause of the patients in Kibera, remains a messianic figure, who literally lays down for these suffering patients without ever involving them in the war over their lives. These victims soon disappear completely from the film, after laying the set for the film's main story:— the story of Tessa and Justin's heroic fight against global capitalism and its social injustices in Africa.

In *The Constant Gardener* the victims are gradually relegated to the periphery of the frame, negating the most fundamental principle of any meaningful intervention. According to Boal, any effective intervention should transform the victims from the position of spectators to spec-actors. In this film, however, the victims remain as spectators in a tragic drama of their own lives. They gaze at Tessa when she visits Kibera, at Justin when he visits Lorbeer at Lokichoggio. The question that begs answers is why this film frames its intervention in ways that deliberately obliterate the presence of the victims and, more important, possibilities of their agency? Perhaps a direct answer to this question would be that this is a deliberate strategy in the tradition of Hollywood films to legitimize and validate the presence of Western white heroes and heroines in the enterprise of intervention in Africa. As Josef Gugler reminds us:

> With the assumption of colonial control European voices came to dominate the discourses about Africa: to this day they shape our image of Africa. Imperialists proclaimed superiority over the colonized. Henceforth they would affirm that Africa had no history, that they were enlightening the "Dark Continent," and that they were on a civilizing mission, that they were carrying the "white man's burden." (2003, 19)

It is amazing how *The Constant Gardener* accurately confirms Gugler's observation of Africa as a white man's burden. Musila (2008, 158) rightly reminds us that the film "rehashes the question of messianic intervention in Africa by the West reminiscent of the pre-colonial missionaries and their cause of saving the so-called Dark Continent from heathen ways of savagery." To prepare Africa for this messianic intervention, the film frames its visual images in such a way that the locals are reduced to passive victims who do not have much control over their fate and who are apparently waiting for intervention to come from elsewhere. In Kibera, for instance, the camera focuses on the glaring image of a vast squalid space, filthy and abject with masses of people walking without any indication of where they are going to, while others are presented lazing about in the narrow alleys of the slum. A similar image is created in Turkana where once again the camera focuses on a mass of idle people waiting for relief food.

Tessa therefore becomes the typical messiah who comes to save these "natives" from inevitable destruction. She stands up for the rights of the poor and exploited victims. Her messianic image becomes more pronounced when she comes to Africa. She visits Kibera slums where very few whites dare set foot. In Kibera she becomes the center of attention and attraction, stealing the limelight from the local artists performing HIV-AIDS intervention drama pieces. The camera zooms in on her, shifting focus and attention from this performance that had attracted a huge audience. With the camera focused on her, she becomes the "star" of an alternative performance; she gets "anointed," and "enthroned" by the kids in a gift-giving ritual.

Her messianic role becomes more obvious when she asks Jomo to go for the HIV-AIDS test, advice that he accepts promptly, though there are indications that Dr. Bruhm might have already asked him to go for the test but in vain. The theater performers are presented more as entertainers whose messages Jomo seems to have ignored before he hastily acts when instructed by Tessa. At the cocktail party at the High Commission, once again, it is only Tessa who seems to be daring enough to confront those in power, questioning them in regard to perceived corruption in the Ministry of Health. Indeed at this point Dr. Bruhm takes a supporting role, though it is obvious that he has been involved in this struggle much longer. In addition, Tessa is portrayed as the one more sensitive and conscious than all the other characters in film. Thus it is unsurprising that only Tessa seems to be equipped with agency since "Dr Bluhm has been conveniently relegated as her subordinate, playing the role of a loyal foot-soldier, reminiscent of the ever loyal Uncle Tom figure" (Musila 2007, 69). Tessa's messianic figure is amplified further when she stubbornly insists on going to give birth at the public Uhuru Hospital as a gesture of her solidarity with the poor masses of Kibera. She is shown in the hospital playing a mother's role, breastfeeding the newborn baby of the dying Wanza Kilulu.

Whereas Tessa seems to project the image of a messiah quite aptly, she still remains alienated from the people whose cause she is vigorously propagating. For instance, in the Kibera slums, other than her conversations with Jomo she hardly develops any meaningful relationships with the larger community. At the hospital, it is intriguing that though she is seen breastfeeding Wanza Kilulu's baby Baraka, we do not see her interacting with other patients, not even Wanza herself. It appears as if the other patients are simply there to act as a backdrop for the drama of the white protagonists and antagonists. Though she does not relate to these people, she is paradoxically ready to stand up for them. For instance, she is the one who narrates the melancholic story of Wanza Kilulu to us, accentuating how she (Wanza) had been used as a guinea pig by the pharmaceutical company carrying out a trial of TB treatment on unsuspecting poor people living in the slums infected by HIV. The image of Tessa, as a savior sacrificing her life for the Africans, is reinforced when we see her thoroughly drenched after being rained on after a visit to Kibera where she had gone to investigate the syndicate between the Western Pharmaceutical Company (KND/3BEES) and the governments of Kenya, Britain, and Canada. At the end of it all Tessa is killed because of her efforts to intervene on behalf of the poor Kenyans. She thus ends up a martyr. Africa therefore becomes a site where Tessa's activism finds prominence as opposed to her own country where she receives no recognition as an activist.

It is noteworthy that after Tessa's death it is Justin who takes over her role. Once again the victims are driven further onto the margins of the film's central frame. Justin, who has been nonchalant about Tessa's activism, whose passion is in gardening rather than in saving exploited Africans, now takes up the starring role. With his entry, the film's plot that was initially structured on Tessa's story of intervention takes a new turn; instead of focusing on the victims of the pharmaceutical company, the images now intermittently shift, through the use of flashbacks, reminding the viewer of Tessa's and Justin's love life, while at the same time employing flashforwards to justify Justin's transformation from a laid-back personality to a more determined one in search of the truth about his wife's death (with the result that much of film's suspense hinges on whether Tessa betrayed Justin with Arnold).

Arguably, *The Constant Gardener* is framed in such a way that white people become the dominant figures in the project of intervention in Africa. Musila (2008) affirms this position when she argues that *The Constant Gardener* as a cultural and (ideological) form participates in the legacy of colonial romanticism and condescension that continues to shape and reinforce postcolonial constructions of the continent as, on the one hand, a tourist paradise and, on the other, the prototypical sociopolitically inept state(s) marked by violence, inefficiency, corruption, poverty, and disease. The visual representation of Africa in terms of abjection validates and legitimizes the external intervention as evinced in the figure and actions of Tessa Quayle. In this film the images of abjection in both the Kibera slums and Turkana are deliberately chosen to portray the paralysis, apathy, and lethargy of the Kenyan government, implying that it is uncaring and thus neglects its populations because the officials are more interested in cutting corrupt deals than providing efficient services. Indeed, in this film all the Africans in positions of authority are portrayed as incorrigibly corrupt, inefficient, or compromised in one way or another. This is supposed to portray the country as insecure, lawless, and in fact a bandit nation. More than that, all these people in authority are portrayed as unfeeling and callous: the police officers who collect the bodies in Lokichoggio simply carry the bodies without showing any feelings toward the dead; at the mortuary the police officer who accompanies Justin to identify Tessa's body is also very unfeeling and uncaring, and lacking in professional ethics; the minister of health is portrayed as corrupt and does not care much about the health of his people and is part of the pharmaceutical drug's conspiracy; the woman at the hospital registry is not only incompetent and inefficient but literally confused; the policeman who picks up Justin in Kibera when he goes in search of information to unravel the mystery of Tessa's death is portrayed as unashamedly corrupt. The pilot who evacuates the aid workers from Lokichoggio is portrayed as unfeeling and insensitive when he vehemently refuses to take Abuk along, but before that Justin blatantly attempts to bribe him because as far as Justin is concerned, corruption is normalized in Kenya; the doctor in Kibera in charge of TB treatment is also portrayed as lacking in professional ethics as he refuses to give treatment to patients who have not consented to be used in TB drug trials.

During Tessa's funeral the Africans are once more presented as part of the backdrop; at the downtown hotel where Justin meets Ghita again the Africans simply act as some kind of a backdrop to the set; in Lokichoggio the same portrayal of Africans is replicated when Justin goes to see Lorbeer. In all these instances the Africans are presented as lacking in agency before they are eventually erased out of the film's frame. It is in this sense that *The Constant Gardener* continues in the tradition of Hollywood films that claim to speak to unjust Western practices in Africa but ironically end up circulating the West's self-affirming ideology of superiority. Thus it is apparent that this film, like others in its tradition, revisits and repeats the earlier Western tropes of Africa as a site waiting to be civilized, enlightened, and modernized by a white person.

It is no wonder, therefore, that a film shot in postcolonial Kenya forty years after independence omits the middle class and upper class of Kenya from its frame. Their presence would contradict the Western imaginary template of the abject and derelict Africa that cries out for external intervention. The presence of well-educated, highly conscious, and active Kenyans undoubtedly would undermine the presence of external interveners. As Musila (2007, 69) reminds us:

> In the same spirit, the film lingers on the poverty and suffering of the Kenyans in the slums, completely denying the possibility of a local economic middle class with the exception of the politicians and diplomats. These characters are tainted by the brush of corruption, and represent the emblematic African politician, in all his greed. In excluding the possibility of an African middle class that earns from its sweat, the film reinforces notions of the continent as suffering mass of humanity—awaiting Western humanitarian intervention—dotted with little islands of corruptly acquired opulence. Undeniably, there exists a wide socio-economic gap on the continent and we do have

politicians who have accumulated wealth corruptly. But we also have a significant black middle class, whose fingers are not stained by the grime of corruption, and it is a gross misconception to present the continent as populated only by the dying poor and thieving rich.

Similar to other films in the tradition of Hollywood interventions in Africa, this one too presents Africans as a homogeneous mass of humanity. Both in Kibera and Lokichoggio the Africans are presented as large seas of humanity, while white people are differentiated through close-up camera techniques, therefore highlighting their individualities. In Lokichoggio we also encounter a mass of people either sitting idle waiting for relief food or singing and therefore reaffirming the stereotypes and myths of Africa in the Western imagination as lazy or merry-makers. The same applies to the visual images that project the Kenyan street, marketplace, the schools, hospital, and hotel. Musila's (2007, 69) description of this phenomenon is most illuminating.

> The film achieves this "suffering of humanity" image by denying the Kenyans characters any sense of individuality. Yet the various British characters are complex people, generously granted depth and even a long enough stay in the film to grow as characters. We are treated to Justin Quayle's idiosyncratic Etonian gentility, in all its suffocating courtesy and political mildness and we watch as he slowly gains political consciousness. Similarly, we watch Sandy Woodrow's gradual growth from a spineless bureaucratic diplomat to a politically conscientised man, who redeems himself by demolishing the High Commission's web of deceit and pretended ignorance. The African characters on the other hand, remain flat tropes cast in stereotypical categories: the minister of health, as the typically corrupt politician, Mustapha the loyal servant, Wanza the long suffering African woman, Kioko and Abu, the innocent faces of the African child, who never fails to inspire patronizing benevolence and humanitarian generosity in the West.

Through the use of ambiguity, as a device of talking about one thing and implying several ways of judging or feeling, it can be argued that *The Constant Gardener* does not depart in any radical way from the ideological orientations of traditional Hollywood "Africa" films. Instead, it participates in that tradition. Gugler observes:

> Since colonial days films produced in the US, Europe and South Africa have propagated images of "Black Africa" dominated by people

of European descent with whom Western viewers could easily identify with. The portrayals of Africans repeated and reinforced negative
stereotypes: they appeared as barbaric, savage and blood thirsty; as
servants, most incompetent; or simply as part of the décor. (2005, 12)

Perhaps Africans are simply being used as a backdrop for the romance drama
of Western protagonists. At the end, one is left to wonder about the effects
of such films that romanticize Western intervention against injustices committed against Africans. As the film comes to an end, we are once again presented with visual images of abjection—but now played out in Zimbabwe—
where the exploitative corporation has now transferred its activities.

NOTES

1. Gates 1988 and White 2004 offer pertinent and significant insights into the concept
of the trickster as a theoretical construct in literary criticism.

REFERENCES

Barlet, Olivier. 2000 [1996]. *African Cinemas: Decolonizing the Gaze.* Translated by Chris
Tuner. London: Zed Books.
Boal, Augusto. 1979. *Theatre of the Oppressed.* London: Pluto Press.
Dalamba, J. 2000. "Race and Representation in Sankofa." Unpublished thesis.
Dixon, Norm. 1995. "Film and Racism in South Africa—2 August 1995." In *Darkest
Hollywood: Cinema and Apartheid,* ABC TV, August 7 (preview).
Empson, William. 1949. *Seven Types of Ambiguity.* London: Chatto and Windus.
Freire, Paulo. 1972. *Pedagogy of the Oppressed.* Translated by Myra Bergman Ramos. Har-
mondsworth: Penguin.
Froude, J. Anthony. 1888. *The English in the West Indies.* London: Longman.
Gates, Louis Henry, Jr. 1988. *The Signifying Monkey: A Theory of African-American Literary
Criticism.* Oxford: Oxford University Press.
Gugler, Josef. 2003. *African Film: Re-imagining a Continent.* Bloomington: Indiana Univer-
sity Press.
Musila, Grace. 2007. "*The Constant Gardener* (2005): A Review." *Jahazi* 1 (2): 68–69.
———. 2008. "Representations of Africa in the Western Imagination." In *Towards Africa-
Oriented Risk Analysis Models,* edited by Korwa G. Adar, Richard O. Iroanya, and
Francis Nwonwu, 149–62. Africa Institute of South Africa.
White, Bob W. 2004. "Modernity's Trickster: 'Dipping' and 'Throwing' in Congolese
Popular Dance Music." In *African Drama and Performance,* edited by John Conteh-
Morgan and Tejumola Olaniyan, 198–215. Bloomington: Indiana University Press.
Young, Lola. 1996. *Fear of the Dark: 'Race', Gender and Sexuality in the Cinema.* London/
New York: Routledge.

# SEVEN

# Minstrelsy and Mythic Appetites

*The Last King of Scotland*'s Heart of Darkness in the Jubilee Year
of African Independence

RICARDO GUTHRIE

The stunning success of *The Last King of Scotland* (2006)—a fictional biopic starring acclaimed African American actor Forest Whitaker, who won an Oscar for his portrayal of Ugandan dictator Idi Amin—perhaps represents a paradigm shift in how films "based on real events" can affect audiences' geopolitical sensibilities, and vice versa. The Hollywood film industry continually feeds America's appetite for mythic stories set in exotic locales (in this case, Uganda during the heady 1970s) while recycling narratives that reinforce its own "heart of darkness."[1] Rather than summoning cultural-historical themes that illuminate the rich complexities of Afro-Diasporic peoples while exploding the myth of Africa as a site for exorcising shame, fear, and loathing, the film instead focuses on the image of an African mad-man who acclaims Western sensibilities (Amin extols the virtues of the Scottish people and strikes up a problematic friendship with a Scottish physician) while slaughtering his own kinsmen in fits of paranoia. The fictional story line, based on Giles Foden's novel, attempts to create multidimensional characterizations of Amin. We must ask, however, what is the significance of this dictator's pseudobiography airing in 2006—the year before Ghana, the first sub-Saharan African colony to achieve independence, prepared to celebrate fifty years of nationhood?

Perhaps it's because there's an audience, and appetite, for such stories set in Africa, as Whitaker himself proclaimed in an interview: "There is a deep, mythical quality sometimes to the stories. . . . They become like some mythic parable somebody would tell or write in some book that children would read in a thousand years from now" (Germain 2006). But Whitaker was concerned with stories about African liberators such as Stephen Biko or Nelson Mandela, not Idi Amin, and there's the rub: Why can't Hollywood tell stories that are full of the richness and complexities of African liberation and independence that reflect global interactions, collaborations, and transnational implications?

A film is not a history book, one might argue, and *The Last King of Scotland* is a fictionalized story, not "real" history. According to Gabriel (1995), the purpose of Hollywood films is, first and foremost, to produce entertainment that will turn a profit. Movie genres—action, horror, romance, mystery, westerns, and thrillers—attract audiences and consuming publics in order to maximize profits. Such Hollywood genres are particularly suited for films set in Africa because they can be marketed to viewers who may never set foot there. Then what's at stake, if it's only a film or a popular, fictionalized adaptation of a moment in history? "Struggles over meaning" in popular culture "are also struggles over resources," as Lipsitz reminds us: "They arbitrate what is permitted and what is forbidden; they help determine who will be included and who will be excluded; they influence who gets to speak and who gets silenced" (1990, 632). And in the realm of postcolonial filmic reality, dictators, criminals, smugglers, and madmen get center stage while liberators and revolutionaries are silenced and resources made scarce for films highlighting freedom and independence instead of paternalism and dependence (Martin 1995).

As Cameron (1994) notes, authenticity in such films is a manufactured commodity designed to buttress elements of action, plot, character, and myth. If that's all *The Last King of Scotland* represents, then its appeal to certain audiences would be understandable, but there was a disproportionate receptiveness that exceeded all expectations. In many ways, the narrative logic of *Last King* appears to have attracted audiences seeking comprehension of a post–Cold War reality. But *Last King* does something more: it propels a cultural ethos resurrected from the days of colonialism and empire, while updating twenty-first-century impulses of Western imperialists (and fading imperialists such as Great Britain) seeking justification for intervention around the world. For that matter, *Last King* offers easy vindication for Western political intervention globally, and that version of events offers a certain appeal to Western moviegoers who approve of those interventions. That version is also very marketable. *The Last King of Scotland*, therefore, provides a unique vehicle for comprehending ways in which imperialism on film reinscribes powerful themes of the past, while setting the stage for new empires of the present. *Last King* updates the spectacle of Hollywood in Africa and recycles imperialist cultural logics to fit a changing, neoconservative post–Cold War reality. The questions of empire, intervention, and humanitarian assistance are conflicted and contradictory—giving rise to the political-cultural intrigue that drives *Last King*'s plotline, and which confounds attempts to combine history, biography, and filmic reality. *Last King* appears to deftly maneuver between these three aspects under the guise of a Conradian heart of darkness formula. It seems to attack British imperialism, while raising disturbing questions about postindependence Africa—but, rather than refuting imperialist interventions, it instead provides a rationale for using empire to settle old scores and align new political configurations. In addition, rather than simply reinvigorating Joseph Conrad's *Heart of Darkness* story line, *Last King* focuses on a Scotsman who goes to Africa and discovers the eccentric, charismatic, but violent Idi Amin—a fellow postcolonial subject who shares his distaste for British imperialists. The film updates the story with very flawed postcolonial protagonists who attempt to challenge neocolonialism.

Further, by casting an American Black actor as Idi Amin, *Last King* raises unsettling issues about Black identity, Afro-Diasporic sentiment, and racial ventriloquism that harks back to Hollywood's days of blackface minstrelsy— only this time portrayed by an African American actor (Saxton 1990). The desire to create an international film exploring British imperialism, African independence, and Afro-Diasporic identification, helps create a cultural product heralded as "The Emperor Jones in Africa"—linking *Last King* with the 1920s Eugene O'Neill play, which starred Paul Robeson as a savage Caribbean dictator. The resurrection of racial regimes to unite a fictive white imaginary through film is a daunting yet powerful project, as Robinson (2007) examined in pre–World War II American films. He provides compelling evidence of the utility of film as a venue for bolstering regimes of race before 1945 and the modern quest for African independence. In this context, *Last King* is a test case for revitalizing race concerns against the backdrop of post–Cold War neoconservatism. These thematic elements—postcolonial subjectivity and global Afro-Diasporic identification in the neocon moment—are major concerns. I will also address the historical significance of African independence, particularly the story of Kwame Nkrumah and Ghana—and how Nkrumah's Pan-Africanist struggle against Western imperialism represents a complex narrative of Afro-Diasporic freedom and the problematic quest for leadership in postcolonial Africa.

It's 80 percent fiction, but 100 percent the truth!
—Giles Foden, explaining the premise for his novel, *The Last King of Scotland* (*Last King of Scotland* DVD)

The story of independence on film has its own mythic arc (a type of Third World romanticism of 1960s revolutionary movements, not only in Africa but in Latin America and Asia), competing with the more prevalent mythos of reinscribed savagery dooming such "revolutionary" movements to failure. Even as Hollywood strove to capitalize on the 1960s and '70s as an era of social and political change, films on Africa rarely promoted stories that challenged the savage paradigm. *Cry Freedom* (1987), *A Dry White Season* (1989), and *Cry, the Beloved Country* (1995) were notable exceptions, according to Cameron (1994)—perhaps because of their focus on the apartheid regime. Their limited success depended on their catering to the "dominant" Eurocentric audience.

> The Eurocentrism of audiences can . . . inflect cinematic production. Here the dominant audience, whose ideological assumptions must be respected if a film is to be successful, or even made at all, exerts a kind of indirect hegemony. "Universal" becomes a codeword for palatable to the Western spectator as the "spoiled child" of the apparatus. [These films] betray traces of "representational adjustments" as the values of a radical liberation struggle are watered down for a predominantly liberal American audience. (Shohat and Stam 1994, 186–87)

*Last King* is attractive because it references so many genres: It is an adventure/travelogue; it is a male-bonding film with oedipal conflicts; it is a horror movie with intimations of humanity's monstrous evil and future indications of an antiterrorist genre; and it is, in the words of the filmmaker, a "thriller" with spy intrigue. There is also the utility of returning to the "heart of darkness" theme—the film and the novel provide justification for placing Africa in quarantine while denying economic trade until its rulers prove themselves amenable to democracy. Viewers identify with Garrigan as he comes to the painful realization that Amin is a likable but very dangerous madman. The heart of darkness paradigm—traveling to Africa to uncover the savage evil that lurks within, held in check by Western civilization—has enduring appeal to Westerners and imperialist voyeurs across the globe, and it is still a powerful trope central to numerous Hollywood films (Coppola's *Apocalypse Now*, set in the jungles of Vietnam, being one of the most successful of this genre).

A second attraction, to some, are the old clichés of African incompetence, brutality, and tragicomedy set in exotic time/space, which seemingly explain Africa's dilemma. There's the colonial/imperial logic that Africa can be civilized only under the auspices of Western authorities (the World Bank, the United Nations, if not direct intervention by the United States). Third, there is the collective colonial guilt that must be continually assuaged for past wrongdoing. One would think that guilt would dissipate after several decades, but despite progress, color lines have yet to be fully eroded, and so, the West versus The Rest dialectic still produces conflict, shame, and remorse for continued asymmetrical power relations (Gabriel 1995).

And last, while imperialist desires may be questioned, such films ultimately provide justification for going after "madmen" in other parts of the world: for example, the removal of Saddam Hussein from power through the preemptive US military invasion of Iraq. As a figure positioned between the British meddlers and the Ugandan dictator, Garrigan may appear to be a suitable mediator. The diplomats portrayed in *Last King* first try to build Anglo solidarity with Garrigan, but they are rejected. Garrigan, like Amin, has nothing but disgust and contempt for the meddlesome British: "I'm *not* British," he exclaims at one point. "I'm Scottish!" As a victim of British imperialism, he thinks his postcolonial status exempts him from Western excess, but his own behavior in Uganda (trying to seduce the wife of a colleague, sleeping with Amin's wife, and dismissing allegations of Amin's political assassinations while enjoying gifts from Amin) betrays his own moral bankruptcy. Later, when Garrigan realizes that Amin will never let him leave Uganda, he pitifully begs the British to help him, but the stakes have been raised. "You're his white monkey! You must earn your passage," the lead diplomat/spy declares and suggests that Garrigan poison Amin in exchange for help. This scenario allows viewers to consider that the colonialists may have been calculating and unscrupulous, but Amin's postcolonial thuggery is worse; thus, viewers might ask: Can Western intervention through assassination of a brutal dictator be justified?

The post-9/11 geopolitical and discursive landscape reflects post–Cold War aesthetics that affirmed and rationalized Bush-Cheney's "neocon" political agenda—just as the Western/Frontier trope of the Last Cold War Cowboy, Ronald Reagan, helped cement and rationalize his heroic struggle against the "Evil Empire" (Russia and Communism). Indeed, *Last King* reads like a "Cowboys in Africa Western"—there are numerous references to American cowboy culture (at one point, Amin dresses up in cowboy hat, rides a horse, and lassoes a member of his cabinet; later, seminude African women dressed in cowboy hats and boots dance and gyrate around a fire while distorted rock guitar music wails on the soundtrack); and the film constantly juxtaposes primitive and modern life, using visual cues and plot sequences highlighting the collision of white and black worlds. The film perhaps serves as a cautionary tale of the corrupting influence of Western power, which traps both the Scotsman and the Ugandan.

This is not to say that the tragedies of postcolonial Africa are solely due to imperialist meddling. Idi Amin was not a misunderstood African nationalist punished by the West because he dared to stand up to Britain and Western colonialists—he was put into power by the British who helped overthrow the government of Milton Obote, who had grown independent and resistant to British economic priorities. Amin, installed after a military coup, was erratic and unpredictable. He demonstrated that he understood the power of violence and coercion all too well. In a crucial plot twist from *The Last King of Scotland,* one of Idi Amin's wives has an affair with Garrigan, gets pregnant, and is subsequently killed, hacked to pieces, and then has her limbs sewn back onto her fractured body (the arms are sewn where the legs should go, the legs sewn onto the shoulders, etc.), creating a gruesome visual montage—one that lingers in the mind long after the film is over. But the story line is emblematic of both the success and the failure of the film as fictionalized reality. As Whitaker himself discusses in one of the "behind-the-scenes" interviews appearing on *The Last King of Scotland* DVD, the scenes of the wife's affair and brutal death were contrived, and loosely based on the facts: (1) One of Idi Amin's wives *did* have an affair, but not with a white man; (2) She was brutally hacked to death but under different circumstances, not as depicted in the film; and (3) Her limbs were sewn back onto her body correctly, so that it could be dressed for burial—not as a grotesque reassemblage.

So, if this film was "inspired by true events," then why were these changes made in the story line, and to what effect? This film and these scenes typify what happens when Africa is depicted by Hollywood—it represents a type of reality, but it is a gruesome, distorted one, much like the body of Amin's late wife; and one must ask: "Why is it necessary to hack off pieces of African reality and stitch them back together into grotesque assemblages?" In many ways, this reassemblage demonstrates how Hollywood's sense of history is used to reinforce mass conceptions of Africa. In fact, the scriptwriters and film producers can be well-intentioned—it doesn't matter; the story still has to be adjusted to fit Western expectations, as noted by Foden. As Cameron (1994) observes, even though films on Africa have historically reflected literary constructions of myths masquerading as the truth, moviegoers are willing to accept these mythic visions as authentic, particularly when they provide comforting distance between savage Africa and themselves. In recent years, his observation has been validated, and films produced during this jubilee period of African independence (post-2006) are no exception. African nations, despite some fifty years of independence, are depicted as frontiers of the "wild, wild West" still in need of discipline and military intervention by Western authorities. Uganda, Ghana, and other sub-Saharan countries represented the epitome of African resistance to colonial and postcolonial oppression, but their continued political and economic problems typified all that has gone wrong in many African countries since the age of independence. It's a complex story, one that foregrounds Western collusion with unstable political regimes over five decades. This story, in fact, has yet to be told on film.

## MINSTRELSY IN *THE LAST KING OF SCOTLAND*

Ultimately, Whitaker's attempt to humanize Amin is undermined by his blackface makeup, even though he has terrific vocal coaching, is effective in his mannerisms and jocular vitality, and embodies Amin's explosive temper exceptionally well. Why did the film need an African American in blackface to play Amin? Whitaker's portrayal was sincere—he worked hard to capture Amin's crowd appeal and physicality, while demonstrating why he ruled for nearly a decade. On a certain level, *Last King* is not just about imperialism; it is part minstrel show and racial ventriloquism as well. Whitaker's star appeal lends credence to an otherwise mundane heart of darkness narrative. A native African *could* have played the role, but the film's depiction of Amin as an eccentric buffoon evokes black caricatures from nineteenth-century American theater and early twentieth-century film (Chude-Sokei 2006; Stewart 1998). For example, Charles Gilpin and Paul Robeson, talented Black actors from the 1920s, were both cast in Eugene O'Neill's play *The Emperor Jones,* based on Haiti's President Sam, a tyrant who briefly held power in 1915 (Delson 2008). *Emperor Jones* relies on themes from an early imperialist project: A bloodthirsty Black tyrant (Brutus Jones) destroys a fledgling Black republic while ruling with superstition and brutality over his countrymen.

Gilpin originated the role in the 1920s and fought with O'Neill over the stereotypical rendering of Jones. Although he did not have to put on black-face for the role (a common-enough practice during the early days of theater and Hollywood), he bitterly resisted the buffoonery inherent in the Emperor Jones character. Robeson took over the stage play after O'Neill fired Gilpin, and later portrayed Emperor Jones on film. He felt he could accommodate the character's childish behavior and evince a more believable, complex figure. Audiences, however, disagreed about whether Brutus Jones was anything other than a gross caricature of a flawed Black leader. Still, Robeson's portrayal catapulted him to international fame, and he reprised the role on tour in Europe during the 1930s (Delson 2008; Stewart 1998; Dorinson and Pencak 2002).

Acknowledging the continuing appeal of O'Neill's play, the book jacket for the 1998 *Last King of Scotland* novel describes the Idi Amin story as an *"Emperor Jones in Africa,"* while the 2006 film lures audiences anticipating Whitaker's genius at portraying powerful Black icons—including those with questionable pedigree. African savagery is one thing, but combined with ec-centric buffoonery and minstrel blackface, it must have seemed lucrative to film producers—such stereotypical caricatures have successfully attracted viewers to Hollywood movies. According to Chude-Sokei, one of the lega-cies of minstrelsy and racial ventriloquism is that it is also a recognizable vehicle for African American actors to establish their relationship within the African diaspora while allowing others to measure their own status within society. In writing about Bert Williams, the leading minstrel performer in the early 1900s, Chude-Sokei notes:

> For this comedic performer, blackface masquerade was as much a means of negotiating relationships between and among diaspora blacks in Harlem as it was an attempt to erase the internationally projected racist fiction of the "stage Negro" (or "darky") from within the conventions of popular performance, from behind a mask pro-duced and maintained by competitive projections and denials of black subjectivity. . . . Williams's minstrelsy maps out yet another pan-Africanist sensibility. (Chude-Sokei 2006, 9)

It is interesting that Whitaker darkened his skin to get in character as an African leader, and that "blacking up" as Idi Amin perhaps aided the authentication process—as did putting on the uniform, or learning to speak Kiswahili. Also, the use of blackface provided an opportunity to embody an ironic decon-struction of the objectified racial subject. Blackface buffoonery subordinates Black humanity, but it also allows the performer to mediate between the audi-ence and the character. In the nineteenth century, the purpose of minstrelsy were to defuse serious matters without denying them. Blackface minstrelsy also reflected a people (African Americans) and a region—the South—that were "encased in a mythology . . . fascinatingly different, closely wedded to nature, and above all, timeless" (Saxton 1990, 173). In many ways blackface al-lowed Whitaker to critique perceptions of Africans, and to put his own spin on African-Diasporic identity. In a way, he became "more African than the Africans." He never tried to imitate Amin directly, but to capture the essence of a powerful African leader who may have been deranged or paranoid be-cause of the political conflicts of the era.

Is blackface minstrelsy a useful way to assess Whitaker's performance? According to Saxton, in addition to evoking a sense of the "timeless," min-strelsy succeeded because it exploited and suppressed African elements even as it borrowed from African culture—rhythms, dance patterns, music, lan-guage, etc., that were transformed by nineteenth-century Americans. Above all, minstrelsy was always political—it provided a rationale for defending slavery and, later, Jim Crow (Saxton 1990, 170). In *Last King*, Whitaker's black-faced, costumed figure of Amin builds on well-worn media caricatures of the dictator as madman, while constructing an Afro-Diasporic identification with Blackness that is deeply rooted in cultural idioms of Uganda and Africa in general—he learned Kiswahili, met with Ugandan families, familiarized himself with the country's history, and embodied an Africa that Blacks might recognize and learn from (*Last King* DVD).

But there's more to this minstrel show than meets the eye: clearly, Whita-ker is a proven Hollywood star, and would draw audiences regardless of his performance or skin tone. Whitaker appeared in Oliver Stone's Vietnam War epic *Platoon* (1986), portrayed troubled jazz artist Charlie Parker in Clint East-wood's *Bird* (1988), came to fame as a Black Britisher captured as a hostage by the IRA in Neil Jordan's *The Crying Game* (1992), and later directed the popular film *Waiting to Exhale* (1995). Having Whitaker's name on the marquee helped attract US audiences to *Last King*—a market not guaranteed if a lesser-known, African actor played the title role. So, in some ways, the Hollywood produc-tion opened the door for Whitaker to perform as an African and allowed him to extend the legacy of an "emergent diaspora sensibility that was in fact de-pendent on artifice, impersonation" (Chude-Soke 2006, 13)—ideas that were earlier embraced by Robeson, who insisted on playing a flawed role because he felt he could humanize it. Whitaker, similarly, felt compelled to go to Africa and to portray a more human side to an African leader.

> I was given this unbelievable amazing opportunity as an African-American, because I'd never been to the African continent. To go there and . . . for it to be my job to understand what it's like to be African. (Guillén 2006)

But is this film about Africa? *Last King of Scotland* is set in Africa, but it is about the heart of prototypical Westerners; to be exact, its success is an ironic commentary about the heart of darkness at the center of the Hollywood dream machine. Colonial nostalgia still sells tickets, and it sells even better if the audience can put themselves above the flawed characters and reflect on what they can do *now* to combat evil and savagery that yet endures in the heart of men across the Atlantic. Africa is merely the backdrop. But it is an enduring backdrop, and for this reason, we have not seen the last of films such as *The Last King of Scotland*. But we can hope for better.

LEARNING FROM HISTORY: "FORWARD EVER, BACKWARD NEVER!"

> This fine country . . . had lived up so well to the memory of Sir Seretse Khama, that great statesman, who had stood with such dignity on that night when the new flag had been unfurled and Botswana had come into existence. . . . [Mma Ramotswe] had imagined that the world had been watching Botswana on that night and had shared the feelings of her people. Now she knew that this was never true, that nobody had been at all interested, except a few perhaps, and that the world had never paid much attention to places like Botswana, where everything went so well and where people did not squabble and fight. (McCall Smith 2006, 220)

What other stories can Hollywood tell about Africa? Stories that call upon narratives already provided by history—stories that require what Massey (1994) calls a "double-articulation" of time and space to connect us to the myriad of African nations with specific politics and distinct cultures. Stories that require an "extroverted history" of our global connection to Africa. Stories that embrace our collective "Afro-Diasporic" consciousness (Chude-Sokei

2006). There is richness that abounds in telling these complex stories and in intelligently critiquing what's being produced. But, as McCall Smith's *No. 1 Ladies' Detective Agency* investigator, Precious Ramotswe, declares, "the world had never paid much attention" to stories of Africa that did not focus on squabbling natives. There are alternatives to such stories, such as those contained in McCall Smith's charming, nostalgic detective series set in Botswana. But nostalgia is not the only way to frame kind-hearted, complex stories about Africa; there are other ways, a few of which I will discuss below.

Audiences can learn to cultivate their "Afro-Diasporic" consciousness—we all share a history of Africa's destiny that was stolen and subverted through slavery, colonialism, and postcolonial consequences. It is a consciousness that can appeal to any race, especially since the Human Genome Project provides proof that there is only one race of human beings. It will require not just another reworking of Alex Haley's *Roots* story. I'm thinking here of Henry Louis Gates's remarkable TV series, *African American Lives* (2006), about the African roots of Black celebrities including Oprah Winfrey, Whoopi Goldberg, Chris Tucker, Quincy Jones, Morgan Freeman, Don Cheadle, and Maya Angelou. It's remarkable because it depends on an archaic view of race as biology and DNA, rather than race as culture, society, and politics. Though genetic scientists have concluded that *all* human beings can be traced back to Africa, and that all humans come from the same "tribe," Gates's TV series resurrects a genetic-based racial essentialism. (At one point he declares, based on his DNA profile: "I'm fifty percent European . . . I guess I'm not Black!" and then goes to a pub in Ireland to tell inhabitants he has more in common with Ireland than with Africa.) Based on both genetic and historical analysis, everyone can acknowledge their African ancestors, not just the dark-skinned Americans who are the descendants of slaves.

For Blacks and Whites, an Afro-Diasporic consciousness places us at the center of the story line—not as heroes or villains, but as complex human beings who are capable of doing good or bad. This turns the heart of darkness inside out—there is no evil lurking within, held in check by civilization; no essential badness to humanity but the human capacity for making choices. Under what circumstances do we choose goodness to confront evil? Not just when it is in our interests to do so, but when the greater glory of humankind stands to benefit. These themes currently exist in Hollywood genres—so why not articulate them in films set in Africa too?

What is required is a sense of "double articulation," or as W. E. B. Du Bois (1903) defined it: "dual consciousness"—to embrace the tension between being

American and African at the same time. (Du Bois wrote in the language of the time: the tension between being "Negro" and American.) This is also partly what Massey (1994) called double articulation: to elevate the historical connections between local and global communities—that the interrelation between local and global is never static or essential; it is always changing, being renegotiated through the *stories* that we tell about ourselves and about the geographical spaces and historical places we call home. And that's why it does matter what Hollywood films say about the nature of humanity and civilization—particularly the humanity found in Africa in comparison to the rest of the world. It's okay to use specific genres to tell history, but we can afford histories that exceed conventions and racial regimes (Robinson 2007), especially those filmic regimes that reinforce the status quo and seemingly justify military intervention around the world. Hollywood's treatment of African peoples is still generally one-dimensional: Africans are objects of history and Western intrigue; they provide the backdrop for romance or heroic conflict between Western protagonists; or they appear as savage combatants or tribal victims fated to genocidal destruction (Cameron 1994).

As Malcolm X stated, *"Of all our studies, history is best prepared to reward our research."* And in that regard, Hollywood wouldn't have to dig very far to uncover historical dramas to eclipse the tragicomic allure of films such as *Last King of Scotland*. How about the story of Ghana's independence? Imagine: the story focuses on an African minister, Francis Kwame Nkrumah, touted at a young age as having almost mystical qualities; sent to the United States to be schooled; trained at an HBCU (historically Black college/university)—Lincoln University; mentored by luminaries such as W. E. B. Du Bois, C. L. R. James, and George Padmore; sent to Britain for graduate schooling, where he joins other young African leaders: Jomo Kenyatta, Nnamdi Azikiwe, and others who would return to Africa after World War II to lead their countries to independence—Idi Amin's story pales in comparison. Nkrumah leads Gold Coast/Ghana to independence in March 1957, calls for African Unity and the destruction of colonialism and imperialism, and immediately develops a model for African independence: socially, politically, and economically. He also cultivates a charismatic, mystical following, but he is not a bloodthirsty tyrant who enriches himself by stealing his nation's wealth. He was soon opposed by the West, and fell victim to Cold War intrigue. He was the subject of assassination attempts, and a CIA-backed coup removed him from office in 1966 (Rahman 2007). There is romance, political intrigue, Cold War spy drama with "Mission Impossible" plotting and scheming, and a flawed, epic hero at the center of it all. Why not tell this story? Why is Idi Amin more widely known than Nkrumah?

Is it because many observers think, after viewing repetitive representations of wars in Africa, that all African governments after Independence have gone excessively awry? The exceptions—such as Botswana—do not receive much attention. The media often portrays Africa as a world apart, as a singular place dominated by corrupt, incompetent rulers who immerse their countries in bloody conflict. We could consider another story that Americans are familiar with, but fail to apply to postindependence dramas set in Africa. As the story goes: thirteen American colonies declare themselves independent of Britain in 1776, and four-score-and-seven-years later, in the 1860s, this fledgling country fights a bloody, fratricidal war—brother against brother—that results in over 600,000 deaths in little over four years. Shortly after America's very own "Civil War"—fueled not by blood diamonds, but by slavery, cotton, and tobacco—for nearly one hundred more years, US rulers commit genocide against Indigenous peoples, condone racial terrorism and violence against African Americans, and engage in discrimination against every new immigrant group brought to these shores. Independence dramas can be tragic, bloody, and mythic—Africa does not have a monopoly on postindependence conflict and brutality.

Where does that leave moviegoers? We go to the movies to be entertained, not to be politically educated, many will protest. And the movie industry does not differentiate between conscientious viewers and those who are simply voyeurs—both audiences can be mobilized at the same time to purchase tickets and watch the latest depiction of Africa on film. But perhaps viewers can be enticed by alternative stories to those currently in vogue. Perhaps producers and audiences will, together, exorcise Hollywood's heart of darkness, and insist on stories that acknowledge humanity's Afro-Diasporic heritage; stories that rely on extroverted histories exceeding narrow, localized, or patriotic interests; and stories recognizing human beings with fully articulated identities that are complex and that extend beyond static racial boundaries. And ultimately, film audiences can learn to reject films based on guilt-tripping or racist projection of the evil within.

I think we can begin to do this, and begin to embrace heroic yet humble stories that can stir the heart, as typified by the novels of McCall Smith, even as they depict an idealized narrative of African culture and identity. It is a simple narrative that is complicated by modernity and a postcolonial world order that obscures the poignant realities of everyday Africans.

"Will you go back to your village one day?" she asked. . . . And
Mma Ramotswe replied, "I shall go back. Yes, one of these days I shall
go back."
And in her mind's eye she saw the winding paths of Mochudi,
and the cattle pens, and the small walled-off plot of ground where a
modest stone bore the inscription [of her father] *Obed Ramotswe*. And
beside the stone there were wild flowers growing, small flowers of
such beauty and perfection that they broke the heart. They broke the
heart. (McCall Smith 2006, 227)

These are important contributions to the narratives that inscribe Africa,
even as they replace savage themes with "picturesque pleasures and upstand-
ing virtues," as noted in the *New York Times Book Review* (quoted inside book
flap, McCall Smith 2008). *The No. 1 Ladies' Detective Agency* has, in fact, been
adapted for television—the pilot was first screened on the BBC in 2008, and
the series aired one season on HBO in 2009.[2] As a narrative paradigm for
Africa of the twenty-first century, it may influence the emergence of a new
filmic language that can affirm humanity in the complex relationships of
Africans grappling with the joys, challenges, and contradictions of independence and postcolonialism. And compared to that, blackfaced imitations of
bloody dictators will not appear to be so appetizing after all.

### NOTES

1. In assessing "Hollywood films," I am using a loose definition that includes film
productions that are international in scope but that follow the Hollywood film genre:
large-scale productions and distribution networks, Americo-centric themes, high production values and high-tech special effects, explosions, gadgetry, or chase scenes, and cast
members who play to an audience that is decidedly Western or reflective of Western
sensibilities (Shohat and Stam 1994). *The Last King of Scotland* is a coproduction of US and
British film companies but uses Hollywood conventions to propel its story.
2. HBO canceled a second season in 2010 but announced plans for two movies, continuing the series on the silver screen and reuniting the cast, starring African American actors Jill Scott and Anika Noni Rose and African actors Lucian Msamati and Desmond Dube.

### REFERENCES

*African American Lives*. 2006. New York: Kunhardt Productions, PBS, Henry Louis
Gates, Jr.
Cameron, Kenneth. 1994. *Africa on Film: Beyond Black and White*. New York: Continuum
International.

Chude-Sokei, Louis. 2006. *The Last "Darky": Bert Williams, Black-on-Black Minstrelsy, and the African Diaspora*. Durham, NC: Duke University Press.

Delson, Susan. 2008. "The Troubled Reign of *The Emperor Jones*." *American Legacy* (Fall): 48–60.

Dorinson, Joseph, and William Pencak, eds. 2002. *Paul Robeson: Essays on His Life and Legacy*. Jefferson, NC: McFarland.

Du Bois, W. E. B. 1997 [1903]. *The Souls of Black Folk*. Edited by David W. Blight and Robert Gooding-Williams. Boston: Bedford Books.

Gabriel, Teshome. 1995. "Towards a Critical Theory of Third World Films." In *Cinemas of the Black Diaspora: Diversity, Dependence, and Oppositionality*, edited by Michael T. Martin, 70–90. Detroit, MI: Wayne State University Press.

Germain, David. 2006. "Africa Is Suddenly Hot." *San Diego Union-Tribune*, October 27, arts section.

Guillén, Michael. 2006. "Forest Whitaker Interview." October 7. http://twitchfilm.net /archives/007779.html.

*Last King of Scotland, The*. 2006. DVD interviews and commentaries. Fox Searchlight Pictures.

Lipsitz, George. 1990. "Listening to Learn and Learning to Listen: Popular Culture, Cultural Theory, and American Studies." *American Quarterly* 42 (4): 615–36.

Martin, Michael T., ed. 1995. *Cinemas of the Black Diaspora*. Detroit, MI: Wayne State University Press.

Massey, Doreen. 1994. "Double Articulation: A Place in the World." In *Displacements: Cultural Identities in Question*, edited by Angelika Bammar. Bloomington: Indiana University Press.

McCall Smith, Alexander. 2003. *The No. 1 Ladies' Detective Agency*. New York: Anchor Books.

———. 2006. *Blue Shoes and Happiness*. New York: Anchor Books.

———. 2008. *The Good Husband of Zebra Drive*. New York: Anchor Books.

Rahman, Ahmad A. 2007. *The Regime Change of Kwame Nkrumah: Epic Heroism in Africa and the Diaspora*. New York: Palgrave Macmillan.

Rebort. 2006. "Last King Shall Be First." Interview with Kevin Macdonald on making *The Last King of Scotland*, the first feature film completely shot in Uganda. October 16. http://www.iofilm.co.uk/io/mit/001/kevinmacdonald_last_king_of_scotland _20061016.phpOscar-winner.

Robinson, Cedric. 2007. *Forgeries of Memory and Meaning: Blacks and the Regimes of Race in American Theater and Film before World War II*. Chapel Hill: University of North Carolina Press.

Saxton, Alexander. 1990. *The Rise and Fall of the White Republic: Class Politics and Mass Culture in Nineteenth-Century America*. London: Verso.

Shohat, Ella, and Robert Stam. 1994. *Unthinking Eurocentrism: Multiculturalism and the Media*. New York: Routledge.

Stewart, Jeffrey C., ed. 1998. *Paul Robeson: Artist and Citizen*. New Brunswick, NJ: Rutgers University Press.

# EIGHT

# "An Image of Africa"

Representations of Modern Colonialism in Africa in Peter Jackson's *King Kong*

CLIFFORD T. MANLOVE

Looked at from the vantage point of historical context, it makes sense that Merian C. Cooper made his masterwork *King Kong* in 1933,[1] given that its narrative portrays the intersecting histories of narrative cinema and colonialism in the Modern period (1885–1935). Cooper's *Kong* is a masterwork for two principal reasons, aside from its pioneering commercial use of stop-motion photography, rear-screen and miniature projection, the traveling matte, and the Williams Process. First, it incorporates filmmaking as a major theme; and, second, Cooper explicitly links the Modern colonial project in Africa to filmmaking and the cinematic experience. Cooper cowrote, codirected, and coproduced *King Kong* in the context of several key historical events and technological developments relevant to film history and the colonization of Africa: famous "explorers" and ethnographers with cameras, guns, and magazine/book contracts crisscrossed the remaining unmapped globe during the 1870s through the 1920s and '30s, making great names and fortunes for themselves; the Conference of Berlin (1885) and the "Scramble for Africa" were followed quickly by Maxim's invention of the fully automatic machine gun in 1889; the first films were screened for mass audiences by the Lumière brothers in 1895; the word "savage" retained scientific value among anthropologists, paleontologists, and others in the human sciences until 1930 (Stocking 1968); "Social Darwinism" popularized the use of evolution to explain class and racial differences and the evolutionary metaphor "survival of the fittest" was used by some public intellectuals to justify colonialism (Shohat and Stam 1994, 104–7); and black migration from the American South to major northern cities such as Chicago and New York intensified between 1920 and 1930 (Snead 1994, 20–21). These are but a few of the well-documented influences setting the stage for Cooper's *Kong* that provide context for the themes of filmmaking and colonialism in the film.

Given these historical contexts, how can Peter Jackson's 2005 "remake" of *King Kong* be explained (apart from Jackson's well-documented interest in the film as a youth? [Vaz 2005, xiii]). What about American culture and history in the first decade of the twenty-first century is analogous to the 1930s that could produce a new *Kong*?[2] What about the manner of Hollywood's representation of Africa in 2005 recalls 1933; or, is Jackson's version simply a "period" film? Jackson's choice to remake *Kong* raises the question of whether the practice of colonialism in Africa is merely a historical relic, something no longer with us in the twenty-first century in the same way that, say, the transatlantic slave trade appeared to be for the twentieth. It suggests a cultural and historical kinship between the worlds of 1933 and 2005. Likewise, "Skull Island" is more than some distant, exotic island, location and history unknown.[3] I argue that Jackson uses Skull Island as a means to draw attention to Cooper's use of it to allegorize Africa's "unexplored jungles." In fact, it is Jackson who gives the island that name; it is unnamed in Cooper's version, reinforcing my argument. Kong's island is analogous to Africa in both versions of the film, raising the question of how, if at all, Hollywood representations of Africa have been revised during the last eighty years. At first blush, Jackson's choice to set his narrative in the 1930s makes his version appear to be merely a nostalgic homage to Hollywood and Cooper rather than a contemporary cultural critique. The persistence of colonialism decades after independence can easily be glossed over by Hollywood's stylized, "period film" representations of the formerly colonized. Hollywood accomplishes this using the silver screen, a space on which the audience can simultaneously focus their own fears and fantasies, under the guise of showing what has never been seen before (Rony 1996). Jackson's *King Kong* simultaneously embodies and challenges this effacement, particularly with respect to Africa. Ultimately, however, I will argue that the case Chinua Achebe makes for *Heart of Darkness* (1899) as a failed representation of Africa could also be applied to Jackson's *Kong*. This is especially ironic, given Jackson's decision to include Conrad's *Heart* in his new *Kong* narrative.

All versions of *King Kong* use representations of Skull Island and New York City to portray the relationship between Africa and "Modernity," implicating narrative cinema, and Hollywood in particular, with the modern colonial project in Africa. Further, Jackson's version makes the case that Hollywood views Africa, and its position with respect to the northern world, in much the same way in 2005 as was the case in 1933. My essay analyzes three discursive debates in *King Kong* that illustrate these arguments. First, to what extent do Cooper's own biography and Africa's place in the American public imagination between 1880 and 1930 conspire to create Kong and Skull Island? Second, how does the prevalent thematic struggle between "savagery" and "civilization" in Cooper and Jackson's versions reflect not only the Africa/Modernity polarity, but the reflexive and transgressive perspectives on that relationship? Third, how are we to read Jackson's inclusion of Joseph Conrad's *Heart of Darkness*? How does *Heart* color *Kong*? How do the two imaginative works parallel or speak to each other? In each case, Jackson enhances the reflexivity Cooper uses simply to draw our attention to the role of artifice in the creation of cinematic spectacle. What distinguishes spectacle from other forms of visual entertainment, Cooper argues in *Kong*, is that spectacle reaches out and touches the spectator from the Real. Jackson's version expands Cooper's focus on cinematic entertainment predicated on racial difference to include the role of cinema in Modern colonialism.

COOPER AND "MODERNITY'S" FASCINATION WITH AFRICA

Raised from birth on the family plantation in Jacksonville, Florida, Merian Coldwell Cooper was born in 1893—the same year that Edison built his "Black Maria"—roughly five years after the partition of Africa and five years before the Spanish-American War, officially announcing America's entry into the Modern colonial project. Colonial images of Africa played a crucial role in Cooper's childhood and in his return to journalism after his adventurous military career, ultimately playing an influential role in his development as a filmmaker. There is much critical speculation that Cooper "invented" the name "Kong"—Cooper always claimed to have invented it—as a result of having unconsciously internalized stories he read as a six-year-old about the exploration of the Congo. Such a book of stories was given to Cooper by a great-uncle, Merian R. Cooper, who, at the age of sixteen, had enlisted as a private in the Confederate army, was twice wounded in battle, survived, and was promoted to the rank of captain (Vaz 2005, 7–74). *Explorations and Adventures in Equatorial Africa* (1861) by the French explorer, Paul Du Chaillu, is his story of hunting gorillas—"the king of the African forest"—in the Congo region of Central Africa. What is especially interesting about this book—besides the fact that it was first published in English—is the inclusion by Du Chaillu of more than a dozen lithographs portraying encounters between Europeans and Africans, and also between Europeans and African animals, scattered throughout the book. Du Chaillu's recollection of his first encounter with a gorilla must have made an impression on young Cooper: "Then the underbrush swayed rapidly just ahead, and presently before us stood an immense male gorilla. He had gone through the jungle on his all-fours; but when he saw our party he erected himself and looked at us boldly in the face. . . . He was not afraid of us. He stood there, and beat his breast with his huge fists till it resounded like an immense bass-drum, which is their mode of offering defiance" (1969, 98). Du Chaillu's image of this first encounter is evocative of Kong's first appearance in Cooper's film to claim his bride, down to the "swaying" brush and defiant drumming by Kong of his breast and by the Skull Islanders. According to film historian Rudy Behlmer, on reading Du Chaillu, Cooper recalls, "'I made up my mind right then that I wanted to be an explorer'" (Vaz 2005, 14). Cooper especially remembered the vivid lithographs depicting large apes scattered through the book and a tale Du Chaillu relates of a gorilla carrying a woman off into the jungle.

Perhaps a more obscure source for the name and concept of "Kong" is as a place-name for geographical and political features in West Africa. "Kong" is and has been variously used as a place-name for a town, a region, an ethnic group, and even for a major mountain range in West Africa, at roughly 10 degrees north of the equator, near the northern borders of modern Côte d'Ivoire and Ghana, stretching east into Sudan and Ethiopia. Given that Skull Island is dominated by a large, steep mountain—Kong's home—the "Kong Mountains" are especially significant. According to Bassett and Porter, "The mountains first appear in two maps drawn by James Rennell for Mungo Park's account of his legendary journey to the Niger River. They subsequently appear on nearly all of the major commercial maps of the nineteenth century beginning with Aaron Arrowsmith's four-sheet map of the African continent and ending in the early twentieth century" (1991, 367). The existence of the Kong Mountains was never established by direct observation; instead, its cartographic existence was a product of anecdote and lore—much like Skull Island—and an increasingly pressing desire to learn about the sources and basins of the great African rivers: the Niger, the Nile, and the Congo. Bassett and Porter continue,

> The Kong Mountains were popularly viewed as a great drainage divide separating streams flowing to the Niger River and Gulf of Guinea.

They were also believed to be rich in gold, covered with snow, and an "insuperable barrier" hindering commerce between the coast and the interior. What is intriguing about the Kong Mountains is that they never existed except in the imaginations of explorers, mapmakers and merchants. (1991, 367)

This makes metaphorical and symbolic connections between Skull Island and Africa even more tempting and substantive. In the same way that the imaginary Kong Mountains served as an "insuperable barrier" between North and sub-Saharan Africa—and between the Niger River and the sea—Skull Island is dominated by a massive mountain shaped like a primate skull and a vast wall reminiscent of ancient Egyptian architecture, according to Captain Englehorn in Cooper's version of *Kong*. Just as Skull Island is an imaginative creation by Hollywood—one that reifies popular clichés about "primeval" Africa—so too were the Kong Mountains a creation born of nineteenth-century Eurocentric views of African geography and the perceived necessity for "exploration" of it. Bassett and Porter's thesis concerning the importance of the Kong Mountains in the broader history of cartography is telling with respect to Jackson's version of *King Kong* and his use of Conrad's *Heart of Darkness*.

After receiving an invitation from Haile Selassie in February 1923, Cooper traveled to Ethiopia to meet the heir of King Solomon—aka Ras Tafari, who would later be revered by Rastafarians as the Living God—and to hunt adventure for the camera and for publication. Cooper and Ernest B. Schoedsack made their first of many cinematic collaborations, filming "the army of Abyssinia assemble[d] for maneuvers" (Vaz 2005, 95). In one of a series of articles detailing his observations of Ethiopia that he produced for the magazine *Asia*, Cooper exclaims, "'It isn't real,' I said to myself, 'it's a dream—of living in an age long, long dead.' . . . A dream—a vision—a memory of the Age of Kings!'" (1923, 707–8). Even ten years prior to *Kong*, Cooper sees Africa and its relationship to Western Modernity in evolutionary terms suggestive of the scientific discourses surrounding extinctions resulting from nineteenth-century colonialism (Lindqvist 1997). The fact that Ras Tafari would be crowned emperor of Ethiopia in 1930, 225th in a direct line of succession from King Solomon and Queen Sheba, brings life to Cooper's Modern fantasy about Africa being a veritable, living museum of natural history for Modernity. If we take Jackson's use of Conrad's *Heart* as commentary on Cooper's *Kong* seriously, the question of whether Cooper read Conrad becomes interesting when considering whether Skull Island is a symbol for Africa. Although we cannot know whether he read Joseph Conrad, Conrad's novels were advertised for sale alongside Cooper's first of three essays about Ras Tafari and Abyssinia in *Asia* (1923, 775). We can know that, like Conrad's youthful travels up the Congo River, Cooper's African travels would lead to the creation of his best-known film work.

Cooper began preliminary conceptual work that would lead to *Kong* while shooting *The Four Feathers* (1929) in East Africa (A. E. W. Mason's novel, *The Four Feathers,* had been adapted for the silver screen before and would be adapted again in 2002). According to Ray Morton, "In the course of production, Cooper became intrigued by a tribe of baboons that lived near the location, and he began studying their lifestyle, behavior, and social interactions. In 1929, while living in New York, Cooper wrote an 85,000-word monograph recording his observations" (2005, 17). This is evocative of the district commissioner's ethnographic observations of Umuofia at the conclusion of Chinua Achebe's *Things Fall Apart,* where he reduces the Igbo culture to the subject of a book. *King Kong* is not only a film about filmmaking, about story-making, it shows the dependence of Hollywood on the "exotic," the "savage," and the unexplored, the never-before-filmed or taboo, the very point Carl Denham makes in Cooper's *Kong* when he proclaims his desire to shoot (or capture) "what no white man has seen before." As it turns out, the "great apes" of "Equatorial Africa" would provide the perfect, ironic dramatic tension for Cooper's *Kong,* embodying utter savagery yet in human form, "Other" yet "kin," precisely the point Achebe makes about *Heart of Darkness* and Marlow's ambivalent liberalism (Achebe 1977, 783). Marlow criticizes the hypocrisy of European colonialism's profiting from the flesh and the very lives of the people it professed to save, while also recoiling from his black "kin."

THE "SAVAGE" VERSUS "CIVILIZED" THEME AND REFLEXIVITY

Modern production and consumption of film and narrative entertainment is a reflexive theme in all three versions of *King Kong,* and most especially Jackson's. All three major versions of *Kong* feature several reflexive elements: Cooper foregrounds Denham's quest to make an authentic "jungle" film in an exotic location, Dino De Laurentiis's 1976 version moves the reflexive focus to Fred Wilson's—equivalent of the Denham character—desire to use Kong for corporate public relations and advertising, and Jackson returns the focus to Denham's project to make a film that has "never been seen before," using the narrative to elaborate on and critique the production details of Denham's filmmaking. In the context of the horror genre, J. P. Telotte puts it this way: "In short, *Kong* forces us to refocus our vision, to shift our perceptions, and in the process hints of a reflexive impulse at work. What makes this element even more explicit in *King Kong* is the extent to which the film seems aware of its power over how we see. In fact, we might argue that *Kong* is *about* seeing, and particularly about its limitations and dangers" (1988, 390). At its most essential level, *King Kong* is a film about filmmaking and the dangerous affiliation cinema shares with the practice of colonialism. There is a distinct linkage between the Modern drives to see, shoot film, and to colonize what appears to be new. Telotte elaborates: "This drive to see—despite the dangers and difficulties, despite native prohibitions, even despite the island's great wall built to prevent encounters with what lies beyond—is central to *King Kong*" (391). Each version of *Kong* not only dramatizes this "drive to see"— the narrative moves by way of the visual drive—the films also implicate the audience in pushing this desire beyond "civilized" limits. Telotte goes on to link the drive to see to genre: "It points to something that the horror film, in varying degrees, has always been concerned with: I call it an imperative of seeing—our desire to see things we are not supposed to, and especially to see into life's shadows, regardless of the menace this hiddenness might hold" (1988, 391). What all versions of *Kong* make clear is that colonial narratives are structured like the horror genre in film. Just as the horror genre is about an insistence on seeing the taboo, Modern colonial narratives seek to make the taboo useful, representable, and commercial. "*Kong* suggests the danger in this insistent seeing, a possibility that we might 'spoil' or violate the work in trying to look beyond our normal boundaries. In effect, it warns us about its own threatening aspect" (Telotte 1988, 391). Similarly, Modern colonialism is not simply a matter of nationalism, economic expansion, and the alleged advance of history, what makes colonialism Modern is its employment of spectacular mass entertainment at the expense of the taboo (Shohat and Stam 1994, 100–101). Two inventions of the late nineteenth century shaped the narrative of Modern colonialism as a horror film: the motion-picture camera and the fully automatic machine gun.

The camera / gun trope—based on Marey's *"fusil cinématographique"* ("camera gun")[4]—portrayed in *King Kong* also parallels the historically close, even reflexive relationship between national militaries and cinemas. Cooper's long infatuation with making a natural drama about a giant ape takes on an epic, timeless dynamic when coupled with Modernity in its most salient forms: imperial commerce (the Empire State Building),[5] Hollywood (Denham's drive to film "what no white man has seen before"), and the military (Cooper's choice to use combat airplanes in the narrative—he and Schoedsack cameo as the pilots who shoot Kong to death). According to Lawrence Suid, "From the infancy of the [film] industry, producers have sought assistance from the military in the form of technical advice, men, and equipment" (1977, 14). To explain this, Suid makes the obvious point with respect to national cinemas, that film has inherent propaganda value: "The military believed providing such assistance to commercial films aided recruiting and helped inform the American people of its activities and procedures" (1977, 14). But, the connection of cinema and the military goes beyond material "assistance" or PR. The cinematic process and the colonial process each rely on similar mechanical and philosophical necessities. Both have the capability—using the ability to manipulate time and space for an audience—to revise and reconfigure the given horizon of the world. Cinema and Modern colonialism are interested in carving, creating something patterned and organized out of what lies beyond the limits of their knowledge, and profiting from the results.

Modern colonialism in Africa and cinema also owe their existence to a crucial invention in 1889 by Sir Hiram Stevens Maxim, the fully automatic machine gun. The same intermittent mechanism used to quickly advance a strip of cartridges into the firing chamber of a gun at rapid, precisely regular intervals could also be used to run a strip of film stock through a camera or a projector. This pair of inventions—the machine gun and the moving-picture camera—made "savage" triumph over "civilization" appear impossible (and in the film, in the case of Kong's brief occupation of the Empire State Building). Jackson's version of Kong emphasizes the crucial linkages between exploration, the camera, and the machine gun in its narrative, adding a film crew for Denham to the sailor/soldier crew of the Venture. Cynthia Erb presents a detailed analysis of what she terms "the camera/gun trope" in Cooper's version of the film, "a cliché from safari adventures of the 1920s. . . . Though articulated in many different forms, the camera/gun trope is a representation usually composed of a cameraman photographing animals in the jungle or on the African veldt, accompanied by a white hunter who provides gun cover. Sometimes, as in King Kong, one man wields both gun and camera" (1998, 67).[6] The power and pervasiveness of this trope can be seen in the extensive cluster of metaphors and figurative language comparing the various functions of the gun and the camera. For example, according to the OED, while the word "shoot" regarding guns comes into the English language in verb and noun forms during the sixteenth century, it comes to be associated with photography as early as 1890—"To take a snapshot (of) with a camera; to photograph (a scene, action, person, etc.) with a cinematographic camera;

to take (cinematographic film), to film; occas. with the actor as subject"—and 1929 ("The action of shooting a film"). Jackson's version emphasizes the camera/gun trope beyond even Cooper's use of it. In Jackson's version, the film crew of Denham's expedition is never without the camera and tripod, and Englehorn's crew is armed with machine guns. Whereas, in Cooper's version, the *Venture*'s crew carries single-action carbines as they explore and attempt to subdue/exploit Skull Island. As the ship's crew arms and equips, and Denham's camera crew packs photographic gear to pursue Kong and Darrow, Jackson uses a sequence of shots to graphically match film canisters and cylinder gun clips. Given these linkages between the tools of cinema and Modern colonialism, it is not just a metaphor to speak of each version of *King Kong* as showcasing "Hollywood's Africa."

CONRAD AND MODERN COLONIALISM IN *KING KONG*

> Monsters belong in "B" movies.
>
> —Carl Denham, "B movie" director, *King Kong* (2005)

Peter Jackson's version of *King Kong* serves as a running commentary on images of Africa, race, gender, and colonialism used by Cooper in 1933.[7] Perhaps unintentionally, Jackson's version also serves as a metacommentary, a critique of twenty-first-century representations of Africa and the "developing" world in Hollywood. While Jackson makes his veneration for Cooper's original version clear by way of numerous allusions in his 2005 version—even emphasizing and fleshing out Cooper's emphasis on the theme of filmmaking—Jackson's inclusion of Conrad's *Heart of Darkness* in the narrative also draws attention to Cooper's representation of Africa, race, gender, and colonialism.[8] In Cooper's eye, Africa has yet to be developed; it and its people are prehistoric; and spreading civilization is the duty of the civilized (Kipling's "White Man's Burden").

Jackson's choice to make Conrad's *Heart* a part of *Kong* reinforces the question of reflexivity: In what way is *Kong* like *Heart*? In what new ways is Skull Island kin to Africa?[9] What meaning do these metaphoric pairs share? Like Conrad's representation of the Congo, "Skull Island" is depicted as one of the few "blank spaces" left in the world at the start of the twentieth century and, like the colonial explorers of the late nineteenth century, film director Carl Denham wants to film "what no one has seen before," edit the footage, and charge admission to New York audiences. While Jackson's version may strike the term "white man," much of the racialized and colonial senti-ment of Cooper's version is highlighted nevertheless. In Jackson, the crew becomes suspicious of the ship's course and Denham's desire to shoot his film on location, and they confront him. Denham replies, "Gentlemen, please, we're not looking for trouble." "No, you're looking for something else," Crewman Jimmy replies, uncannily wise for his age. (In fact, Jimmy has "borrowed" a copy of Conrad's *Heart* on "long-term loan" from the New York Public Library, enhancing NYC's status as a center of civilization and co-lonialism, linking it to London, where Marlow tells his tale.) Denham admits and boasts simultaneously, "Yes we are. We're going to find Skull Island. Find it, film it, and show it to the world! For twenty-five cents you get to see the last blank space on the map!" (Jackson 2005). Modern colonialism is not only about economics, it is about the economy of entertainment, of spectacle, and the presentation of "others" for mass consumption. Conrad's Marlow tells a similar tale, a memory stirred by seeing a map in a shop window in Central London: "Now when I was a little chap I had a passion for maps. I would look for hours at South America, or Africa, or Australia and lose my-self in the glories of exploration. At that time there were many blank spaces on the earth and when I saw one that looked particularly inviting on a map (but they all look that) I would put my finger on it and say: When I grow up I will go there" (1988, 11). Just as maps embody and engender narratives, so too do pictures (moving pictures, in particular). A map serves the same function as a screen for cinema—what is a "blank space" but a screen, waiting to be filled, whether by an audience, a filmmaker, or an explorer. Marlow contin-ues, reflecting on his desire to explore:

> "But there was one yet—the biggest—the most blank, so to speak—
> that I had a hankering after. True, by this time it was not a blank
> space any more. It had got filled since my boyhood with rivers and
> lakes and names. It had ceased to be a blank space of delightful
> mystery—a white patch for a boy to dream gloriously over. It had
> become a place of darkness. . . . And as I looked at the map of it in a
> shop-window it fascinated me as a snake would a bird—a silly little
> bird." (1988, 11–12)

It seems appropriate that this screen for young Marlow should be in a "shop-window," a mise-en-scène fit for the spectacle of commerce that bears some resemblance to Denham's cinematic desires. While Skull Island somehow remains a "blank space," it also is "a place of darkness," outside of history (as Africa was for European historians of the nineteenth century). Crewman Lumpy makes precisely this observation in response to Denham's boast to film the last unfilmed place on the map, "I wouldn't be so sure of that. . . . Seven years ago, me and Mr. Hayes were working our passage on a Norwegian barque." The chief mate, Mr. Hayes, interjects, "We picked up a castaway, found him in the water. He'd been drifting for days." Lumpy continues, "His ship had run aground on an island, way west of Sumatra, an island hidden in fog. He spoke of a huge wall, built so long ago no one knew who made it, a wall a hundred foot high; as strong today as it was ages ago" (Jackson 2005).[10] Like Africa, Skull Island bears the intrinsically visual burdens of blankness and blackness, and serves as a temptation to see something new, to see the other beyond the walls defending against "savage" nature. How "far west" of Sumatra is Skull Island? How close is it to Africa? One indication is that in the time it takes the *Venture* to steam west from Sumatra, Jack Driscoll writes an entire advanced draft of a "stage comedy" inspired by Ann Darrow.

Peter Jackson's use of Joseph Conrad explicitly demonstrates the link between filmmaking and the cinematic gaze in European colonization of Africa. We are introduced to *Heart of Darkness* in *King Kong* by way of the "wild" young crewman, Jimmy, that Carl Denham's writer, Jack Driscoll, meets in his "stateroom." We learn that Jimmy first joins the crew of the *Venture* as a stowaway and that his rough origins are unknown. The introduction is given by Mr. Hays, the chief, who catches Jimmy palming an expensive pen owned by Driscoll while delivering his dinner of "lamb's brains in walnut sauce." Because of a lack of space on board—a result of the need for extra hands required by Denham's project—Driscoll is forced to stay in an animal cage below decks, parodying both the subservient role of the screenwriter and the turn-of-the century colonial interest in putting "natives" on display in mock African villages in museums and world's fairs. After returning the stolen pen to Driscoll, Mr. Hays takes Jimmy deckside to handle some ropes. Mr. Hays challenges Jimmy: "You gotta straighten up. Jimmy, you don't want to be on this ship the rest of your life. . . . You gotta be smart, get yourself educated, give yourself some options, take this seriously." Jimmy replies enthusiastically, "I do, Mr. Hays. Look, I've been reading," and he hands Mr. Hays a hardback copy of *Heart of Darkness and Two Other Stories* (including Conrad's *Youth: A Narrative* and "The End of the Tether"). Just as it was the fashion in literary studies to view *Heart* as a stylistic exemplar, so too does Jimmy measure being "educated" and "serious" by way of Conrad's quintessentially difficult, stylized text. Ironically, the "wild" Jimmy demonstrates his accession to being serious about joining "civilization" by way of a story about a man who loses his civilized veneer. In the manner of grand foreshadowing, as if to reassure that what he is reading will educate him, Jimmy points out to Mr. Hays on the back of his copy of *Heart*, "Look, 'Adventures on a tramp steamer,' just like us" (Jackson 2005). The adventure that is in store for Jimmy, Mr. Hays, and the *Venture* will be just like Marlow's, Jackson implies.

Not coincidentally, this scene is followed below deck by Ann Darrow rehearsing her first encounter with Driscoll—whom she admires greatly as a playwright—in front of a mirror, while holding up a copy of one of Driscoll's plays plainly in front of her, reflecting in the mirror. The play is entitled *Isolation* (a perfect title from the standpoint of Achebe's reading of Kurtz in *Heart*). As she rehearses, Denham and Driscoll work to write the screenplay Denham hopes to shoot at their yet-to-be-disclosed destination. As Denham paces outside exotic cages, Driscoll sits in his cage, writing an early scene for their nature film. A sign on his cage reads: "WILD ANIMALS INSIDE / THE PETTY OFFICER MUST BE / PRESENT WHILE UNLOADING / THIS CRATE." Running through exposition for his story, Denham finally declares: "And that's when she sees it." "Sees what?" Driscoll asks. "The island," Denham intones quietly, seriously, as if just making this discovery for the first time. Driscoll inquires, "What's wrong with it?" "Nothing is *officially* wrong with it," Denham argues, "because 'officially' it hasn't been discovered." Tellingly, on this note, Driscoll decides to write the name of the island. As he types the name, "S-K-U-L-L," the moment is stylized by Jackson using a slow-motion zoom to Driscoll, moving to each finger punching each typewriter key at a canted angle (akin to how moments of high tension are shot in Jackson's *Lord of the Rings*), during which we crosscut to similar slow-motion zoom close-ups of the faces of Denham and Jimmy (whose eyes appear to show recognition at Denham's description of the island). Denham's eyes meet Jimmy's and, for the first time, Denham seems apprehensive (Jackson 2005). It should be noted that European cartographers of the seventeenth and eighteenth centuries likened the shape of the African continent to that of a human skull.

Chinua Achebe's argument that *Heart* presents a racist picture of Africa applies also, more or less, to all three versions of *Kong*. According to Achebe, "*Heart of Darkness* projects the image of Africa as 'the other world,' the antithesis of Europe and therefore civilization, a place where man's vaunted intelligence and refinement are finally mocked by triumphant bestiality" (1977, 783). Similarly, all three versions of *Kong* portray the savage Skull Island as the "antithesis" in every respect to civilized New York City and Manhattan Island. Several of Marlow's descriptions of travel up the Congo are suggestive of Achebe's reading of *Heart* and Denham and Company's time on Skull Island.

> "We were wanderers on a prehistoric earth, on an earth that wore the aspect of an unknown planet. We could have fancied ourselves the first of men taking possession of an accursed inheritance, to be subdued at the cost of profound anguish and of excessive toil. But suddenly as we struggled round a bend there would be a glimpse of rush walls, of peaked grass-roofs, a burst of yells, a whirl of black limbs, a mass of hands clapping, of feet stamping, of bodies swaying, of eyes rolling under the droop of heavy and motionless foliage." (Conrad 1988, 37)

It should be noted that these are Marlow's words, not Conrad's, though *Heart* obviously raises a question about the relationship between an author and a narrator. The Congo and Skull Island are not only "blank spaces" to be mapped and incorporated; they are also perceived as utterly alien—journeying to them is akin not only to interplanetary travel but also to time travel as well. While the tone differs dramatically, Marlow's evolutionary, anthropological descriptions of travel upriver are shared by Cooper when he meets Ras Tafari, "It's a dream—of living long, long ago" (1923, 707). According to Marlow,

> "The Steamer toiled along slowly on the edge of a black and incomprehensible frenzy. The prehistoric man was cursing us, praying to us, welcoming us—who could tell? We were cut off from the comprehension of our surroundings; we glided past like phantoms, wondering and secretly appalled, as sane men would be before an enthusiastic outbreak in a madhouse. We could not understand because we were too far and could not remember because we were travelling in the night of first ages, of those ages that are gone." (Conrad 1988, 37)

This passage in particular must resonate with Jimmy as he reads it—let alone later, after actually "discovering" Skull Island. Indeed, just as the *Venture* is about to "discover" Skull Island, Jimmy is at a lookout post, reading *Heart* during a long, uneventful shift at the top of the main mast. As the *Venture* approaches the fog-shrouded island, Jimmy is the first to see Skull Island, to see the skull-shaped rocks looming out of the dark, and to see the massive wall. But, he sees it too late; the *Venture* runs aground on the rocks. Unlike *Heart*, in which the "savage" spirit of the Congo River basin never actually threatens the "refinement" of the venerable River Thames, Kong's bestiality literally threatens not just the blond Darrow; Kong "mocks" and briefly "triumphs" over "The Empire State." Kong's breast-thumping bravado stands in tragic, ironic contrast to the ease with which he is machine-gunned by US Navy combat aircraft, which is demonstrated by a final, very long shot to show Kong's tiny, insignificant body fall nearly the length of the Empire State Building in a manner that Schleier suggests is evocative of Depression-era images of suicides in New York (2008, 51).

Achebe argues that, in the final analysis, what is most troubling about *Heart* is that it is a story that purports to be about the African "heart of darkness" but really takes place on the River Thames, just to the east of London. Conrad's *Heart* is more about Europe, Marlow, and Kurtz than it is anything African. As Achebe puts it, "Africa as a setting and backdrop which eliminates the human factor. Africa as a metaphysical battlefield devoid of all recognizable humanity, into which the wandering European wanders at his peril. Can nobody see the preposterous and perverse arrogance in thus reducing Africa to the role of props for the break-up of one petty European mind?" (1977, 789). This, in the end, is true of Skull Island as well; Skull Island represents Africa as *Heart of Darkness* does. Rather than being windows on Africa (or even Skull Island), *Kong* and *Heart* instead serve as mirrors for their own audience's views of that vast, distinctive continent.

EVOLUTION, REFLEXIVITY, AND CRITIQUE OF COLONIALISM

While Merian C. Cooper uses reflexivity to represent Modernity and his own philosophy of filmmaking, Peter Jackson uses the same reflexivity to criticize—and perhaps reify—Modern colonialism. Like Kong and Darrow, like Skull and Manhattan Islands, *Heart of Darkness* and *King Kong* are mirror images of each other. Conrad's *Heart* is predicated on the process of an otherwise "civilized" individual being revealed for his true, base savageness; Modern colonialism is founded on a selfish hypocrisy, not philanthropy. Jackson's *Kong* focuses on the rapid progress a monster can achieve in desiring civility and humanity modeled by Darrow (Morton 2005). Jackson's version of Cooper's *Kong* redefines the concepts of sentience and humanity, even as it reifies the "civilized" subject's own fantastical self-image that it is "the best of all possible worlds." Even as self-proclaimed civilization builds walls to protect itself from the other, it seeks the other out for resources, for research, and for spectacle. Although Jackson's version has an awareness and critique of the racist nature of the original Kong's representation and narrative fate, it may also reify a certain racism and sexism. This is a result of Jackson's representation of the primitive as destined to lose out in the "struggle for existence"—Kong is the last of his kind—in the manner of M. C. Cooper and T. H. Huxley.[11] According to Huxley, the civilized and the primitive are in unavoidable, moral conflict.

> Society differs from nature in having a definite moral object; whence it comes about that the course shaped by the ethical man—the member of society or citizen—necessarily runs counter to that which the non-ethical man—the primitive savage, or man as a mere member of the animal kingdom—tends to adopt. The latter fights out the struggle for existence to the bitter end, like any other animal; the former devotes his best energies to the object of setting limits to the struggle. (1888, 165)

In Jackson, the primitive appears fated to be unable to resist the sexy spectacle of civilization. And, despite the walls—like anthropologists, psychoanalysts, and priests, the wall "limits," or regulates, struggle with the "savage"— civilization is morally (and scientifically) compelled to drive savage nature "to the bitter end."

The fact that Jackson's 2005 version of *Kong* represents the effects of theories of evolution and extinction on Skull Island in a manner evocative of how Africa and "primitive" people were represented in debates over Social Darwinism in the second half of the nineteenth century is not simply an issue of nostalgia or a critique of a long distant past. By 1888—when T. H. Huxley published his evolutionary manifesto, "The Struggle for Existence: A Programme," evolutionary theory had already been used to explain quite a number of colonial "extinctions" around the world. If extinction is the inevitable fate of all unsuccessful species, according to evolutionary science, then Modern colonial activity is exempt from any charges of genocide or criminal neglect (Lindqvist 1997). It is precisely this Modernist fantasy that leads to Denham's decision to capture Kong. When Jackson shows us a large humanoid skull on Kong's island—something Cooper never shows—we are meant to know that he is the last of his kind. This links the process of extinction, Modern colonialism, and the exotic appetites of Hollywood cinema to film the original, never-before-filmed image before it disappears. In the Hollywood imagination, Africa remains that "primeval" place which, as Hegel puts it, "has no history," like Skull Island. In the same way that Africa has been shown by contemporary paleontology to be the birthplace of modern humanity, so too has time stopped for it, in Hollywood's eye. This makes the image of Africa—in the Hollywood imagination—an exotic anachronism, a specimen from an otherwise lost, ancient world that always remains on the verge of extinction.

NOTES

1. Cooper's 1933 version was recognized in June 2008 by the American Film Institute to be the fourth best "fantasy" film of all time in its "America's 10 Greatest Films in 10 Classic Genres" list, trailing *The Wizard of Oz, Lord of the Rings: The Fellowship of the Ring,* and *It's a Wonderful Life.* It is interesting to note that the filmmaker of *Lord of the Rings*—Peter Jackson—remade *King Kong* in 2005.

2. David Rosen makes precisely this point in his "KING KONG: Race, Sex, Rebellion," implicitly explaining the making of De Laurentiis's 1976 version: "But what is especially interesting about an interpretation of a film like KING KONG in terms of its historicity is how our more recent experience enables us to retrieve and appreciate its 'original' meaning and compare it with our own understanding of it; the racial configurations of the 1960s, the resurgence of a radical movement in the United States, and the deepening social—and now economic—crisis stimulate and make possible such an understanding" (1975, 10). Jackson's version argues that similar racial, sexual, and class questions arose in 1933, 1976, and 2005.

3. See Rony for her argument that Skull Island is located in Indonesia, just off the coast of Sumatra (1996, 177). All three versions of *Kong* are quite vague about the location of Skull Island. However, Rony convincingly cites Captain Englehorn's observation in Cooper's version that the language of the Skull Islanders is related to an Indonesian dialect. My argument here—which Rony acknowledges—is that American audiences would read Skull Island as Africa, regardless of how close it was to the continent of Africa in "reality." Several plot elements in Cooper's *Kong* reinforce seeing Skull Island as representative of Africa. For instance, Denham describes its location: "Way west of Sumatra." Rather than represent the Skull Islanders racially as kin to Sumatrans or the islanders of Southeast Asia, Cooper decides to use black actors, of either African or Aboriginal descent. Being "way west" of Sumatra might as well put Skull Island perhaps as far west as Madagascar or Comoros off the east coast of Africa, at least in the Hollywood imagination.

4. Etienne-Jules Marey, a French physiologist and photographer of distinct animal movements, "called his 1882 camera a 'fusil cinématographique,' because of its gun-like apparatus, which made twelve rapid exposures on a circular glass plate that revolved like a bullet cylinder" (Shohat and Stam 1994, 132).

5. According to Schleier (2008), both Kong and the skyscraper "were dual ciphers of the Depression era's heroic and exploited multiethnic construction workers" (29). For a very thorough discussion of the role of the skyscraper in *Kong* and Hollywood during the Depression see Schleier 2008. As if to mark its currency as a beacon of Modernity, the owners of the Empire State Building have announced that it is "going green," spending $20 million to replace 6,500 windows with insulated glass and to upgrade ventilation, water, and lighting systems, cutting operating costs by $4 million a year and carbon dioxide emissions by 100,000 tons over the next fifteen years (according to CNN on 6 April 2008).

6. Erb credits initial analysis of this trope to Donna Haraway's *Primate Visions*, in which Haraway figures the camera/gun trope using the various African expeditions of Carl Akeley in the 1920s.

7. Dino De Laurentiis's 1976 version of *King Kong* also critiques images of Africa and colonialism in Cooper, primarily from an environmental point of view. And, unlike Cooper and Jackson, De Laurentiis chooses to include the return voyage from Skull Island to NYC, showing a chained Kong in the hold of an oil tanker that is evocative of the Middle Passage and the transatlantic slave trade. De Laurentiis's version of the narrative also emphasizes the development of a close relationship between Kong and Dwan (Ann in Cooper and Jackson).

8. Jackson's representation of "orcs" in his film version of J. R. R. Tolkien's *Lord of the Rings*—often sporting "dread" locks, especially in *The Two Towers*—is evocative of some images of race in Tolkien. The racial geography of Tolkien's "Middle Earth" can be read as his analogy for our earth—it is the darker-skinned, "swarthy" "Southrons" and the "Haradrim" who choose to ally with Mordor.

9. Some describing the geographical shape of the African continent in the nineteenth century likened it to a human skull. The image of a black man with a full set of dreadlocks piled on his right shoulder in the shape of the African continent is a common image in Rastafarian art and imagery.

10. The vast wall on Skull Island can also be seen as an analog for the topography of the African coastal regions, which made it hard for colonial exploitation prior to the invention of steamships. Essentially, the continent of Africa is a vast plateau, rising several hundred feet above sea level, creating many cataracts and falls on all the major, navigable rivers into the continent to block most river commerce.

11. Thomas Henry Huxley (1825–1895) was the evolutionary biologist and fierce proponent of general science education in Britain who earned the nickname "Darwin's Bulldog" defending Charles Darwin against religious attack by Bishop Wilberforce.

## REFERENCES

Achebe, Chinua. 1977. "An Image of Africa: Racism in Conrad's *Heart of Darkness.*" *Massachusetts Review* 18: 782–94.
———. 1994 [1959]. *Things Fall Apart*. New York: Anchor-Doubleday.
Bassett, Thomas J., and Philip W. Porter. 1991. "'From the Best Authorities': The Mountains of Kong in the Cartography of West Africa." *Journal of African History* 32 (3): 367–413.
Carroll, Noel. 1984. "*King Kong*: Ape and Essence." In *Planks of Reason: Essays on the Horror Film*, edited by Barry Heith Grant, 215–44. Metuchen: Scarecrow Press.

Conrad, Joseph. 1988 [1899]. *Heart of Darkness*. Edited by Robert Kimbrough. 3rd ed. Norton Critical Edition. New York: Norton.

Cooper, Merian C. 1923. "From King Solomon to Ras Tafari." *Asia* (October): 707–13+.

———, dir. and prod. 1929. *The Four Feathers*. Paramount.

———, dir. and prod. 1933. *King Kong: The Eighth Wonder of the World*. RKO.

Cooper, Merian C., Earnest B. Shoedsack, and Marguerite Harrison. 1925. *Grass: A Nation's Struggle for Life*. Paramount-Famous Players-Lasky.

De Laurentiis, Dino. 1976. Prod. *King Kong*. Paramount.

Du Chaillu, Paul B. 1969 [1861]. *Explorations and Adventures in Equatorial Africa: Accounts of the Manners and Customs of the people, and of the Chase of the Gorilla, the Crocodile, Leopard, Elephant, Hippopotamus, and Other Animals*. New York: Negro Universities Press.

Erb, Cynthia. 1998. *Tracking King Kong: A Hollywood Icon in World Culture*. Contemporary Approaches to Film and Television Series. Detroit, MI: Wayne State University Press.

Haraway, Donna. 1989. *Primate Visions: Gender, Race, and Nature in the World of Modern Science*. New York: Routledge.

Huxley, T. H. 1888. "The Struggle for Existence: A Programme." *Nineteenth Century* 23 (132): 161–80.

Jackson, Peter, dir. 2005. *King Kong*. Universal.

———, dir. 2003. *The Lord of the Rings: The Return of the King*. New Line.

———, dir. 2002. *The Lord of the Rings: The Two Towers*. New Line.

Lindqvist, Sven. 1997. *"Exterminate All the Brutes": One Man's Odyssey into the Heart of Darkness and the Origins of European Genocide*. Translated by Joan Tate. New York: New Press.

Morton, Ray. 2005. *King Kong: The History of a Movie Icon from Fay Wray to Peter Jackson*. New York: Applause Theater and Cinema.

Rony, Fatimah Tobing. 1996. *The Third Eye: Race, Cinema, and Ethnographic Spectacle*. Durham, NC: Duke University Press.

Rosen, David N. 1975. "KING KONG: Race, Sex, and Rebellion." *Jump Cut: A Review of Contemporary Cinema* 6: 8–10.

Schleier, Merrill. 2008. "The Empire State Building, Working-Class Masculinity, and *King Kong*." *Mosaic* 41 (2): 29–51.

Seelye, John. 1990. "Moby-Kong." *College Literature* 17 (1): 34–40.

Shohat, Ella, and Robert Stam. 1994. *Unthinking Eurocentrism: Multiculturalism and the Media*. Sightlines. London: Routledge.

Snead, James. 1994. *White Screens/Black Images: Hollywood from the Dark Side*. Edited by Colin MacCabe and Cornel West. New York: Routledge.

Stocking, George W., Jr. 1968. "The Dark-Skinned Savage: The Image of Primitive Man in Evolutionary Anthropology." In *Race, Culture, and Evolution: Essay in the History of Anthropology*, 110–32. New York: Free Press-Macmillan.

Suid, Lawrence. 1977. "*King Kong* and the Military." *American Classic Screen* 2 (July–August): 14–16.

Telotte, J. P. 1988. "The Movies as Monster: Seeing in *King Kong*." *Georgia Review* 42 (2): 388–98.

Tolkien, J. R. R. 1965. *The Lord of the Rings: The Return of the King*. New York: Ballantine.

———. 1965. *The Lord of the Rings: The Two Towers*. New York: Ballantine.

Vaz, Mark Cotta. 2005. *Living Dangerously: The Adventures of Merian C. Cooper, Creator of King Kong*. Introduction by Peter Jackson. New York: Villard.

# NINE

# Plus Ça Change, Plus C'est la Même Chose

## Hollywood's Constructions of Africa in *Lord of War*

EARL CONTEH-MORGAN

In the world in general, and as one moves from one culture to another, mutual cultural stereotyping abounds. In other words, there is often a pervasive discrepancy between one's experiences in a particular culture and the distorted representations of that culture by others in literature, art, or poetry, and especially in the ubiquitous arena of cinema. Constant repetitions (positive or negative), whether in public political speeches or popular entertainment, degenerate into unconscious internalizations so that over the decades (or centuries) little changes about the perception of a region of the world. Although some of the content in Hollywood films set in Africa has changed, there is still an undercurrent in the films that is déjà vu. It is often a rehashing of a familiar, sweeping portrait of Africa as hideous, exotic, corrupt, primitive, or uncivilized clothed in different attire.

The objectives of this chapter are: (1) to examine some of the origins of the cinematic construction of savage, primitive, or uncivilized Africa; (2) to ascertain whether this negative portrayal of Africa still continues even after Peter Davis and Daniel Riesenfeld's 1993 documentary, *In Darkest Hollywood: Cinema and Apartheid;* (3) to evaluate what changes have taken place in Hollywood's cinematic construction of Africa; and (4) to reflect on how "Africa" is constructed in one cinematic portrayal of Sierra Leone and Liberia. The chapter will focus on the following questions: Are negative portrayals of Africa in film still widespread and profound? If so, how do they compare to pre-twenty-first-century portrayals? What are the possible motivations underlying negative constructions in the twenty-first century? The chapter will in particular focus on the film *Lord of War* (2005) to examine, ascertain, and evaluate current and/or recent cinematic constructions of Africa by Hollywood.

An attempt will be made to generally underscore the subtle meanings, ideas, and intended and unintended consequences that most traditional analysts in the social sciences would gloss over when confronting an enduring issue such as Africa's place in the international system.[1] Cinematic construction includes social relations produced by the process of human engagement with the tangible world. These social relations are "instrumental," "rationally based," or socially constructed and therefore are not inherent biological drives or primordial.[2] The negative misrepresentations of Africa in film, to constructivists, are formed/created/constructed as part of the process of social interactions between racial collectivities that have produced powerful myths and stereotypes and even institutionalized cinematic misrepresentations. The cinematic construction of a culture involves conceptual lenses, which to a large extent are subjective. A collectivity of conceptual lenses on a particular issue leads to intersubjective transmissibility as others such as the young or new arrivals in the sociocultural context are indoctrinated into the cognitive structure containing the conceptual lens. According to Nicholas Onuf, we live in a "world of our making." In other words, individuals, groups, or collectivities construct their social world, their reality, often at odds with the real.[3] The outcome is intersubjective understanding and/or transmissibility reinforced by cognitive structures that shape perceptions, expectations, roles, and positions. Overall, the analysis here intersects with James Ferguson's searching question about Africa: "Do accounts that cast Africa as a land of failed states, uncontrollable violence, horrific disease, and unending poverty simply recycle old clichés of Western presence and eternal African absence—as if the earth, like the moon, had a permanently darkened half, a shadowed land fated never to receive its turn to come into the 'light' of peace and prosperity?" (2006, 10).

MISPERCEPTIONS OF AFRICA: AN OVERVIEW

The human propensity to divide people into "friends" and "aliens," in-group vs. out-group, resulted in the African being viewed by the European as the other, especially as the comical, threatening, naive, subhuman, or savage other. The reason for this is that the African was black and therefore in terms of pigmentation, different. Different as different not in a neutral or positive way, but as the out-group or antithesis to the lighter (white) skin of European pigmentation.⁴ Insofar as they (Africans) constituted the other and were viewed in ethnocentric lenses, they became related to darkness, savagery, the immoral, the incongruous, the exotic. Accordingly, they became the subject of constant Western distortions and perverseness that culminated in the inhumanity of the slave trade. The tragedy was that despite the phenomenal growth in knowledge between the seventeenth and early nineteenth centuries, the freedom to inquire and investigate, and the pervasive spirit of the Enlightenment, Europeans tended not to handle difference in a positive way. The inability to objectively handle Africa's racial and cultural attributes, or rather unwillingness to rationally evaluate new and different values, resulted in the emphasis by the European on the comically erroneous, and the propensity to think of and portray the African in caricature. Caricature in turn became so pervasive that it eventually became an integral part of industry and commerce. The extensive interplay of misperceptions, caricatures, fascinations with the exotic, or cultural ethnocentrism became so ingrained in literature, and later cinema and media, that it became increasingly difficult for many, even some of the most educated, to distinguish fact from fiction in representations of Africans.

Initially, "the African condition" was constructed on the foundation of myths crafted especially by Europeans of the eighteenth and nineteenth centuries and transmitted to succeeding generations.⁵ Public policies or institutional policies designed to achieve some measure of racial equality between blacks and whites confront a gargantuan task involving the attempt to reconstruct a more just society by deconstructing or unlearning the multitude of myths and stereotypes internalized by many, including Africans themselves, regarding skin color and supposed inherent inferiority or superiority. Ideas, myths, and stereotypes regarding black inferiority/white superiority have over the centuries sunk so deep into the Western psyche that even with the mountain of scientific evidence underscoring the genetic equality of the human race, the tacit acceptance of black inferiority still reigns supreme in the minds of many.

During the eighteenth and nineteenth centuries, both European intellectuals and explorers articulated myths and stereotypes of African inferiority and savagery in the most denigrating language. For example, the Scottish philosopher David Hume (1711–1776) in his *Essay and Treatises* (1768) wrote:

> I am apt to suspect the Negroes . . . to be naturally inferior to the white. There never was a civilized nation of any other complexion

than white, nor even any individual eminent either in action or speculation. No ingenious manufacturers among them, no arts, no sciences.

Such articulation no doubt contributed not only to perpetuating the stereotypical image of Africa but was also a manifestation of the widespread ignorance about Africa and its peoples. Moreover, it contributed greatly to all of the dehumanizing effects of the Atlantic slave trade directed at the Africans. While prejudice and ignorance about Africa and Africans abounded during the Middle Ages and the Renaissance period, it did not result in their physical dehumanization. Often European art of the Renaissance period depicted the races with equal dignity.

Prejudice, fabrications, and the spread of theories of black inferiority seem to have become more vicious in the nineteenth century. In 1831, the German philosopher Georg Wilhelm Friedrich Hegel (1770–1831) described Africa as a "land lying beyond the daylight . . . , enveloped in the black color of night . . . and where men are children." In his roughly four-hundred-page book, *Philosophy of History,* he gave Africa only eight pages, and concluded the brief section on Africa thus: "At this point we leave Africa, not to mention it again. For it is no historical part of the world; it has no movement or development to exhibit." Both Hume and Hegel seem to have been influenced by intersubjective understanding and transmission of the myths and stereotypes about Africa because they never traveled to Africa, nor were they serious scholars of Africa. They became the purveyors of the major keynote of their times.

In addition to philosophers, European explorers also contributed to the spread of prejudice against Africa and Africans. Richard Burton (1821–1890), an English explorer, wrote that "the study of the Negro is the study of man's rudimentary mind." He further stated that the Negro is "a degeneracy from the civilized man . . . part of the childish races." Similarly, Samuel Baker (1821–1893), another English explorer, wrote that the nature of the Negro is "human nature viewed at its crudest state." He, the Negro, has a nature "at the level with that of the brute, and not to be compared with the noble mind of the dog."[6] Arthur de Gobineau (1818–1882) and Houston Chamberlain (1855–1927) made a distinction between "white, yellow, and black" races, underscoring the superiority of the white race. According to Gobineau, race determined the success or failure of civilizations, because races were not created equal. In the late nineteenth century, ideas like these pervaded European society. These ideas were further strengthened by racist interpretations of social Darwinism, which cast the struggle between individuals as a wider struggle between racial groups, even in the minds of new generations. Cheikh Anta Diop (1956) observed that "many of the guiding lights of Western civilization—scholars, scientists, and public officials—continued to believe in the classification of the races, with blacks occupying the lower rung and much of the terminology applied to Africa is still stereotypic."

The driving force behind the construction of African inferiority vis-à-vis other races, especially Europeans, was the Atlantic slave trade, which began in 1502 and for over three hundred years manifested organized and systematic cruelty against Africans.[7] To justify the domination, plunder, and dispossession of Africans, the Europeans created myths and denied that Africans had a history or that they contributed anything to world civilization. Thus, even before the nineteenth century when many Christian missionaries began their journeys to Africa, it was already ingrained in the minds of many of them that Africa was the continent of savages, inferior people, or individuals who are less than human.

These myths and stereotypes influenced European attitudes toward Africans, which in turn shaped the relationship between the two races. A superiority-inferiority relationship eventually developed out of the psychological power of myths and stereotypes. It is interesting to note that profound and extensive bilateral relationships did not shape the myths and stereotypes; they were developed and ingrained in the European psyche during the era of slavery and colonial rule. The unequal power relationship which manifested itself in the institutionalization of the Atlantic slave trade was legitimized in the minds of slave owners in part as a result of the impact of myths and stereotypes about Africans. Those Europeans and Americans who owned slaves generally regarded them as inferior and therefore not worthy of any meaningful employment. Myths and stereotypes could support economic agendas; blacks were portrayed in comical roles for financial gain, as well as to satisfy the demand for cheap labor. This racist cognitive structure was transmitted consciously into European and American domestic institutions such as schools, churches, governmental institutions, and the entertainment industry, among others. In the United States, even the founding fathers could not escape the impact of racist myths and stereotypes about blacks. For instance, in 1784, Thomas Jefferson in his notes on the State of Virginia wrote that "never yet could I find that a black man could utter a thought above the level of plain narration; never saw an elementary trait of painting or sculpture."[8] It is therefore not surprising that blacks in Western societies are still regarded by some as inferior, even today. The intersubjective transmission of the stereotypes and prejudice is continuous and self-perpetuating, resulting in unequal treatment, stratification, and implicit and explicit racism reflected in many Hollywood films.

During the nineteenth century and early twentieth century, Europeans targeted Africa for territorial, resource, and cultural colonization. To justify the multilevel domination of the continent, France, for example, claimed it was embarking on a *mission civilisatrice* (civilizing mission). Generally, European colonizers operated on the assumption that savage or "darkest Africa" was in need of civilization, Christianity, or the benefits of European Enlightenment. The subsequent European hegemony over Africa resulted in further transmission of distorted images about Africa to Europe, fueled especially by the captivating effect of the film industry and its global reach. Moreover, along with the scramble for land and resources went the motion picture photographer in search of the most exotic, bizarre, or sensational images of Africa to present to Europeans for their entertainment.[9] These images also created the false impression that Africans were indeed savages, brutes, or even subhumans in need of salvation. In time, the deliberate caricature of the African in film, literature, and other avenues was institutionalized as a justification for the plunder and colonial domination of Africa.

In other words, the African as the exotic, the comical, the savage, or the brute, and other categories are constructs of the world capitalist system. Global capitalism "created" the intersubjective reality and perception of African incongruity. The consequence has been the perpetuation of this grotesque image of the African in the film industry manifested in the relegation of the least-coveted roles to blacks in many Hollywood films, especially those bearing on Africa.

Film has a particularly universal reach, coupled with its vividness and appeal to the senses. As the reach and impact of film deepened, it further institutionalized the putative civilizational divide between Europe and Africa, "civilized" and "savage" respectively. As Africans became increasingly marginalized within their own continent in terms of power, wealth, and prestige, so did their portrayals in films by Hollywood further relegate them to a marginal role as the villains, the buffoons, or the savages, among other stock characters. By the mid-twentieth century the distortions and misrepresentations of Africans had become so pervasive and permeative that they were assumed standard operating procedure for Hollywood films on Africa. The question to be explored in this chapter is whether in this age of globalization, and in the early twenty-first century in particular, Hollywood films on Africa are still tainted by misrepresentation. This question will be examined via a critical analysis of the Hollywood film *Lord of War* (2005).

In the first decade of the twenty-first century, Northern cinema producers released memorable films such as *Hotel Rwanda, Lord of War, The Constant Gardener, The Last King of Scotland,* and *Blood Diamond.* These are films that focus primarily on issues affecting Africa and therefore contain scenes that portray various dimensions of the continent and its peoples. While the themes they expose are often very significant, such as the issue of child soldiers, resource wars, ethnocentric violence, and state collapse, they nonetheless convey the impression that they can only educate, publicize, or try to change attitudes about these issues by stereotyping Africans. The result is miseducation through cinematic misrepresentation, at times in the most grotesque manner.

Generally, *Lord of War,* written and directed by Andrew Niccol and starring Nicolas Cage as Yuri Orlov, has many superlatives to its credit. Reviewers applaud the film's entertainment value: it is interesting, engaging, a great performance, captivating, fantastic, and a thriller, among many others.[10] The film has also been described as a tirade directed at the arms trade, or a critical examination of the trade in weapons that not only transforms children into killers, but directly contributes to the scope and intensity of violence in war zones. In general, *Lord of War* deals with a very salient international topic—arms dealing—which merits serious discussion. It is a transnational issue linked to brutal civil wars, child soldiers, and the competition for "Third World" resources.[11] In many ways, it is an excellent film because it underscores the trafficking of weapons by the international arms industry. The arms-dealing activity of the Ukrainian American, Yuri Orlov, is a microcosm of how Africa is ever being infiltrated by the North, either in the form of eighteenth- and nineteenth-century slave trading, nineteenth- and twentieth-century colonial rule, or the proxy wars of Northern superpowers. However, one is forced to wonder why most of the negative scenes, caricatures, and exaggerations in the film are relegated to Africa and African characters. It seems as if whenever someone from the Northern nations has something serious to say about the global arms trade, it is generally said in regards to a selective negative perception of Africa.

Granted, we cannot expect art to present history, and it is widely understood that feature filmmakers have poetic license to distort the evidence. Yet the long history of Hollywood's caricature of Africans has led to a gross miseducation of the Western audience about even the most basic facts about Africa. For example, Africa, the second largest continent, is often referred to as a single country pervaded by war, disease, corruption, and starvation, among other things. Even significant anchor states like Nigeria, Kenya, Ethiopia, and South Africa are often not referred to by their sovereign names but simply as Africa. Orlov is in many ways a symbol of the attitude of many to Africa's problems. In this sense, Lord of War is a profound film. Like Orlov, many in the North display a savvy and cunning attitude toward Africa, and capitalize on the plight of its weak and troubled nations. The severe poverty and resource wars in Africa are often the target of, or enablers of, individuals or groups out to capitalize on them for profit. At the end of the film, Yuri Orlov is arrested and interrogated by officials who are supposed to stop illegal arms dealing with poor disadvantaged countries. It is a distortion to include in the film the relentless pursuit of Orlov by a federal agent portrayed as very determined to stop illegal arms dealing. This segment of the film portrays the official channels of leading nations in a very positive light while at the same time stereotyping African leadership and the African characters. Orlov is released, however, and straightaway resumes arms dealing. His release is significant because it means that the arms trade, whether by nations or individuals, can never be pronounced illegal because the very nations who profit the most from the trade are leading nations. In other words, the hegemonic nations and the warlords in countries undergoing civil wars have a vested interest in arms dealing. They are, as Orlov states, "vile, sadistic men calling themselves leaders," who encourage the trade in arms that prolongs civil wars. Most likely because of its compelling indictment of the international arms trade, Amnesty International recommends Lord of War as an educational tool and has supplied a teacher's guide to the film.[12]

What is missing from such an educational approach to the film is a critical look at cognitive structures and a conceptual lens implied in: (1) representations and/or misrepresentations of Africa or African characters in the film; (2) Yuri Orlov's attitude toward Africa and Africans in the film; and (3) the casual reference to the idea that the film is based on facts, when in fact it engages in distortions and decontextualizations, especially in relation to African figures in the film. There is no doubt that Liberia and Sierra

Leone experienced serious civil conflict between the early 1990s and the early 2000s. The documentary aspect of the film ignores the international political context of war in the subregion that would explain the demand for weapons in the region. Violence in the region was closely tied to (1) superpower retrenchment at the end of the Cold War; (2) the negative impact of the sudden and adverse effects of an imposed new world order of neoliberal internationalism, which resulted in state failure in Liberia and Sierra Leone; and (3) the instability that results from externally imposed artificial states where geography and cultural and political affiliations do not coincide. Orlov's statements, which sound often like those of a narrator in a documentary, do not bring out these facts. In other words, like most popular Hollywood films about Africa, it engages in sociocultural decontextualization. As a result, the impression is created in the film that "Africa" has always been a barbaric, perennial war zone prone to bloodletting. "Africa" is the site that is held up as the quintessential example of extreme violence. One is therefore tempted to ask, why didn't the film include scenes of violence in the former Yugoslavia, Chechnya, Iraq, or Sri Lanka, among others? Perhaps the answer to that would be that the past still informs the present in Hollywood when it comes to Africa. Africa, even in 2005, is still relegated to the role of the barbaric, uncivilized, or "dark continent" because of ingrained perceptions. Whether the repetition of these perceptions is motivated by the need to maximize profits through popular narrative formulas or to sway the emotions of viewers toward a human rights agenda, it comes at the expense of Africans.

Where Africa is concerned, Hollywood often presents scenes as if they are complete in themselves, ignoring the antecedents or entire political/historical contexts. Wars seem to emanate spontaneously from the ambitions of sinister antagonists, such as the fictional President Andre Baptiste Jr. (arguably modeled on Charles Taylor, Liberian warlord and later president), who is shown to be so psychologically unstable that he shoots an inattentive aide on impulse.[13] In interactions between Orlov and President Baptiste, the latter is portrayed as a barely literate, psychotic killer with an equally psychotic son. He is also portrayed as uncouth, uneducated, and speaking ungrammatical English. If the allusion is to Charles Taylor, then in real life, American-educated Charles Taylor is far more informed and articulate than what is portrayed in the film. Often such distortions by Hollywood of "African" characters, violence, savagery, and the like are a continuation of the centuries-old stereotypes, myths, and lies about Africa, often for comical effect or to magnify the horrific. The sensational and grotesque, the exaggerated presentation, is lucrative for ratings and profits. Such mercenary, Machiavellian, profit-oriented actions are taken for granted and acceptable in Hollywood's mind-set. The subtle and not so subtle representations of African leaders abound in Hollywood films on Africa, and *Lord of War* is no exception. For instance, it is interesting that the title of the film is connected to the character Andre Baptiste's description of himself as a "lord of war," a preference over Orlov's term "warlord." One plausible explanation is that Baptiste is repeatedly presented (assumed to typify African leaders generally) as a manipulative megalomaniac. Thus, he prefers "lord of war" because it implies more importance than a mere warlord among many others in Africa's civil wars. The title appeals more to his egocentric disposition. Baptiste is also portrayed as incapable of discerning the difference between "lord of war" and warlord. Even if it is Orlov, the unscrupulous arms dealer, who symbolizes the ultimate lord of war, the film implies that African leaders in general are not just dictatorial and power hungry, but are inherently warlike, mentally unbalanced, or "savage" in comparison with other leaders in other regions of the world. Such negative depictions, although glaringly exaggerated for comical or dramatic effect, tend to undermine the central message of *Lord of War,* which is the fact that arms transfers fuel wars and contribute to the deaths and maiming of many thousands of humans worldwide.

The civil conflicts of Liberia and Sierra Leone were indeed brutal and involved heinous acts by the warring factions. Nevertheless, one would be correct to argue that civil wars everywhere are brutal. What Hollywood does is to engage in selective treatment of Africa because the continent and its people are viewed with an ethnocentric lens. In sum, while *Lord of War* can be described as a dramatic satire against the arms trade, it at the same time achieves its thriller effect by demonizing the African segment of the entire exposé. The film constructs and imposes a distorted cognitive structure and conceptual lens of Africa on the screen: viewers see unseemly, unethical practices of arms traders internationally but also are led to the conclusion that selling weapons to African leaders—the ultimate villains—is especially horrible. The result is hyperbole presented as fact. In this regard, the observations of Lemuel Johnson about conceptions of black people still apply to Africans today, at least with regards to films such as *Lord of War:* "The Negro, insofar as he was black and physically different, became an incarnation of the incongruous and the antithetical. He was seen as an apt metaphor for esthetic and ethical caricature. Insofar as he was black, he was a metaphor for darkness and for the unholy" (1971, 19).

Although *Lord of War* is full of many distortions and exaggerations, it nonetheless contains significant positive educational content related to arms trafficking and its negative ramifications of civil wars, and the problem of child soldiers. Accordingly, the film begins with an emphasis on the scope of arms trafficking, as when Yuri Orlov in the opening scene says: "There are over 550 million firearms in world circulation. That's one firearm for every 12 people on the planet. The only question is: How do you arm the other eleven?" The problem of arms transfers or trafficking is one of the most insidious and tragic dilemmas of the international system because it is not only heavily endorsed by the great powers, but it is also very profitable to them. The countries that benefit the most from the sale of small arms to developing countries are the United States, Russia, France, Britain, and China in that order. Light (small) arms are especially in great demand because of the perennial interethnic and/or identity problems that plague the "Third World." Therefore, despite its many exaggerations, *Lord of War* succeeds in educating viewers about the profit-oriented politics of arms trafficking that enable so many human rights violations. The dramatic and sensational in film manage to galvanize the attention of the international community against arms trafficking. Internet news articles on Viktor Bout, the Russian arms dealer who is thought to have inspired the main character, Orlov, connect the arms dealer with the imagination of a popular reading public through references to *Lord of War*. There was a collective sigh of relief that this key, if not the most important, arms trafficker was captured in Thailand in March 2008. The film also educates about the perennial problems of arms trafficking by pointing out the dilemmas of the arms dealers themselves summarized in the rationale that someone else will sell weapons to warring factions even if they stop doing so. Another problem underscored in the film is the personal involvement and even vested economic interest of dealers in the outcome of a war. For example, in *Lord of War*, Simeon tells Yuri that he sold weapons to both sides in the Iran-Iraq War. He wanted the war to have no end, meaning that no side should be allowed to win so that he could continue to profit. To a very large extent, the film, despite some serious misrepresentations, definitely succeeds in its grasp of the "reality" of the small arms trade and its disastrous effect of fueling governmental oppression.

## *LORD OF WAR*: AN EVALUATION

To the portrayal of the African as the savage, the buffoon, or the subhuman has now been added the psychotic warlord and the sinister arms buyer, among other stereotypes. In other words, Hollywood's films about Africa and the African have been characterized by deliberate concoction of fact and fiction with an overall inclination toward accentuation of the exotic, the bizarre, the comical, or the horrific. If the reason is for commercial profit, then such a deliberate choice has taken on the presentation of grotesque fictionalized material on Africa as part of an exposé of the "truth," or nonfiction. Even in films with a serious political content, the richness and subtleties of African culture or the centrality of the political economic issues became obscured. Ward Churchill's observations of Euro-Americans and American Indians in North America are quite relevant regarding Hollywood's portrayal of Africans in films. According to Churchill:

> The cinematic depiction of indigenous peoples in America is objectively racist at all levels. . . . In this, film is linked closely to literature of both the fictional and ostensibly nonfictional varieties, upon which most scripts are based. It is thus both fair and accurate to observe that all modes of projecting images and attendant conceptualizations of native people to the "mainstream" public fit the same mold. Moreover, it is readily observable that within the confines of this mold are included only the narrowest and most negative range of graphic / thematic possibilities. (1998, 167)

The results are distortions, reductionisms, and exaggerations driven by Hollywood's unwillingness to handle difference and complexity in a socially conscious way, or at its worst, a penchant to exploit Africa for entertainment and profit by accentuating the sensational. Hollywood presents many scenes devoid of context, leading to pretext. Pretext in turn degenerates into caricatures of the Africans as fools, psychopaths, or extremely violent devils, among many other things. There is little focus on the individuality of ordinary people who are affected by resource wars or arms dealing. And there are virtually no narratives about Africans in peaceful states who lead ordinary, fulfilling lives. Their daily routines, family lives, and life-affirming cultural practices are largely ignored.

The outcome is that Hollywood reconstructs African realities (norms, issues, actors, etc.) to fit its own preconceived ideas. Finally, Hollywood is still far from producing a film based on the life of the Africans long before Europeans arrived and along the lines of *Helen of Troy, Cleopatra, Julius Caesar,* and other Western epics. Hollywood could, for instance, produce films depicting the great civilization of Ancient Zimbabwe based on the ruins found in that country, the wonderful art of Ife in West Africa, the Akan kings of present-day Ghana, or the great emperors of the Western Sudan, among many other potential subjects. All these are well documented in African history. With the exception of Nelson Mandela, the African leader is hardly portrayed as courageous, wise, good, or accomplished, as in many Western epics about Western leaders. Where Africa is concerned, Hollywood engages in selective perception and largely underscores the negatives. The blending of half-truths in an overly exaggerated manner or the deliberate distortion of truth for melodramatic effect ends up as mythology. In the final analysis, Hollywood films about Africa, even in the early twenty-first century, could still be described as *plus ça change, plus c'est la même chose.*

## NOTES

1. See, for example, positivist social science as reflected in neorealist and neoliberal analysis. Specific examples are Waltz 1979 and Keohane 1984.

2. For differing perspectives on ethnoracial relations, see Bates 1983.

3. For further details, see Durkheim 1938 and Ruggie 1998.

4. For details, see Johnson 1971.

5. See, for example, Harris 1998 and Curtin 2004.

6. See Killingray 1997 and Obichere 1977, 15.

7. For details, see Davidson 1984.

8. See Thomas Jefferson's Notes on the State of Virginia written in 1781: http://www.pbs.org/wgbh/aia/part3/3h490t.html.

9. See Davis 1996.

10. See, for example, the many reviews on *Lord of War*, such as in the *New Yorker* at www.newyorker.com/critics/cinema/articles/050926crci_cinema; or http://www.bbc.co.uk/films/2005/10/03/lord_of_war_2005_review.shtml.

11. On the impact of arms transfers see Henrikson 2007.

12. See http://www.amnestyusa.org/pdfs/lordofwar_edguide.pdf.

13. For details on Charles Taylor and the Liberian conflict, see "Liberia's Uneasy Peace: A Profile of Charles Taylor," on the website of *The NewsHour with Jim Lehrer.* www.pbs.org/newshour/bb/africa/liberia/taylor-bio.html.

## REFERENCES

Bates, Robert. 1983. "Modernization, Ethnic Competition and the Rationality of Politics in Contemporary Africa," In *State vs. Ethnic Claims: African Policy Dilemmas,* edited by Donald Rothchild and Victor A. Olorunsola. Boulder, CO: Westview.

Chamberlain, Houston. 1912. *The Foundations of the Nineteenth Century.* 2nd ed. London: Published by John Lane, The Bodley Head.

Churchill, Ward. 1998. *Fantasies of the Master Race: Literature, Cinema, and the Colonization of American Indians.* San Francisco: City Lights Books.

Curtin, Philip. 2004. *The Images of Africa: British Ideas and Action, 1780–1850.* Madison: University of Wisconsin Press.

Davidson, Basil. 1984. *The Search for Africa: History, Culture, Politics.* New York: Random House.

Davis, Peter. 1996. *In Darkest Hollywood: Exploring the Jungles of Cinema's South Africa.* Athens: Ohio University Press.

Diop, Cheikh Anta. 1956. "The Cultural Contributions and Prospects of Africa." Proceedings of the International Conference of Negro Writers and Artists, *Présence Africaine,* Special Issue, June–November: 347–54.

Durkheim, Emile. 1938. *The Rules of Sociological Method.* Translated by E. G. Catlin. New York: Free Press.

Ferguson, James. 2006. *Global Shadows: Africa in the Neoliberal World Order.* Durham, NC: Duke University Press.

Gobineau, Arthur, Count. 1913. *The Renaissance.* Translated by Paul V. Cohn. London: Heinemann.

Harris, Joseph E. 1998. *Africans and Their History.* New York: Penguin.

Hegel, G. W. F. 1990. *The Philosophy of History.* Translated William Carew Hazlitt. Whitefish, MT: Kessinger Publishing.

Henrikson, Emma. Sept. 2007. "Corruption in the Arms Trade—Undermining African Democracy." International Peace Bureau, Geneva, Switzerland.

Hume, David. 1854. "Of National Characters." In *The Philosophical Works of David Hume.* Boston: Little, Brown.

Johnson, Lemuel A. 1971. *The Devil, The Gargoyle, and the Buffoon: The Negro as Metaphor in Western Literature.* Port Washington, NY: Kennikat Press.

Keohane, Robert O. 1984. *After Hegemony: Cooperation and Discord in the World Political Economy.* Princeton: Princeton University Press.

Killingray, David. 1997. *A Plague of Europeans: Westerners in Africa since the Fifteenth Century.* Baltimore: Penguin Books.

Obichere, Boniface I. 1977. "African Critics of Victorian Imperialism: An Analysis." *Journal of African Studies* 4 (15): 1–20.

Onuf, Nicholas G. 1989. *World of Our Making: Rules and Rule in Social Theory and International Relations.* Columbia: University of South Carolina Press.

Ruggie, John. 1998. *Constructing the World Polity: Essays on International Institutionalization.* New York: Routledge.

Waltz, Kenneth. 1979. *Theory of International Politics.* Reading, MA: Addison-Wesley.

# TEN

# New Jack African Cinema

*Dangerous Ground; Cry, the Beloved Country;* and *Blood Diamond*

BENNETTA JULES-ROSETTE, J.R. OSBORN, AND LEA MARIE RUIZ-ADE

It is a truism that actions speak louder than words. In the case of film, action cinema has the power to override dialogue and deconstruct plot structure through the shock value of violence, explosion, and conflict. The violence itself becomes an anthropometric narrative actor as well as an agent of change. In this context, New Jack African cinema treats Africa at once as a liminal space, a purgatory from which to escape, and a potential utopia. This genre, which has its roots in Hollywood action films and Hong Kong martial arts cinema, uses the agency of explosive violence to mask genuine African social problems. It has one foot in Hollywood and the other on the African continent, melding a variety of Hollywood cinematic devices with a cinema of resistance. Although conventional plot structures such as quest, vengeance, and coming of age are incorporated into New Jack African cinema, peak events involving violence overshadow all other narrative concerns and devices.

New Jack films trace their origin to Mario Van Peebles's 1991 film *New Jack City,* starring Wesley Snipes and rapper Ice-T. As spin-offs of the blaxploitation genre of the 1970s and Hollywood action films of the 1980s, these films are closely related to the larger genre of 'hood films.[1] Manthia Diawara states that 'hood films, exemplified by John Singleton's 1991 *Boyz N the Hood* and other commodities related to the global spread of hip-hop culture, "are an expression of poor people's desire for the good life" (1998, 238). Drugs, crime, and male-oriented popular culture are centerpieces of these films, in which hip-hop and rap stars emerge as cinematic heroes. Paul Smith points out that pulp genres, such as spaghetti westerns and New Jack action films, are mutable (1993, 20). New filmic genres often disguise older ones by making referential allusions to the past or remaking new films in vastly different settings that evoke the superficial appearance of new genre types.[2] Thus, Boer trek films in the colonialist South African genre discussed by Peter Davis operate as disguised westerns (1996, 128–30). Similarly, Ice Cube transports the American New Jack genre to Africa in *Dangerous Ground* (1997).[3]

Although New Jack African films partake of this genre mutability, they are characterized by certain basic operating principles: (1) New Jack African films displace the locus of crime and destruction from the US inner city to African urban and rural sites. (2) Within these sites, the films manipulate time and space to create internal moments of actualization, reconstruction, and reconciliation. Bar scenes are often deployed in this manner. (3) Traditional African communities are presented as twilight zones within idyllic fantasies and are often iconized through the figure of the African mother. Even the shooting styles, focus, and lighting of village scenes, along with the B-roll intercuts, may be muted in order to convey the impression of a vague and waning traditional community. (4) Conventional social interactions across genders and generations are also muted and manipulated in order to open up new pathways for their transformation. (5) Peak events center on conflict, explosion, and mass destruction so that the possibility of an alternative reality may be introduced to resolve the conflict. (6) After the explosion, this alternative reality may never actually be attained. It remains virtual, but it is alluded to through Hollywood-style cinematic suture devices that allow the antihero to save the day, often through death or extreme sacrifice.[4]

While there are genuine heroes and villains in New Jack films, their identities are flawed, reworked, and transformed through violent peak narrative events. Within these narrative and genre conventions, New Jack films deploy truncated and ironic dialogue, which contributes to the pulp-like quality of the scenario and reinforces the anachronisms and interpersonal conflicts highlighted by the manipulation of time and space. Truncated dialogue may also make characters appear one-dimensional as they navigate the fault lines of New Jack cinematic deconstruction and destruction. However, these one-dimensional characters are actually multilayered, thereby concealing the depth of their cinematic complexity and the essential relationships of their composite identities to the narratively driven filmic explosions. This process of occultation resembles strategies used in popular African painting and music to conceal subversive political messages.[5]

New Jack African cinema deals not only with the destruction of community but also with its restitution.[6] A narrative problem arises, however, because the communities to which order might ultimately be restored exist only in a twilight zone of evanescent stereotypes. The "traditional" African village, which is threatened and eventually comes under fire, is juxtaposed to already exploding urban spaces that are the loci of crime, violence, and disorder, but also the objects of dreams of extraordinary wealth and success. The narrative complexity of the New Jack genre combines multiple subjects and story lines, each vying for a distinct resolution. The resulting tension produces a situation in which the various narrative strands become strained, and they must be snapped or exploded in order to reach resolution.

Elements of colonial film are also retained in New Jack African cinema, in particular with regard to the landscaping of lost and idyllic utopias.[7] In *Dangerous Ground* (1997) and the comic film *Yankee Zulu* (1993), Sun City, with its casinos and easy wealth, is depicted as an El Dorado. In *Blood Diamond* (2006), the remote diamond fields of Sierra Leone are the source of wealth. But these utopian spaces, which are the fabric of cinematic dreams, are not venues in which wealth may be spent. They contain objects of desire that promise to transform actual communities, such as traditional villages and burgeoning cities, into utopias. This model of cinematic desire contrasts with the themes of African auteur films (for example, works by Sembène, Rouch, and Mambety), in which El Dorado is fictively located in Europe.

New Jack African cinema operates as a mutable genre mediating across African auteur films and Hollywood cinema. This mediation results in a post-colonial filmic export that introduces controversial images of Africa to an international viewing public. Examples of the New Jack African paradigm will be used to delineate the structure, social context, and appeal of these films in relation to conventional Hollywood genres. The objective here is not to salvage Hollywood cinema, but rather to illustrate the ways in which its narratives change through interaction with other narrative formats and, in turn, generate a syncretic genre that introduces new filmic discourses. Whether the shelf life of African New Jack films coincides with that of hip-hop genres, pronounced by certain pundits to be culturally dead as of 2007, is an open question (Sanneh 2007).

IN AND OUT OF HOLLYWOOD: MUTABLE GENRES AND NEW JACK CINEMA

Much has been written about colonial cinema in Africa. The perpetuation of stereotypes and the reaffirmation of rigid social boundaries are the hall-marks of colonial cinema. This approach is also reflected in neocolonial cinema, which thinly veils the stereotypes and continues to reinforce social, economic, and racial barriers. Neocolonial cinema may contain pertinent information and salutary messages. Films such as Sydney Pollack's *Out of Africa* (1985) and Zoltan Korda and Alan Paton's *Cry, the Beloved Country* (1951) are docudramas describing the limitations of restrictive colonialist settings as seen through the eyes of reluctant reformers. These films rely on aesthetic conventions and plot structures characteristic of Hollywood cinema, and they deploy a Western commercial film language.[8]

Teshome H. Gabriel considers "point of view" to be a distinguishing feature of revolutionary, third world, and African cinema in which the spectator is exhorted to political action (1979, 7). This type of cinematic process is not characteristic of the colonial genre, which seeks to maintain a social and political status quo. More than stereotypes and plot structure are involved. If we contrast Korda and Paton's 1951 version of *Cry, the Beloved Country* with Darrell Roodt's 1995 film by the same name, it becomes clear that cinematic adaptations of the novel with identical characters and plot structure convey very different messages in relation to the period and social context of their release. In both films, as in the novel, Reverend Stephen Kumalo departs in search of his wayward son Absalom, who has become involved in a life of crime in Johannesburg. Absalom's participation in the murder of Arthur Trevelyan Jarvis leads to a litany of tragedy and redemption on the parts of both Reverend Kumalo and Arthur's father, plantation owner James Jarvis. In the 1951 version, Stephen Kumalo, played by Canada Lee, is portrayed as a naive and passive seeker who stumbles upon the world of crime in which his son is implicated. However, in the 1995 version, Reverend Kumalo, portrayed by James Earl Jones, becomes a prophetic religious figure whose source of strength issues from his solitary meditations on a mountaintop.

James Jarvis's redemption may be interpreted as a forecast of the crumbling of apartheid in the 1951 version of the film, but it becomes a strong metaphor for "truth and reconciliation" in Darrell Roodt's 1995 version. Roodt is a cosmopolitan director and producer whose other credits include *Sarafina* (1992), *Dangerous Ground* (1997), *Blood Diamond* (2006), and *Winnie* (2012). In these films, Roodt applies Hollywood-style musical and docudrama approaches to the social and political issues of apartheid and the African diamond trade. His vantage point of working across South Africa, Europe, and Hollywood gives him a unique perspective, and his postapartheid adaptation of *Cry, the Beloved Country* offers a precursor to his later New Jack–styled films. In describing the 1995 adaptation of Alan Paton's novel, Roodt states:

I was able to approach the film with massive hindsight, to look back and shake my head. . . . It is the pain of remembrance with which I have imbued the picture. . . . We are trying to understand the past, and for me, the new direction of films in South Africa will be about retelling history. (Beittel 2003, 82)

Based on the social context of the film, and the reinterpretation of the plot in 1995, Stephen Kumalo emerges as a silent revolutionary rather than a passive victim. Sidney Poitier's portrayal of the priest Theophilus Msimangu overshadows Stephen Kumalo in the first film. Activism is represented by Stephen's brother John, who works as a laborer in Johannesburg, where he has also become a local antiapartheid leader. While John is depicted as insincere and conniving in both films, his role is more nuanced in the second version, in which Stephen emerges as a political victor and survivor in the style of Nelson Mandela. In 1995, Theophilus is played by Vusi Kunene, a South African actor, whose portrayal is more sage and passive than that of Poitier. Davis states that although Poitier's character appears passive, his demeanor and posturing are aggressive.

> Just as there may be a distortion of memory about exactly what Poitier did, films can carry messages that even contradict what is being said or done. Here was a black man whose body language carried lessons not intended by the film-makers, possibly not even recognised by them, and the implications of which Poitier himself may not have realised. Poitier's movements, his behaviour, his demeanour, said, "Here is a black man who as a hero is the equal of any white man you have hitherto seen." (1996, 43)

This comparison suggests that shifts in filmic genres are not driven exclusively by plot structure. They also depend on the subtleties of character portrayal and the historical contextualization of the film (Beittel 2003, 72). In the closing sequence, or the fifteenth day scene, Stephen Kumalo climbs to a mountaintop to pray for peace and reconciliation on the day of his son's execution. On the way up, he encounters Jarvis on horseback. At first glance, Jarvis conducts a conversation with Kumalo from this superior position, indicating his status as a white South African landowner. Mark Beittel criticizes Roodt's 1995 retelling of the history of apartheid at the final meeting between Kumalo and Jarvis based on the signifier of the horse and the use of camera angles (2003, 85–87). However, the power of Jarvis's transformation and the potential future of South Africa after Absalom's climactic death are apparent in this scene. The camera focuses on Jarvis in mid to long shots on his horse four times in the conversation sequence, which also includes fourteen shot-reverse shot intercuts with Jarvis and Kumalo at eye level, or nearly so. Cinematically, these eye-level close-ups represent the potential for emerging equality and respect between the two men after the explosive deaths of their sons.

> Shot 1: *Jarvis on horseback. Mid-range.*
> JARVIS: For I knew that you would go up to the mountain on the fifteenth day.
> *Series of intercuts between Jarvis and Kumalo, ending with Jarvis from his horse.*
> JARVIS: I have here a letter for the people of your church. The letter asks if you desire a new church. . . .
> *Series of intercut close-ups between Jarvis and Kumalo as dialogue continues.*
> JARVIS: You will know what to do. Perhaps there could be a stone with the name of my son who had the brightness in him.
> *Cut to close-up of Kumalo.*
> KUMALO: It shall be done, umnumzana.
> JARVIS: Go well, umfundizi.
> *Closing of dialogue sequence and fourth shot of Jarvis on the horse as he leaves the frame.*

After the meeting, Stephen continues up the mountain, and the emotional tone of the final sequence sets up a juxtaposition between conflict and quiescence more fully developed in Roodt's New Jack films. The rapid pace of the intercuts and parallel editing linking Absalom's death, his wife's labor pains, and Stephen's prayer implodes the space of the three events. In a culminating moment of violence (Absalom's death), the idyllic home of the traditional community, which is shot in soft focus, gives birth to the hope of a new South Africa.

Darrell Roodt directed the 1995 version of *Cry, the Beloved Country* just two years before he released *Dangerous Ground* (1997). The plot structure of *Dangerous Ground* bears a striking resemblance to *Cry, the Beloved Country*. In both films, an errant son has become involved with criminal activity in

Johannesburg and is sought out by his family. Vusi, the film's hero played by Ice Cube (O'Shea Jackson), is both a father figure and an older brother. His return from the United States for his father's funeral establishes the parallel between Vusi and the farmer James Jarvis as cultural outsiders to the South African black community. Karen, portrayed by Elizabeth Hurley, the girlfriend of Vusi's lost brother Stephen, replaces Absalom's wife. But unlike both versions of *Cry,* in which racial stereotypes remain fixed within the model of apartheid, *Dangerous Ground* unfolds within a "new South Africa" in which the oppression of apartheid is replaced by multiracial crime.

As a New Jack film, *Dangerous Ground* explodes stereotypes and addresses political conflicts with subtle inversion and humor. This challenging of stereotypes creates "a liberated space" in which film can explore new social forms and narrative structures (Gabriel 1979, 7).[9] Quest narratives, such as those involving the search for a hidden treasure, take place within a closed universe in which a subject and an antisubject may vie for the same valued object. A. J. Greimas explains: "This treasure is often kept and sometimes given by a supernatural being who does not belong to the society of the subject of the quest. Be he keeper or giver of the treasure, this character plays the role of mediator between the universe of transcendent values and the immanent universe into which the new values are introduced into circulation" (1987, 93). Several solutions are possible in this type of narrative. In one instance, the subject, or group of subjects, may in fact obtain and retain the valued treasure. The simplest form of this resolution is represented by colonial films such as *King Solomon's Mines,* in which the hidden treasure is not conceived of as belonging to the indigenous population but instead to the mythical figure of King Solomon. This narrative construction allows colonial adventurers to appropriate the treasure without guilt or social conflict. Another version of this narrative simply removes the hidden treasure, if conflict arises, by demonstrating that the treasure was truly mythical, never existed, or has been destroyed.

In New Jack films, however, the multiple subjects and antisubjects compete for the same valued object, for example diamonds. No subject is endowed with moral superiority in the quest, and the proliferation of subjects complicates and overextends the narrative to the point of rupture. Once again, a viable solution to this narrative problem would be the destruction or removal of the treasure itself. More generally, narrative resolution is achieved through an explosion in which the valued object may remain intact for whoever is left standing after the dust settles. The subject who eventually acquires the treasure does so through a morally questionable show of force rather than moral superiority. As a result, the value of the treasure may be transformed. According to Greimas, the objects of value become "polarized" in microuniverses in which the narrative inverts their perceived values (1987, 93–94). The positive value of the treasure (that is, money for diamonds) is thus inverted into a negative value (that is, blood for diamonds). This inversion of values distinguishes New Jack cinema from colonial narratives, traditional Hollywood images of Africa, and African auteur films.

In colonial films, adventurers claim and extract the treasure from an indigenous landscape in which its value is unrecognized. In African auteur films, such as Djibril Diop Mambety's *Touki Bouki* (1973), the object of value shifts from a hidden African location to a foreign European landscape, and the object recedes from the African subjects seeking to acquire it. Although the subjects and meaning of the quest differ across these two forms, the narrative structure remains in place. If the treasure is ultimately lost, this loss is explained by the transgression against a moral taboo.

Camera techniques reinforce these narrative structures. Hollywood constructs action sequences in such a way that they unfold around multiple cameras. Audiences enter the world of the film rather than watch it from afar. This approach differs considerably from the narrative structure of conventional colonial cinema, where stories play out on African soil. Africa provides the setting and backdrop for a foreign story, and the camera views African scenes from a distance (Rouch 2003, 56). Auteur filmmaker Jean Rouch used innovative camera movements to modify the conception of colonial subjects and stories.[10] Rouch positioned his camera within the center of the action and opened new avenues for ethnographic and filmic representation of African ritual, modernity, and change.[11] In New Jack films such as *Dangerous Ground* and *Blood Diamond,* the landscape and tensions of Africa swirl around the camera. The viewer is transported to the center of unresolved African dilemmas, in which social tension, colonialism, crime, and violence have lasting legacies and chaotic consequences for characters and locales. These issues remain open filmic and narrative questions, unanswered by the organizing gaze of colonial administrators or the best intentions of multinational NGOs.

Both Teshome H. Gabriel (1979, 7) and Peter Davis (1996, 2) compare the eye of the camera to the barrel of a gun, suggesting the political use of film as a weapon for African liberation. But the camera may also open on a field of dialogue and shared dreams, as Rouch so fervently argued.[12] Via a rain of bullets and explosions, New Jack African cinema bridges the cultural and geographic divide separating Los Angeles from Johannesburg. The action genre inserts audiences within an African landscape where the all-too-familiar tale of destroying a criminal menace replaces the grand colonial quest for wealth and power. Audiences encounter a story unfolding within and across Africa rather than a morality play about Africa. Instead of becoming a gun, the camera focuses on the gun. As buildings and characters explode on screen, stereotypes implode. New Jack African cinema utilizes a Hollywood exaggeration of action and violence, but it redirects and refocuses these tropes through a display of Africanized wealth, the cosmopolitan negotiation of African identities, and the flow of global capital in and out of Africa.[13] Channeled through a cinematic lens, the perils and possibilities of Africa are exposed.

THE "DANGEROUS GROUND" OF NEW JACK AFRICAN CINEMA

Darrell Roodt's *Dangerous Ground* (1997), which was produced by Anant Singh, superimposes a plot reminiscent of Mario Van Peebles's *New Jack City* (1991) on the landscape of a "new South Africa." Both films revolve around the violent takedown of a drug ringleader as a means of social redemption. But in the African adaptation, the streetwise police officers have been replaced by Vusi Madlazi (Ice Cube), a South African student who returns from California for his father's funeral, and his brother Ernest (Sechaba Morojele), an ex-freedom fighter and antiapartheid activist. Following the funeral, Vusi heads off in search of his errant brother Stephen (Eric Miyeni) and eventually confronts the crime lord Muki (Ving Rhames) in order to free his brother of an outstanding debt. Throughout the film, reference is made in dialogue and visually to the "new South Africa." Both black-on-black crime and interracial violence are addressed as Vusi weaves his way through this labyrinth. The contested meaning of multiculturalism in the reconstructed South African state is problematic, and its scaffolding is fragile. The oft-repeated phrase "Welcome to the new South Africa" simultaneously identifies, effaces, and purifies all that accompanies the postapartheid transition: violence, crime, drugs, prostitution, and global capital. As Ice Cube explores this imaginary homeland, he demonstrates that some of the closest multicultural bonds may be found in an underworld of crime and violence that mutes economic and ethnic differences.

Interestingly, both the leading protagonist and villain in this film are portrayed by African Americans. The casting of African Americans as Africans has a long history, which may be traced to the arrival of minstrelsy in South Africa in the 1880s and the roles played by early African American performers, such as Josephine Baker in her 1935 film *Princesse Tam-Tam* and Paul Robeson in the 1937 version of *King Solomon's Mines* (Jules-Rosette 2007, 92–94; Davis 1996, 16; Lipsitz 1994, 43). More recently, African American performers including Sidney Poitier, Canada Lee, James Earl Jones, Danny Glover, Whoopi Goldberg, Denzel Washington, Derek Luke, Dennis Haysbert, Terrence Howard, and Jennifer Hudson have played the roles of South African blacks, including Nelson and Winnie Mandela, Steve Biko, and African freedom fighters. An interesting cultural and performative question centers on why African American performers have been selected to play these roles, and how their performances reflect diasporic transnationalism, identity construction, and global capitalism. In the apartheid era, the use of African American actors allowed production companies to sidestep many of the legal and political problems accompanying the employment of black South Africans (Davis 1996, 43–44). As foreign nationals, African Americans could not be victimized for portraying outspoken political positions, and they were less likely to be prosecuted for participation in antiapartheid productions.

One reason the selection of African American performers continues during the postapartheid era may be that they are popular international box-office draws. Ice Cube's portrayal of Vusi advances this tradition through incorporation of what Diawara labels "homeboy cosmopolitanism" (1998, 246–48). Throughout his journey of return and redemption, Vusi confronts the social tensions of the new South Africa via anecdotal philosophizing. Commenting on this performative strategy, Diawara states:

> Ice Cube . . . embodies the Homeboy both on screen and off. He combines an ordinary appearance and a scruffy style of dress with the musical flair of a fiery preacher. . . . His antihero persona—flamboyant, yet capable of getting the job done—binds him to segments of the Black community that identify with lawbreakers. Ice Cube's critical cypher treats both African-American and the dominant society as equal culprits in the destruction of African-American culture. (1998, 269–70)

In *Dangerous Ground*, Ice Cube transports his persona and critical stance from the streets of Los Angeles to an African terrain. As a political refugee returning to South Africa from California, Ice Cube's character Vusi experiences the culture shock typical of diasporic transnationalism. Diawara refers to this type of transposition as "transtextuality," or the fluid movement of expressions from one character and subculture to another across films, literary texts, and musical genres (1998, 271). He goes on to discuss how this transtextuality exemplifies a particular form of "black maleness," or gender stereotyping. In *Dangerous Ground*, Ice Cube problematizes gender issues and violence with ambivalence and value conflicts amid a shower of gunfire. He raises issues of moral and political responsibility in the contexts of immigration and social change.

Ice Cube forcefully voices the challenges and identity problems facing South Africa in his opening dialogue and confrontation with Ernest. In response to his younger brother's call for continued armed revolution as a means of liberation, Vusi tersely replies, "What you need to do is get yourself back in school. That's how you fight a war, with education." With these lines, Vusi distances himself from his brother's call for justice through violence, shifting political action from the frame of a military movement to a quest for social, educational, and economic equality.[14] Ironically, it remains violent gunfire, albeit divorced from military organization, that eventually answers the needs of Vusi's family and enables the return of the lost brother Stephen.

Women are important narrative actors as both mother figures and partners. The mother iconically represents the promise of communal values. Women also participate in New Jack violence as active partners. In Diawara's discussion, homegirls constitute the diegetic opposite of homeboys and reaffirm male-dominated narratives (1998, 267–70). There is, however, another type of homegirl who challenges the philosophies and outlooks of homeboys and destabilizes their discourses, not only through criticism but also through an aggressive attitude. This type of homegirl does not rely on the agency and actions of the homeboy for her responses but is, instead, an initiator of action and a source of narrative change. A parallel may be drawn between Karen (Elizabeth Hurley) in *Dangerous Ground* and Absalom's common-law wife Katie (or Mary, as she is called in the 1951 adaptation) in *Cry, the Beloved Country*.[15] As played by Lelita Khumalo in the 1995 version, Katie is a passive-aggressive mother figure. Her silent agreement to marry Absalom further unveils his transgressions and both potentially destabilizes the Kumalo family and offers the possibility of a new generation. Katie's decision to leave the city and return to the rural home of the Kumalo family parallels Karen's trajectory, which similarly results in relocation to the rural village of the Madlazi family. Both Karen and Katie are active figures that contribute to narrative transformations. They are semiotic adjuvants whose presence is essential to moving forward the development of the plot and the other characters.

In *Dangerous Ground,* Karen portrays an active homegirl cosmopolitan. She is an ambivalent and ambiguous figure—a downwardly mobile white South African whose origins and identity remain mysterious. At the same time, her "critical cypher" targets Vusi's assessment of South African society and enlightens him about the behavior and circumstances of his brother Stephen. Her knowledge of the new South Africa surpasses Vusi's and becomes a source of narrative complication. During the scene where Vusi finds Stephen stranded in a Sun City hotel, Karen asserts her active role.

> VUSI: You're pathetic, man. *Throws the syringe and lunges for Stephen who darts across the room.* I thought you was a man. *Stephen gets behind Karen.*
> STEPHEN: I am a man.
> VUSI: I thought you was a man! *Vusi strikes Stephen over Karen's shoulder.*
> KAREN: If you hit him again, I'm gonna hit you, okay!
> *Close-up of Vusi.*
> VUSI: Get out of the way before I break your little ass in two. This is family business.
> *Reverse shot past Vusi's arm to Karen looking up at him from Stephen's lap.*
> KAREN: Well, I'm a part of this family. *Karen glances at Stephen, then back at Vusi. (In a reproachful tone.)* You've got a lot of catching up to do, Vusi.
> VUSI: Give me this shit! *Throws drugs across the room.* I thought you was going to help me. Look like you're just helping yourself. *A series of shot-reverse-shots between Karen and Vusi.*
> KAREN *(quietly)*: I'm sorry.
> *Close reverse shot of Vusi.*
> VUSI: Could you at least pack his bags, please?
> *After a pause, Karen slowly moves out from between them, glancing back and forth at them as she goes.*

Karen's physical position in relationship to the brothers reinforces her mediatory role linking Vusi with his family, country, and culture. Although she spends the bulk of this scene physically looking up at Vusi, she also exerts control over the situation. She removes herself to the side of the room only when it is clear that Vusi will not hurt his brother. Reluctantly, Vusi concedes that he cannot succeed in his quest without her help. The unstated possibility that Karen, as Stephen's girlfriend, may also be pregnant deepens her attachment to Vusi's family and introduces a source of disruption and reconciliation.[16]

Vusi's initial meeting with Karen in a Johannesburg bar and strip club is a pivotal scene of identity construction and a cosmopolitan encounter. As with the persona of Ice Cube's archetypal homeboy, the character of the bar itself has traveled, replicating both form and function from South Central L.A. to Johannesburg, S.A. The Hollywood and cinematic daydream of the darkened bar as a gangster's paradise renegotiates the filmic journey, and the plot shifts from a story of diasporic return to one of underworld encounters and unbridled action. The bar provides a training ground for learning and understanding life in a global South Africa, where new encounters, identities, and fantasies are available to anyone willing and able to pay the price. The bar itself is a "dangerous ground," organized by the seamless logic of the gangster movie genre, where every encounter hides the possibility of danger and sinister motivations. Even the dancing carries an ulterior motive, and the sharing of a drink buys more than just alcohol.

After the pivotal bar scene, the logic of the New Jack genre reorganizes the motives and meaning of Vusi's quest, pulling loose ends into place. Stephen crossed the wrong man (West African crime lord Muki) and, for this reason, he disappeared. Muki's criminal reign needs to be dealt with—one way or another—in order for both Stephen and his family to be redeemed. But this shift complicates the narrative by introducing multiple subjects in search of a similar treasure. Although Muki is clearly the villain of the story, his attributes are not all negative. In the economy of the new South Africa, he maintains a level of material wealth and social status to which Vusi and his brothers aspire. In contrast, when Stephen is located in the global megabar of a Sun City casino, he is a broke and hunted victim. Stephen, Vusi, and Karen attempt to achieve redemption by repaying the money that is owed. But Muki rejects the monetary offering, and Stephen is killed at his hand. This leaves Stephen's family in need of justice and retribution. The answer to their predicament rests no further away than Ernest's cache of military weaponry. To obtain the promised gifts of the hidden treasure, they adopt the morally questionable means of their adversaries. In place of redemption through moral transformation, Vusi, Ernest, and Karen obtain their goal with a New Jack show of weaponry.[17]

Vusi takes the lead in charging into Muki's apartment, guns blazing. As a barrage of gunfire kills Muki's henchmen, fast-paced electronic music chants the lyric "the brothers gonna work it out." This violent resolution also destroys a collection of art and ritual objects that have been appropriated and desecrated by the drug lord. The explosive destruction of traditional objects and of the corruption represented by Muki and his thugs sets the stage for future growth and rebirth. Both elements are redeemed as Vusi slays the drug lord with the symbolic spear of his father. The success of the film, like the success of the brothers, arises from the vision of a new South Africa exaggerated and channeled through scenes of explosive action.

CONFLICT DIAMONDS AND CONFLICT NARRATIVES IN *BLOOD DIAMOND*

*Blood Diamond* is a redemptive New Jack African film that explores how conflict diamonds fuel civil war in West Africa. Unlike *Lord of War* (2005), a Hollywood take on diamonds, wealth, and violence starring Nicolas Cage, the diamonds and conflict of *Blood Diamond* are viewed from various perspectives, and Africa remains the major terrain of action. The morality and consequences of the climactic events are sustained by the conjoined subplots of smuggling and survival. Diamond smuggler Danny Archer (Leonardo DiCaprio) and Sierra Leonean fisherman Solomon Vandy (Djimon Hounsou) represent the two poles in this struggle. Solomon seeks to protect his family and the integrity of the mother figure by reclaiming his lost son.

As in *Dangerous Ground*, bar scenes play a pivotal role in character development and identity construction. The bar scenes are also markers for transitions in the filmic narrative. At a beach bar in Freetown, journalist Maddy Bowen (Jennifer Connelly) meets Danny Archer for the first time and questions his motives.

> *Danny approaches Maddy. Mid-range.*
> DANNY: Can I offer you a cigarette?
> MADDY: I'm fine. No Thanks. Are you listening to this? *[Shot of Bill Clinton on CNN apologizing for the Monica Lewinsky affair.]* The world is falling apart and all we hear about is Blowjobgate.
> *Series of intercut close-ups between Danny and Maddy as dialogue continues.*
> DANNY: When was the last time the world wasn't falling apart?
> MADDY: Oh, a cynic. Why don't you sit down and make me miserable?

DANNY: Danny Archer.
MADDY: Maddy Bowen.
BOTH: Pleased to meet you.
DANNY: American?
MADDY: Guilty.
DANNY: Americans usually are.
MADDY: Says the white South African.
DANNY: *(clicks no)* I'm from Rhodesia.
MADDY: We say Zimbabwe now, don't we?
DANNY: Do we?
MADDY: *(Laughs)* Last time I checked.
DANNY: So don't tell me you're here to make a difference.
MADDY: And you're here to make a buck.
DANNY: I'm here for lack of a better idea.
MADDY: That's a shame.
DANNY: Not really. Peace Corps types only stay around long enough
    to realize they are not helping anyone. Government only wants
    to stay in power until they've stolen enough to go into exile
    somewhere else. The rebels, they're not sure they want to take
    over, otherwise they would have to govern this mess. But T.I.A.,
    right M'ed?
M'ED: T.I.A.
MADDY: What's T.I.A.?
DANNY: This is Africa.

In this scene, Maddy plays a conventional role in which she reaffirms stereotypes about diamond smuggling. Her idealistic observations contrast
with Danny's cynical and ambivalent remarks. The slogan "T.I.A." codifies
his moral stance on a wide range of experiences of deception, corruption,
and violence.

A later scene features a nighttime party at the same bar just before the
invasion of Freetown by the Revolutionary United Front (RUF). Danny receives a gun from the bartender M'ed (Ntare Mwine) for cash they exchanged
in the initial bar scene. He asks if M'ed will be evacuating his family due
to the imminent threat of invasion, and the bartender replies that he will
stay: "This is my country, man. Be here long before you came, long after
you're gone." Unlike Danny who has just returned from business in South
Africa, M'ed is settled in Freetown. His life, like that of the majority of Sierra

Leone's population, will adapt to whatever political situations arise after the explosion. M'ed states: "Half the people who be soldiers today, be out of work tomorrow." The beach bar appears a third and final time after RUF rebels take the capital. The bar is burned as part of a riotous victory celebration, and M'ed is briefly shown lying on the bar, presumably dead. Danny and Solomon view the bar from a distance and skirt the area unnoticed during their escape from town.

The use of the bar to bookend the invasion and rebel takeover of Freetown highlights its filmic role. Not only does the African street literally explode during the invasion sequence, it is also the key event that focuses Danny, Solomon, and Maddy on a shared narrative quest for the lost diamond and Solomon's missing family. Prior to the invasion, the stories of the three protagonists are parallel but not fully intertwined. Once the city explodes during the rebel invasion, the three narratives implode. Like the film itself, the bar is consumed in violence and flames. From the moment Danny and Solomon begin to run, their purpose crystallizes.

Between the invasion of Freetown and the closing sequence, the characters are united in a search for lost treasure, and the film follows them like fugitives on the run. Their quest continues to be interspersed with dialogue and banter covering a host of Africa's problems—from child soldiers to diamond smuggling, the complicity of the press, and the failure of education. But these problems remain unresolved, as dialogues are truncated and punctuated by increasingly regular intervals of gunfire and violence. Although the morality of violence remains uncertain for the film's characters, the filmic logic no longer questions its necessity during the final shootout on the diamond fields. Even Solomon, who is synchronically positioned as a peaceful fisherman in counterpoint to Danny's mercenary lifestyle, beats both rebel leader Captain Poison (David Harewood) and South African Colonel Coetzee (Arnold Voslo) with a shovel. In doing so, he reclaims his lost son, who unlike Arthur Jarvis and Stephen Madzlai is ultimately spared from death. More important, however, he escapes with the promise of future wealth, prosperity, and moral vindication, symbolically represented by the reclaimed diamond.

Bookending the pivotal invasion of Freetown between New Jack–style bar scenes creates parallels in the narrative structure of *Blood Diamond*. Between an early scene depicting the meeting of diamond executives in Belgium and the unresolved coda, in which Solomon arrives in Europe, the entirety of the film occurs on the African continent. Africa is the site of action. The international discussions influence the African conflict, but those meetings remain intact and free of explosion. Africa, in contrast, hides the lost treasure, violently explodes in the foreign removal of that treasure, and offers the hope of future redemption. The political and social commentary of *Blood Diamond* frames this New Jack story line without pronouncing an airtight solution. Smugglers may in fact be heroes, and the foreign buyers of diamond engagement rings remain complicit with African military regimes. Danny Archer's final sacrifice does not redeem the continent, and Solomon's story is ultimately never heard. Instead, the explosion and implosion of multiple African story lines destroy simple answers and provoke the imagination of alternative futures.

EXPLODING GENRES

New Jack African cinema transfers the tropes of Hollywood and hip-hop blockbusters, such as homeboy and homegirl cosmopolitanism, racial tension, drug running, and exaggerated gangland violence, to the landscape of Africa. A preview of this shift can be glimpsed through the subtle Africanization of Kumalo's religiosity in the fifteenth-day scene in Roodt's 1995 production of *Cry, the Beloved Country.* Although the religious quest and moral attitude of the film remain consistent with the 1951 version, the story shifts from a colonial perspective to metaphors of African Christian syncretism. But Roodt's New Jack cinema does not simply extend or alter the quest narrative; it explodes the narrative. There is a sense in which New Jack African cinema is "postapocalyptic." It combines the combats and conflagrations of the world's end with a glimmer of hope for new beginnings. The final blowout scene of *Dangerous Ground* depicts the crime lord Muki's ejection from a window, destroying a source of corruption, drugs, and crime in South Africa. Vusi's brother Ernest, the rebel without a cause, helps Vusi exterminate the source of crime. Through the use of strategic intercutting, African soccer fans depicted on a nearby television become cheering spectators of Muki's death. In *Blood Diamond,* Danny Archer dies in a violent shootout with corrupt diamond thieves. His death leads to their potential extermination and a revindication by the forces of justice in Europe. Even though these forces are, in fact, compromised, their control over the decriminalization of blood diamonds foreshadows hope for the future.

Modernist dramas make Africa a land of fantasy in which colonial domination displaces the indigenous "other." In contrast, New Jack African cinema levels the playing field, imbuing heroes, antiheroes, and villains with equal culpability for Africa's plight. It challenges Hollywood conventions through violence and resistance. Yet, New Jack cinema continues to exploit Hollywood's narratives, audiences, and resources. With its ambivalent conclusions, the struggles between capital and community, identity and domination continue to unfurl. When the present is exploded, the future becomes full of possibility. Avoiding moralistic and documentary solutions, New Jack African cinema conveys the feel of explosive changes in Africa without assessing the relations of power and the social conditions that generate these changes. It is interesting to speculate about future transformations of New Jack cinema in which a rapprochement between action narratives and international audiences could either widen the gap or bring Hollywood closer to what Jean Rouch has described as the "ciné-truth" of African cinema and its social realties.

NOTES

This essay draws on a symposium on *Dangerous Ground* and African action cinema organized by the Art, Culture, and Knowledge (ACK) group of the African and African-American Studies Research Center (AAASRC) at the University of California, San Diego.

1. Diawara (1998, 268–73) analyzes *Boyz N the Hood* (1991) as a key example of American 'hood films. African filmmakers such as Djibril Diop Mambety have also dealt with scenes and travails of urban life. These works could be seen as related to American 'hood films. The South African production *Tsotsi* (2005), directed by Gavin Hood, offers a more recent example of African 'hood films. What distinguishes New Jack cinema from both American and African 'hood films is a reliance on violence to explode social problems and offer hope for the future.

2. Paul Smith (1993, 20) describes *Casablanca* as a "disguised Western" that uses the narrative structure of a western transported from the nineteenth-century American West to twentieth-century Morocco but invoking the same primal conflicts.

3. The New Jack genre has also been transported to France in *banlieue* cinema, exemplified by Pierre Morel's film *Banlieue 13* (2004).

4. In this discussion, the term "virtual" refers to A. J. Greimas's (1987, 91) semiotic distinction between the realization and virtualization of narrative elements rather than a description of digitally animated virtual realities. For Greimas, virtual values are values that either remain unrealized or are yet to be realized in a narrative.

5. Tricia Rose (1994, 39) and George Lipsitz (1994, 36–38) describe the process of layering, through which rappers establish beats, sounds, and dialogues in which hidden messages are transmitted. Bogumil Jewsiewicki (1991, 130–51) describes similar processes of layering and occultation in popular African painting.

6. Paul Smith (1993, 42–44) discusses the importance of similar processes of destruction and restitution in spaghetti westerns. In these westerns, the community may be restored by a lone gunfighter who leads the community to the brink of destruction but also restores its moral order.

7. Peter Davis (1996, 17–18) describes the early colonial films focusing on a search for fabulous wealth and hidden treasures. He parallels these films with Hollywood westerns in terms of the themes of the exploitation of an indigenous population. See also Nixon (1994, 31–36) for discussion of the influence of classic Hollywood gangster films on black South African popular culture.

8. See Christian Metz (1982, 37–39) for a discussion of spectators' responses to conventional Hollywood film language.

9. Teshome H. Gabriel (1979, 6–7) discusses liberated cinematic spaces with regard to revolutionary African cinema. See also Robert Stam's analysis of theories of Third Cinema (Stam 1993, 233–53).

10. Although there is ongoing discussion of Rouch's role in African cinema, Rouch situated himself as a companion of the African filmmakers with whom he collaborated or trained (Rouch 1968, 523–37).

11. "Ciné-Trance: A Tribute to Jean Rouch (1917–2004)," ed. Jeff Himpele and Faye Ginsburg, presents a series of reflections commenting on the openings made possible by Rouch's pioneering work in visual anthropology and film. The tribute appeared in the March 2005 issue of *American Anthropologist* (107, no. 1).

12. Commenting on the relationship between his work and cinematic fiction, Rouch (2003, 185) states: "For me, as an ethnographer, there is almost no boundary between documentary film and films of fiction. The cinema, the art of the double, is already the transition from the real world to the imaginary world, and ethnography, the science of the thought systems of others, is a permanent crossing point from one conceptual universe to another."

13. The exaggeration of violence distances New Jack African cinema from the pseudo-realistic depictions of African docudramas. This prevents New Jack films from falling victim to the cinematic pessimism of some docudramas (Dargis 2007) and frees them to imagine new identities, social alternatives, and new visions of Africa.

14. In the 2005 University of California San Diego *Dangerous Ground* film symposium, Jonathan Markovitz discussed the ambivalent role played by Vusi's brother Ernest as a postapartheid revolutionary without a cause. The crumbling of apartheid also diminished the impact of antiracist organizations in South Africa.

15. Alan Paton does not name Absalom's girlfriend in his novel *Cry, the Beloved Country*. As a result, her name varies across cinematic and theatrical productions. Her name is Katie in the 1995 Darrell Roodt film. In the Korda 1951 version, however, her name is Mary. And she is listed under the name Irina for the musical adaptation *Lost in the Stars*.

16. In the 2005 University of California San Diego *Dangerous Ground* film symposium, Lea Marie Ruiz-Ade introduced the possibility of Karen's pregnancy, which is reinforced by cinematic cues such as her return to the rural Madlazi home and her incorporation as a member of the family.

17. It is interesting to note that Ernest's cache of weapons was buried in the forest. The act of retrieving the weapons is in itself an act of finding buried treasure. In the Scene Selections menu of the *Dangerous Ground* DVD, that scene is referred to as "Buried Treasure."

REFERENCES

Beittel, Mark. 2003. "What Sort of Memorial? *Cry, the Beloved Country* on Film." In *To Change Reels: Film and Film Culture in South Africa*, edited by Isabel Balseiro and Ntongela Masilela, 70–87. Detroit, MI: Wayne State University Press.
Dargis, Manola. 2007. "Africa at the Cineplex." *New York Times*. February 4.
Davis, Peter. 1996. *In Darkest Hollywood: Exploring the Jungles of Cinema's South Africa Location of Culture*. Athens: Ohio University Press.

Diawara, Manthia. 1992. *African Cinema: Politics and Culture.* Bloomington: Indiana University Press.

———. 1998. *In Search of Africa.* Cambridge, MA: Harvard University Press.

Gabriel, Teshome H. 1979. *Third Cinema in the Third World.* Ann Arbor, MI: UMI Research Press.

Greimas, Algirdas Julien. 1987. *On Meaning: Selected Writings in Semiotic Theory.* Translated from the French *Du Sens I* (1970) and *Du Sens II* (1983) by Paul J. Perron and Frank H. Collins. Minneapolis: University of Minnesota Press.

Himpele, Jeff, and Faye Ginsburg, eds. 2005. "Ciné-Trance: A Tribute to Jean Rouch (1917–2004)." *American Anthropologist* 107 (1): 108–29.

Jewsiewicki, Bogumil. 1991. "Painting in Zaire: From the Invention of the West to the Representation of Social Self." In *Africa Explores: Twentieth Century African Art,* edited by Susan Vogel, 130–51. New York: Center for African Art.

Jules-Rosette, Bennetta. 2007. *Josephine Baker in Art and Life: The Icon and the Image.* Urbana: University of Illinois Press.

Korda, Zoltan, director. 1951. *Cry, the Beloved Country.* Script by Alan Paton and John Howard Lawson. London: London Film Productions.

Lipsitz, George. 1994. *Dangerous Crossroads: Popular Music, Postmodernism and the Poetics of Place.* London: Verso Press.

Metz, Christian. 1982. *The Imaginary Signifier: Psychoanalysis and Cinema.* Translated from the French by Cecla Briton, Annwyl Wiliams, Ben Brewster, and Alfred Guzzetti. Bloomington: Indiana University Press.

Nixon, Rob. 1994. *Homelands, Harlem, and Hollywood: South African Culture and the World Beyond.* London: Routledge.

Roodt, Darrell, director. 1995. *Cry, the Beloved Country.* Script by Ronald Harwood. Los Angeles: Miramax Films.

———, director. 1997. *Dangerous Ground.* Script by Greg Latter and Darrell Roodt. Los Angeles: New Line Cinema.

Rose, Tricia. 1994. *Black Noise: Rap Music and Black Culture in Contemporary America.* Hanover, NH: University Press of New England.

Rouch, Jean. 1968. "Films Inspired by Africa." In *First World Festival of Negro Arts: Colloquium on Negro Art,* edited by Société Africaine de Culture, 523–37. Paris: Présence Africaine. First presented as a paper, "Le Cinéma d'inspiration africaine," at the First World Festival of Negro Arts, Colloquium on Negro Art, Dakar, Senegal, 1966. File GN 460-A315-F41-M85, Musée de l'Homme, Paris.

———. 2003. *Ciné-Ethnography.* Edited and translated by Steven Feld. Minneapolis: University of Minnesota Press.

Sanneh, Kelefa. 2007. "The Shrinking Market Is Changing the Face of Hip-Hop." *New York Times.* December 30.

Smith, Paul. 1993. *Clint Eastwood: A Cultural Production.* Minneapolis: University of Minnesota Press.

Stam, Robert. 1993. "Eurocentrism, Afrocentrism, Polycentrism: Theories of Third Cinema." In *Otherness and the Media: The Ethnography of the Imagined and the Imaged,* edited by Hamid Naficy and Teshome H. Gabriel. Chur, Switzerland: Harwood Academic.

Zwick, Edward, director. 2006. *Blood Diamond.* Script by Charles Leavitt and C. Gaby Mitchell. Los Angeles: Warner Brothers.

# ELEVEN

# "It Is a Very Rough Game, Almost as Rough as Politics"

Rugby as Visual Metaphor and the Future of the New South Africa in *Invictus*

CHRISTOPHER GARLAND

Clint Eastwood's *Invictus* (2009) tells the story of Nelson Mandela's role in transforming the image of South Africa's national rugby team, the Springboks, from a divisive, apartheid-era hangover to a symbol of national unity. In the film, which stars Morgan Freeman as Mandela and Matt Damon as Springbok captain François Pienaar, rugby serves as a visual metaphor for the politically turbulent transition from the postapartheid interregnum period to the beginning of the new South Africa.[1] This essay explores how *Invictus*, although perhaps not Eastwood's most inventive or visually creative directorial project, is notable because of the way it renders this significant moment in the short history of the new South Africa: the country's hosting of the 1995 Rugby World Cup. In drawing from two Hollywood genres—the "based on a true story" sports movie and the interracial buddy film—Eastwood synthesizes elements of these two popular genres in a way that diverges from some of the conventions in the former and avoids the racist stereotyping of the latter. Yet even if the film is not entirely successful as a biopic—the narrative reifies Mandela's popular sainthood by ignoring any of the leader's political or personal failings—it underscores one of his great achievements. Mandela's adoption of the Springboks helped dismantle the pervasive notion of the team as a cultural manifestation of conservative Afrikaner nationhood and its apartheid regime.

How rugby functions as a visual metaphor is epitomized by the film's climactic scene, where the underdog Springboks play the New Zealand All Blacks in the final of the World Cup. A series of close-up shots are intercut with reaction shots of fans, both black and white, watching the game at private homes and bars around the country. On the playing field, the cinematography focuses on the brutal art of scrimmaging, wherein players from opposing teams lock heads and shoulders in an attempt to gain possession of the ball. Although these slow-motion sequences ostensibly depict the physical toll on the Springboks and demonstrate the team's newfound commitment to winning, they are the most striking of all the sequences where rugby is a visual metaphor for the early years of the new South Africa.[2] Like the Springboks' scrum, which is a violent movement seemingly tenuous in its stability, the Rainbow Nation prevails. Intercutting the rugby play with shots of "ordinary" blacks, whites, and blacks and whites together, the metaphor of rugby as both a force and emblem of national unity is heightened by the drama of the Springboks' last-minute victory.

The fact that the playing of rugby is not just reserved for the country's mostly white national team is crucial in the mise-en-scène of the film's final sequence that follows shortly after the Springboks' triumph. As the credits roll, a group of black South Africans play an informal game of touch rugby. Although this scene is a far cry from the Springboks' dramatic, hyperphysical battles depicted earlier in the narrative, the implication of the inclusion of this scene as the film's final image is clear. In the diegesis of *Invictus,* rugby not only helped to provide a bridge between black and white South Africans during the World Cup, but it is also a way of looking at the country's future through the successful appropriation of a symbol from South Africa's recent, segregated past.

As in the case of all the countries where the game is played, rugby in South Africa has a direct connection to colonialism, with English schools in Cape Town first holding matches in the 1860s. Since that time, rugby has retained a prominent position in white culture. In *The Land and People of South Africa* (1972) renowned South African writer Alan Paton succinctly states that white South Africans are "madly enthusiastic about playing rugby" (42). Writing about rugby's place in contemporary South Africa, J. M. Coetzee poses a question: "Why does this crippled game flourish, and flourish particularly in South Africa?" (1992, 22). While Coetzee's short essay does not dwell on the important question of the racial divide between rugby and soccer in that country, his question could nonetheless be updated to address the idea of contemporary South Africa: "How did a sport popular only with a small minority come to flourish as part of the popular discourse about the origins of the new South Africa?" As one of the most enduring legacies of British imperialism in Southern Africa, rugby nonetheless became, in the words of Bill Keller, "the secular religion of the Afrikaners, the [other] white tribe that invented and enforced apartheid" (2008).

During the apartheid regime, rugby was not merely a colonial sport adopted with fervor by the white settler community, as was the case with New Zealand and Australia, but also a bastion of Afrikaner nationhood.[3] Although white English-speaking or "British" South Africans have played and followed the sport since introducing the game to southern Africa, the top teams, whether in the schoolboy ranks or the representative teams from all across the different South African provinces—Transvaal, Orange Free State, Natal, and Cape Province—came to be dominated by Afrikaners. In particular, the Springboks, as the formal collection of the best players in the country, essentially became an Afrikaner team. John Carlin, in *Playing the Enemy: Nelson Mandela and the Game That Made a Nation* (2008), the book on which *Invictus* is based, states:

> They feared God, but they loved rugby. . . . Successive South African national teams had built up the reputation . . . as the most bruisingly physical rugby players in the world. Mostly they were Afrikaners, though occasionally an unusually hefty, or tough, or fast "Englishman" (as the Afrikaners called them, when they were being polite) would sneak into the national side. And mostly, being Afrikaners, they were big-boned men of horny-handed farmer stock, who as children learned the game playing barefoot on hard, dry pitches where if you fell, you bled. (42)

Along with a deep-seated passion for rugby, Afrikaners, the elder of South Africa's two white tribes, also offered the most overt resistance to black minority rule. After Mandela's release from prison in 1990, it was a right-wing, separatist faction, led by Afrikaner nationalist General Constand Viljoen, with whom Mandela had to negotiate in order to prevent civil war during his ascent to national leadership. In the interregnum period before Mandela and the African National Congress's electoral victory over the ruling National Party led by de Klerk, a moment in history touched on only briefly at the beginning of *Invictus,* the greatest threat to the republic was posed by right-wing Afrikaners prepared to devolve South Africa in civil war in order to achieve an independent state within the country's borders. The threat of a race war is not heavily emphasized in the film's narrative, but it forms an important context for the significance of Mandela's achievement: the Springboks are no longer synonymous with apartheid, but rather a team all South Africans can embrace.

But whether black South Africa adopts rugby (as players or fans) is less important than reimagining rugby outside an exclusionary mark of apartheid-era Afrikanerdom.[4] The final sequence calls attention to the radical potential of a new future for South Africa: here, rugby, popular with both the architects and enforcers of apartheid, stands in for the wider claiming by black South Africans during the postapartheid era of an image of the past. In his "Theses on the Philosophy of History," Walter Benjamin argues that "to articulate what is past does not mean to recognize 'the way it really was.' It means to seize hold of a memory as it flashes up at a moment of danger" (1969, 255). By the end of the 1995 Rugby World Cup, Mandela may not have transformed the country's black majority into die-hard rugby fans, but he was able to "seize hold" of the image of a sport deeply associated with a racist regime and reinscribe it with a message of national unification. During this "moment of danger"—a time when it was a very real possibility that white and black South Africa "would have made war" (Carlin 2008, 95)—Mandela's support of the Springboks enabled rugby to take on different meanings and associations than it ever had before. Whether in scenes where he appeals to the country's sports council and advises them not to change the colors or name of the Springboks or by ensuring that the Springboks visit black townships, the film captures Mandela's attempt at national reconciliation and compromise. As the leader of the host country for the largest and most significant rugby event in the world, Mandela had reckoned to "use sport for the purpose of nation-building and promoting all the ideas which we think will lead to peace and stability in our country" (cited in Carlin 2008, 163).

Mandela's emotional appeal to Afrikaners via rugby is as memorable as the film's overt dramatic tension: the Springboks' unexpected run through the world cup tournament culminating in the upset of the All Blacks. This narrative focus on the interplay between rugby and politics is established from the film's opening scene. The film's first shot is a long shot from near ground level—a slightly disorienting angle used repeatedly in the later action sequences of the Springboks' games—of a rugby scrum (a situation similar to the line of scrimmage in American football). The scrum is set up in the top right corner of the frame. The camera is positioned behind the players awaiting the attacking play of the opposition and then tracks across the field as the action moves to the sideline, ending with the ball going out of bounds.

The shrill blast of the coach's whistle, which was used to start the play at the opening of the shot, sounds out again to indicate that the play is dead. After tracking across the field, the camera rises above the fence at the edge of the practice field and simultaneously pans to the left. The shot is now an elevated view across a two-lane road, where, situated lower down than the rugby field, black children play soccer on a field that is much less lush than the ground that the whites are playing on. After the camera tilts and fixes the long shot on the soccer play and the basic school buildings behind them, there is a superimposed title in the center of the bottom third of the frame: South Africa, February 11, 1990.

While the total length of the take is only seventeen seconds, this moving shot sets up a number of the film's important premises: the color line in apartheid South Africa applies not only to education but also to participation in sports. The superimposed title given at the end of the shot—the date of the official release from prison of Mandela—signals the starting point for a narrative in ways that again connect rugby and politics. Marking the start of Mandela's path to national leadership and the abolition of apartheid, this moment also has a direct effect on South African rugby. An international sporting boycott had made South Africa a pariah state in world rugby and resulted in the Springboks being excluded from the first two Rugby World Cups in 1987 and 1991. The redemption of South African rugby began with the end of apartheid, allowing the Springboks to freely play matches around the world and allow nonwhite overseas players to play in South Africa. (The latter point had been a major point of contention, particularly between the Springboks and the multiracial New Zealand teams.)

In addition to setting up the historical context through the superimposed date, the camera's movement during the course of this shot indicates the direction of the film that is fulfilled by the film's aforementioned final shot, where black rugby players become the camera's primary focus. After showing some rugby play, there is a cut back to the white schoolboy rugby team running through a passing drill. The frame is divided in half from top to bottom, emphasizing the imposing school buildings behind. A jump cut to a shot of the black boys playing soccer is followed by a shot of the beginning of the motorcade along the road that divides these separate worlds.

In the following sequence, there are shots of the black boys abandoning their game, and rushing to the fence to watch the passing motorcade; the next shot mirrors this action, showing that the white boys on the other side of the road have also made their way to the fence. A tracking shot of the white boys—they are focused on the black boys cheering on the motorcade from the other side of the road—shows their faces expressing a mixture of anxiety and hostility. The following exchange between the white coach and a young player illustrates the way in which parts of white South Africa reacted to Mandela's release. When one of the schoolboys asks who is traveling in the motorcade, the Afrikaner coach, in the film's first piece of dialogue, responds, "It is that terrorist, Mandela. They let him out. Remember this day, boys. This is the day that our country went to the dogs. Come, let's go, come."

This opening sequence begins the film's dialectical narrative pattern. In *Hollywood's Vision of Team Sports: Heroes, Race, and Gender* Deborah V. Tudor asserts that "certain patterns do reoccur many times within sports films; certain paired attributes often appear in the same film where they function to constrain each other" (1997, xix). Here, the treasured cultural practice of white South Africa, rugby, presents as the antithesis to the emergence of black political agency. Thus the sphere of national politics and the world of sports are paired in the film's narrative, with Mandela attempting to put these two concepts in dialogue with each other in order to achieve synthesis for contemporary South Africa. After the opening scene, the film's focus turns from visually demonstrating the intersection of rugby and apartheid to a short sequence that demonstrates the foundations of the Mandela era. Beginning with news footage of F. W. de Klerk at a press conference announcing Mandela's release, the sequence includes a montage of shots showing the power struggle between the ANC and "their black rivals."

In this sequence the still image and live action footage of Morgan Freeman as Mandela has been digitally inserted into archival news footage depicting events in South Africa's immediate postapartheid history.

The use of documentary footage in the transitional sequence between this fictional opening scene and the introduction of Mandela, the primary biopic subject, places the representation of the "true" story of Mandela and the Springboks as one of the film's major concerns. The narrative foregrounds the historical crisis of the power transition between the ancien régime headed by F. W. de Klerk and the ascendant African National Congress. Writing about the tendencies of Hollywood cinema, Robert Ray argues that to "a great extent, American history's major crises appear in American movies only as 'structuring absences'" (1985, 31). In *Invictus* and a number of other European- or American-funded films that have a sub-Saharan African nation as a primary setting—including *The Last King of Scotland* (Kevin Macdonald, 2006), *Blood Diamond* (Edward Zwick, 2006), and *District 9* (Neill Blomkamp,

2009)—moments of historical crisis in Africa in fact serve as a structuring presence. The opening scene and subsequent documentary sequence are integral to the narrative structure of *Invictus*, providing both historical context and emphasizing the difficulty of Mandela's task of nation building. Moreover, although the majority of the film is set around five years after the moment portrayed in the opening scene, in the film's diegesis Mandela's release is posited as the point of origin for the new South Africa. When Mandela's motorcade moves along the road, he is literally traversing and surveying the gap between the social experience and sporting passions of segregated black and white South Africa. And when Freeman as Mandela quotes directly and accurately from Mandela's famous speech in Durban in the synthesized documentary sequence—"Take your guns, your knives, and your pangas, and throw them into the sea!"—the film is locating itself as a very specific moment of crisis in South Africa's recent history.

Writing about the link between historical representations and the depiction of sports in Hollywood film, Aaron Baker argues that sports films "look back in time through the lens of present concerns" (2003, 7). Baker's identification of the filtering of past and present in Hollywood sports films is worth considering in one of the most compelling scenes in *Invictus*— the Springboks' visit to Robben Island (the main location for Mandela's imprisonment). The scene evokes the ongoing project of reconciliation that was central to Mandela's vision for the new South Africa. The same year as the world cup, Mandela passed the Promotion of National Unity and Reconciliation Act (no. 34), which would lead to public testimony about crimes committed under the auspices of the apartheid regime. When the Springboks players are being given a guided tour of the apartheid-era prison complex, the twenty-eight-year-old Afrikaner Springbok captain, François Pienaar, asks if he can see the president's cell. Once he is left alone, Pienaar watches a number of prisoners—the "ghosts" of Robben Island—breaking rocks in the bright sunlight. Discussing the role of ghosts in a popular literary text, Sibylle Fischer argues, "The ghost will ensure that the events will never truly be over and that the story will continue to be told" (2004, 157).

This, too, is true of contemporary South Africa. The story and residual effects of apartheid haunt the country today, "rooted in individual and collective memory" of those who "suffered arbitrary arrests, beatings, assassinations, and torture" as well as being "subjected to the structural and systematic violence of poverty" and its associated maladies (Dowdall cited in Hamber 1998, 351). The presence of the ghosts in *Invictus* calls to mind the trauma of apartheid and its effect on the country's present; in turn, the ghosts have a didactic effect on the Springbok captain. The apparitions are an image of history that inspires Pienaar: the new South Africa, which has its roots in the ending of apartheid's evils, has a pending future that requires an acknowledgment of past ills.

The voice of Mandela reading William Ernest Henley's 1892 poem "Invictus" permeates the scene's diegetic sound, evoking an eerie sense of Mandela as an omniscient presence for the Springbok captain. As the reading of the poem continues, Pienaar turns toward the bed and camera pans to the right and tilts down diagonally to a ghostly Mandela sitting on the basic cot and facing the wall. There is a cut when Pienaar turns to look out the window and sees the ghostly prisoners. Mandela, who is among the prisoners, looks up at the window, before dissolving and disappearing completely. The earlier shot is repeated, panning left and tilting diagonally down to the right, but now the space is empty. In the next scene, the Springbok team is outside, on a small hill overlooking the yard where prisoners were breaking rocks. In the cut to Pienaar's point of view, he again sees the ghosts of the prisoners; a reaction shot follows, with the rest of the team walking past the Springbok captain, before a low-angle shot of the ghostly Mandela. The presence of Mandela in the narrative is both omnipotent and omnipresent: wherever Pienaar goes to reflect, Mandela appears before him. The ghostly shocks because it is a visitation of the past upon the present: Pienaar is forced to face Mandela not as president or black liberator, but rather as a political prisoner of apartheid.

The appearance of the ghostly Mandela during the Springboks' visit to Robben Island diverts the narrative from the realism of the Hollywood sports film and into the realm of allegory. The ghosts of *Invictus* can be read to allegorically evoke the unearthing of the past through a project that began the year after the country's hosting of the Rugby World Cup, the Truth and Reconciliation Commission (TRC). Coming on the heels of the Promotion of National Unity and Reconciliation Act, the TRC gave the opportunity to victims of apartheid to confront the perpetrators of crimes—police officers, members of the military, as well as South African citizens who did not hold official positions of authority—and bear witness to their confessions. Furthermore, one of the primary purposes of the TRC was to allow the victim the ability to narrate his or her experience, an attempt to demonstrate that South Africa "decided to say no to amnesia and yes to remembrance; to say no to full-scale prosecutions and trials and yes to forgiveness" (Boraine 2000,

156). When the ghosts appear, Pienaar, as with those exposed to the testimony and confessions from the TRC hearings, undergoes a visceral shock from the country's recent past.

Moreover, the Robben Island scene is an example of what Adam Lowenstein calls the allegorical moment as "a shocking collision of film, spectator, and history where registers of bodily space and historical time are disrupted, confronted, and intertwined" (2005, 2). The uncanny reappearances of the ghostly Mandela and fellow Robben Island prisoners in *Invictus* calls to mind the whole monstrous apparatus of apartheid as it worked upon the black subject. What is more, in this newly postapartheid setting Pienaar (and the audience) experience the shock of seeing a specter still present at the scene of the crime. But the film's Robben Island part also reemphasizes the bond between Pienaar and Mandela. This bond, as shown in this scene, is both metaphysical and exclusive to Pienaar's experience: it is, after all, the Springbok captain alone who sees the ghosts of Mandela and his fellow inmates. Here, the representation of nonfiction (the Springboks really did visit Robben Island during the World Cup) and fiction (Pienaar's visions of ghosts) enable further interaction between the film's protagonists.

Discussing the nonfictional and fictional narratives about team sports that inform Hollywood sports films, Deborah Tudor asserts that "the construction of the hero" is consistently placed in the foreground (1997, xii). *Invictus* follows this convention of the Hollywood sports film by presenting two primary heroes in Mandela and Pienaar. Yet unlike other Hollywood sports films that focus on the success of an underdog team, including *Remember the Titans* (Boaz Yakin, 2000), *Miracle* (Gavin O'Connor, 2004), and *Any Given Sunday* (Oliver Stone, 1999), in Eastwood's film the role of the coach barely registers on the film's narrative. Mandela's relationship with Pienaar replaces another convention of this genre: the building of a link between the coach and the star or favorite player. Mandela does not fill the role of the traditional team sports coach figure, such as the fictional coach Norman Dale from *Hoosiers* (David Anspaugh, 1986) or the fictionalized coach Ara Perseghian from *Rudy* (David Anspaugh, 1993), both of whom direct rousing speeches to the sports team and attempt to share a love of the game with their players, but Mandela does provide Pienaar with a copy of the poem ("Invictus") that inspired him during his time in prison.

This gifting of Henley's poem not only underscores the relationship between Mandela and Pienaar but also links this interracial bond with the film's final scene, where Mandela watches the crowd of black and white South

Africans celebrating the Springboks' victory. As in the Robben Island scene, this sequence is accompanied by a voiceover of Freeman as Mandela reading from Henley's poem. The final lines—"I am the master of my fate: I am the captain of my soul"—now serving as a dual metaphor for both political and sporting triumphs. Furthermore, Pienaar and Mandela's relationship presents a variation on another genre, the "interracial buddy film." In "Hegemony in Black and White: Interracial Buddy Films and the New Racism" B. Lee Artz, discussing American race relations and Hollywood film, argues that

> celluloid images of successful Blacks working in established institutions help construct harmonious race relations. Buddy movies, in particular, help Blacks (and Whites) accept existing social conditions. Behind the façade of entertainment lies a persuasive political argument that Blacks are benefitting materially, politically, and culturally from existing social arrangements and practices. . . . Pleasing to Blacks and comforting to Whites, the fictions of interracial buddy movies simplify race relations. (1998, 68)

Artz identifies the 1980s and 1990s as the era in Hollywood cinema when the interracial buddy film genre became produced en masse: *48 Hours* (Walter Hill, 1982), *Beverly Hills Cop* (Martin Brest, 1984), *Die Hard with a Vengeance* (John McTiernan, 1995), and the *Lethal Weapon* series (Richard Donner) may be among the best known, but *Trading Places* (John Landis, 1983) and *The Last Boy Scout* (Tony Scott, 1991) are also prominent films featuring black and white buddies. More recent examples include the *Men in Black* films (Barry Sonnenfeld, 1997, 2002) and *Miami Vice* (Michael Mann, 2006).

Yet several of the central characteristics that Artz employs in order to define the new racism of the Hollywood interracial buddy film—"Recognizable Black culture" (Artz references the speech and dress of black characters), "Weak White characters," "White authority," and "Isolated Black characters" (72)—are difficult to locate in the rendering of the Mandela/Pienaar dynamic and its mid-1990s South African setting. For American audiences, black South African culture is not an easily "recognizable black culture," especially considering the unfamiliar S.A. accent. The character of Pienaar may not be a particularly incisive psychological portrait, but he is not the white buddy who is "weak, naive, or dishonest" (72). While the tension between the black and white members of the security forces is palpable, both sides cede to Mandela's wishes. For example, in a scene early in the film, the white staff members at the governmental Union Building in Pretoria are shown to be packing up their personal items in anticipation of being fired. Mandela subsequently tells them that none of the staff will be losing his or her job, and he insists that the black and white security work out of the same office. Moreover, throughout the film Mandela is frequently accompanied by his chief of staff, Brenda Mazikubo (Adjoa Andoh), and black members of his administration and security detail, one of whom is notable as an allegorical representation of black South African fandom, expressing his initial disdain but eventual enthusiasm for the Springboks' World Cup success.

Perhaps one of the primary reasons why *Invictus* does not fit the mold of the typical Hollywood interracial buddy film is because of the way it deviates from another genre to which it belongs: a Hollywood depiction of Africa. In an article that attempts to highlight the need for "film producers with African knowledge" in order to improve the representations of Africa in film, Kristin Skare Orgeret argues that "another rather problematic tendency in films produced in the north is that Africa's most important stories often are told by foreigners and through actors from the same global north" (Orgeret 2009, 505, 507). Leaving aside the author's problematic assertion about the necessity of film producers who possess a so-called "African knowledge," Orgeret begins with two early examples of Hollywood depictions of Africa, *Casablanca* (Michael Curtiz, 1942) and *The African Queen* (John Huston, 1951), where "Africans are presented either as naive child-like characters in need of help from the north, or as savage, wild and violent figures" (506, 507). Orgeret then turns to the example of Antoine Fuqua's *Tears of the Sun* (2003), a film starring Bruce Willis as a US Navy SEAL sent on a mission to Nigeria in order to remove a US citizen (played by Monica Bellucci) from the midst of a civil war. Orgeret argues that by the end of *Tears of the Sun*, "Africa is totally reduced to coulisse here, and Africans to extras within the limited repertoire of helpless victims and cruel warlords: this emphasizes American patriotism and courage" (507).

This binary in which Africans are characterized in Hollywood cinema—as reliant on whites and/or in a constant state of war—is the manifestation of a widespread, simplistic view of a geographically diverse, multiethnic, multilingual, and multinational continent. Rebutting the generalizations that mark discourse about Africa and its many countries and peoples, John Ryle argues that in "truth Africa is far less homogeneous—geographically, culturally, religiously and politically—than Europe or the Americas. South Africa and Burkina Faso have as much in common as Spain and Uzbekistan" (2005, 9). That generalizations about Africa's poverty, war, and mass killings are found in both classical and contemporary Hollywood's visions of Africa is unsurprising. What Ryle calls "the tendency for Westerners—and often Africans too—to seek to impose a single reality, general explanation, on the whole place" can be traced from the start of European imperialism to today's mainstream media representations of the continent, where all too often Africa and Africans are treated with broad strokes (9).

Whereas it is not difficult to see how the one-dimensional portrayal of Africans as "cruel warlords" plays out in *Tears of the Sun* or the grotesque cartoonish depiction of Nigerians as cannibalistic gangsters in Neill Blom-kamp's *District 9* (2009), the objectification of Africans as either "cruel warlord" or "victim" does not occur in *Invictus*. Mandela utilizes his political dynamism to incorporate the Springboks into his larger plan for reconcilia-tion. In Eastwood's film, Mandela and the country's black majority are far from victims. It is black South Africans, whether the national sports council (who almost change the Springboks' colors and name), the fans (who choose to follow Mandela's lead and support the team), or the black rugby players in the film's last shot (who choose to play the game), who are shown to possess the agency to adopt or reject rugby.

This criticism of the positioning of Hollywood stars in these films relates to the Hollywood model of production itself: films must sell in order to recoup the considerable expense of their production and make a profit, and stars are used to sell films to a wide audience. Orgeret objects to Mandela's being por-trayed by an American film star, which also occurs in Joseph Sargeant's 1997 film *Mandela and de Klerk,* in which Sidney Poitier plays Mandela. In addition, as Orgeret rightly points out, there are a significant number of films in which African Americans, including Denzel Washington and Morgan Freeman, play African characters. There are also a number of films where white American Hollywood stars portray "white Africans." For example, in addition to Matt Damon's portrayal of Pienaar, Leonardo DiCaprio plays a white Zimbabwean soldier turned smuggler in *Blood Diamond,* and Kevin Kline stars as the white South African newspaper editor Donald Woods in Richard Attenborough's *Cry Freedom* (1987).[5] Hollywood stars remain among the most recognizable public figures internationally, and studios are more likely to bank on the draw-ing power of Denzel Washington and Leonardo DiCaprio than an actor un-known in most markets around the world.[6]

While not negating the importance of the debate about casting an Ameri-can or European actor over "homegrown" talent, the presence of the star is a critical factor in the commercial viability of Hollywood film production.

The marketing of *Invictus* focused on Matt Damon, who is extremely popular with younger audiences due to his role as the main star in the immensely successful *The Bourne Trilogy* (Doug Liman, 2002; Paul Greengrass, 2004, 2007). *Invictus* posters advertising the film prominently feature Damon, and the main extra feature on the basic DVD release features a minidocumentary about the American actor learning rugby in order to believably portray Pienaar. In conjunction with the casting of Damon, Freeman's popularity among a wide-ranging audience fits the Hollywood production model, especially when considering that, as Morgan Freeman stated at the film's UK premiere, this is a film that is "based on Mandela" (2010). From the opening scene, where the newly released Mandela's motorcade is heralded by the chanting of the black, soccer-playing schoolboys, through to the still image of (the real) Mandela that precedes the final scene of the young black men playing rugby, he is the film's omnipresence. And although *Invictus* provides a variation on the Hollywood sports film player / coach dynamic, Mandela has all along been coaching the secondary protagonist, Pienaar: if not about the play on the field, then certainly about his vision for the new South Africa.

The film consistently returns to short scenes that visually demonstrate Mandela's political skill in appropriating for the new South Africa Springbok team that when employed as "a metaphor for apartheid's crushing brutality . . . worked very well" (Carlin 2008, 42). During the first meeting between Pienaar and Mandela at the presidential offices in Pretoria, the president captures the rugby captain's respect and attention through an anecdote about the crowd greeting him with a rendition of *Nkosi Sikelel' iAfrika* (now the national anthem, alongside the Afrikaans *Die Stem van Suid-Afrika*) at the 1992 Barcelona Olympics. It was a time when, as Mandela admits to Pienaar, "the future—our future—seemed very bleak." Mandela's analogy draws a comparison between the outlook for the Springboks leading up to the World Cup (scenes at the beginning of the film show the team losing multiple matches) and the interregnum before the country's first free election in 1994.

Prior to the World Cup final against the All Blacks, Mandela looks out the window to see his security detail throwing around a rugby ball. Eastwood employs the sort of camera movement used to show the Springboks' games—medium close-ups shot at the eye level of the players—but with the white members of Mandela's detail explaining some of the rules of rugby to their black colleagues. Cutting to a shot of Mandela inside his office, the film shows the president asking a rhetorical question as a response to his critics, both black and white, who have questioned his motives in promoting the ideology of "One Team, One Country": Mandela asks, "Still think I'm wasting my time with the rugby?" In a subsequent scene, this marrying of rugby to the country's political future is reiterated. Looking out the hotel window at Johannesburg on the evening before the game, Pienaar, the platonic ideal of the rugby-mad Afrikaner, admits to his wife that he was not thinking about the upcoming game against the All Blacks, but was "thinking about how you spend thirty years in a tiny cell, and come out ready to forgive the people who put you there."

The shot of Pienaar echoes the earlier shot of the Springbok captain looking out the window of Mandela's prison cell at Robben Island, as well as the aforementioned shot of Mandela looking out the window at the formerly divided security detail "playing" rugby. The film's dialectical narrative pattern—rugby, a part of the historical, conservative antithesis to democracy, becoming synthesized in the political dynamic new South Africa—is reemphasized through the way these shots are put in conversation through thematic and aesthetic construction. With rugby providing a metaphor for the "rough" transition to a nascent democracy, *Invictus* conveys Mandela's political achievement in reclaiming a symbol of apartheid and demonstrates, in the words of Walter Benjamin, the power of seizing "hold of a memory as it flashes up at a moment of danger" (255).

### NOTES

1. The title of this essay comes from a conversation between Mandela and Pienaar during the film's first act.

2. The cinematography (particularly when the teams are engaged in scrum sequences) accentuates the physicality of the game but probably at the expense of clarity about the nuances and rules of the game. For an audience unfamiliar with rugby, the patterns and flow of the game may remain obscure. Rugby combines a roughness equaled by few other full contact sports—unlike American football, a sport descended from rugby, there are no pads used—with an array of complicated rules regarding tackling, kicking, and ball possession. Despite having a cult status in the United States and other countries, rugby has never achieved the global appeal of soccer and basketball.

3. Rugby is extremely popular throughout many of the former colonies of the British Empire, particularly in the other former white settler colonies of Canada, Australia, and New Zealand. The ninety-year rivalry between New Zealand and South Africa over world rugby supremacy underscores the dramatic tension of the showdown between the Springboks and the All Blacks in the film's climactic scene. In addition, see Grundlingh (1994) for more about the centrality of rugby in Afrikaner culture and politics.

4. Despite the enthusiasm for the Springboks among blacks that the film depicts in chronicling the team's run through the world cup, today rugby is not South Africa's most

popular sport. Even though there are a number of black players on both the national and international scene, rugby has not replaced soccer as the primary sporting interest of the country's majority, perhaps because the history of the Springboks cannot be readily forgotten as a whole. The enforcement of racial quotas on rugby teams in South Africa, a practice that was discontinued in 2007, did make some inroads in promoting the playing of rugby beyond the traditionally white schools and clubs; yet twenty out of the twenty-two players on South Africa's world champion team that same year were white. For evidence of the overwhelming fervor for soccer rather than rugby for the majority of South Africans, one need only turn to the country's recent, successful hosting of the FIFA World Cup. However, while not proportionate to the country's racial demographics, a number of "nonwhite" players and coaches, including former Springboks coach Peter de Villiers, have played a major role in South African rugby since 1995.

5. Attenborough's film is also one of the interracial buddy films listed by Artz.

6. One of the remarkable elements of the financial success of *District 9* is not only that the actor taking the leading role, Sharlto Copley, was unknown as an actor in both South Africa or abroad, but also that it was his acting debut.

REFERENCES

Artz, B. Lee. 1998. "Hegemony in Black and White: Interracial Buddy Films and the New Racism." In *Cultural Diversity and the U.S. Media*, edited by Yahya Kamalipour and Theresa Carilli, 67–79. Albany: State University of New York Press.
Baker, Aaron. 2003. *Contesting Identities: Sports in American film*. Urbana: University of Illinois Press.
Benjamin, Walter. 1969. *Illuminations*. Edited by Hannah Arendt. New York: Schocken Books.
Boraine, Alex. 2000. "Truth and Reconciliation in South Africa: The Third Way." In *Truth v. Justice: The Morality of Truth Commissions*, edited by Robert I. Rotberg and Dennis F. Thompson, 141–58. Princeton: Princeton University Press.
Carlin, John. 2008. *Playing the Enemy: Nelson Mandela and the Game That Made a Nation*. New York: Penguin Press.
Coetzee, J. M. 1992. *Doubling the Point: Essays and Interviews*. Edited by David Attwell. Cambridge, MA: Harvard University Press.
Fischer, Sibylle. 2004. *Modernity Disavowed*. Durham, NC: Duke University Press.
Grundlingh, Albert. 1994. "Playing for Power? Rugby, Afrikaner Nationalism, and Masculinity in South Africa, c.1900–1970." *International Journal of the History of Sport* 11 (3): 408–30.
Hamber, Brandon. 1998. "'Dr. Jekyll and Mr. Hyde': Problems of Violence Prevention and Reconciliation in South Africa's Transition to Democracy." In *Violence in South Africa: A Variety of Perspectives*, edited by Elirea Bornman, Rene van Eeden, and Marie Wentzel, 349–71. Pretoria, South Africa: HSRC.
Hassim, Shireen Tawana Kupe, and Eric Worby. 2008. *Go Home or Die Here: Violence, Xenophobia and the Reinvention of Difference in South Africa*. Johannesburg: Wits University Press.
*Invictus*. 2009. Directed by Clint Eastwood. Screenplay by Anthony Peckham. Burbank, CA: Warner Bros. Pictures.

"Invictus Premiere: Morgan Freeman Still Says He Knows 'Little to Nothing' about Rugby." *Telegraph.co.uk*. Jan. 31, 2010: http://www.telegraph.co.uk/culture/film/film-news/7122654/Invictus-premiere-Morgan-Freeman-says-he-still-knows-little-to-nothing-about-rugby.html.

Keller, Bill. 2008. "Entering the Scrum." *New York Times*, Aug. 17, BR9.

Lowenstein, Adam. 2005. *Shocking Representation: Historical Trauma, National Cinema, and the Modern Horror Film*. New York: Columbia University Press.

Orgeret, Kristin Skare. 2009. "Films Out of Africa." *Journal of African Media Studies* 1 (3): 505–9.

Paton, Alan. 1972. *The People and Land of South Africa*. New York: HarperCollins.

Ray, Robert B. 1985. *A Certain Tendency of the Hollywood Cinema, 1930–1980*. Princeton: Princeton University Press.

Ryle, John. 2005. "Introduction: The Many Voices of Africa." *Granta: The Magazine of New Writing* 92 (Winter): 9–15.

Tudor, Deborah V. 1997. *Hollywood's Vision of Team Sports*. New York: Routledge.

# TWELVE

# "Every Brother Ain't a Brother"

Cultural Dissonance and Nigerian Malaise in *District 9*'s New South Africa

KIMBERLY NICHELE BROWN

> I've said many times that the word "apartheid" means good neighborliness.
>
> —P. W. Botha

Hailed as the sleeper hit of the summer of 2009, *District 9* uses a quasi documentary style to chart the demise of Wikus van der Merwe (Sharlto Copley), a slightly inept Afrikaner bureaucrat charged with the relocation of the sentient alien population known derogatorily as "Prawns." Viewers learn that the insectoid aliens were stranded in the impoverished Johannesburg township of District 9 in 1982, twenty-eight years prior to the film's diegetic present, when the aliens' spaceship became inoperable and they were rescued subsequently by the South Africans. Wikus becomes empathetic to the plight of the aliens when he inadvertently ingests a liquid that causes his metamorphosis into an insectoid, which the audience witnesses throughout the course of the movie. In an attempt to undo the transformation, Wikus befriends the alien, Christopher, who has been secretly gathering alien technology that has been scattered throughout the township in the hopes of one day using the technology to repower his ship to return his brethren to their home world.

Nominated for four Oscars, the sci-fi thriller was produced by TriStar Pictures and directed by South African–born Canadian émigré Neill Blomkamp. Blomkamp moved to Canada with his family in 1997 at the age of eighteen, four years after the first democratic elections, open to people of all races, were held in South Africa. The Blomkamps' relocation is indicative of the massive emigration of whites from South Africa since the end of apartheid's reign. On February 14, 2009, *Newsweek* reported that "Some 800,000 out of a total white population of 4 million have left since 1995, by one count."[1] In an interview with Andrew O'Hehir for Salon.com, Blomkamp states,

My upbringing in that city [Johannesburg] had a massive effect on me, and I started to realize that everything to do with segregation and apartheid, and now the new xenophobic stuff that's happening in the city, all of that dominates my mind, quite a lot of the time. Then there's the fact that science fiction is the other big part of my mind, and I started to realize that the two fit well together. There's no message, per se, that I'm trying to get across with the movie. It's rather that I want to present science fiction, and put it in the environment that affected me. In the process, maybe I highlight all the topics that interest me, but I'm not giving any answers. You can take from it what you will.

Blomkamp works hard to achieve verisimilitude, as evidenced by his suturing of a mockumentary with traditional cinema, punctuated by cinema vérité.[2] Rather than see the mockumentary format as incidental, one could read Blomkamp's employment of the technique in much the same way that Armida De la Garza reads its usage in Sergio Arau's *A Day without Mexicans* (1998). De la Garza argues that Arau's film is emblematic of a "possible post-national imaginary, co-existing with, if not replacing, forms of national belonging" (2009, 119). I would argue that *District 9* is another "post-national imaginary," but one that functions to reinscribe old ways of national belonging in South Africa.

Contrary to its director's assertion that the film contains "no message, per se," *District 9* offers a metanarrative concerning both the apprehension of and hope for a new South Africa. *District 9* offers an interesting confluence of the science fiction trope of "first contact" and the ensuing anxieties such an encounter produces in humans (i.e., interspecies miscegenation as a threat to *human* rather than *racial* purity) with the rising xenophobia of a country struggling to develop a national identity in the face of encroaching alien populations (from both off-world and other African nations). Additionally, Wikus van der Merwe's twofold metamorphosis from a white Afrikaner to an alien Other and from *company man* to *enemy of the state* represents an attempt to reconcile South Africa's racist past and white complicity in the apartheid state with a newer, albeit counterfeit, representation of white masculinity as empathetic to the plight of the Other.[3]

In *Cinema in a Democratic South Africa* (2010), Lucia Saks investigates the trajectory of postapartheid cinema from 1994 to the present. She argues that this cinema seeks to move beyond race and to unify a nation under a common national identity, without eradicating the nation's multiracial complexion. Saks explains that within South Africa "there is a race to establish new terms of representation that will lead the way to harmony, however temporal, transient, and idealized" (2). She contends that the goal of South African cinema is to create a new national story that is essentially postracial in its desire to "disgorge the old styles of thinking and showing, illustrating and believing, and to supplant them with new images and ideas; a race to get people to reassign values to others and to their place in the new dispensation" (2). On the surface, Blomkamp's decision to make a Hollywood film that mimics movies that position white protagonists as the savior of blacks and other people of color seems incongruous with the stated goals of postapartheid cinema and its desire to offer counternarratives and depictions that challenge old notions of white supremacy and black inferiority.

Leonard Thompson explains that one of the goals of the Mandela government was to "attract massive infusions of foreign investments," which meant "opening South Africa to the global market and exposing South African industry to foreign competition" (2000, 278, 279). It is in this context that the new South African cinema project emerged as a way for South Africa to enact control over its global image. However, Mbye Cham reminds us that the postapartheid South African film industry is dominated by whites "and despite feeble challenges, American Hollywood products and models still dominate the country's mediascape. . . . The historically advantaged white filmmakers, most of whom have the advantage of better training and experience, continue to enjoy relatively easier access to resources, as rare and limited as these are for all" (viii–ix). In new millennial films, white directors still tend to serve as translators of black experiences for audiences in the United States. Although scholars such as John Rieder and black science fiction writers like Nalo Hopkinson have argued that science fiction actively critiques issues of colonialism, imperialism, and now globalization, change of genre aside, *District 9* bears much in common with films that feature white messiahs rescuing the Other (i.e., *Avatar, Blood Diamond, The Blind Side, The Help,* etc.).[4] Michael Valdez Moses explains that in the "prevailing 'progressive' reading of *District 9*, Wikus is transformed from a staunch (and unreflective) defender of the segregationist regime that employs him into a courageous dissenter and freedom fighter who struggles on behalf of the liberation of the aliens" (2010, 157). Like Moses, I challenge this reading and instead want to argue that *District 9* is emblematic of what Carter A. Wilson defines as "meta-racism" where "adversive" forms of racism have been supplanted by subtler manifestations in the wake of postracial discourse. Thus, while critics have hailed *District 9* as a strong indictment against the apartheid regime, I read the film as covertly pro-apartheid.

When the film opens, the audience is treated to the diegetic sound of Wikus, off camera, fumbling with his microphone. His clumsiness, lack of pretension, dowdy attire, and his admission that he is nervous mark Wikus as the proverbial everyman. However, he is also the recognizable company man; in fact we soon learn that Wikus has risen up the ranks of middle management through nepotism (his wife's father, Piet Smit [Dirk Minnaar] appoints him to his new position) to become the public face of Multinational United (MNU) in the Department of Alien affairs. Wikus explains that at MNU "we try to engage with the prawn on behalf of MNU and behalf of humans." Thus the film sets him up as an interstitial figure, whose role as corporate liaison will be reassessed throughout the course of the film and actually come to fruition with his eventual transformation into an insectoid.

After Wikus's contextualization of the role of MNU, the film switches momentarily from the documentary format to an establishing shot of the sort Hollywood audiences are more familiar with, even while being transported to the unfamiliar terrain of South Africa. The long shot of a bustling Johannesburg with the alien spacecraft hovering on the horizon is accompanied by the nondiegetic music from an African song sung in a tongue native to South Africa. The skyscrapers pictured amid busy highways reinscribe Africa, or precisely, South Africa, as a site of urbanization and technological advancement rather than the primitive jungle of the West's imagination. A voice-over explains, "To everyone's surprise, the ship didn't come to stop over Manhattan or Washington, or Chicago, but instead coasted to a halt directly over the city of Johannesburg." Another expert explains, "There was a lot of international pressure on us at the time. The entire world was looking at Johannesburg so we had to do the right thing." In several interviews, Blomkamp explains that he modeled *District 9* after the premise of the 1988 film *Alien Nation* (dir. Graham Baker). Unlike *Alien Nation,* whose premise is based on integrating the alien population into the US mainstream, "doing the right thing" means setting up the aliens in "temporary" housing in the township of District 9 for approximately twenty-eight years rather than integrating them into South African society in an egalitarian fashion. Much like Botha's deadpanned comment that "apartheid means neighborliness," humanitarian rhetoric is used to rationalize the encampment of the aliens. Johannesburg, then, as the site of "first contact" is a very deliberate choice for Blomkamp. In an interview with Tasha Robinson, Blomkamp states, "In my opinion, the film doesn't exist without Joburg. It's not like I had a story, and then I was trying to pick a city. It's totally the other way around. . . .

I actually think Johannesburg represents the future. My version of what I think the world is going to become looks like Johannesburg."[5]

The title of my essay derives in part from Public Enemy's 1989 rap song "Welcome to the Terrordome" that cautions against forming solidarity on the basis of race alone because, "every brother ain't a brother." I make playful use of this phrase because it can be applicable to the loss of a structured way of thinking about solidarity along racial lines that was part and parcel of the apartheid regime. Yvette Christiansë argues that with the 1993 Truth and Reconciliation Hearings "all subjects were faced with the task of having to reconsider their relation to the past, specifically its power to proscribe identity" (375). Given that Botha's notion of apartheid as "neighborliness" has become obsolete, I am interested in the ways Blomkamp mimics Botha in his act of filmic subterfuge; the film masks its own its own xenophobia with the supposed cathartic and dramatic gesture of having Wikus walk in his neighbor's shoes by becoming the Other in a very literal and visceral sense.

But, every brother, ain't a brother. In fact Botha's definition of apartheid permeates the narrative. Catharsis is temporal at best but not preferable to the maintenance of the status quo, as the film offers no hope for improving the lot of the "Prawns" except deportment. *District 9* employs aliens as allegorical referents in order to flesh out contemporary problems of race and globalization in South Africa. One of the many problematic elements about *District 9* is that it never really fixes the conundrum of using "Prawns" as a *metaphor* for disenfranchised blacks in the face of the existence of real blacks in South Africa who are still mainly disenfranchised in the contemporary postapartheid state. What the movie does instead is typical of films starring white Africans as protagonist; it relegates blacks to the background.[6] Additionally, and the most damning barrier to achieving brotherhood: the "Prawn" cannot be understood outside of the context of racist labeling—the audience is never told what the so-called "Prawn" calls himself. In fact, it is nearly impossible to tell one "Prawn" from another. Humanizing, decolonizing, or liberating the "Prawn" is not really the issue.

Nigerian immigrants serve as the film's archetypal menace; they are depicted as engaging in acts of sexual deviance (i.e., interspecies prostitution), cannibalism, bizarre rituals of animal sacrifice, auto theft, and general scams, as well as arms and drug trafficking. Although the murder rate in South Africa is excessively high (almost 27,000 in 1995–96)[7] and the rise in violent crime has resulted in a mass exodus of both blacks and whites, in *District 9* Nigerians are singled out as the only criminal element in Johannesburg.

Their presence as quintessential villains is rivaled only slightly by the depiction of Colonel Koobus Venter (David James), who symbolizes the old Boer regime. The literal annihilation of both entities within the fictive realm of the movie underscores the belief that Nigerian immigration and overt espousals of white supremacist rhetoric must be curtailed in order for a new South African national identity to emerge.

It should be noted that the largest group of recent black immigrants to South Africa hails from Mozambique and Zimbabwe rather than Nigeria.[8] In an interview with Salon.com, Blomkamp has described the discrimination that black Zimbabwean immigrants face at the hands of black South Africans as ironic; in the light of their recent experience with apartheid, one would expect the latter to be less likely to discriminate. However, Blomkamp's observation does not take into account the fact that whites still hold much of the wealth and land in South Africa, leaving the majority population to compete with black immigrants for limited resources. He essentially reinforces the rhetoric of black on black violence (US) and tribalism (African), which puts the onus of intraracial conflict on blacks rather than on an unequal economic system that still privileges whites. Black South Africans are depicted as being just as intolerant of the aliens as whites were of blacks both before and during apartheid, thus neutralizing the complicity of white South Africans in either era—discrimination is treated as a natural human condition.

In the light of Blomkamp's disapproval of the xenophobia that has arisen because of the influx of these of populations, his decision to target Nigerian immigrants for censure and demonization is suspect. Carina Ray reminds her readers that Nigeria "not only led the 1986 boycott of the Commonwealth Games in protest over Britain's refusal to enact full sanctions against apartheid South Africa, it also chaired the U.N. anti-apartheid committee and supported the anti-apartheid movement and southern African liberation movements financially." She further asserts that Blomkamp's characterization of the cannibalistic crime lord, Obesanjo (Eugene Khumbanyiwa), is actually a thinly veiled reference to Nigeria's former military ruler, Olusegun Obasanjo, who "in the late 1970s . . . ramped up his country's support for the anti-apartheid movement, which continued until apartheid fell."

While I agree with Ray's assessment, I would also argue that Nigeria becomes a target because its growing economy problematizes the widespread belief that African nations were better managed under white colonial rule, and positions Nigeria (with the success of Nollywood) in direct competition with South Africa on the global market, as well as a threat to Hollywood's domination in the same arena. In 2009 Nollywood managed to surpass Hollywood as the second largest film industry in the world, and the Lagos-based industry is rapidly catching up to that of India. Jonathan Haynes suggests that rather than see Nollywood as imitative of Hollywood or Bollywood, the name reveals "that we live in a multipolar world where the old patterns of cultural imperialism have changed and viewers have a much greater choice in the media they consume" (2007b, 106). In the global film industry, particularly in relation to Africa, "old patterns of cultural imperialism" included the use of costly film stock and other production material, as well as the cost of cinematic training and the dependence on foreign backing and the film festival circuit for authenticity. Onookome Okome explains that Nollywood's use of video film and its refusal to look to the West for legitimacy in cinema circles, opting instead to cultivate an audience of postcolonial viewers worldwide, has made it an autonomous entity (2007, 1). Haynes concurs, stating,

> Nollywood is an extraordinary example of the sort of coping mechanism that keeps Africa alive: out of the impossibility of producing celluloid films in Nigeria (because of economic collapse and social insecurity) came a huge industry, constructed on the slenderest of means and without anyone's permission. Cruelly constrained in its material circumstances, it is a heroic act of self-assertion—on the part of Nigeria in general, and of the individual filmmakers. (2007a, 131)

Although Nollywood's detractors and film purists might cast a disparaging eye on its use of video film, Okome argues that with the emergence of this technology, "the discourse on African cinema will need to be rephrased in very radical ways" (2007, 3).

In the 1990s two seemingly disconnected things—Nollywood and internet bank scams—served to mark Nigerians as hypercapitalistic and corrupt. The internet bank scams have been featured in US television programs such as *Law and Order* and *Homicide: Life on the Street* as early as 1992, and more recently, on Oprah Winfrey's talk show on April 13, 2007, and on the pilot episode for the show *Leverage* in 2008.[9] An anonymous film critic on the website *NigeriansTalk* argues that movies like *Tears of the Sun* (2003) and *X-Men Origins: Wolverine* (2009) show that Nigerians have supplanted Russians as Hollywood's new super villain.[10] Gary Baines argues that the banking scams "play upon several weaknesses of human nature, especially the belief by many businessmen that a bunch of hicks from Africa could never fool a shrewd

American businessman" (2003, vii). I would argue more explicitly that they play on Western conceit that continues to position Africa as primitive and technologically unsophisticated.

In *District 9* Blomkamp alludes playfully to the bank scams by demonstrating the "Cat-nip" con the Nigerians run routinely on the aliens, thus exploiting the aliens' obsession for the product. *District 9* reinscribes notions of the black primitive in order to neutralize the Nigerian menace. In his book *Colonialism and the Emergence of Science Fiction,* Rieder argues that "the key element linking colonial ideology to science fiction's fascination with new technology is the new technology's scarcity. The thrill of the technological breakthrough is not that it benefits everyone but that it produces a singular, drastic difference between those who possess the new invention . . . and those who do not" (32). Struggling for legitimacy in the global marketplace, the South African government finds itself in competition with the Nigerian immigrants who have found success in the criminal sector within South Africa, so much so that when Wikus and the MNU military unit run across Obsjenjo, they give him a wide berth. However, the Nigerian threat is neutralized because Blomkamp cinematically sequesters the Nigerians within the township in a way that, as Jordache Abner Ellapen might argue, is indicative of Africkaner Nationalist ideologies in relation to blacks in general within the sociopolitical site of the township.

Ellapen explains that "the 'township space' is a modern invention constructed through Afrikaner Nationalist ideologies to blacks from whites, but the project of the township was to construct black identity and culture as pre-modern. The 'township space' mobilized myths associated with the 'otherness' of black identity" (114). Wikus and MNU are able to ignore the Nigerian mafia that has arisen in District 9 because, while detrimental to those who populate District 9, Nigerian vice is restricted to the confines of the township. Additionally, while Blomkamp might concede that the Nigerian crime lord is badass, he is depicted as technologically unsophisticated.[11] The irony presented by the Nigerians is that although they amass technology in large numbers, they do not have the ability to use it. Although the movie explains that alien weaponry works in tandem with alien DNA, therefore making it impossible for humans to operate, white South Africans are engaged in scientific research to overcome this obstacle, whereas the Nigerians resort to cannibalistic rituals based on the superstitious belief that ingesting alien body parts will enable them to operate the weapons. Here Blomkamp enacts the well-worn Cartesian duality in which the Nigerian immigrant is depicted as emotive and instinctual, while the white-led MNU scientists, although equally brutal, are the intellectuals.

Despite being negatively received by Nigerians both on the continent and abroad, *District 9* was nominated for four Academy Awards in 2010 and maintains a four-star rating on major cable venues. Indeed, one could argue that Hollywood tends to bestow the highest honors on films that have problematic racial representations and that cast white protagonists as saviors of racial Others. Additionally, as Carina Ray has established, there has been scant mention of the movie's "egregious portrayal" of Nigerians by mainstream US movie critics. With the exception of the *District 9 eSymposium*, posted by Paul Zeleza, very little scholarly attention has been given to the movie and what it says about Hollywood's continued stereotypical representations of blacks and its visual depictions of the "new South Africa."

Because films like *District 9* persist in replicating black stereotypes, claims of postraciality within the South African cinema project must be met with skepticism. Speaking of South Africa's goals toward postraciality, Grant Farred writes that "'Post'-racialism, however contentious such a condition might be, constitutes the dialogic project of recognizing race as the primary discourse to be at once engaged and disarticulated" (2006, 52). To buttress his argument, Farred quotes Paul Gilroy when he states that postracialism cannot be achieved "without violating the precious forms of solidarity and community" (52). However, in the case of *District 9*'s new South Africa, I am persuaded by Juliet Hooker's concept of "racialized solidarity" in which she explains that the solidarity and community that whites form with each other rather than those "essential to sustaining a black biopolitics," as Farred argues, is what really must be considered (52).

In his roundtable response to *District 9*, published in *Safundi: A Journal of South African and American Studies,* Ralph Goodman places the movie within the context of the Truth and Reconciliation Hearings. If good fences make good neighbors, as the old adage states, then Wikus's supposed naïveté regarding MNU's hidden agenda seems believable—the "fences" shield whites against the reality of township living. Goodman explains that the Truth and Reconciliation Hearings shocked a "majority of Afrikanerdom" with the double revelation of (1) "their previous lack of full awareness" and (2) "the fact that when it came to white Afrikaners, the general public often made no distinction between major perpetrators of evil deeds, and those who, like most whites were guilty of quiescence, moral laziness, or willful silence in the face of clear discrimination against the majority of the populace" (2010, 171).

Goodman insists that this double revelation has prompted a "critical mass" of Afrikaners to "slowly and painfully" alter how they respond to the racial Other. He further contends that this transformation among the Afrikaner population has "begun to earn Afrikaners as a whole a new respect within many postapartheid South African circles."

It is in this vein that Goodman is able to put a positive spin on *District 9*'s ending. Goodman unwittingly conflates the audience's acceptance of Wikus once he has transformed into the racial Other as a hopeful sign that white audiences can be conditioned to accept and like racial Others that exist in the real world. Goodman writes, "He becomes hybrid, one of 'them,' and yet still remains the likeable antihero Wikus. The last point is crucial: despite his own disgust and the sheer abjectness of his transformation, the viewer's sympathies remain with Wikus. This might well be the single most radical aspect of the film" (174). Technical details aside, Blomkamp fully acknowledges that he and his production team used special effects and other movie magic to mitigate the general aversion that most moviegoers have to insects by enlarging the eyes of not just insectoid Wikus, but all of the aliens to make them more palatable or "lovable." The audience, then, has been manipulated into its identification with Wikus by these effects arguably as much as by witnessing his transformation and subsequent hardship.

While Wikus has lost the cachet of white humanity within the *filmic* realm, at the heart of things, they know Wikus is still Wikus, which is to say that he is still white, and still human. Therefore, one could argue that rather than empathy, the audience experiences Wikus's chagrin at losing his privilege. Further, we are more horrified that Wikus, who is *passing* as alien, is traumatized by his experience than we are horrified by the plight of the insectoids who have been discriminated against for years. Unlike Goodman, then, I would argue that Wikus's transformation follows the themes of malaise and cultural dissonance present in the film. Becoming the Other is the process of disorientation rather than enlightenment, and entails the loss of home and family to ensure against the spread of contagion. In the last scene of the movie, the audience identifies Wikus from other prawns because he is holding a handmade flower; his wife has explained earlier that he has a penchant for making handmade gifts as a symbol of his love for her. The flower shows the audience that he is still human; Wikus is banking on Christopher's promise to return and restore his humanity. If human privilege is a metaphor in the film for white privilege, the flower also marks his whiteness.

Therefore, in the end, the audience experiences Wikus's situation as one of lack, rather than using him as a vehicle through which to gain an empathetic understanding of the Other. The audience laments Wikus's loss as debasement, and what the loss of that privilege means in southern Africa and the world over: not only do you become homeless, a scavenger, a thief, a would-be revolutionary, an enemy of the state, but you also lose the privilege of seeing humanity as your birthright. At the end of the movie, the audience is hoping, like Wikus, for Christopher's speedy return to earth so that he can reverse Wikus's inhuman condition and regain all that he has lost. In tandem with its desire to see a sequel, the audience wants things back to normal.

It is significant to remember that unlike Jake Sully (Sam Worthington), the protagonist in *Avatar* (James Cameron, 2009), Wikus's transformation is involuntary. While postracial discourse and neoliberalism have trained us to root for the Other and to express concern for the condition of the Other (at least in public), no one really wants to *be* the Other. Despite *District 9*'s easy reliance on the buddy trope reflected in the homosocial bonding that occurs between Christopher and Wikus, the movie's treatment of Nigerians and the fact that even if we concede that Wikus's friendship with Christopher is genuine and not born out of necessity, Wikus still does not want to *be* Christopher.

In his last conversation with his wife, she asks Wikus, "How can we go back?" Moses contends that "the implication is that Wikus and Tania [Vanessa Haywood] would happily return to a world in which humans and aliens do not mix, indeed have no reason to interact" (2010, 160). Wikus's interaction with his wife at this juncture also reinforces their shared belief in racial purity. While insectoids can mate with humans, it is not only illegal but also deemed perverse; throughout the film both Nigerian prostitutes and Wikus are vilified for having real and alleged sexual liaisons with aliens. For Nigerian women, this accusation plays on long-standing stereotypes of black women as lascivious and sexually deviant; these women offer a contrast to Tania, whom Wikus refers to as "angelic." Wikus's reverence of Tania recalls the fervor with which white men both during apartheid and in the segregated U.S. South "protected" white womanhood against the threat of black male rape. For example, Timothy Keegan describes how white masculinity in South Africa "was in a state of malaise" due to the perceived sexual threat that black men posed to white female "honour" before the start of the First World War and in the face of dissolving racial boundaries (2001, 459). Suffering from a similar malaise, it does not occur to Wikus to suggest that she sully herself (in reputation or deed) by taking him back, even though they are still married, thereby modeling the *proper* behavior of the Other toward white women.

John Marx contends that "the movie ends with something like the question of whether viewers are more terrified of the pernicious administration they know, or by the prospect of revolutionary—that is to say alien—change" (2010, 166). This final interaction between Wikus and his wife demonstrates the real malaise—the failure for either of them to have a true catharsis; both would rather fall back on old racial scripts than embrace a brotherhood based on equality rather than on the maintenance of good fences. So in summation, let me quote Malcolm X: "I believe in the brotherhood of all men, but I don't believe in wasting brotherhood on anyone who doesn't want to practice it with me. Brotherhood is a two-way street." In *District 9*, brotherhood is definitely not a two-way street, because in the end, every brother ain't a *revolutionary* brother.

## NOTES

1. These numbers are inconclusive; actual figures might be higher given that the South African government has been unable to compile accurate data on migration out of the country. See http://www.newsweek.com/2009/02/13/fleeing-from-south-africa.html.

2. Additionally, one cannot help but make comparisons between the township of District 9 depicted in the film and the actual township of District 6.

3. *District 9* joins works like the film *Stander* and J. M. Coetzee's novel *Disgrace* (1999) in that envisioning. *Disgrace* was later made into a movie in 2008 directed by Steve Jacobs.

4. For more research on the "white messiah" figure in contemporary Hollywood film, see Vera and Gordon 2003.

5. For the interview in its entirety, see http://www.avclub.com/articles/district-9-director-neill-blomkamp,31606/.

6. Films such as *Stander, In My Country,* and *Disgrace* participate in the marginalization of blacks because the films' focus on the figure of the white African supplants the experiences of the majority black population.

7. See http://www.bbc.co.uk/news/world-africa-11243513.

8. Zimbabwean immigration has risen as many seek to escape the regime of President Robert Mugabe, while immigration from Mozambique has been on the rise since the eruption of civil war in 1977.

9. For example, please refer to the *Law and Order* season 3 episode "Consultation" *and the* Homicide: Life on the Street *season* 5 episode "Deception."

10. See http://nigerianstalk.org/2010/09/29naughty-at-50-%E2%80%93-evolution-of-nigerian-notoriety-on-american-screens/.

11. It is instructive that Robert Stam has a similar reading regarding how Bantus and biracial figures are represented in the 1984 movie *The Gods Must Be Crazy*. Stam argues that the movie "relays colonial discourse of official White South Africa. The racist discourse of the film posits a Manichean binarism contrasting happy and noble but impotent Bantusian 'Bushman,' living in splendid isolation, with dangerous but incompetent mulatto-led revolutionaries. Yet the film camouflages its racism by a superficial critique of White technological civilization" (180–81).

REFERENCES

Baines, Gary. 2003. *Nigerian Scams Revisited*. New York: Novinka Books.
Cartelli, Philip. 2007. "Nollywood Comes to the Caribbean." *Film International* 5 (4): 112–14.
Cham, Mbye. 2009. Foreword to *Zulu Love Letter: A Screen Play*, by Bhekizizwe Peterson and Ramadan Suleman, vi–x. Johannesburg: University of the Witwatersrand Press.
Christiansë, Yvette. 2003. "Passing Away: The Unspeakable (Losses) of Postapartheid South Africa." In *Loss: The Politics of Mourning*, edited by David L. Eng and David Kazanjian, 372–95. Berkeley: University of California Press.
De la Garza, Armida. 2009. "Mockumentary as Post-nationalism: National Identity in *A Day without a Mexican* by Sergio Arau." In *Visual Synergies in Fiction and Documentary Film from Latin America*, edited by Miriam Haddu and Joanna Page, 119–32. New York: Palgrave Macmillan.
Ellapen, Jordache Abner. June 2007. "The Cinematic Township: Cinematic Representations of the 'Township Space' and Who Can Claim the Rights to Representation in Post-apartheid South African Cinema." *Journal of African Cultural Studies* 19 (1): 113–38.
Farred, Grant. 1997. "Bulletproof Settlers: The Politics of Offense in the New South Africa." In *Whiteness: A Critical Reader*, edited by Mike Hill, 67–78. New York: New York University Press.
———. 2006. "'Shooting the White Girl First': Race in Postapartheid South Africa." In *Globalization and Race: Transformations in the Cultural Production of Blackness*, edited by Kamari Maxine Clarke and Deborah A. Thomas, 49–71. Durham, NC: Duke University Press.
Fischer, Claude S. 1973. "Urban Malaise." *Social Forces* 52 (2): 221–35.
Gaylard, Gerald. 2010. "*District 9* and the Parktown Prawns." *Safundi: The Journal of South African and American Studies* 11 (1): 167–70.
Goodman, Ralph. 2010. "The Allegory of District 9." *Safundi: The Journal of South African and American Studies* 11 (1): 170–72.
Halpern, Jodi, and Harvey M. Weinstein. 2004. "Rehumanizing the Other: Empathy and Reconciliation." *Human Rights Quarterly* 26 (3): 561–83.
Haynes, Jonathan. 2007a. "Nollywood in Lagos, Lagos in Nollywood Films." *Africa Today* 54 (2): 131–50.
———. 2007b. "'Nollywood': What's in a Name?" *Film International* 5 (4): 106–8.
Helgesson, Stefan. 2010. "*District 9*: The Global South as Science Fiction." *Safundi: The Journal of South African and American Studies* 11 (1): 172–75.
Hooker, Juliet. 2009. *Race and the Politics of Solidarity (Transgressing Boundaries: Studies in Black Politics and Black Communities)*. Oxford: Oxford University Press.
Keegan, Timothy. 2001. "Gender, Degeneration and Sexual Danger: Imagining Race and Class in South Africa, ca. 1912." *Journal of Southern African Studies* 27 (3): 459–77.
Marx, John. 2010. "Alien Rule." *Safundi: The Journal of South African and American Studies* 11 (1): 164–67.
Moses, Michael Valdez. 2010. "The Strange Ride of Wikus Van De Merwe." *Safundi: The Journal of South African and American Studies* 11 (1): 155–75.
"Naughty at 50—Evolution of Nigerian Notoriety in American Screens." 2010. http://nigerianstalk.org/2010/09/29/naughty-at-50-%E2%80%93-evolution-of-nigerian-notoriety-on-american-screens/.

O'Hehir, Andrew. 2009. "Is Apartheid Acceptable—for Giant Bugs?" *Salon*, August 12. http://www.salon.com/2009/08/12/blomkamp/.

Okome, Onookome. 2007. "Nollywood: Spectatorship, Audience and the Sites of Consumption." *Postcolonial Text* 3 (2): 1–21.

Osinubi, Tokunbo Simbowale, and Oladipupo Sunday Osinubi. 2006. "Ethnic Conflicts in Contemporary Africa: The Nigerian Experience." *Journal of Social Science* 12 (2): 101–14.

Ray, Carina. "Humanizing Aliens or Alienating Africans? *District 9* and the Politics of Representation." *The Zeleza Post*. (eSymposium on *District 9*). Vol. 3 presentation. http://www.zeleza.com/symposium/949.

Rieder, John. 2008. *Colonialism and the Emergence of Science Fiction*. Middletown, CT: Wesleyan University Press.

Saks, Lucia. 2010. *Cinema in a Democratic South Africa*. Bloomington: Indiana University Press.

Simoes Da Silva, Tony. 2005. "Narrating a White Africa: Autobiography, Race and History." *Third World Quarterly* 26 (3): 471–78.

Stam, Robert, and Elle Shohat, eds. 1995. *Unthinking Eurocentrism: Multiculturalism and the Media*. London: Routledge.

Thompson, Leonard. 2000. *A History of South Africa*. New Haven: Yale University Press.

Valji, Nahla. 2008. "Creating the Nation: The Rise of Violent Xenophobia in the New South Africa." Centre for the Study of Violence and Reconciliation. September 8.

Vera, Hernán, and Andrew M. Gordon. 2003. "The Beautiful American: Sincere Fictions of the White Messiah in Hollywood Movies." In *White Out: The Continuing Significance of Racism,* edited by Ashley "Woody" Doane and Eduardo Bonilla-Silva, 113–28. New York: Routledge.

Wilson, Carter. 1996. *Racism: From Slavery to Advanced Capitalism*. Thousand Oaks, CA: Sage Publications.

THIRTEEN

# Coaxing the Beast Out of the Cage
Secrecy and Disclosure in *Red Dust* and *Catch a Fire*
JANE BRYCE

Any discussion of two films in tandem suggests a comparative approach, the teasing out of similar or opposing motifs and shared or divergent meanings.[1] The bracketing of *Red Dust* and *Catch a Fire* in one essay is, however, more than a gesture toward a shared thematics and provenance. It rests on the fact that both films participate in an ongoing project of representing South Africa through the struggles, experience, and political project of Ruth First, Joe Slovo, and their daughters, Shawn, Gillian, and Robyn. In the same breath, this statement has to be qualified by acknowledging the essentially collective process of film production and the inevitable mediation therefore of any idea of an overarching individual narrative. It has to be further qualified by the salient differences between the daughters and their parents, even between the parents themselves. If, as a result, this essay is more an exercise in respecting difference than in claiming likeness, it nonetheless works on the assumption of filiation: that there is a connecting thread between the anti-apartheid activist, left-identified, revolutionary first generation, the raised-in-exile second generation, and their differently inflected but common interest in promoting a postracial, postapartheid politics.

Shawn and Gillian Slovo have both produced memoirs—a film and a literary narrative—of their childhood, in which they reflect on the impact of their parents' political commitment on their lives as children and since. Shawn Slovo's film, *A World Apart* (1988), focuses on the period after Joe had gone into exile, and the daily contradictions of the life Ruth and the three daughters continued to lead in Johannesburg, especially the exclusion of the children from any information regarding the whereabouts of their father or their mother's political activities. It shows the toll this took on Shawn as the eldest daughter, especially when Ruth was imprisoned for 117 days under the so-called 90-Day Act, leaving the girls and their grandmother to survive as best they could. In her memoir, *Every Secret Thing: My Family, My Country* (1997), Gillian Slovo recounts how, after the deaths of her parents, an ANC comrade of theirs, Mac Maharaj, described watching *A World Apart:*

> Mac said he had enjoyed the film but then he added something differ-
> ent: some of his African comrades, he said, had decided that what the
> young girl in the film needed was a "good slap." . . . Mac said quickly
> that of course he disagreed. Our childhoods were particularly dif-
> ficult, he said, for the very reason that we were white and therefore
> isolated in our community. Not so the kids of African comrades, he
> continued. They all knew the score. "Africans lived in a community
> that warned you," he said, "that was with you, even if only in spirit.
> You didn't." (Gillian Slovo 1997, 97–98)

This incident points to a subject that has gained in prominence since the end of apartheid—the role of whites in the new South Africa, their responsibility for and acknowledgment of the crimes of the past, and the reconfiguring of "whiteness" outside of privilege and power. The cultural critic Sarah Nuttall says of this process:

> Far from being normative or consistent, [whiteness] emerges within
> a range of formations or constellations, in particular those which
> have to do with masking, concealment, transfiguration, and secrecy,
> on the one hand, and with the politics and practice of visibility . . .
> on the other. (Nuttall 2001, 116)

The children of activists, like the Slovo sisters, stand in a particular relation-ship to this process of redefinition. With regard to past relations between black and white activists, Gillian asks, "How could we win? Compared to the poverty, degradation and discrimination they endured, our suffering was negligible. When it came down to it, the scale was weighted permanently against us" (98). Yet suffering there was, as both these memoirs testify, aris-ing from the fear and the secrecy that dogged their lives, the dread of ad-mitting to the name Slovo, and the longing for normality represented by a white community to which they did not truly belong. Ruth and her three daughters, aged fourteen, twelve, and eleven, followed Joe into exile in 1964. After several years in England, both parents returned to Africa: Ruth to a post at Maputo University from which she maintained her active support for the freedom struggle, and Joe at first to Angola as leader of Umkhonto we Sizwe (MK), the armed wing of the ANC, before he too moved to Maputo. Ruth was assassinated by a letter bomb in her office in 1982; Joe, who lived to see the end of apartheid and was appointed Minister of Housing in the first democratic government, died of cancer in 1995.

It is hardly surprising that such a highly politicized family and national affiliation should continue to inform the lives and work of the Slovo sisters. All three sisters are cultural workers: Shawn and Gillian are writers; Robyn an independent film producer. The fact that their shared concerns and feelings (as signified by the subtitle of Gillian's memoir, *My Family, My Country*) have been articulated in memoir and fiction, film and literary text, makes the two films discussed here inseparable from their individual and collective expressive project. Though neither *Red Dust* (2004) nor *Catch a Fire* (2006) is overtly autobiographical, and though both are directed by non–South African male directors (Philip Noyce, Australian, and Tom Hooper, British/Australian), the concept and the screenplay of both films originate with the Slovos and are to a considerable extent shaped by their peculiar perspective on South Africa. Troy Kennedy-Martin's screenplay for *Red Dust* is based on the novel of the same title by Gillian Slovo, while Shawn Slovo wrote the screenplay for *Catch a Fire,* which is produced by her sister Robyn.

*Red Dust* dramatizes the operation of the Truth and Reconciliation Commission (TRC, 1996–2003) through a focus on the amnesty plea of one special branch policeman/torturer and the ramifications of his open-court statements in the lives of his victims and their families. In his essay, "Looking the Beast in the (Fictional) Eye: The Truth and Reconciliation Commission on Film," David Philips (2007) explains the workings of the commission in detail and its relation to *Red Dust,* and two other films that came out in 2004, *In My Country* (John Boorman, 2004) and *Forgiveness* (Ian Gabriel, 2004). I will therefore confine myself to noting the distinction he makes between the Human Rights Violation Committee, to which victims told their stories, and the Amnesty Committee, dramatized in *Red Dust,* to which perpetrators of crimes could appeal for amnesty (Philips 2007, 304). The two criteria for the granting of amnesty were full disclosure and proving that the crime was politically motivated. Victims attended and could oppose the granting of amnesty, as Alex Mpondo initially does in *Red Dust.* The TRC represented a compromise between the outgoing Nationalist government, which wanted a general amnesty for all its operatives, and the incoming ANC government, which refused, but offered individual amnesties on a case by case basis. The replacing of retributive justice by reconciliation has been much criticized by those in South Africa who feel they were robbed of justice through this process. The Slovos could be said to be among them.[2] In 1998, they attended and testified at a TRC appeal by the men who had murdered their mother—dubbed by Gillian Desk-Man and Bomb-Maker—with the intention of opposing their amnesty. Recalling the process in a lecture recorded in Chicago, Gillian analyzes its shortcomings as follows.[3] First, she says, the days on end they spent in the hearing meant they got to know the men at a level of intimacy "most difficult to endure." Second, although the TRC granted amnesty on the basis of full disclosure—telling the whole truth—and demonstrating a political purpose, "I do not believe that they killed for a political purpose. And I don't believe they told the truth" (G. Slovo 2006). At the time, Robyn Slovo was quoted as saying, "We were deeply shocked by the amnesties which are completely unwarranted and unfair" (Brittain 2000). Shawn describes how after sitting in a room for ten days with her mother's killers, "They were given amnesty, but all I know at the end is that they are our mother's killers and they are free."[4]

The *untruth* that emerged from this encounter with the TRC was, according to Gillian, that it obscured the fact that "they had killed for hatred" (2006). The novel she subsequently wrote—*Red Dust*—was conceived as a fiction that would express her misgivings but keep her personal experience at a distance, but she found herself unable to write the book that way, and it ended up, she says, "shot through with my own feelings." Her themes, "how we carry the past into the present" and "intimacy between enemies," arose from the encounter with her mother's killers, which remains the story's subtext (2006). The release of the film in 2004, a year after the TRC finally closed its doors, and ten years after the first democratic elections in postapartheid South Africa, puts it close to its material in terms of time; in terms of place, it brings vividly to the screen the emblematic red dust of the Karoo, and the small-town spaces and relationships of the fictional Smitsrivier, for which the Eastern Cape town of Graaff-Reinet stands in.[5] However, though time and place may bear a close resemblance to "reality," neither novel nor film purports to be "history." Rather, Slovo's experience is refracted through a cast of characters offering multiple points of view which can never be reconciled. Special branch policeman Dirk Hendricks (Jamie Bartlett), serving time for a different crime, is claiming amnesty for the torture of ANC activist and now MP, Alex Mpondo (Chiwetel Ejiofor). Mr. and Mrs. Sizela (Mawongo Tyala and Nomhle Nkyonyeni), parents of Steve, arrested with Alex and never released, are seeking to know what happened to him and the whereabouts of his body. They have appealed to "lefty lawyer" Ben Hoffman (Marius Weyers) for support, and he, elderly and sick, has appealed to his protégée, Sarah Barcant (Hilary Swank), to return from New York and help with the case. Alex is appearing as witness and "victim," he claims, "to block the amnesty of a sadistic bastard." Hendricks's senior officer, Piet Muller (Ian Roberts), now putting his skills to use as director of a security firm, is determined his name will not be called at the tribunal.

This cast of characters is caught in a tension between desire for and dread of disclosure. Sarah Barcant, whose job as a lawyer is to pursue the truth, is herself a reluctant returnee. Marked by her difference (her American accent), she has deliberately distanced herself from the country she says she hates by emigrating to and identifying with the USA, returning now only in deference to Ben. As her role in the film makes clear, it was not only blacks who suffered, and Alex Mpondo gradually gets to the truth of her rejection of her origins. After she was arrested for "dating a black boy," her mother lost custody of her and emigrated. Her boyfriend, Johnny Naniso, got a nine-month sentence and, like Steve, disappeared. Ben continually exerts moral blackmail on Sarah to return and help in making the new South Africa, and at the end of the film, Alex also urges, "This country is changing and you should be part of it." Sarah's reply comes straight from *Every Secret Thing:* "I always felt that what happened to me was such a small thing compared to what happened to you." Alex's response, "We have the right to say that it hurt," gives her the permission she needs to admit her own pain, which she has kept at bay through her role as lawyer, and tried to bury by living elsewhere. It also signals the new structures of power in postapartheid South Africa, whereby white belonging—as the Afrikaner writer Antje Krog has shown[6]—can only be at the invitation of the black majority, and only on condition of "full disclosure," of which Sarah is no less afraid than anyone else.

Slovo's theme of "how we carry the past into the present" is dramatized in the film through the use of repeated short flashbacks, while "intimacy between enemies" is conveyed through the use of close-ups and the gaze. As trauma narratives, *Red Dust* and *Catch a Fire* seek to give expression to the unsaid, unsayable experiences of the past as part of a process of healing, and in this they share the objectives of the TRC itself. At the symbolic level, the swimming pool where Alex Mpondo repeatedly immerses himself may be read as his own unconscious, where his memories of the past are repressed. But these repressed memories return unbidden in the form of fiery flashes of scenes from a torture being enacted on his own abject body, and, as his memory returns, on the body of Steve Sizela. These flashbacks are not only cinematic, they represent a symptom of posttraumatic stress disorder; by claiming that he too suffers from PTSD in the form of nightmares, Hendricks tries to make himself a victim. Ironically, Alex, designated victim by the TRC, angrily rejects the "Victim" label on his place at the hearing, and objects to Hendricks's lawyer referring to him as such. Yet victim and perpetrator are both ambiguous labels, as a later incident makes clear. Although he succeeds in presenting evidence that he did not break under torture, Alex nonetheless discloses that, confronted by Steve after prolonged torture, he did admit that he was a comrade a moment before Steve died of his wounds. When Alex is subsequently tormented by ex-comrades calling him a traitor, he reacts by dragging one of them to a water trough and ducking him, in simulation of the water torture he himself was forced to undergo for twenty-eight days. Afterwards he makes this enigmatic comment to Sarah: "One thing you don't know, I became a torturer a long time ago."

This blurring of the line between torturer and victim is arguably a feature of the inversion of power relations that characterizes the TRC itself. As a victim under apartheid, value was invested in *not* speaking, *non*-disclosure, *not* giving way under torture. At the TRC hearing, value is invested in full *dis*closure. As Alex remorselessly leads Hendricks to a point where he has to admit recall of what he did, we see victim transformed to interrogator. In a further parallel, Piet Muller, the man responsible for Steve's death, similarly dreads disclosure of his role, and goes as far as stopping the prison van carrying Hendricks to the hearing, to warn him not to bring up his name. This, the first dialogue scene in the film, occurs after a sequence showing the TRC trailer rolling through the desert on its way to Smitsrivier, intercut with a point-of-view shot of Hendricks in the blacked-out van, where a loose strip of canvas lets in intermittent flashes of light resembling Alex's flashbacks in their painful intensity and brevity. This scene signifies at a visual level the interplay between secrecy and revelation which drives the action, the way the past irrupts in the present in moments of blinding light. Furthermore, the intimacy between Alex and Hendricks is highlighted by the long look, rendered in slow motion, which they exchange on first arriving in court, while the revelation of what actually went on between them fourteen years earlier is conducted in shot/reverse shot mode to signify the mutuality of their pain-ful journey back into the past. This intimacy is also shared by Sarah, another victim/interrogator, when she goes to interview Hendricks in jail. During an episode filmed for the most part in close-up as they face each other across a narrow table, Hendricks asks, "Do you remember the first time I met you, Sarah?" and later Sarah also uses his first name, "Can I be frank with you, Dirk?" as she leans forward, smiling.

The use of the gaze in *Red Dust* signifies recognition and complicity, but also misrecognition and exclusion. As Sarah Nuttall puts it, "We see that a re-lationship to country, to nation, can also involve the capacity to exit the frame-work it sets up . . . in order to undertake or achieve the setting up of the self, of who one is" (Nuttall 2001, 124). By removing herself from South Africa, Sarah Barcant has sought concealment, privacy, secrecy and invisibility. On returning, her immediate visibility means she is subjected to comments from passers-by who point out, "That's the Barcant girl," meaning, "the one who ran around with blacks." When she goes to visit her old home and—in another reenact-ment of Gillian Slovo's own experience visiting her former home in Johan-nesburg—she is allowed in only as far as the garden; the new occupier looks at her and says, "You're the Barcant girl aren't you? So what's wrong with white boys?" Sarah's reply, "Nothing, I just never found one that turned me on," turns the question on its head. Rather than accepting that her behavior was transgressive, she refutes the norms of white femininity and asserts her right freely to express desire. She is less in control on a subsequent occasion with Piet Muller, when she runs from a street riot straight into him, and he takes the opportunity to remind her of her proper role as a white woman—to be pro-tected. "You're running away from a black man? We'll protect you now just like we protected you then." If in this instance she is disarmed by being the object of the white (Afrikaner) male gaze, by contrast, in her role as lawyer, she is the one empowered to speak on behalf of the elderly Sizelas, who sit in the court-room silently watching her. Yet, in the setting of their home after the discovery of their son's body, it is the Sizelas who must speak the words of forgiveness if Alex is to be released from his trauma of betrayal. And in the final scene, it is Alex who must speak to release Sarah from her concealed and long-buried pain. The film shows that power is contested and passes from one character to another depending on the context. It is a measure of the film's respect for these diverse positions that the final embrace between Alex and Sarah is read, not as romantic cliché, but as a gesture of comradeship and equality between survivors of a brutal past that has damaged them both.

If *Red Dust* addresses itself to the way the new South Africa is dealing with its past, *Catch a Fire* looks back to the period of apartheid itself, specifically 1980–81, and the acts of sabotage by Umkhonto we Sizwe (MK), on key South African civilian, military, industrial, and infrastructural sites. Its focus, however, is again on the individual, in this case Patrick Chamusso, a worker at the Secunda coal-to-oil refinery north of Johannesburg, his wife and family, and the consequences for them of his wrongful arrest and torture for a sabotage attack on Secunda in 1980. Radicalized by his torture at the hands of the Special Branch, Chamusso joined MK and undertook the mission to destroy the plant based on his inside knowledge of its layout. He single-handedly infiltrated the plant and succeeded in blowing up one section of it in 1981. According to Shawn:

> The mastermind behind the attack, from his base in exile in Mozambique, was Joe Slovo, my father. . . . One year later, I am visiting Joe. "If you ever want to tell a story about this period in our history, he says, you must tell the story of operative Patrick Chamusso, code-name Hot Stuff. He's a character. A maverick. A live wire."[7]

Arrested for the bombing, Chamusso describes how when he was taken to Middleburg police station the only thing he would tell them was, "Joe Slovo sent me.'[8] He was jailed for twenty-four years on Robben Island, and when he was released in 1993, one of the first people he met was Shawn Slovo, who started to fulfill her father's behest by recording his story over the space of three days. Eventually, a script was commissioned by Working Title Films, the company for which Robyn Slovo works, and twelve years later, in 2005, the film was shot. However, as Shawn acknowledges in a joint interview with director Philip Noyce, "When Philip came on board we did a whole new level of research to get to the truth of the story," including retracing the journey back to Maputo with the "real" Chamusso (*Groucho Reviews* 2006, 3). There is an intriguing difference between Shawn's assumption that "the truth of the story" is there to be accessed by research and Gillian's more skeptical approach, which suggests rather that the truth can never finally be pinned down. This perspectival difference is manifest in the generic differences between the two films, one fictional, one "based on a true story." Is *Catch a Fire* constrained by the historical facts to tell the story in a particular way, with a particular outcome? And if so, how is this manifest in the visual shaping of the film?

The montage of archival images and footage with which *Catch a Fire* opens is a conventional means of emphasizing the historical nature of the events it dramatizes. Similarly, the newscast voice-over, shading into the voice of the actor playing Patrick Chamusso telling his own story, impresses on the viewer that what we are watching is the "truth." The image accompanying the voice-over, the Secunda oil refinery, informs the viewer of the extent to which the power of the apartheid state is underpinned by its industrial complex, as well as Patrick's role in supporting it. As the camera pans down from the vast smoking chimneys to a small convoy of cars driving beneath them, we are impressed by the contrast, the way human life is dwarfed by the gigantic complex. Like *Red Dust,* the film's action begins with this motorcade, the thunderous implacability of the TRC trailer replaced by four family sedans sporting balloons on their way to a wedding. The first car contains a family group: a husband (Patrick) and wife (Precious) in the front, wife driving, grandmother in the back with two young children, all singing along to music on the car radio. As an image of apartheid South Africa, it is radically unconventional, both the car (later, a policeman will query how Patrick can be the owner of such an expensive consumer item) and the sheer normality of a black family group on an outing. The early scenes of dancing at the wedding, the singer belting out the '80s hit "Hot Stuff" (Patrick's MK code name and the original title of the film) and Precious's jealousy of Patrick's dancing with another woman, emphasize this normality. Subsequent scenes of the Chamussos at home or out shopping reveal both how ordinary life carries on in defiance of the world outside, and how the world outside intrudes on the private domestic world until it can no longer be ignored. Meanwhile, Precious's jealousy of Patrick's outside woman and her child is emblematic of the larger story of betrayal, and ultimately the cause of Patrick's downfall.

Returning from the wedding next day, the Chamussos' car is stopped at a roadblock and searched. A railway line has been blown up in the night and the police are searching for the culprits. Both here and later, dealing with security at work, Patrick is cast in the light of the "good kaffir," soft-spoken and submissive, punctuating his utterances with the phrase "yes baas!" which echoes in other contexts—the "yes coach!" of the football team and the "yes commander!" of the MK trainees in Maputo. He explains that he can afford a car because he works as a foreman at Secunda, but both the car, signifying social mobility and status, and the camera they find in its boot provoke the police to humiliate him. The camera, with which he innocently took snapshots at the wedding, becomes a key visual motif and the mode of his entrapment. Colonel Nic Vos, shown in the next scene interrogating an MK saboteur, stands for the panopticon of the apartheid security machine, the all-seeing eye which, like the helicopter searchlight that beams down on Patrick at his arrest, reveals everything and leaves nothing secret. In *Red Dust,* the *look* between Alex and Hendricks dismantles the hierarchy built on that power; here, the look is the property of Vos, denoting absolute power served by covert surveillance, manipulation, and betrayal. At the farm the security police use as an interrogation center (called the Carpentry Shop by its victims), Vos's interrogation is watched on a screen by men in another room, as if it were television entertainment. Patrick's ownership of a camera, an apparatus for looking, framing, and recording, is hence a contravention of hierarchy and a misappropriation of power. Even after Patrick goes to Angola Vos's gaze pursues him, as shown by the photographs of Patrick's movements which he scrutinizes, and he knows when Patrick crosses back into South Africa. The symbiosis between the photographic image and betrayal is most explicit when Vos, knowing that jealousy is the weak point of Precious and Patrick's relationship, sends Precious pictures of Patrick apparently in intimate conversation with a pregnant woman. This is enough for Precious to reveal to Vos where Patrick may be found after his attempt to blow up Secunda—at his mistress's home.

This is not the only time Vos uses Precious to get to Patrick. When he is picked up on suspicion of involvement in the earlier explosion (the 1980 incident in which he was not involved), Patrick is tortured by ducking and suspension in scenes reminiscent of the flashbacks in *Red Dust.* When he offers no information, Vos brings Precious to the farm and brutalizes her, before shoving Patrick into the room with her and watching the effect on the television screen next door. The value placed on femininity in both *Red Dust* and *Catch a Fire*—as in *A World Apart*—is a significant marker of culture, and of the double standard practiced by the Afrikaner police. Patrick's response, "What kind of man are you?" points to a basic principle by which he defines himself as a man—that women are weaker and therefore to be protected. This principle, though made ambiguous by his infidelity to Precious, constitutes a boundary over which Vos has stepped, and seals his determination to join the ANC cause. That the same principle operates in Afrikaner culture is used ironically to underline the doublethink of a racist mind-set. In the scenes of Vos with his family—at the shooting range, at a picnic, at home—his elder daughter is shown as dissenting from the ideology of violence. When she refuses to handle a gun, saying, "I hate this, all this talk of guns and killing," Vos is the gentler, more tolerant parent. When later she is traumatized by shooting a (black) intruder, he comforts and congratulates her. Femininity, within this cultural framework, is to be protected at all cost, and the death of a black man is a small price. The flouting of this principle when it comes to black femininity is a sign of a one-dimensional ideology that dehumanizes the Other, not only through the abjection of the black male body under torture but through the abuse of black women and white women who do not conform. This explains Muller's contempt for Sarah Bercant in *Red Dust;* in *A World Apart,* the interrogator tries to appeal to Ruth First in detention by hinting at how much more he could do to her when he says, "You're lucky we have respect for women." The category "women," however, does not include Precious; Vos's daughter, on the verge of a realization of this contradiction, is brought back into the fold by killing a black man.

Perhaps the most sinister of Vos's techniques is his crossing of the line between black and white domestic space, a line fundamental to the principle of separation on which apartheid was built. By appearing to Precious as she takes in washing at home to ask her about Patrick, he shows that nothing is sacred, there is nowhere to hide, and the safe domestic space is provisional and vulnerable. In contrast, in the scene where he takes Patrick home for Sunday lunch, the sacred space of the white family is held up to Patrick's gaze as the reward of good behavior, the site of true civilization. In this disturbing scene, civility and hospitality are travestied as a form of mental torture as they sit in the garden after lunch, swimming pool behind them, and Vos continues his interrogation. In *A World Apart* this scene happens in reverse—the white child, Shawn, is taken by the black maid to her home in the township, where she is welcomed as a part of the family. Perhaps nothing could more clearly dramatize the difference between white and black cultural concepts of human behavior in the context of apartheid. The gap between them is what the TRC tried to address through the concept of reconciliation or *ubuntu,* the indigenous humanist philosophy by which it was driven. Apartheid was, as much as anything, a struggle over meaning, in which certain patriarchal and racial categories were normalized and all others outlawed. These two films, in attempting to represent the facts and consequences of apartheid, are part of that struggle for meaning. This in turn raises questions about the potential and the limitations of cinema to represent revolutionary struggle, history, and "truth."

HOLLYWOOD REPRESENTATIONS OF AFRICA?

In thinking about what links these two films, we might therefore ask what *kind* of representations they are and whether they qualify to be described as "Hollywood's Africa." The fact that director and cast of *Catch a Fire* testify to the importance of Chamusso's participation in the film, as of South Africa as location, points to one of the important ways in which this is not a conventional "Hollywood" film. The apparatus synonymous with "Hollywood"—the machinery of production, the size of the budget, the celebrity of the stars—also refers implicitly to a hierarchy dominated by "America"/ foreign money/commercial production values. Notably, this hierarchy was interrogated both in the production process and the product that emerged. Tim Robbins, for example, the American actor who plays Nic Vos, speaks of the impact on his thinking of "discovering what the white South African culture was. . . . I simply couldn't judge the way I'd judged before. I had to understand the people in all their complexities" (Groucho Reviews, 2). Derek Luke, the actor who plays Chamusso, similarly testifies to the way the experience of visiting townships and immersing himself in black South African culture changed his sense of his own role: "I thought I was bringing something to South Africa, but South Africa actually brought something to me. It gave me a balance. It took all the complaining out of me."[9] Responding to the question, "Why did I want to go back there, to that time?" Philip Noyce recalls growing up in Australia where "we had our own form of apartheid. . . . Black South Africans have shown us how to forgive and how to transition through a revolution to the other side." This, he says, is "a miracle I wanted to create and that I wanted to celebrate."[10]

The optimism of this sentiment may perhaps be the one element that brings Catch a Fire into a "Hollywood" frame, as the Slovos' reaction to their TRC experience makes clear. In her Chicago lecture, Gillian Slovo talks of her novel, Red Dust, as being "about the complexities of the TRC," and the fact that it did not lead to an optimistic conclusion. Though the film was "good," it was both "more optimistic and more simplistic, shot through with the desire South Africa represents for the world." While, "I certainly don't mean to decry the miracle," for her the TRC was based more in wish-fulfillment than in any real reconciliation (G. Slovo 2006). At the same time, Robyn Slovo recognizes her own experience in the film: "[Catch a Fire] is a very personal film for me. . . . I vividly remember those people coming to the house searching everything and taking either one or two parents away. . . . The images that work in this film were conveyed to Philip who then talked to all these people who were able to re-create that apartheid South Africa."[11] Moreover, the scenes in Maputo feature those very parents, who were both living there by 1981. Joe is shown in his role of MK chief of staff, debriefing new recruits, and in attendance at the funeral of the twelve ANC comrades who were killed in the raid on the training camp. Robyn, who attended her own mother's funeral in 1982, only a year later, and saw her buried alongside the twelve comrades, appears in the film version of the ANC funeral as Ruth First.

As concerns *Red Dust*, "Truth and Reconciliation" describes a process very different from the standard Hollywood courtroom drama, whose purpose is either to underline the objectivity and essential fairness of the US legal system, or, by providing a platform for the brilliance of the legal argument, to demonstrate how an exceptional individual can prevail against the odds. In *Red Dust*, the emphasis is less on Sarah Barcant's skills as a prosecutor and more on the emotional implications of a gradual uncovering of layers of buried truth. Both films, however, confront the question of how "history," whether refracted through fiction or conveyed as "reality," is inevitably (re)shaped by the exigencies of genre and audience. This is illustrated in both films by the fact that the principal actors are American stars while the supporting roles are played by South Africans. The perceived need for foreign actors speaks to issues of visibility and recognition by which the films can be expected to be judged outside South Africa. This underlines an ironic aspect of the project—that the struggle for meaning in which the films participate has to be conveyed in the form of a commercial cinema with "external appeal." The fact that this cinema is part of the normative ideological apparatus of Western cultural imperialism makes its role deeply problematic. At the same time, these are not technically "Hollywood films" but British independent films with American actors, which intrinsically sets them at a tangent to mainstream "Hollywood" cinema.

Undeniably, the films perform the important gesture of making visible aspects of the past which were repressed under apartheid, and bringing these to the attention of audiences. Moreover, they do this by to an extent reversing the usual terms of engagement—focusing on what South Africa offers to the world as opposed to what the world offers Africa. For instance, they show how a sacred tenet of US statehood—its right to kill its enemies—can be forgone and something else substituted for revenge. At the end of *Catch a Fire*, the liberated Chamusso comes upon his old enemy Vos out fishing and has the chance of killing him, but does not. Although following facts, the film thereby sidesteps the action movie cliché that concludes in violent retribution delivered by the hero acting, as Noyce puts it, as "judge, jury and executioner."[12] Moreover, the epilogue to the film featuring the "real" Chamusso destroys the illusion of fiction and the expectations of genre and brings home to us the fact that the story is not yet finished. As the "real"

Chamusso says, "The whole film is the truth and I can't stand watching it because those are the things that happened to me."[13] If *Catch a Fire* attempts to represent one man's truth, *Red Dust* is closer to Gillian Slovo's realization that "memory, experience, interpretation could never be fixed or frozen into one, unchanging truth. They kept on moving, relentlessly metamorphosing into something other, so that the jagged edges of each fragment would never, ever slot together" (G. Slovo 1997, 281).

NOTES

1. The title for this essay is derived from the Foreword by Archbishop Desmond Tutu to Truth and Reconciliation Commission of South Africa Report, para 91. "Having looked the beast of the past in the eye, having asked and received forgiveness and having made amends, let us shut the door on the past—not in order to forget it but in order not to allow it to imprison us." It appears in text on screen at the end of *Red Dust*.

2. The granting of amnesty to the killers of Ruth First and Jeanette Schoon, another white activist based in Luanda, and her six-year-old daughter, Katryn, became a focus for the disillusionment of many ordinary South Africans. As the British newspaper, the *Guardian*, reported: "Within hours of the announcement of amnesty, local radio station presenters were crying and songs were being dedicated to the victims' families. The outrage being expressed about these two high-profile cases reflects the disillusion of many township victims profoundly disappointed by their own experience of amnesties given to police, and by the slowness and inadequacy of reparations payments" (Brittain 2000).

3. G. Slovo 2006.

4. Extra material on DVD of *Catch A Fire*.

5. The title *Red Dust* denotes a particular landscape, that of the Karoo desert of the Eastern Cape, of which the wide horizons and sculpted mountain peaks provide the dramatic backdrop to the film. Though Gillian asserts that she chose this setting purely by chance (see note 3, above), it cannot escape the overdetermining associations of an earlier work, Olive Schreiner's *The Story of an African Farm* (1883). This novel, set in the Karoo, has attained iconic status as a founding narrative of the Afrikaner relationship to the land. Moreover, Ruth First coauthored, with Ann Scott, *Olive Schreiner: A Biography* (1980).

6. Antjie Krog ends her account of the TRC, *Country of My Skull* (1998, also released as a film under the title *In My Country*, 2004) with a poem: "A new skin / I am changed forever. I want to say: / forgive me / forgive me / forgive me / You whom I have wronged, please / take me / with you" (229).

7. S. Slovo 2006. http://www.workingtitlefilms.com/features/qanda/id/15/hotstuff -an-introduction-by-shawn-slovo.

8. Extra material on DVD of *Catch a Fire*.

9. Ibid.

10. Ibid.

11. Ibid.

12. Ibid.

13. Ibid.

REFERENCES

Brittain, Victoria. 2000. "Outrage over Amnesty for Apartheid Killer." *Guardian* online, 13/6/2000: http://www.guardian.co.uk/world/2000/jun/13/victoriabrittain.
*Catch a Fire*. 2006. Directed by Philip Noyce. Writtten by Shawn Slovo. France/UK/SA/USA. Universal/Working Title Films.
First, Ruth, and Ann Scott. 1980. *Olive Schreiner: A Biography*. New York: Deutsch.
*Forgiveness*. 2004. Directed by Ian Gabriel. Written by Greg Latter. SA. Giant Films/Dv8.
*Groucho Reviews*. 2006. Interview with Tim Robbins, Philip Noyce, Shawn Slovo and Robyn Slovo, November 10, 1–4. http://www.grouchoreviews.com/interviews/186.
*In My Country*. 2004. Directed by John Boorman. Written by Antjie Krog (novel) and Anne Peacock (screenplay). UK/Ireland/USA. Chartoff Productions/Film Afrika/Film Consortium.
Krog, Antjie. 1998. *Country of My Skull*. Johannesburg: Random House.
Nuttall, Sarah. 2001. "Subjectivities of Whiteness." *African Studies Review* 44 (2): 115–40.
Philips, David. 2007. "Looking the Beast in the (Fictional) Eye: The Truth and Reconciliation Commission on Film." In *Black and White in Colour: African History on Screen*, edited by Vivian Bickford Smith and Richard Mendelsohn, 300–322. Athens: Ohio University Press.
*Red Dust*. 2004. Directed by Tom Hooper. Written by Gillian Slovo (novel) and Troy Kennedy Martin (screenplay). UK/SA. BBC/Distant Horizon/Videovision.
Schreiner, Olive. 1883. *The Story of an African Farm*. London.
Slovo, Gillian. 1997. *Every Secret Thing: My Family, My Country*. London: Little, Brown.
————. 2000. *Red Dust*. London: Virago.
————. 2006. "Truth and Reconciliation." November 12. http://www.chicagohumanities.org/en/Genres/Public-Affairs/Gillian-Slovo-Truth-and-Reconciliation.aspx.
Slovo, Shawn. 2006. "Hotstuff—An Introduction." http://www.workingtitlefilms.com/features/qanda/id/15/hotstuff-an-introduction-by-shawn-slovo.
————. 1988. *A World Apart*. Directed by Chris Menges. Written by Shawn Slovo.

# FOURTEEN

# Situating Agency in *Blood Diamond* and *Ezra*

IYUNOLU OSAGIE

In its four decades of postindependence history, Sierra Leone has been marred by government corruption and greed, a widening gap between the small ruling elite and the poor masses, and an underlying ethnic tension at the political level (though not at the social and cultural level). After seventeen years of Siaka Stevens's inglorious one-party rule, he handed over a failing economy to his hand-picked successor, Joseph Momoh. Momoh lacked the shrewdness with which Stevens had managed to keep both enemies and friends at bay. Consequently, Momoh's weak managerial style easily translated into government paralysis. This obvious weakness intensified national fears about the fiscal health of his government and fueled concerns about a small but growing war in Eastern Sierra Leone, spearheaded by Foday Sankoh, a former corporal in the army and a professional photographer. Many dispirited junior officers of the Sierra Leone Army (SLA) were losing their lives to Sankoh's rebel war. As the leader of the Revolutionary United Front (RUF), Sankoh was receiving arms, finances, and logistical help from his Liberian rebel counterpart, Charles Taylor. The coup of April 29, 1992, staged by young disgruntled soldiers in the SLA, because they had not received their food rations or paychecks from the Momoh government, was the beginning of the unraveling of a failed state. With this military intervention, the National Provisional Ruling Council (NPRC), as the coup plotters called their government, installed itself in power, but under national and international pressure the NPRC later conceded power to the democratically elected government of Ahmed Tejan Kabbah in 1996 (Hirsch 2001; Gberie 2005).

Meanwhile, the continuing political destabilization in Liberia was having a profound and direct effect on the political stability of the Sierra Leonean government and the flow of resources for its sustainability. Outside of the capital city, Freetown, the RUF had expanded its territorial hold over much of the country. Its leader Sankoh had dreams of ruling the country, and he was a force to be reckoned with since his rebel unit controlled the diamond areas. Major peace talks did not produce the expected results. The army was also divided in its resolve to support Kabbah's government; some were hoping to repeat the disastrous rule of the NPRC, with the intention of plundering the national treasury for personal gratification. On May 25, 1997, therefore, some elements of the SLA, the Armed Forces Revolutionary Council (AFRC), joined forces with the RUF to dethrone Kabbah. This joint force met with surprising resistance from many quarters. First, paramilitary forces and other loyal segments of the SLA joined forces with the Nigerian-led West African task force, ECOMOG, to militarily engage the AFRC and RUF. Second, the civilian population protested en masse in a civil disobedience campaign. Third, international protests further pressured the unelected regime to step down. Eventually, Kabbah's government was reinstated in February 1998. A semblance of civility returned for about ten months, but on January 6, 1999, a regrouped RUF descended with vengeance on the city of Freetown, ruthlessly destroying life and property. Taking the government and military forces by surprise, the RUF inflicted unimaginable violence on the people (Koroma 2004).

In *The Amistad Revolt* (2000), I argue that the ascendancy of the NPRC in 1992, aided by the cultural icons of the Amistad story and other related symbols, marked a turning point in the resolve of ordinary Sierra Leoneans to actively contend for national democracy (Osagie 2000). It was in this same spirit of commitment to true liberation that the people also rejected both the AFRC and the RUF. However, the people's refusal to cooperate with the renegade segment of the army and the RUF further intensified the RUF's reign of terror in the nation: the dismemberment of the limbs of both young and old (their signature entrance into many communities), the looting and incineration of villages, the reckless killing by its drugged-up forces, the forced enlistment of young boys and girls, and the gang rape of women and young girls were everyday stories left in their trail (Kandeh 2004). Moral outrage around the world finally galvanized the support of international bodies, such as the UN and the former colonial power, Britain, to intervene in the crisis. These interventions, including the second reinstatement of President Kabbah, and later the death of Sankoh, finally brought some stability to Sierra Leone (Koroma 2004). Today, the nation is struggling to heal from this very traumatic past.

Looking back, it is pertinent to note that theater, an important institution for political awareness in Sierra Leone, was a significant contributor to the shape of the resistance against the RUF and to the faith and determination of civilians that their communal resolve would result in a democratic outcome. Even before the recent civil war in Sierra Leone, the revolutionary character of the theater was already evident. For example, Charlie Haffner's *Amistad Kata Kata* played an incidental but pivotal role in the 1992 coup that brought an end to Stevens's distasteful legacy—the Momoh government (Opala 1994; Osagie 2000). Sierra Leone theater has not only mirrored the social and political stages of this young nation (Spencer 1988), it has, so often, been the political conscience of the country. In the late 1960s, through the 1980s in particular, as the country became mired in corruption and the social fabric of the nation began to unravel, young voices in the theater satirized government policies and raised political awareness among a disenfranchised people. For example, novelist and playwright Yulisa Amadu Maddy, in his collection of plays, *Obasai and Other Plays* (1971), examines class tensions, ethnic elitism, and other topical social and political issues. Maddy speaks for the oppressed, the poor, the voiceless. He later formed *Gbakanda Theater,* which is grounded in the protest theater style. Many artists have followed in his steps. As the country struggled with its identity, the legacy of colonial decadence, the death of a short-lived democracy, nepotism, ethnic discrimination, and the political amnesia that set in during the 1970s and '80s, given the highhanded rule of Siaka Stevens's ruling party, the All People's Congress, Sierra Leonean artists turned more and more to themes that reflected their historical struggles. They also drew strength from stories that highlighted the resilience (if not the victories) of past heroes, such as Kai Londo, Bai Bureh, and Mammy Yoko. Artists such as Julius Spencer in *The Patriots,* John Kolosa Kargbo in *Let Me Die Alone,* and Charlie Haffner in *Amistad Kata Kata* took up the challenge of tackling difficult historical subjects by reinterpreting and revising the sometimes controversial and contradictory relations of these national figures to the colonial enterprise that produced them.

This purposeful use of theater to inform audiences of the country's history and political temper has certainly contributed to the formation of a strong sense of collective identity. In *Theatre for Development in Africa* (1988), Kamlongera highlights the role of the theater in reaching all sorts of communities in Africa. Artists' engagement with the "theatre for development," sometimes called "popular theatre," has further sharpened their sensitivity to the pivotal role they are playing in shaping their respective countries. It is against this backdrop of a productive artistic sense of agency in Sierra Leone that I examine two recent civil war movies on Sierra Leone, the Hollywood-produced *Blood Diamond* (2006), directed by Edward Zwick, and the independent film *Ezra* (2007), by the Nigerian filmmaker Newton Aduaka. How do Zwick and Aduaka situate agency in their respective movies? What is at stake in each film, and what ideological purpose does each serve?

By now, none can deny the might of Hollywood in its mediation of knowledge, its capitalistic lure, and its powers of dissemination, so that we have to acknowledge that whether Hollywood tells a story well or not the fact that it tells a story on Africa, any story at all, has a lasting impact. As a powerful social institution alert to the winds of global changes, Hollywood is quick not only to readjust its ideological mirror but also to net the economic benefits that come with the tide. In this way, Hollywood continues to affect the construction of social meaning on a global scale. Through its creation of cultural symbols and its authoritative control of those symbols, Hollywood influences and shapes the political, economic, and social perceptions of society. Subsequently, Zwick's blockbuster movie *Blood Diamond,* with its $100,000,000 budget and A-list lead actors, has brought global attention to the issue of conflict diamonds and indeed raised awareness of the political struggle of the small nation of Sierra Leone. It is a well-made movie; but is it a well-told story? Zwick's Hollywood perspective on the war in Sierra Leone is challenged by Aduaka's small independent film *Ezra*. With a budget well under £2,000,000, Aduaka cannot have the same global impact as a Hollywood-financed movie, but the Nigerian filmmaker still insists on weighing in with his own narrative of the war, thereby resisting a Hollywood monopoly on the conflict. By using California Newsreel as a distributing agency, Aduaka at least hopes to reach the intellectual community in the West, in addition to local audiences in Africa.

Since both directors engage the civil war in Sierra Leone, there are obvious similarities in the two stories. Both films portray the price that can be paid by ordinary people in conflict zones when national and international interests target valuable resources, such as diamonds. They further portray the issue of conflict diamonds, the brutality inflicted on civilians in this war-torn country, and the implications of child soldiering. Both film directors highlight the challenges civilians face when they attempt to exercise their democratic right to vote—rebel forces literally cut off the hands of civilians in their "no hand, no vote" political strategy, while portraying themselves as the hand of justice, change, and restoration under conditions of state collapse. Zwick and Aduaka also position Western characters as the recipients of the fortunes in Africa, if not some of the key initiators of the violence waged for control of those fortunes. They both highlight the irony of Africa's rich endowment in natural resources as catastrophic. In Sierra Leone in particular, the diamond-rich eastern region of the country epitomizes a bane rather than a boom. Since all these narrative moments are important historical identifiers of the eleven-year-old civil war in Sierra Leone, both Zwick and Aduaka richly frame their stories with them. The commonalities between the two films, however, stop here.

In terms of aesthetic attributes—film quality, sound mixing, casting options, etc.—we do not expect a movie with *Ezra's* budget to best *Blood Diamond*, and it doesn't. *Blood Diamond's* gross revenue was close to double its production cost. The film received five Oscar nominations, including Best Achievement in Sound Mixing, Sound Editing, and Editing. By comparison, *Ezra's* film quality is determined by its shoestring budget. Critics point to the film's poor technicality (the sound selections end up being too repetitive, for example), its disappointing portrayal of Ezra's mental state, and its some-times confusing nonlinear plot. However, confusion is part of the intended effect of the movie, especially since most of the plot happens "inside Ezra's brainwashed, drug-scarred mind as he futilely tries to remember what hap-pened" during the war (Holden 2008, E4). Aduaka also had to use an inexpe-rienced cast (with the exception of Richard Gant) and the narrative strategy of discontinuity (and he does so quite effectively), so as to keep film produc-tion costs down. Still, within the smaller circle of competitions in which *Ezra* was entered, the film won Best Film at the 28th Annual Durban International Film Festival, and the Grand Prize at Africa's major film festival, FESPACO, in addition to other smaller awards.

Partly, *Blood Diamond's* mass appeal can be attributed to the fact that Holly-wood has, to some extent, shifted its ideological grounds to accommodate new global interactions that have brought what were formerly seen as ad-versarial relationships into working alliances. Hollywood has come a long way from its marginal or nonrepresentation of Africans, African Americans, Native Americans, and other non-European groups to actually making these groups important subject matter for its viewing audiences. Today, Hollywood appears to have mitigated its former racist image by increasing the number of significant roles that minorities play. This trend, which began in the 1970s and penetrated Hollywood with New Left radicalism, is particularly evident today in racial "buddy" movies. By the 1990s racial "buddy" movies (movies starring black and white male lead roles) had become not just palatable, but a cultural staple. This "positive packaging" of minorities in Hollywood, however, needs to be examined closely. Such "buddy" movies tend to subvert any serious examination of racism in American society and equally elide any significant critique of America's imperialist projects. In fact, "buddy" movies risk further consolidating racial stereotypes.[1] Zwick's *Blood Diamond* is a case in point. The "buddy" movie frame (starring Leonardo DiCaprio and Djimon Hounsou) covers some of the deep-seated Hollywood stereotypes about Africa and Africans that are prevalent in the film. Since *Blood Diamond* attempts to focus attention on the international diamond trade that precipitated civil war in Sierra Leone in the 1990s, audiences would most likely interpret Zwick's movie as a performance of resistance against the omnipotence of multinational corporations. Zwick uses both black and white bodies as sites of revolution, and he successfully implicates film audiences not simply as spectators and consumers of an entertainment product, not merely as co-conspirators and participants in the diamond trade, but more important as co-conscripts in the fight against international capitalist forces that have precipitated much bloodshed and government collapse in several regions in Africa. It is thus easy for the audience to embrace this mobilization against one capitalist corporation—the diamond industry—while forgetting the uninterrupted capital flows to the Hollywood industry, which is first and foremost a business. In racial "buddy" movies, Hollywood seemingly puts its racist image under erasure, but I argue that this image reconsolidates elsewhere. Racial erasure works through a kind of democratic dispersal of narrative equity—both black and white actors are *there* for all to see; however, familiar racial stereotypes still surface in the hegemonic relations within the narrative.

Zwick's film has received rave reviews for its topicality, its gripping story line, its educational content, and activist stance. However, as in Steven Spielberg's 1996 *Amistad,* white paternalism, a major Hollywood product when it comes to race relations, is prevalent yet again (Osagie 2000). Although the main protagonist, Danny Archer, is from Southern Africa and expresses much skepticism about American society, he is a white man who hopes to end his violent life in Africa (that unsettling dark continent) by finding the biggest diamond he can to buy his way to America. The second protagonist, Solomon Vandy, outlives his white African "partner," but the story line is such that his helplessness makes the instrumentality of a white patron (a white American female in this case, Maddy Bowen) essential. Hollywood logic dictates that market forces determine the casting decisions that are made, but this claim only helps to solidify the attitude that black bodies cannot be celebrated as agents of their own destiny. Hollywood's economic explanation for its casting decisions, and ultimately its narrative decisions, so often dismisses even the relevance of African agents in their own struggle against global adversaries.

As can be expected, the aims and agendas of *Ezra* and *Blood Diamond* are different. In *Blood Diamond* Zwick relies on well-known Hollywood techniques to ensure box office success. *Blood Diamond* is packaged as a fast-moving thriller with lots of "fire power" to keep its audiences engaged. The narrative moves forward in time, with the two main protagonists battling almost impossible odds to reach their goal of claiming a prized diamond hidden in the heart of the war zone. In *Ezra*, Aduaka begins in a time-forward mode that serves only as a preface to a dominant time-backward frame. The attack that begins on July 13, 1992, with young Ezra traipsing late to school as he enjoys the alluring scenery, serves as a footnote to the events, seven years later, when Ezra, at age sixteen, faces the Truth and Reconciliation Commission Hearing, trying to come to terms with his life as a boy soldier in one of the rebel factions in the war. By using a discontinuous narrative mode—a series of flashbacks impelled by the courtroom scene—Aduaka is able both to move the plot along and to explore the inner psyche of the main character, Ezra. *Ezra* engages audiences using alternative methods; its narrative mode demands a settled, reflective response from its audience. The complexity of the plot, the complicity of its brainwashed protagonist, and the fragile hopes of the commission—that the logical articulation of the events of a particular day of infamy in Sierra Leone history (January 6, 1999) will unveil the truth and bring closure and healing to the battered psyche of the nation—offer little catharsis but plenty of reflection. Avoiding a tidy closure to the movie, Aduaka concludes on an ambivalent note.

These differing stylistic approaches to the same basic story access different value systems. Zwick admits that as a filmmaker he wants to "entertain people first and foremost. If out of that comes a greater awareness and understanding of a time or a circumstance, then the hope is that change can happen. Obviously, a single piece of work can't change the world, but what you try to do is add your voice to the chorus" (Levy 2008). Clearly, Zwick's use of the civil war and its unfortunate circumstances are primarily tools in the *business* of entertainment. Aduaka, in contrast, is anxious to move away from any art for entertainment's sake dynamic.

> What I'm trying to talk about concerns everyone. . . . I want people to realize that wars don't end with ceasefires, that deep psychological problems remain. . . . In the West these kids [child soldiers] would

get years of psychological counseling. In West Africa they end up scarred and are left to go fight as mercenaries in one conflict after another, just fuelling more wars. (Sanogo 2007)

Through an exploration of Ezra's turmoil after the war, Aduaka demonstrates that the burden of the war is far-reaching and that consequently the catalyst for the war—in this case the world's insatiable need for diamonds—is as important to address as Ezra's need to investigate (know of, admit to, come to terms with) the killing of his parents. Pedagogically, both movies mobilize a different set of social, political, and aesthetic capital as each, in its own way, attempts to offer meaning through audience engagement.

*Blood Diamond* starts with a pristine scene of morning life in Solomon Vandy's village. Solomon's dream is to see his son become a medical doctor. It is in their conversation, after he walks his son home from school, that the audience begins to understand that the serene setting of a peaceful village life belies their anxieties about a looming war. As he and his son Dia playfully bond on their way home, war comes to the village in the shape of two truckloads of rebels who wreak havoc on the village, indiscriminately killing young and old, dismembering limbs, and forcefully enlisting able-bodied men and youths into their ranks. In this first of many heart-thumping war scenarios in the movie, Dia, his mother, and his two sisters escape, while Solomon is captured and driven away to work in a diamond-mining site under the control of rebel forces.

Ed Zwick's *Blood Diamond* successfully retells a portion of the story of Sierra Leone's civil war of the 1990s. Indeed, the trade in illicit diamonds precipitated the war and enabled rebel forces to unleash a reign of terror in the country for a protracted eleven years. Zwick introduces a complex plot in which international mercenaries are pitched against the indigenous rebel forces, who are in turn pitched against the government of Sierra Leone for control of mining sites and, in essence, for control of the government itself. Zwick also enhances the plot by making one mercenary figure, Danny Archer, in rebellion against his mercenary boss from South Africa, Colonel Coetzee. As a white Zimbabwean who has fought in many wars in southern Africa, Archer wants to get out of the mercenary business by finding that prized diamond that can get him out of Africa. His quest will link him up with Solomon. Solomon has found a very large diamond during his mining days and has hidden it. Under the pressure of unfavorable circumstances attributable to the intensifying war, Solomon becomes a reluctant partner to Danny. His first concern is to find and reunite with his family. Recognizing this desire as a weakness, Danny exploits Solomon's desire by promising to find his family for him. Moreover, Danny convinces Solomon that the only way Solomon can get the diamond safely out of the country is through him. Danny's confidence rests on the singular fact that he is white. He impudently tells Solomon: "I know people, white people. Without me you are just another black man in Africa." In reaction to Solomon's reluctance to partner with him, Danny later adds: "You need my help whether you like it or not." Thus the American "buddy" movie concept is transplanted to the African landscape; this casting strategy—what we already know of the typical American "buddy" movie—merely reveals white privileging at work.

Yet this movie does not fail to thrill. Perhaps its main success lies in the fact that the star character is portrayed not as a saint or a redeemer, but as a character whose hardened life and criminal background as a diamond smuggler make him a nebulous, unpredictable individual. His lies and murders come as no surprise to the audience, and his occasional kindness and unexpected partnership with the decent, humane family man, co-protagonist Solomon, gives the plot not only its ironic twist but also its complex reading of a civil war that was without moral clarity. With the history of military and political struggles in Southern Africa fresh on his mind, Danny is perceptively accurate about his place as a "foot soldier" in a mercenary army. He and others in his position were constantly lied to, to make them believe that the fight against black Africans in Angola and South Africa carried moral weight. They were fighting a communist threat, they thought. In reality, they were pawns in the hands of those who had found a way to steal African resources by spilling the blood of both black Africans and young, sometimes poor, white males in southern Africa. Engulfed by violence all his life, Danny's only way out of such violence is to inflict violence on all who stand in his way. Danny is without illusions about African society: he knows that corruption is rampant across border states; he knows of the exploitation of Africa by the rich and powerful in the Western world; he knows that Africa is an economic pariah on the world stage. This knowledge, however, does not redeem him or transform his life; rather, he lies, kills, cheats, and invokes the privileges of whiteness to get ahead. By using a flawed character like Danny, Zwick presents the plight of Africa's underprivileged masses, without the intense "preachiness" evident in Fernando Meirelles's movie *The Constant Gardener* (2006), and without the messiah complex in Spielberg's *Amistad* (1997) or Michael Caton-Jones's *Shooting Dogs* (2005).

This is not to say that Zwick does not deploy these two elements—"preachiness" and a messiah complex. Both these elements are present in *Blood*

*Diamond* but they are well masked, and sometimes appear latent. These familiar Hollywood stereotypes of white hegemony in African and other non-Western spaces are often obscurely presented. Zwick achieves this effect through his characterization of Danny Archer as criminalized. Danny is a white African caught in the moral dilemma of being the descendant of colonizers, yet unfortunate enough to be trapped politically and economically in a postapartheid society. His schizophrenic personality divulges a double displacement: first, his deep-seated knowledge of how big financial barons in Europe, America, and other major economic trade zones around the world operate leaves him no illusions about the criminality of Western capitalism and, in essence, his own identity; second, his knowledge of, and identification with, Africa, exemplified by his connection to the soil, puts him in a moral predicament. If he truly belongs to Africa, his birthplace, and if his identity is rooted in the African soil, why does he want to move to America, especially through the desperate measures he undertakes? If he truly does not care about America, as he claims in conversations with the American Maddy Bowen, why is the financial ease he imagines on the other side of the Atlantic so intensely appealing that he is willing to kill Africans and fellow mercenaries alike to get to America? These questions we ask of the character Danny should compel us to think about the way in which Hollywood's blockbuster mentality drives its production decisions as well. In the final analysis, capital flows to Hollywood trump sentimental ties, altruistic objectives, and revolutionary logic, just as Danny's materialism overshadows his rhetorical love of Africa. Danny's desire to claim a diamond that is not his is analogous to Western industry's indifference to its source of wealth.

In his quest for wealth, Danny runs into Maddy Bowen, an American journalist, who is hoping to make a difference by telling the world about conflict diamonds. Driven by both compassion and a nose for a good story, Maddy targets Danny as an important key to unlocking the door to a dangerous syndicate of diamond smugglers, a role Danny balks at. Zwick presents Danny as a reluctant redeemer, but a redeemer nonetheless, who eventually offers up his body as sacrifice. Unlike the defense lawyer Roger Baldwin in *Amistad,* whose obsession is to save the hapless African slaves, and unlike Tessa Quayle, the female protagonist of *The Constant Gardener,* whose "hysterical" drive to save the oppressed of the world brings her to Kenya, Danny is, at least at first, simply too self-absorbed and too angry with his lot in life to care about the next person. When he eventually (moments from his dying breath) helps save Solomon and his son Dia by returning the diamond that rightfully belongs to Solomon, the big cathartic moment in the movie is achieved: Danny becomes a savior. Audiences may or may not consider that Danny returns the diamond when he is dying and can no longer use it. In this way, familiar mechanisms of the messiah complex are masked.

The ambiguity that the movie maintains up to this point is quickly cast aside when Danny is remembered as a hero. After Danny dies, it is Maddy, and not Solomon, who dominates the narrative. Maddy becomes the new messiah, and the new face of white heroism. As a journalist dealing in sensational material, Maddy is "preachy," a Hollywood type American audiences are used to. Like Danny, she is a good talker, a go-getter. Yet Maddy wants to save the world. Her investigative reporting takes her down the trail of names and places listed in Danny's "black book," which he gives her halfway through his mission. Through her journalistic endeavor, it becomes Maddy's job to discourage American girls who want a diamond-studded storybook wedding, to expose African strongmen, warlords, and corrupt governments, but more important, to track down the diamond lords in London and other European cities who fix prices in the global markets. Maddy makes it possible for Solomon's family to be rescued and for Solomon to sell the diamond he rightfully owns. Of course, Solomon remains the prism, the living testimony, through which she narrates a captivating story on conflict diamonds—not unlike Hollywood's mission in this film.

The actor Djimon Hounsou (*Blood Diamond* is considered one of his best performances) remains stuck in the supporting role he often plays in movies. Solomon does not say much for a good portion of the movie. Except for his initial daring, self-impelled move—having enough gumption to bury the biggest diamond ever seen against the odds of being caught by his ruthless RUF boss, Captain Poison—and his subsequent foray into the rebel camp to find his son, he hardly takes the initiative. After all, he is just a countrified fellow who finds it hard to live a lie. He becomes dependent on Danny to find his family and even, ironically, to find his way back through a war zone to dig up his hidden diamond. This so-called partnership between Danny and Solomon is more often portrayed as a master-slave relationship. Although Danny desperately needs Solomon to find the treasure, he calls the shots and maps their every move. Danny is the one with the paraphernalia of power: guns, contacts, a helicopter, and many technological gadgets. In short, he has everything except the diamond. This vital information Solomon keeps to himself, and Danny's precarious position in the relationship often throws him into fits of anger and even violence against Solomon. He constantly tries to assert his superiority through his arsenal of white privilege by accessing all the icons of white military power—he can summon the whole South African mercenary force. When Solomon decides that finding his son Dia is more important than going after the diamond, he and Danny get into a fight:

> DANNY: "You listen my boy . . ."
> SOLOMON: "You are not the master."
> DANNY: "Right now that's exactly what I am and you better remember it, *kaffir*."

Their "buddy" relationship stacks up as master-slave relationship on the African landscape. This master-slave formula continues to haunt Africa half a century after independence.

Even the rhetoric of the demented RUF leader, Captain Poison, ironically bears the branding of this history of bondage. In brainwashing his victims that working in the mines is far better than living under a corrupt Sierra Leonean government, he states: "No more slave and master here." On the one hand, RUF gives a window into the colonial legacy of government corruption and the neglect of the people, but at the same time, its forced incarceration of children and adults in the mining camps is nothing short of the slavery it claims to abhor. Spewing scorn on the democratic process of voting to make one's voice heard, Captain Poison cuts off hands, while abducting able bodies at will to extract diamonds for a foreign market. In today's world, the colonial master-slave structure is merely replaced by a postcolonial relocation in which the slave master now lives overseas, with the overseers (people like the RUF leader) doing his bidding. This imbrication of slavery as deeply ingrained in the African landscape is well portrayed when even the RUF leader (despite his position of dominance) admits his desire to get out of his place in the global food chain: "If I look like the devil," he says, "it is only because I have lived in hell." He, too, wants to get out of the cycle of violence that has engulfed his country.

By the end of the movie it is Solomon and his family who are out of Africa, out of the hell that their country has become. Their relocation may bring relief to Western audiences, as Solomon and his family reunite, and with reassuring amounts of money to live well. In contrast, most Sierra Leoneans, if they get to see the movie, cannot see themselves in this resolution, nor can they see this migration as a viable solution to a national catastrophe. We are asked to believe that Solomon, who shows up as a victim-survivor of the diamond crisis, then becomes the voice of protest on conflict diamonds at the Kimberley conference in South Africa. The movie ends with Solomon, voiceless and speechless, facing an applauding audience. Zwick misses the opportunity here to give Solomon the last word.

In Aduaka's movie *Ezra*, the approach to agency is quite different. Although whites show up in the movie on two occasions—in one instance, to deliver drugs in a rebel camp and in another to identify a diamond-mining site through Ezra—their role remains peripheral to the plot. We are made aware of the fact that the war in which Ezra is engaged is tied to the global diamond trade, but Aduaka insists on focusing on the plight of child soldiering in Africa by taking us into the mind of one of its tortured victims, Ezra. Although *Blood Diamond* touches on the problem of child soldiers through some dramatic scenes with Dia and other child soldiers, it is only a subplot that is not fully developed for the audience to fully understand the trauma that accompanies such a career. In *Ezra* the audience enters the world of war and violence largely through the narrative lens of children who are making history, according to their commander Rufus, through "the barrel of the gun."

These children's lenses, however, are fraught with misrememberings, misrecognitions, and misinformation. The long hard road to becoming a ruthless killer, for Sierra Leone's children and others, is solidified by a steady diet of indoctrination. Children like Ezra, Moses, and Cynthia are reprogrammed in a rebel camp run by Rufus not just to participate in the revolution, to overthrow the Western-backed political elite of the country, and to believe in a utopian future of basic human rights (education, health care, and dignity, among other things) but also to claim the revolution as their own making. Consequently, we are not at all surprised when Ezra attempts to defend the very rebel war that has destroyed his family and his innocence. Unlike most children who are kidnapped into the cause, however, children like Mariam, Ezra's rebel-wife,[2] joins the cause willingly to avenge the "death of her activist father" (she's not sure he is dead), who is described as an outspoken antiestablishment journalist. In either case, whether children are kidnapped or self-enlist, they come to believe strongly in the strident morality of their cause and in the infallibility of their leaders (Rosen 2005; Singer 2005). Like Ikemefuna in Chinua Achebe's *Things Fall Apart,* such children end up sacrificing their lives. Aduaka successfully uses the Ikemefuna image to tell his story.

The movie succeeds in conveying the long road to recovery that child soldiers face. It will be almost the close of the war before Ezra and his pregnant rebel-wife Mariam, and his sister Onitsha, attempt to escape from rebel enclaves altogether as, through a series of epiphanies, Ezra's faith in the cause and in the leadership begins to wane. It is in fact Mariam who helps him see what he seems to know already but refuses to admit to himself—that the rebel leaders of all factions are feverishly selling diamonds to white foreigners for their own personal gain, and not for the benefit of their respective rebel groups. In fact, Rufus brutally quells all dissent in the ranks. Ezra soon comes to terms with his own vulnerability, especially when he learns of his parents' death and of Mariam's capture by a rival rebel faction. Losing faith in the brotherhood, he decides to search for his wife, pick up his sister at their village, and escape. In particular, the safety of Ezra's unborn child haunts him, especially when he becomes aware of the fact that a battle between rebel forces and pro-government forces is imminent. Ridding himself of both gun and uniform, his plan is for them to make their way across the border to Conakry and then to Lagos as civilians. This plan ultimately fails as Mariam is shot and killed at a random rebel post and he himself is actually "saved" by government forces that appear on the scene. The main plot of *Ezra* centers on his struggle at a rehabilitation center for child soldiers to recover from his rebel past.

As the Truth and Reconciliation Commission claims, to achieve the closure of his ordeal, Ezra must recall and tell the Commission the events of January 6, 1999, the day when Ezra's rebel force attacked three villages, one of which was his own village. According to Onitsha in her accounts of that tragic day in front of the commission, her brother, whom she had not seen in years, set fire to their house, thus killing both his parents. Ezra vehemently denies this account. He remembers, vaguely, a carnage of villages ordered by Rufus, but having been drugged, he cannot recall any of the details. Refusing to come to terms with the truth, he absolutely denies killing his own parents. But the audience knows, as Onitsha knows, that Ezra certainly participated in their death; however, the audience is also aware that he cannot be fully blamed for his actions because of the complicated hegemonic relations of power at play. Like other child soldiers, Ezra merely obeys the orders of his commander. Aduaka deliberately puts the audience in a position of suspended judgment. We cannot exonerate the unrepentant Ezra, but we cannot hang him or castigate him for actions that are truly beyond his control.

The tension drawn between his action and his motivation (he thinks he is fighting for his village and his people and is ready to avenge his parents' deaths when he learns of it) is paralleled by the tension evident among the representatives of the commission. The leader of the commission is a retired

American general, an African American, whom Ezra takes to task both on the doctrine of democracy and the legitimacy of sanctioned violence. Ezra wants to know if the general has witnessed and killed in war, and why, if he did, his actions would be justifiable, but the rebel soldier's would be unjust. He also wants to know why America props up dictatorships if it claims that the democratic process is the only viable route to social justice and economic equity around the world. These questions go unanswered, as the commission is there not to lay blame (it repeatedly reminds Ezra that it is not a prosecutorial body) but to create a space for the community to come to terms with itself by confronting its loss, its past, and its own children.

In fact, one of the three members of the commission, Elder Ezekiel, who is representing Ezra's village, further complicates the plot because, as a member of Ezra's village, he is also a witness to Ezra's role in the death of his parents. In the seat of neutrality he now occupies, Elder Ezekiel does not and cannot speak as a witness (which would put the blame squarely on Ezra's shoulders), but as a village elder. He falls back on tradition and reminds the audience of a popular and fitting Sierra Leonean proverb: "there is no bad bush to throw a bad child." Indeed, this proverb calls our attention to the fact that, given the right tools—rhetorical or otherwise—Sierra Leoneans in general believe in confronting their problems. Since children represent the nation's future, they cannot be neglected when they are in trouble. As a people, Sierra Leoneans must "hang head," as we say in Krio—that is, deliberate over issues and work through them. Given the fact that Truth Commissions (popularized throughout Africa by the success of the South African model) are today's replica of the familiar village square, they have become the centerpiece of communal therapy and a significant process in national healing. In "Theatres of Truth, Acts of Reconciliation," Catherine Cole defines the Truth and Reconciliation Commission (TRC) as "an instrument of psychological healing, a tribunal of public reckoning, a juridical mechanism for granting amnesty, and a symbol of the need for reparation." These staged hearings are "rhetorical machinations," or "theatricalization of traumatic memory" (2004, 219). The psychological instrument of national reconciliation thus becomes an effective strategy in Aduaka's narrative style. He uses flashbacks as the most natural response to memory, especially since they express the need to take "a step backwards in order to move forwards" (Cole 2004, 222).

The healing process therefore demands that representations of the conflict, like *Ezra,* respond to Sierra Leone's problems by featuring the enormity of the crisis on the ground and by searching for internal solutions within

Africa. This is unlike *Blood Diamond*, a film that finds resolution in charitably taking one family out of the country. In *Ezra*, the panel of "judges" on the commission is a pan-African body that invokes a pan-African solution. While *Blood Diamond* brings closure to the civil war story at the end of the movie, *Ezra* offers no such relief. As intensity builds in the courtroom, Ezra faints, and the audience never actually witnesses the close of the hearings. When we see Ezra again, he is back at the rehabilitation center undergoing recovery. Although in real life the UN-funded rehabilitation project is attested to in Ishmael Beah's *A Long Way Gone* (Beah talks specifically of UNICEF's role in rehabilitating child soldiers), in *Ezra* Aduaka chooses to focus on the role of black doctors and nurses who help Ezra in the recovery process. In this way, the Nigerian director further emphasizes black agency and the role of locals in directing their own destiny.

Aduaka concludes the movie with a most haunting moment. Ezra appeals, hopes, or prays at the end of the movie: "May the spirit of the ancestors forgive me. . . ." The film is over, the screen is blank, but Ezra's statement rings loud and clear, leaving audiences with much to think about, and hopefully act on, as they leave the movie theater. A Sierra Leonean proverb, "the song is over, but words remain in excess," truly captures the mission of this film. The film in essence does not end because there is so much to deliberate on *afterward*. *Ezra* calls us to action.

In situating agency in *Ezra*, then, we can say that the enigma of the boy soldier phenomenon (and the underlying problem of often unscrupulous global competition for Africa's resources) becomes a problem that the entire African world needs to resolve. Though there is much to despair about in this tragic reality in Africa, Aduaka does not present it as unsolvable, nor does he present Africans as mere victims. This rejection of victimhood is particularly projected through Ezra's sister, Onitsha, who, in spite of her tongueless state (her tongue, rather than her limbs, is cut off by a member of Ezra's brotherhood), becomes the star witness in her brother's trial, and the chief advocate seeking a course of inner healing for her brother. Onitsha's name is also telling. Onitsha is a popular city in Eastern Nigeria that has gained notoriety mostly because of its noisy marketplace. So, even though Onitsha's tongue is cut out, she essentially remains the unstoppable voice of reason, announcing Africa's troubles and insisting on a resolution.

As a filmmaker, Aduaka's sentiment in producing the film is in sync with the ideology of African cinema: the objective of filmmaking is undertaken with a serious political responsibility to educate audiences about Africa's problems and to raise awareness about social, cultural, economic, and political dilemmas that Africans face (Harrow 2007). This objective is no less different from the objectives of theater practitioners in Sierra Leone. Although for economic reasons Sierra Leonean artists have not enjoyed significant film-making opportunities evident in other parts of the continent, their projections in the theater world have equally articulated their commitment to, and sacrifices for, the good of their country. For example, during the last phase of the civil war in Sierra Leone, Julius Spencer (a well-known playwright and director) found himself resisting both rebel and renegade government forces through his decision to be the voice, literally, of the legitimate exiled government. Working with ECOMOG, he volunteered to intercept the rebels in power through radio messages that he was broadcasting from an undisclosed location. His rhetorical talent as an artist in the art of persuasion played a pivotal role in convincing Sierra Leoneans to stay in the struggle for peace and democracy. Indeed, Sierra Leonean artists have perfected the theatrical art form as entertainment device, educational tool, and activist stance. In the Sierra Leonean context in particular, theater engenders a revolutionary ideology demanding change in a failed system. Sierra Leonean artists see themselves and the Sierra Leonean people as responsible for that change; they see themselves as agents of their own destinies (Osagie 2000).

NOTES

1. See Peter Davis's chapter, "Buddies," in *In Darkest Hollywood*, which chronicles the deceptive nature of black/white "partnership" in South Africa movies during the apartheid years. Blacks are mostly represented as "faithful servants" or "adjuncts" that "exist to a large degree to boost the central white character" and "reflect the humanity of the white protagonist" (1996, 119).

2. The child-wife phenomenon is common in conflict zones in Africa. A young girl could "marry" (through coercion, or being forced into a sexual relationship) a male rebel that the leadership in the camp approves of. In Sierra Leone such girls were also called "rebel wives."

REFERENCES

Beah, Ishmael. 2007. *A Long Way Gone: Memoirs of a Boy Soldier.* New York: Sarah Crichton Books.
*Blood Diamond.* 2006. Directed by Edward Zwick. DVD. Warner Bros. Pictures.
Cole, Catherine. 2004. "Theatres of Truth, Acts of Reconciliation: The TRC in South Africa." In *African Drama and Performance,* edited by John Conteh-Morgan and Tejumola Olaniyan. Bloomington: Indiana University Press.

Davis, Peter. 1996. *In Darkest Hollywood: Exploring the Jungles of Cinema's South Africa*. Athens: Ohio University Press.

*Ezra*. 2008. Directed by Newton Aduaka. DVD. Amour Fou Filmproduktion, 2007. California Newsreel Production.

Farah, Douglas. 2004. *Blood from Stones: The Secret Financial Network of Terror*. New York: Broadway Books.

Gberie, Lansana. 2005. *A Dirty War in West Africa: The RUF and the Destruction of Sierra Leone*. Bloomington: Indiana University Press.

Harrow, Kenneth. 2007. *Postcolonial African Cinema: From Political Engagement to Postmodernism*. Bloomington: Indiana University Press.

Hirsch, John L. 2001. *Sierra Leone: Diamonds and the Struggle for Democracy*. Boulder, CO: Rienner.

Holden, Stephen. 2008. "Innocence Lost, on a Battlefield Somewhere in Africa." *New York Times*, February 13, B4.

Kamlongera, Christopher. 1988. *Theatre for Development in Africa with Case Studies from Malawi and Zambia*. Bonn, Germany: Education, Science, and Documentation Centre.

Kandeh, Jimmy. 2004. *Coups from Below: Armed Subalterns and State Power in West Africa*. New York: Palgrave.

Koroma, Abdul Karim. 2004. *Crisis and Intervention in Sierra Leone 1997–2003*. Sierra Leone: Adromeda.

Levy, Emanuel. 2008. "Blood Diamond Ed Zwick." *Emanuel Levy*. February 27. emanuellevy.com/interview/blood-diamond-ed-zwick-7.

Maddy, Yulisa Amadu. 1971. *Obasai and Other Plays*. London: Heinemann.

Opala, Joseph A. 1994. *"Ecstatic Renovations!" Street Art Celebrating Sierra Leone's 1992 Revolution*. Freetown: Ro-Marong Industries.

Osagie, Iyunolu. 2000. *The Amistad Revolt: Memory, Slavery, and the Politics of Identity in the United States and Sierra Leone*. Athens: University of Georgia Press.

Pieth, Mark, ed. 2002. *Financing Terrorism*. Norwell, MA: Kluwer Academic.

Rosen, David M. 2005. *Armies of the Young: Child Soldiers in War and Terrorism*. New Brunswick, NJ: Rutgers University Press.

Sanogo, Issouf. 2007. "Blood Diamonds: Nigerian Movie Differs with Hollywood." *SAWF News*. AFP. March 4. http://news.sawf.org/Entertainment/34248.aspx.

Singer, P. W. 2005. *Children at War*. New York: Pantheon.

Spencer, Julius. 1988. "A Historical Background to the Contemporary Theatre in Sierra Leone." *International Journal of Sierra Leone Studies* 1:26–35.

# FIFTEEN

# Bye Bye Hollywood

African Cinema and Its Double in Mahamet-Saleh Haroun's *Bye Bye Africa*

DAYNA OSCHERWITZ

Western cinema has lately rediscovered Africa, or so it would seem. In the past fifteen years, a number of films, including Ridley Scott's *Black Hawk Down* (2001), Terry George's *Hotel Rwanda* (2004), Fernando Meirelles's *The Constant Gardener* (2005), Edward Zwick's *Blood Diamond* (2006), and Kevin Macdonald's *The Last King of Scotland* (2006), have been set in Africa and have taken African reality, or at least a certain vision of African reality, as their subject. This new wave of Hollywood-Africa films has occurred, interestingly, at a moment when African films, which is to say films made by Africans, have been increasing in visibility and prestige in Europe and the United States. African films are often screened at film festivals and on college campuses. They are shown in independent cinemas in major cities across continents. They are increasingly available on DVD through independent distributors, and in 2006, a South African film, Gavin Hood's *Tsotsi* (2005), won the Oscar for Best Foreign Film. While it is true that African films are still not part of mainstream viewing in the West, they have become a staple of the independent film circuit.

Of course, Africa is not new to Hollywood or to Western cinema. Some of the first films made for mass distribution presented images of Africa and Africans. Africa was introduced to the silver screen late in 1896 when the Lumière brothers sent cameraman Alexandre Promio to Egypt to record short films or "views" that were later screened in Europe (Abel 1994, 11; Roberts 1987).[1] The silver screen was introduced to Africa the same year at screenings of Lumière films in Cairo and Alexandria (Armes 2006, 21). Thus began a circulation of images—images of the West exported to Africa, and images of Africa exported to Europe and North America—that transformed Africa into a blank screen onto which the West could project its own image. From the silent era through the 1960s, Europe and Hollywood routinely made "African" films. These range from silent-era films like Promio's documentary shorts, to reenacted *actualités* or newsreel films set in Africa such as *Savage South Africa—Savage Attack and Repulse* (1899), to silent narrative films such as Jacques Feyder's *L'Atlantide* (1921). The sound era saw the production of overtly colonial films, including Pierre Chenal's *La Maison du Maltais* (1927), Robert Stevenson's *King Solomon's Mines* (1937), Julien Duvivier's *Pépé le Moko* (1938), Zoltan Korda's *The Four Feathers* (1939), Jacques de Baroncelli's *L'Homme du Niger* (1940), and Brian Desmond Hurst's *Simba* (1955).[2] Africa became a staple of Hollywood filmmaking, and figured prominently in both "B" movies, including Johnny Weissmuller's "Tarzan" films, which ran in the 1930s, 1940s, and 1950s, and Hollywood classics, such as John Huston's *The African Queen* (1951) and John Ford's *Mogambo* (1953). These Western "African" films became part of "the machinery of cultural hegemony" (Slavin 2001, 3). They satisfied a Western "appetite for fantasy, escape and exoticism with picturesque, sensational material" (Barlet 2000, 5) while simultaneously "indoctrinating Africans into foreign cultures, including their ideals and aesthetics" (Ukadike 1994, 31).

The period of decolonization that began in Africa in the 1960s introduced two oppositional trends in the representation of Africa on film. The first was the emergence of an *African* African cinema, a cinema about Africa by Africans. The first African film to be made by an African in sub-Saharan Africa, Sembène Ousmane's *Borom Saret,* appeared in 1962.[3] It inaugurated a period of fairly intense film production on the continent, primarily in francophone West Africa.[4] The second trend inaugurated by decolonization was a decline in Hollywood and European films about or set in Africa. If Africa had, through the 1950s, figured regularly in feature films made in the West, only a handful of films set in Africa were made in the 1960s and 1970s. The decline in the Western "African" film at the precise moment of the emergence of African cinema raises a number of interesting questions, particularly since African films, from the beginning, have been largely funded by Western governments, and since they rely for both production and distribution on facilities and networks located in Europe. It is worth wondering, for example, whether after decolonization Western audiences were presumed to no longer be interested in Africa, and if so, why Hollywood deemed after the 1990s that such interest had reemerged. It is also worth asking whether African films funded by the West, made by filmmakers who have often trained in the West, and distributed more frequently in the West than in Africa can really be considered to be African films or whether they are more actually African-made Western African films. The question of the virtual disappearance and later reappearance of films about Africa in Western cinema is an interesting one, but it is beyond the scope of this particular essay. Instead, I would like to focus on the second question, which could be restated as the question of what constitutes an African film and what distinguishes it from a Western African film, or more particularly a Hollywood Africa film.

There have been many attempts to answer this question.[5] One of the most interesting answers to have been given has come not in the form of a critical, theoretical intervention, but rather in the form of a film, specifically in Mahamet-Saleh Haroun's *Bye Bye Africa* (1991).[6] Mahamet Saleh-Haroun is a Chadian director often classified as part of the "new" generation of African filmmakers (Armes 2006). He is one of only two Chadians to date to have made films, the other being Issa Serge Coelo, who appears in *Bye Bye Africa*.[7] Quite apart from the nationality of its director, *Bye Bye Africa* is somewhat atypical of African films in that it was one of the first to be shot on digital video. It was, therefore, made outside of the typical funding and production structures most African filmmakers have come to rely on.[8] While Mahamet-Saleh Haroun has stated that he has, in principle, no objection to filmmakers' relying on Western subsidies to make films, he has also noted that accepting such subsidies gives a certain degree of control to the funding institutions and agencies, who, he argues, have an expectation that "[African directors] will create cinema about a certain kind of Africa."[9]

The ideological slant that has tended to dominate film production and consumption does not mean that African directors are doomed to re-presenting and reinforcing (neo)colonial images of Africa. Nor does it mean that African cinema cannot "speak," to borrow Gayatri Chakravorty Spivak's metaphor. However, it does suggest that those African directors who seek to escape what Mahamet-Saleh Haroun has termed "a colonization by images" find ways of making the cinema speak differently.[10] These directors adapt mainstream production norms, technical standards, and narrative conventions to their own particular vision. This, in turn, requires a transformation or re-generation of cinema itself, and it is this process of transformation that is explored in and embodied by *Bye Bye Africa*. The simple decision by director Haroun to film *Bye Bye Africa* using digital video begins this process of transformation. As noted, it moves the film outside the domain of mainstream cinema and therefore distances it to a certain degree from mainstream cinema's ideological norms. This shift away from typical commercial production is marked visually in the film, which has a less polished, less manufactured look than mainstream studio films, therefore seeming closer to reality than cinema. Furthermore, by filming with a handheld camera, Haroun was more mobile than he would have been with a standard movie camera. He was able to move through N'djamena and map the city more freely than he could have with standard production techniques, and he was able to use natural lighting and natural settings, thereby avoiding the need for studio lighting, makeup, and film stock that inherently emphasize whiteness and obscure blackness (Dyer 1997). The technical elements of *Bye Bye Africa* may, then, set it apart from typical studio films. However, they do not, in and of themselves, mark the film as particularly "African." They are not, for example, unique to Haroun's film or even to African filmmaking, but rather, have been used by avant-garde filmmakers of all nationalities since the French New Wave (whom Haroun references at various places in his film). In *Bye Bye Africa*, however, these technical properties are part of a film whose structure and content explores the question of filmmaking in Africa, and it is this interaction, more than anything else, that renders this film distinct.

*Bye Bye Africa* recounts the journey of an expatriate Chadian filmmaker named Haroun as he travels from France back to his native country.[11] In the film's opening scene, Haroun is awoken by a telephone call announcing the death of his mother. He has, apparently, not seen her in some years, and her death is something of a shock. He decides to return to Chad, and this decision prompts another, a decision to make a film about his native country. Haroun announces that his film will be called *"Bye Bye Africa,"* a title that mirrors that of the external, framing film.

The context in which Haroun decides to make the film (the death of his mother), his observation, fairly early in the narrative, that films are a form of memory, and the "Bye Bye" in the film's title all suggest that his motivation in making the film may be to attempt to recover his dead mother and at the same time to reconnect with his native country before he leaves it again for good. This reading seems reinforced by Haroun's own observations that it is his grief over the death of his mother that prompts him to make the film and by the fact that Africa has often been imagined, most notably by Léopold Sédar Senghor, as a woman or a mother. The *Bye Bye Africa* Haroun seeks to make, therefore, is a eulogy, both for his mother and for Africa, a means of capturing on film something that, for him, no longer exists. The film then follows Haroun as he returns to Chad and attempts to reconnect with family and old friends. Haroun films everything he sees as he travels through his hometown, the capital city of N'djamena, using a video camera he has brought with him from France. Haroun ultimately, however, gives up and defers his plans for making a film, announcing his intention to return again to Chad at some point in the future and to make *"Bye Bye Africa"* at that point. In an ambiguous gesture, he leaves his camera behind and goes back to France, promising to return at some later date.

As this summary of the film should make clear, filmmaking and cinema are principal subjects of *Bye Bye Africa,* a fact also made explicit by Haroun, when he says that the subject of the film he plans to make is how to film life. In fact, the issue of filmmaking figures so prominently in the film that many if not most critics have classified *Bye Bye Africa* as a documentary about Chadian cinema. This impression seems borne out by a number of apparent convergences between the life of the director and that of the protagonist. The opinion of the critics notwithstanding, *Bye Bye Africa* is generically ambiguous and might best be characterized as a docu-fiction. The film's dual cameras, the one external to the narrative and the other internal to it, for example, give the film an embedded structure that complicates the relationship between Mahamet-Saleh Haroun, the filmmaker, and Haroun, the character in the narrative.

At first glance, the video camera Haroun carries with him seems to reinforce the idea that the external film entitled *Bye Bye Africa* is a documentary made by Haroun, the same film he repeatedly states he is making within the context of the narrative. However, the images recorded by this camera are marked as distinct from the images filmed by the external camera, since the images filmed by Haroun's camera are presented in black and white while those filmed by the external camera are in color. This creates a distance between the two sets of images, and the respective films that are composed of them. It therefore becomes unclear whether the images Haroun films are part of the external film—even though they are incorporated into it—or whether he ever intends to use them in the film he plans to make. The ambiguity concerning the relationship of the two cameras is reinforced by the fact that they actually record different images, even though they appear to operate in the same space and time. In fact, despite the illusion of convergence, the two cameras may actually belong to two different fictive temporalities, the one the present of the narrative, and the other an external present, which might constitute the future of the narrative within the film.

I have described the images recorded by the film's two cameras as different, but it might be more exact to describe them as divergent. Haroun's camera, the internal camera, for example, tends to capture fragmented, decontextualized images of people and settings. These are unanchored with respect to the external narrative, and they are linked to, but not part of, the film's underlying story. The external camera records Haroun moving in these settings and among these people. This camera films Haroun in the act of filming and ties him to the people and places he films. The two sets of images are, therefore, distinct. If they are images of the same reality, they nonetheless re-present or restage that reality in very different ways.

The tension between the two cameras is evident from the very first scene in which Haroun appears in Chad. In that scene, the external camera films Haroun in the taxi, and captures scenes of ordinary life on the street as the taxi passes by. The taxi driver discusses with Haroun the difficulties faced daily by Chadians, particularly those brought about by the high price of fuel. As he does so, Haroun casually looks around him. Haroun's attention is then caught by a convoy of vehicles moving through the city. The taxi driver announces that they are going to prepare for a major event that will be taking place. Presumably attracted to the spectacle, Haroun pulls out his own camera, which had previously not been visible. However, the taxi driver, misunderstanding the gesture, believes that Haroun has taken the camera out to film him, and he states that he would very much like to see his own image on a film. Probably in order to humor the driver, Haroun does, indeed, film the taxi driver, and for a short moment, the images of the internal and external cameras both focus on him.

This scene introduces a pattern of convergence and divergence between the two cameras that structures much of film. The external camera films the absolutely ordinary, and the images it captures are coherent and form the basis of the narrative. They are images like those the taxi driver says he wishes to see, images of ordinary Chadians engaged in fairly ordinary activities. Haroun, in contrast, attempts to use his camera to catch the extraordinary, the out of the ordinary, as with the convoy of vehicles. In the end, he too, ends up filming the absolutely ordinary, but in a way that is disconnected from reality and ultimately incoherent. This pattern continues throughout much of the film. In fact, the images shot by Haroun's camera are, in many ways, not part of the external film, but rather part of a separate film altogether, a film that is much more documentary and detached than the external film that frames it.

There are essentially two kinds of sequences recorded by this internal camera. The first are nearly silent shots of ordinary Chadians on the streets of N'djamena. These images are presented without any context. It is not explained who the people in these sequences are, what the places in these sequences are, or why they are filmed. Typically, if there is sound in these sequences, it is only Haroun meditating in voice-over about the nature of cinema in Africa. These sequences are almost ethnographic in nature. The gaze through which they are framed is a distant, disconnected, impersonal gaze. The commentary that accompanies such sequences is similarly detached. It is self-reflexive and completely separate from the images, revealing nothing about the people or places filmed.

The second type of sequence recorded by this camera consists, for the most part, of interviews with people who have a connection to cinema in Chad, either owners of theaters or projectionists, for example, or of sequences in which Haroun films actors or potential actors for his films. These are fairly typically documentary sequences, and they explain, perhaps, why the film as a whole has so often been classified as a documentary. These sequences differ from the sequences of ordinary Chadians in that all of them feature people who are somehow connected to cinema in Africa, either through existing contributions or potential future ones. For that reason, it is also clear who these people are and why they are being filmed. These sequences are also disconnected from the external narrative. They are, like the other sequences of the internal camera, filmed in a neutral, detached, depersonalized manner. These sequences tend to foreground the impossibility or improbability of making a film in Africa, since all of them center on the absence of infrastructure or funding, or the decay or what little film infrastructure was once there (cinemas for example). They are, therefore, at odds with the external film, which, by its very nature, affirms the existence of African cinema, although perhaps not in the way imagined by Haroun or those he interviews.

The sequences shot by the external camera, are, as noted, more internally coherent, and it is these images that form the film's narrative. All of those who appear in the sequences shot by this camera are identified, and their function in the film is clear. These images then appear more real than the documentary images they contain. What is interesting, however, is that these images are also marked in a number of ways as fictional. First and foremost, there are a number of characters in these sequences who are played by actors. These include Haroun's father, played by Khayar Oumar Defallah, and the actress Isabelle, played by Aicha Yelena. There are also a number of characters whose status is ambiguous. These include Haroun's friend Garba, played by Garba Issa, and his friend Serge, played by Issa Serge Coelo. These characters seem to be like people who actually exist, but as with Haroun, the similarities between the real people and the characters are superficial, and not sufficient to establish a clear identification between the two. Moreover, there are events depicted in these external images that do not, in reality, occur. The most notable of these is the suicide of the actress Isabelle, which does not occur in reality because she is not a real person.

If the two types of images—fictive and documentary—are interwoven in the film, the tension between them destabilizes the presumed connection between Haroun, the character in the film, and Mahamet-Saleh Haroun, the external filmmaker. The camera used by each is distinct, and the images produced by each camera distinct, which suggests that the two men may be distinct. This undermines what Philippe Lejeune has termed the "auto-biographical pact," according to which the author of an autobiographical narrative must be recognizable as the character within it. Moreover, because the "real" or documentary images are filmed by a character within a narrative marked as fictional, the film's two cameras ultimately call into question the relationship between the external film, *Bye Bye Africa*, the planned and announced film internal to the narrative, and the images shot by Haroun, and they also raise the question of film's relationship to reality, which is one of *Bye Bye Africa*'s central themes.

Genre is not the only element to be destabilized by the use of the double cameras. Time and space and therefore the structure of cinematic narrative are also problematized in *Bye Bye Africa*, as is the relationship between film and reality. It is impossible, for example, according to standard conventions of filmic narration, for Mahamet-Saleh Haroun to be operating both the film's external and internal cameras. First of all, this would require him to be in two places at once, since the external camera films Haroun filming. Second, this would require him to be in two temporalities at once, since it is made clear, during the course of the narrative, that the film *Bye Bye Africa* never gets made during the filmic present, and yet the spectator seems to be watching that very film. This blurring of space, time, and genre, along with the film's use of direct address and voice-over narration, its multivocality and multilinguality, gives to *Bye Bye Africa* many of the characteristics of what Hamid Naficy has termed exilic or "accented cinema." Like such "accented" films, *Bye Bye Africa* tends to destabilize "the narrative system of mainstream [Western] cinema" (Naficy 2001, 25), which suggests that questions concerning cinema and the language of cinema are central to the film. However, unlike typical "accented" films, which function, according to Naficy, to foreground the experience of lived or personal exile, *Bye Bye Africa* foregrounds the exilic or dislocated state of African cinema itself.

In *Bye Bye Africa,* this sense of exile or dislocation is represented first and foremost as a mind-set, a tendency to view Africa through foreign eyes. This is represented spatially in the film's opening sequence, which locates Haroun in France. According to the logic of the film, therefore, literally Haroun comes from France, not Africa. Moreover, there is no actual journey between France and Africa depicted in *Bye Bye Africa.* Instead, the film simply cuts from a scene of Haroun traveling in a taxicab in Paris to one of him traveling in a taxicab in N'djamena. Since journeys in films typically suggest the mental transformation or development of a character, the absence of a journey in *Bye Bye Africa* suggests that Haroun arrives in Chad with a mind-set and worldview identical to the one he had in France.[12] The detached and disjointed nature of Haroun's relationship with his country of origin is also presented directly in the film in a conversation Haroun has with his father, shortly after his arrival. While recounting to him the details of his mother's death, Haroun's father observes that Haroun identifies too closely with the West, that he thinks he belongs there. He also questions the value of Haroun's work in France, observing that he, himself, was unable to understand the only film of Haroun's he has seen, a documentary on Sigmund Freud. He tells Haroun that after watching this film, he has concluded that Haroun does not make films for Africans, but rather for Westerners. Africans, he asserts, would not understand such films, and he goes on to caution Haroun against identifying too closely with the West lest he lose himself.

If we read the words of Haroun's father not as the naive ramblings Haroun takes them for, but rather as a commentary on the nature of film and filmmaking, it is possible to see in them an explanation for the use of *Bye Bye Africa*'s double camera. Haroun's camera, the internal camera, which he has brought with him from France, films in a detached, documentary style that is presumably similar to that he used in making his documentary on Sigmund Freud. There is no sense of the filmmaker's connection to his subject, nothing specifically local, to borrow Manthia Diawara's term, about the sequences filmed by the internal camera, just as there is, it seems, no personal connection between Haroun and Freud. Haroun's father tacitly points this out by asking Haroun if Freud was a friend of his, a tactic he repeats when Haroun quotes Jean-Luc Godard. Rather than statements made by someone ignorant of the nature of cinema, Haroun's father's critiques of his filmmaking may function as wise words from someone who potentially understands the power of cinema better than Haroun himself. Specifically, Haroun's father affirms, there must be a personal connection between a filmmaker and his films if there is to be a connection between an audience and film. It is this connection that Haroun seems to lack.

The sequence that follows this conversation seems to reinforce the substance of Haroun's father's words. In order to convince his father of the value of cinema, Haroun shows him a film of his dead mother. The film is a silent home movie of Haroun's mother at his sister's wedding, and it was shot by Haroun's friend Garba. The intensely personal film resonates with Haroun's father in a way Haroun's own films seem not to. Haroun shows his father this film as a means of demonstrating to him the power of cinema to intervene directly in life, and specifically the power of cinema to transmit memory or create memories. What is ironic, however, is that Haroun, who sets up this lesson, fails himself to understand it. There is a vast difference between Garba's film and the type of film Haroun has set out to make and has, presumably, made in the past. Garba's film is deeply personal. It is a portrait of someone he knows. It is, similarly, viewed by people who are intimately bound to its subject, and in fact, those spectators provide the narrative that accompanies the images, since the film itself is silent. In certain respects, this is similar to the sequences of Chadians filmed by Haroun's internal camera in that the images themselves contain little or no sound, and that the sound that accompanies them comes in voice-over. However, unlike these sequences, the voices that accompany Garba's film are voices of those most connected to the person filmed, and they situate the images of the person in a wider context. Moreover, the film Haroun is working to make is a construction; he has a message he wishes to convey and he attempts to find images with which to create it. Garba's film, on the other hand, is a spontaneous film. There is nothing staged, artificial, or fictional in its content. It simply replays what was in an effort to transmit a memory to others.

In Western films ranging from *Casablanca* to *The Constant Gardener*, Africa and Africans function largely as backdrop. The real subjects of such films are Westerners, and the themes the films explore reflect a Western, rather than an African, perspective. African characters in such films, therefore, tend to be two-dimensional. They appear onscreen but are fairly disconnected from the principal narrative. Haroun's film functions in a similar way. It is not really "about" any of the people who appear in it, people about whom we learn relatively little. Rather, it is a more abstract meditation on the nature of cinema and on the obstacles Haroun encounters trying to make cinema. The Africans who appear in this film are not the subject of the film. They are, in fact, incidental to it. Garba's film, in contrast, is only about Haroun's mother. It has no meaning outside of her. What is more, no meaning is imposed on Haroun's mother by Garba's film. She appears on the screen as she was in life, and she means nothing more nor less in the film than herself. She may, therefore, embody what Ken Harrow has termed "the aesthetics of the surface" (2007, 37), an attempt on the part of the filmmaker to reject Western paradigms of meaning in which everything must stand for or mean something else. Garba's film, therefore, functions as a type of contrasting filmic image that foregrounds the problems and shortcomings of Haroun's own film.

Bye Bye Africa returns to this critique of filmmaking, or at least a certain type of filmmaking, at various points in the narrative. One of the most interesting examples occurs in a scene whose subject is filming and being filmed, a scene that seems to comment directly on the different functions of the internal and external cameras. In this scene, Haroun is filming Chadians from the steps of the Shéhérazade, an old theater in N'djamena. The external camera records Haroun filming from behind, and then the film cuts to the images of the internal camera, which focus on a man in the crowd. This man (Assane Kheiro) moves angrily toward the camera, as he shouts that Haroun is stealing his image, and we see him reach for and grab the camera. The film cuts to the external camera in order to show the man grabbing Haroun's camera and striking him in the process. It then cuts to the man, who is now seated, holding the camera, speaking to Haroun's friend Garba, who attempts to persuade the man to return the camera to Haroun. The man eventually agrees and stands up, walking toward Haroun. He returns the camera to him, telling him he is lucky, and then telling him he had better not steal anyone else's image again. As he speaks, the man looks directly into the external camera; he returns its gaze, in a gesture that mirrors the one that began the scene. However, he makes no comment about the presence of this camera, and he does not object to being filmed by this camera in the way he objected to being filmed by Haroun.

The importance of this scene is marked in the film not only by its literal subject—the act of filming and the differing reactions to the two cameras—but by the fact that Haroun contemplates the man's reaction to being filmed in two subsequent sequences. As with Haroun's father's comments about the cinema, the man's assertion that Haroun is "stealing his image" may, at first, be understood as the reaction of someone who is naive or unfamiliar with technology. Such a reading, however, is undercut by the way the man speaks in direct address to the external camera, acknowledging its presence in a way that defies the conventions of realist cinema. Although the man never mentions the external camera, looking into it and speaking directly to it are forms of recognition. This suggests that the external camera is not invisible to the man, and, moreover, than he does not have an issue with being filmed, per se. Rather, the man has an issue with being filmed by Haroun, someone whom he labels "a stranger," or possibly "a foreigner" since the man speaks French and the word has both meanings in French. What, therefore, seems to concern the man is why Haroun is filming him and what he intends to do with the images he takes.

Haroun's inability to understand the man's reaction demonstrates the degree to which he has become distant from his country of origin. The idea of his alienation is reinforced when his friend, Garba, tells Haroun he has "forgotten" what Chadians are like. Garba attempts to explain the man's reaction to being filmed by stating that Chadians, in general, are wary of the camera and wary of images in cinema. As with the comments of Haroun's father, and as with the comments of the man in front of the theater, there are multiple readings of Garba's comments. It could be he that is asserting that Chadians are not sophisticated enough to understand that film is a fiction, or it could be that Garba is arguing that Chadians understand the force of cinematic images, and that they understand, moreover, that Africa has often been distorted and perhaps even harmed by the images of it cinema has produced. It is not coincidental that the man who refuses to be filmed stands outside of one of N'djamena's theaters, which are presented within *Bye Bye Africa* as spaces dominated largely by images from the West. Posters advertising old French and American films line the walls of these cinemas, and it is repeatedly suggested that the only films screened in these theaters are Western films. The man's reaction to being filmed by Haroun, therefore, reflects a desire not to avoid being filmed—this is clear because he is filmed by the external camera—but rather to control the way in which he is filmed, or essentially to control the images of himself that cinema produces.

If the man in front of the Shéhérazade introduces the idea that Africans must themselves control the images of Africa on film, it is the story of an actress named Isabelle that explores the consequences of cinematic representation on Africa. Isabelle apparently once played a woman infected with

AIDS in one of Haroun's films, and, according to Garba, those in Chad who saw the film, including Isabelle's family and friends, believed afterward that she actually had AIDS. They took the film for reality and scorned her. As noted, Haroun is already identified more closely with the West than with Africa in the film. Therefore the film in which Isabelle appeared, a film that apparently focused on AIDS in Africa, evokes in certain respects recent Western films about Africa including *The Constant Gardener* and *Blood Diamond*. As with such films, Haroun's film seems to have focused on a specific problem or crisis widely associated with Africa, be it AIDS, human exploitation, or civil war. While the problems and issues depicted in such films do exist, and are therefore real, they are not the entire picture. They are, rather, like the documentary images filmed by Haroun's camera, fragmented, decontextualized, divorced from the wider picture.

Isabelle's situation, therefore, seems to suggest that cinema, in general, has presented a distorted image of Africa. However, it also suggests that this distorted image may actually function to impose a reality upon Africa. The average filmgoer in the West has a very limited notion of Africa, and it is also true that this notion derives, in large measure, from the images of Africa shown in Western films and on Western television. However, as *Bye Bye Africa* suggests, these distorted images are also seen by Africans themselves. Isabelle's family and friends, then, may be very much like film audiences in Europe and North America who take the images they see of Africa onscreen for reality. Isabelle points directly to this phenomenon, when she explains her plight to Haroun by stating that cinema is stronger than reality.

Isabelle's story, then, elucidates the reaction of the man on the steps of the Shéhérazade. His refusal to be filmed by Haroun did not, it seems, reflect ignorance or naïveté regarding the nature of the cinematic image. Rather, he refused to be filmed by Haroun because he recognized cinema's power in a way that Haroun did not. He does not, it seems, wish to become like Isabelle, a person whose reality is altered by the fiction of someone else's film. The problem, then, for both Isabelle and the man in front of the Shéhérazade, is the use to which Haroun puts or intends to put their image. While we do not know what Haroun intended to do with the footage he shot of the man in front of the theater and while we know relatively little about the fictional film in which Isabelle appeared, we know a great deal about Haroun's interactions with and attitude toward Isabelle. It becomes clear, for example, that Haroun had a sexual relationship with her at the time she appeared in his film. She was young at the time, only seventeen, and he remembers that he told her he loved her, although he did not mean it. When the film was over, he abandoned her, and never, it seems, thought about her again.

Haroun, in fact, regards Isabelle not as a person, but as an object, an object to be filmed and to be exploited. After Garba tells him what has happened to her, he meets with her again, and he attempts yet again to seduce her. His objectification of and indifference to her is revealed not only by his own behavior but also in the way he films her during this meeting. Haroun's camera, the internal camera, overtly sexualizes Isabelle, tending to shoot her in close-up or extreme close-up, filming her not as a person but as an ensemble of various body parts. The external camera, in contrast, tends to shoot Isabelle in medium or long shot, framing her against her surroundings or emphasizing her interactions with Haroun. Haroun's camera, therefore, objectifies Isabelle in much the same way as he himself objectifies her, whereas the external camera attempts to capture her reality.

It seems logical to conclude that if Haroun's camera objectifies Isabelle in the filmic present, it probably also did so in the past, particularly since the film suggests that he treats her in the present in the same way he did in the past. Unlike the external camera, Haroun's camera has no interest in capturing the reality of Isabelle's life. Instead, it treats her as an object to be exploited. The problem for Isabelle, then, was not that she appeared in a film, but that she appeared in a film made by someone who had no regard for either her or her image. Haroun, the filmmaker, was content to use her image without regard for the consequences of that use on her life, just as he was content to use her without regard for the consequences on her life. He was willing to impose a fiction upon Isabelle, both in his film and in life (by pretending to love her), that negatively affected the reality of her life. Moreover, even when he learns of this, Haroun remains utterly indifferent.

The explanation for Haroun's use of and indifference to Isabelle may be found in the conversation he has with his father about cinema. Haroun's father asserts that Haroun makes films for Westerners, not for Africans. If we assume that Haroun films Isabelle in the same way he had previously filmed her, it would seem that the film in which she appeared objectified her for a Western audience in the same way Haroun himself objectifies her. Haroun's attitude, therefore, justifies his father's charge that he does not make films for Africans, but it also demonstrates the danger to Africa of films that distort its image for foreign consumption. If, as Isabelle asserts, film is stronger than reality—if film, through its imaginary constructions, imposes reality— then films that objectify Africa or Africans ultimately impose that reality on

Africa. This perhaps explains the wariness of Chadians with respect to the camera, the wariness that Garba describes to Haroun.

It is not, moreover, merely Isabelle who is objectified in Haroun's films. In the sequence in which he is interviewing actors and actresses, Haroun asks all those he interviews, male and female, to mime and playact, and to generally pretend to be something they are not. What he is interested in depicting, what his camera records, therefore, is not reality, but a distortion or fiction, a distortion or fiction the film has already suggested is unethical, and one that is created for outsiders, not for Africans themselves. This type of film would necessarily distort and alter the reality of Africa in order to make them understandable to Western viewers. If that is the case, then Haroun's father's assertion that Africans cannot understand his films may not be an assertion that Africans are too naive or uninformed to understand them, but rather an assertion that Haroun's films create an Africa that is unrecognizable to Africans.

How, then, should Africans—or more particularly, African cinema—respond? One potential answer is offered by Isabelle herself. Feeling completely overwhelmed by the version of reality that Haroun's images have imposed on her, Isabelle ultimately confronts him and angrily takes his camera away from him. She then uses the camera to make a film of herself, a film in which she speaks for herself, but also one in which she announces her own death. In taking the camera from Haroun, Isabelle imitates the gesture of the man in front of the Shéhérazade. She prevents him from filming her and therefore asserts a certain degree of control over her own image. However, she goes one step further than the man. She not only blocks and rejects the images imposed on her from the outside, she also seizes the camera in an attempt to create her own images of herself, images that contradict the images she rejects.

Isabelle's gesture in seizing the camera and turning it on herself may be read as a metaphoric rendering of what Melissa Thackway calls "shooting back," a gesture in which Africans make films in order to counter or contradict the images of Africa projected by Western films. Isabelle's actions may, therefore, be read as a metaphor for one way in which African cinema could position itself with respect to the cinema of the West. This type of African cinema, a cinema that returns Europe and Hollywood's gaze, offers more "realistic" images of Africans and Africa than those it seeks to correct. However, this type of African cinema, *Bye Bye Africa* suggests, is little better for Africa than the cinemas of the West. Isabelle's film, after all, is a suicide note. It merely finishes the process of killing Isabelle that Haroun's original film had begun. Similarly, *Bye Bye Africa* suggests, an African cinema that defines itself *against* Western cinema does little to give Africans control over their own images or destinies.

In watching Isabelle's film, Haroun comes to meditate on his past with Isabelle and on his own filmmaking practices, and he seems to come to the conclusion that his father is correct in asserting that he does not make films for Africans. He abandons his plans to make *Bye Bye Africa,* at least in the form originally planned, and he gives his camera to his nephew Ali, who had repeatedly asked for it and who had expressed a desire to become a filmmaker himself. On the surface, this might suggest that Haroun has given up the idea of making a film about Africa, which might in turn be read as the film's assertion that African cinema is impossible. However, there is another way of understanding this gesture.

Haroun's transmission of the camera to his nephew is a sign he has rejected all of the ideas and practices that have marked his filmmaking *up to that point;* it is not necessarily a sign that he has abandoned cinema. He gives the camera to Ali, for example, fully intending for Ali to use it. Ali, who represents the next generation of African filmmakers, has never left Chad, and he therefore assumes the camera without the problematic gaze of the generation that preceded him. Moreover, when Haroun gives Ali the camera, he cautions him to be careful about what he films with it. This suggests that he has learned something about the power of the image, and that he is passing this lesson on. Moreover, if Haroun leaves Chad, he nonetheless declares his intention to return in order to try to make *Bye Bye Africa* again. This new film, the spectator is given to understand, is not the same film Haroun has been trying to make, even if the two share the same title. This suggests that Haroun has not abandoned the cinema, only a certain vision of the cinema, a certain way of making films.

The film's ending brings us back to the question of the difference between African films about Africa and Western or Hollywood films about Africa. For a film to be African, Mahamet-Saleh Haroun suggests, Africans have to be its implied audience, or at least one of its implied audiences. It has to represent Africa in a way that does not distort, sensationalize, or objectify it. It has to consist of images of Africa that Africans recognize and control. Do contemporary Hollywood-style films about Africa meet this standard? That is not the subject of this essay. However, I would say that if films such as *Blood Diamond* and *The Last King of Scotland* differ from Hollywood's earlier African films in that Africa actually figures more as subject than object, they do not, it seems, quite meet the standard set by Haroun the director.

Rather, they tend to resemble the images of Africa shot by *Bye Bye Africa*'s internal camera: disjointed, disconnected, decontextualized images that may be taken from reality, but that are more fictions created for foreign consumption than images of Africa that Africans themselves would project.

This brings us back again to the man in front of the Shéhérazade, the man who refused to allow Haroun to film him but who does not object to being filmed by the film's external camera. His refusal of Haroun's camera, it seems, was a refusal to allow himself to be objectified, to be turned into a commodity for foreign consumption. This may explain why, as he becomes angry, he says he does not wish to be filmed by a stranger. However, it also reveals something about the nature of African film, at least as imagined in *Bye Bye Africa*. For the man, it seems, does not regard the external camera as hostile, nor does he consider the person filming to be a stranger. This raises the question of the origin of that camera, and the identity of the person who wields it. The fact that the man acknowledges both the external and the internal camera in the same sequence suggests that the two cameras do, in fact, exist in the same temporality. This, in turn, would suggest that the external camera is not used by Haroun, but rather by someone else moving through N'djamena at the same time he is. While the film never reveals the identity of this person, it does make reference to the existence of another aspiring filmmaker, Haroun's nephew Ali. Haroun does not give Ali his camera until the end of his journey, but Ali, in the meantime, makes his own camera. He builds it out of local materials, cans and other objects he finds lying around.

Perhaps, in the fictional reality of *Bye Bye Africa,* we are to imagine Ali's camera the external camera that films Haroun as he films, the camera that really films *Bye Bye Africa.* If so, it would seem that Mahamet-Saleh Haroun is arguing, as others have done, that African cinema must position itself completely outside of Western cinema, that it must divorce itself entirely from cinema as it already exists. This, however, seems unlikely, particularly since this ideal camera and the cameraman who uses it are not really part of the fictional world of the film. If their existence is implied or pointed to within the narrative, they both lie permanently outside of it, always outside of the frame. It is not something that is either achievable or desirable, at least not within the film's narrative frame.

In fact, despite appearances, *Bye Bye Africa* is *not* the product of this ideal, external camera. It is, rather, the product of the interaction between this camera and the less than ideal internal camera wielded by Haroun. The film, therefore, ultimately occurs in the space between the two cameras.

Mahamet-Saleh Haroun's vision of African cinema, therefore, is one of a cinema that acknowledges and meditates on the Western influences inherent in cinema at the same time as it attempts to separate itself. It is less a revolutionary Third Cinema, which attempts to seize and co-opt Western cinema, than a cinema of the Third Space, one characterized by an aesthetics of the in-between. This embrace of the in-between is evident in the film's use of the double camera, but also in its hybrid genre—which lies between reality and fiction—in its hybrid temporality—which lies somewhere between present and future—and in its hybrid narrative structure, which is neither completely linear nor completely fragmented. It is also evident in Haroun's own movement in the film. He moves from France to Africa, then from Africa to France, and then, the film suggests, from France back to Africa. His film will, therefore, occur, in the space in between the two just as African cinema must find a way to exist and interact with cinema as a whole.

Moreover, I would suggest that *Bye Bye Africa* implies the creation of this liminal cinema both in the internal and external worlds. In the external world, it is embodied by the film the spectator watches, the *Bye Bye Africa* made by Mahamet-Saleh Haroun. In the internal world, it is the double of that film, which occurs, interestingly, not in the space of the narrative, but just outside of it, in a postfinal sequence that comes after *Bye Bye Africa's* closing sequence. It is a film of Haroun's grandmother, who is never shown in the space of the principal narrative of the film, and it is shot by Haroun at some unspecified point in the future. We see Haroun's grandmother leaving her room, and in voice-over, Haroun describes her and recounts what her role in his life has been. This scene is black and white, like the other sequences filmed by Haroun. However, it is different from any other sequence that he had previously filmed. The images are less steady, the tone slightly different. It is a much more personal scene than any of the others, and although filmed with Haroun's camera, it has much more in common with Garba's film of Haroun's mother than with any other scene in the film. Because of its resemblance to Garba's film of Haroun's mother, it seems to be another film of memory that implies the death of Haroun's grandmother.

This sequence suggests an end to the alienation that had characterized Haroun at the beginning of *Bye Bye Africa,* and the existence of connection to Chad and Africa that he had previously lacked. It is, therefore, a scene that points to a transition in Haroun's filmmaking, away from the depersonalized "Westernized" cinema his father had critiqued and more toward the personal, contextualized filmmaking of Garba or the external filmmaker. The spectator is left wondering when and where Haroun filmed this scene, particularly since he has already left Africa, and since he left his camera behind when he went. The scene, perhaps, represents a glimpse of Haroun's own *Bye Bye Africa*, the film he plans to make, but never realized in the context of the principal narrative. It is, perhaps, this sequence, and not the film that precedes it, that best embodies Mahamet-Saleh Haroun's vision of African cinema, a deeply personal and intimate portrait of Africa made on a naturalized, imported camera, a film that speaks to anyone who watches it, inside or outside of Africa. It is worth noting, however, that Haroun's film ends with a challenge to other African filmmakers, because, in the logic of *Bye Bye Africa*, this type of cinema does not quite yet exist.[13]

NOTES

1. For more on Promio and the films and screenings in Cairo, see Rittaud-Hutinet 1985.

2. For more on British films set in Africa, consult the British Film Institute's website on the subject at http://www.screenonline.org.uk/film/id/474337/index.html. For a study of French colonial films set in Africa, see Slavin 2001.

3. Paulin Soumanou Vieyra's *Afrique sur Seine* (1955) is often cited as the first African film. However, it was shot in France and focuses on an African exile community in France, and it is not, therefore a film about Africa per se. I have therefore cited Sembène Ousmane's *Borom Saret* (1962) as the inaugural film of African cinema. It is worth noting that Vieyra went on to assist Sembène in the production of some of his early films, introducing the strategy of collective production that characterizes many African films.

4. For a more full discussion of these and other early African films, see Gardies 1989.

5. Burkinabé filmmaker Idrissa Ouedraogo has argued that African cinema does not even exist, that the very idea of an Africa cinema is, like Western films about Africa, a (post)colonial fantasy (cited in an interview in *Positif* from March of 1993). See also Gardies 1984; Diawara 1992; Tomaselli, Shepperson, and Eke 1995; Thackway 2003, 3; Barlet 2000; and Harrow 2007.

6. Haroun has made a number of other films, including *Abouna* (2002) and *Daratt* (2006), both of which have also received a fair degree of critical acclaim. His *Un homme qui crie* (*A Screaming Man*, 2010) won the Jury Prize for best film at Cannes in 2010.

7. Issa Serge Coelo's films, to date, include his award-winning short film, *Un taxi pour Aouzou* (1994) and the feature-length films *Daresalam* (2000) and *Tartina City* (2006).

8. Many African filmmakers from former French colonies rely on various types of funding administered through the French Centre National de la Cinématographie, most notably through the Fonds Suds program. Such funding, however, comes with strings, as it gives the CNC a certain amount of control over what types of films are made and what sort of images of Africa they project.

9. Cited from an interview in the *Guardian*, November 15, 2002.

10. Ibid.

11. From this point on, I will use "Haroun" to refer to the character in the film and "Mahamet-Saleh Haroun" to refer to the director of the film.

12. This issue of a foreign mind-set represented by a point of origin in Europe has become something of a minor topos in African films. A variety of films, ranging from Amadou Seck's *Saaraba* (1988) to Djibril Diop Mambety's *Hyenas* (1992) to Moussa Sene Absa's *Tableau Ferraille* (1997) feature principal characters who return to Africa from the West. Other films, such as Idrissa Ouedraogo's *Tilai* (1990) feature protagonists who return home from some unspecified place. In either case, these foreign points of origin tend to suggest the importation of a Western mind-set which is figured as problematic in the context of the narrative.

13. It is worth noting that Ntshaveni Wa Luruli's *The Wooden Camera* (2003) also interrogates the notion of an African cinema, and it does so in similar ways. In that film, the tension between cinema's foreign origins and the desire for a local, authentic cinema is expressed through the metaphor of a locally made case for an imported camera. That film also has an ending that suggests that the resolution to that and other tensions is possible but exists in the future rather than the present.

REFERENCES

Abel, Richard. 1994. *The Ciné Goes to Town: French Cinema 1896–1914.* Berkeley: University of California Press.
Armes, Roy. 2006. *African Filmmaking North and South of the Sahara.* Bloomington: Indiana University Press.
Barlet, Olivier. 2000. *African Cinemas: Decolonizing the Gaze.* London: Zed Books.
Diawara, Manthia. 1992. *African Cinema.* Bloomington: Indiana University Press.
Dyer, Richard. 1997. *White.* London: Routledge.
Gardies, André. 1989. *Cinéma d'Afrique noire francophone: L'espace miroir.* Paris: Harmattan.
Gikandi, Simon. 1996. *Maps of Englishness: Writing Identity in the Culture of Colonialism.* New York: Columbia University Press.
Harrow, Kenneth. 2007. *Postcolonial African Cinema: From Postcolonialism to Postmodernism.* Bloomington: Indiana University Press.
Lejeune, Philippe. 1975. *Le Pacte autobiographique.* Paris: Seuil.
Naficy, Hamid. 2001. *An Accented Cinema: Exilic and Diasporic Filmmaking.* Princeton: Princeton University Press.
Rittaud-Hutinet, Jacques. 1985. *Le Cinéma des origines: Les frères Lumière et leurs opérateurs.* Seyssel: Champ Vallon.
Roberts, Andrew D. 1987. "Africa on Film to 1940." *History in Africa* 14: 189–227.
Slavin, David Henry. 2001. *Colonial Cinema and Imperial France, 1910–1939: White Blind Spots, Male Fantasies, Settler Myths.* Baltimore: Johns Hopkins University Press.
Thackway, Melissa. 2003. *Africa Shoots Back: Alternative Perspectives in Sub-Saharan African Film.* Oxford: James Currey.
Tomaselli, Kenyan, Arnold Shepperson, and Maureen Ngoze Eke. 1995. "Towards a Theory of Orality in African Cinema." *Research in African Literatures* 26 (3): 18–35.
Ukadike, Nwachukwu Frank. 1994. *Black African Cinema.* Berkeley: University of California Press.

JOYCE B. ASHUNTANTANG was born in Kumba Town, Cameroon. She is Associate to the UNESCO Chair and Institute for Comparative Human Rights at the University of Connecticut, and teaches African and English literature at the University of Hartford. She is also an actress, poet, screenwriter, and filmmaker, and author of the book *Landscaping Postcoloniality: The Dissemination of Anglophone Cameroon Literature* (2009). She earned a BA in English from the University of Yaounde, a Master's in Librarianship from the University of Wales, and a PhD in English from the City University of New York. She cofounded Akobat Global Media in Cameroon in 2001 and is the founder of EduART INC, a nonprofit organization that promotes the use of art for social awareness.

KIMBERLY NICHELE BROWN is Associate Professor of Gender, Sexuality and Women's Studies at Virginia Commonwealth University. She is also a founding faculty member and former director of the Africana Studies Program at Texas A & M University. Brown specializes in contemporary African American literature and culture, black feminist theory, Africana film, and American and Africana literatures. In her book *Writing the Black Revolutionary Diva: Women's Subjectivity and the Decolonizing Text* (2010), Brown employs the figure of the "revolutionary diva" as both a moniker for women such as Toni Cade Bambara, Jayne Cortez, Angela Davis, Toni Morrison, and Alice Walker, as well as a trope for revolutionary and feminist agency.

JANE BRYCE is Professor of African Literature and Cinema at the University of the West Indies, Cave Hill, Barbados. Born in Tanzania, she was educated there, the UK, and Nigeria. She has been a freelance journalist and fiction editor and has published in a range of academic journals and essay collections. Her recent publications include articles in *Viewing African Cinema in* the 21st Century: Art Films and the Nollywood Video Revolution, Small Axe: A Caribbean Journal of Criticism, and Black Camera: An International Film Journal. She founded and codirected the Barbados Festival of African and Caribbean Film and curates the Africa World Documentary Film Festival at Cave Hill.

EARL CONTEH-MORGAN is Professor of International Studies at the University of South Florida. He has published in the areas of peace and conflict analysis, American foreign policy, and democratization in Africa. His books include Democratization in Africa: The Theory and Dynamics of Political Transitions (1997) and Collective Political Violence: An Introduction to the Theories and Cases of Violent Conflicts (2004). He coedited Peacekeeping in Africa: ECOMOG in Liberia (1998) and Sierra Leone at the End of the 20th Century: History, Politics, and Society (1999). His articles have appeared in outlets such as the Journal of Social Philosophy, Armed Forces and Society, and the International Journal of Peace Studies. He is currently researching Sino-African relations in the twenty-first century, as well as the human security impact of globalization on Africa.

CHRISTOPHER GARLAND is a PhD candidate in the Department of English at the University of Florida. Born in New Zealand, he has also studied at the University of Auckland and the University of Virginia. His essay "The Rhetoric of Crisis and Foreclosing the Future of Haiti in Ghosts of Cité Soleil" is in the forthcoming edited collection Haiti and the Americas: Histories, Cultures, Imaginations, and "'I have been condemned to live': History, Allegory, and a New (Zealand) Tomorrow in Geoff Murphy's The Quiet Earth" will appear in the journal the Projector. His writing has also appeared in the New Zealand Herald and NYLON. His current research project is focused on contemporary Western visual representations of Haiti.

HARRY GARUBA is Associate Professor at the Centre for African Studies, University of Cape Town, with a joint appointment in the Department of English Language and Literature. In 2005/6, he was a Mellon Fellow at the Harry Ransom Humanities Research Centre at the University of Texas in Austin and later a Mandela Fellow at the W. E. B. DuBois Institute, Harvard University. His publications include "Mapping the Land/Body/Subject: Colonial and Postcolonial Geographies in African Narrative" (Alternation, 2002), "Explorations in Animist Materialism: Notes on Reading/Writing African Literature, Culture, and Society" (Public Culture, 2003), and "The Unbearable Lightness of Being: Re-Figuring Trends in Recent Nigerian Poetry" (English in Africa, 2005).

RICARDO GUTHRIE is Assistant Professor of Ethnic Studies at Northern Arizona University. He studies political narratives of the Black Press and writes about films as cultural political artifacts. He is currently researching the life and influence of physician/publisher Dr. Carlton B. Goodlett at the *San Francisco Sun-Reporter* (1945–66). Guthrie completed his essay on *The Last King of Scotland* during his fellowship as visiting scholar at the Center for Black Studies Research, University of California, Santa Barbara. His poetry and artwork can be viewed on the Museum of the African Diaspora's website: http://www.iveknownrivers.org/.

KENNETH HARROW is Distinguished Professor of English at Michigan State University. His work focuses on African cinema and literature, diaspora, and postcolonial studies. He is the author of *Thresholds of Change in African Literature* (1994), *Less Than One and Double: A Feminist Reading of African Women's Writing* (2002), and *Postcolonial African Cinema: From Political Engagement to Postmodernism* (2007). He has edited the collections *Faces of Islam in African Literature* (1991), *The Marabout and the Muse: New Approaches to Islam in African Literature* (1996), and *African Cinema: Postcolonial and Feminist Readings* (1999). Harrow has published a number of articles dealing with the genocide in Rwanda. He has been the Rwanda and Burundi country specialist for Amnesty International USA since 1993. His latest work, *Trash! African Cinema from Below*, will be published in 2012.

MARYELLEN HIGGINS is Associate Professor of English at the Greater Allegheny campus of Pennsylvania State University, where she teaches human rights and literature, African literature, and international cinema. She has published essays on literary and cinematic representations of human rights and agency in *Research in African Literatures, Tulsa Studies in Women's Literature, African Literature Today, Perspectives on African Literatures at the Millennium*, and *Broadening Our Horizons: Critical Introductions to Amma Darko*, among other journals and books. With Dayna Oscherwitz, she coauthored *The Historical Dictionary of French Cinema* (2007).

MARGARET R. HIGONNET is Professor of English and Comparative Literature at the University of Connecticut, an affiliate of Harvard University's Center for European Studies, and former president of the American Comparative Literature Association. She is the editor of *Lines of Fire: Women Writers of World War I* (1999) and *Nurses at the Front: Writing the Wounds of War* (2001), and coeditor of *Behind the Lines: Gender and the Two World Wars* (1987) and *Comparatively Queer* (2010), among several other volumes. Her interests include feminist theory, Victorian literature, suicide, World War I, and children's literature. The essay in the present volume came out of discussions with her daughter, *Ethel R. Higonnet*, a lawyer working on human rights issues, about the problems that arose in filming *Invisible Crime*, a documentary about violations of women during the civil war in the Ivory Coast.

NATASHA HIMMELMAN holds a BA in English from Dartmouth College and an MPhil in African Literature and Culture from the University of Cape Town (UCT). Currently, she is a doctoral candidate at UCT's Centre for African Studies. She has been a visiting scholar in the Department of Literature at Kenyatta University and in the Department of African American Studies at the University of California, Berkeley, where she has also lectured. Her dissertation focuses on Ngũgĩ wa Thiongo's language project, and her research interests include African literatures, decolonial theory, popular culture, and knowledge production.

BENNETTA JULES-ROSETTE is Distinguished Professor of Sociology and director of the African and African-American Studies Research Center at the University of California, San Diego. Her areas of interest include contemporary sociological theory and sociosemiotic studies of religious discourse, tourism, and African cinema, art, and literature. Her most recent books include *Black Paris: The African Writers' Landscape* (1998) and *Josephine Baker in Art and Life: The Icon and the Image* (2007). She has written over one hundred articles and is past president of the Association for Africanist Anthropology and a former member of the Board of the National Museum of African Art, Smithsonian Institution.

CLIFFORD T. MANLOVE is Associate Professor of English at the Greater Allegheny campus of Pennsylvania State University, where he teaches twentieth-century literature, postcolonial studies, and film theory. In addition to critical and film theory, Manlove's research interests include utopian studies, reggae music and Rastafarian politics, Anglophone colonial/postcolonial literary and film narratives, and the American South. Articles by Manlove have appeared in *South Atlantic Review, minnesota review, College Literature, Cinema Journal,* and *Left Curve.* He is currently writing a book on the classic reggae film, *The Harder They Come,* and is editing an anthology of the journalism, photography, poetry, and letters published in the independent US military newspaper, *Stars and Stripes,* between 1862 and 2012.

CHRISTOPHER ODHIAMBO JOSEPH is Professor of Postcolonial Literatures and Intervention Theater at the Department of Literature, Theatre and

Film Studies at Moi University, Eldoret, in Kenya. He has published essays in the areas of literature, theater, and radio in *Rethinking Eastern African Literary and Intellectual Landscapes* (2012), *Language and Literature: Contemporary Issues from Kenya* (2008), and *Theatre, Performance and New Media in Africa* (2007), among other books. His book *Theatre for Development in Kenya* was published by Bayreuth African Studies Series in 2008.

IYUNOLU OSAGIE is Associate Professor of English at the Pennsylvania State University. Her research and teaching interests include African and African American literatures and theories, black playwrights, women's literatures, contemporary slavery, black diaspora/transnational studies, and African and African American cultural memories. Her award-winning first book is *The Amistad Revolt: Memory, Slavery, and the Politics of Identity in the United States and Sierra Leone* (2000). Her second book, *Theater in Sierra Leone: Five Popular Plays* (2009), is the first edited collection of plays on Sierra Leone. Her play, *The Shield*, has been staged at Penn State and at two Nigerian universities.

J.R. OSBORN is a scholar of communication and a critical media producer. He holds a PhD in communication from the University of California, San Diego and currently teaches in the Communication, Culture & Technology (CCT) program at Georgetown University. His work addresses media history, technology, design, and aesthetics with a regional focus of the Middle East and Africa. He is the webmaster for the Association of Africanist Anthropology and the producer of *Glitter Dust: Finding Art in Dubai* (2012), a feature-length documentary exploring urban space, visual culture, and globalization. He also develops and programs interactive digital terminals for the "Unmixing of African Art."

DAYNA OSCHERWITZ is Associate Professor of French at Southern Methodist University in Dallas, Texas. She is the author of *Past Forward: French Cinema and the (Post)Colonial Heritage* (2010). She has published articles on cinema in *Research in African Literatures, Journal of Contemporary French and Francophone Studies, Mots Pluriels*, and *Memory, Empire, and Postcolonialism*. She is coauthor, with MaryEllen Higgins, of *The Historical Dictionary of French Cinema* (2007) and has published on various aspects of Francophone culture and cinema.

LEA MARIE RUIZ-ADE is a board member of the African and African-American Studies Research Center at the University of California, San Diego. Her areas of interest include gender, electronic communication and media culture, and sociosemiotic studies of cinema, art, tourism, and literature.

Rony, Fatimah Tobing, 140n3
Roodt, Darrell, 5, 160–62, 165, 173
Rorty, Richard, 36
Rose, Anika Noni, 123
Rosen, David, 140n2
Rosenstone, Robert A., 65
Rotibi, Sammi, 75
Rouch, Jean, 36, 38, 159, 164, 174, 175nn10–12
Rousseau, Jean Jacques, 36
Rozario, Kevin, 35
*Rudy*, 185
rugby, 190nn2–4
Ruiz-Ade, Lea Marie, 175n16
Rusesabagina, Paul, 4, 9, 55, 58, 64, 65, 90–92, 95n9
Rutaganda, Georges, 63, 64, 65
Rwanda, 3–4, 5, 8, 44, 47, 54–66, 73, 79, 83–84, 89, 94n5
Rwangyezi, Stephen, 26, 41
Ryle, John, 187–88

*Saaraba*, 259n12
*Sahara*, 7
Said, Edward, 5, 11, 15, 16–17, 20, 31n3
Saks, Lucia, 194–95
Sam, Vilbrun Guillaume, 116
*Sanders of the River*, 94n4
Sankoh, Foday, 222–23
*Sarafina*, 160
Sargeant, Joseph, 188
savage/savagery, images of, 3, 16, 25, 58–59, 61, 63–64, 74–75, 94n4, 104, 109, 112–113, 116, 117, 119, 121, 123, 125, 127, 130–139, 143–148, 150–153, 187, 241
*Savage South Africa*, 241
savior, Westerner as, 8, 10, 58, 63–65, 68, 76, 80, 105, 195, 201, 232
Saxton, Alexander, 118
*Schindler's List*, 55, 58
Schleier, Merrill, 138, 141n5
Schoedsack, Ernest B., 129
Schoon, Jeanette, 220n2
Schreiner, Olive, 220n5
Schroder, Barbet, 40
Schweitzer, Albert, 94n4
Scott, A. O., 79, 81n1
Scott, Jill, 123n2
Scott, Ridley, 5, 10, 68, 76
Scott, Sir Walter, 41
Scramble for Africa, 125, 148

Seck, Amadou, 259n12
Sembène, Ousmane, 159, 241, 258n3
Senghor, Léopold Sédar, 243
*September Tapes, The*, 38
Shaheen, Jack, 80
*Shake Hands with the Devil*, 4, 83, 85–90, 92, 93n3
Shepard, Sam, 71
Shohat, Ella, 7, 113
*Shooting Dogs*, 9, 83, 92, 230
Siad Barre, Mohamed, 77
Sierra Leone, 1–2, 4, 5, 39–40, 45, 65, 79, 143, 150–52, 159, 170–72, 222–38
*Simba*, 241
Singh, Anant, 165
Singleton, John, 157
Sizemore, Tom, 70
slavery, 9, 37, 118, 120, 122, 126, 141n7, 145, 146, 147, 149
Slotkin, Richard, 69, 75
Slovo, Gillian, Robyn, and Shawn, 5, 207–11, 213, 214, 218–20
Slovo, Joe, 5, 207–9, 214
Smith, Adam, 36
Smith, Paul, 157, 174n2, 174n6
Snipes, Wesley, 157
Snow, Harmon Keith, 61, 62
social Darwinism, 125, 139, 147
*Soleils des indépendances, Les*, 94n6
Solomon, 2, 129, 163
Somalia, 5, 6, 11, 68, 70, 73, 76, 77
*Sometimes in April*, 61, 66
Sontag, Susan, 38, 60
South Africa, 1, 5, 10, 11, 40, 113, 150, 158, 159–63, 165–70, 173, 177–90, 193–203, 207–20, 230
Soyan, Moallim, 77
Spencer, Julius, 224, 238
Spielberg, Stephen, 55, 227, 230
*Spirit of the West*, 71
Spivak, Gayatri Chakravorty, 45, 242
Stam, Robert, 7, 113, 204n11
*Stander*, 204n3, 204n6
*Stanley and Livingstone*, 2, 93n4
Steidle, Brian, 3, 41–42, 43–45, 46–48, 49–51
Stein, Ruthe, 32n25
Stern, Ricki, 3, 41–42, 44
Stevens, Siaka, 222, 224
Stevenson, Robert, 241
Stone, Oliver, 118, 185

CPSIA information can be obtained at www.ICGtesting.com
Printed in the USA
LVOW11s1905190415

435235LV00004B/5/P